gather

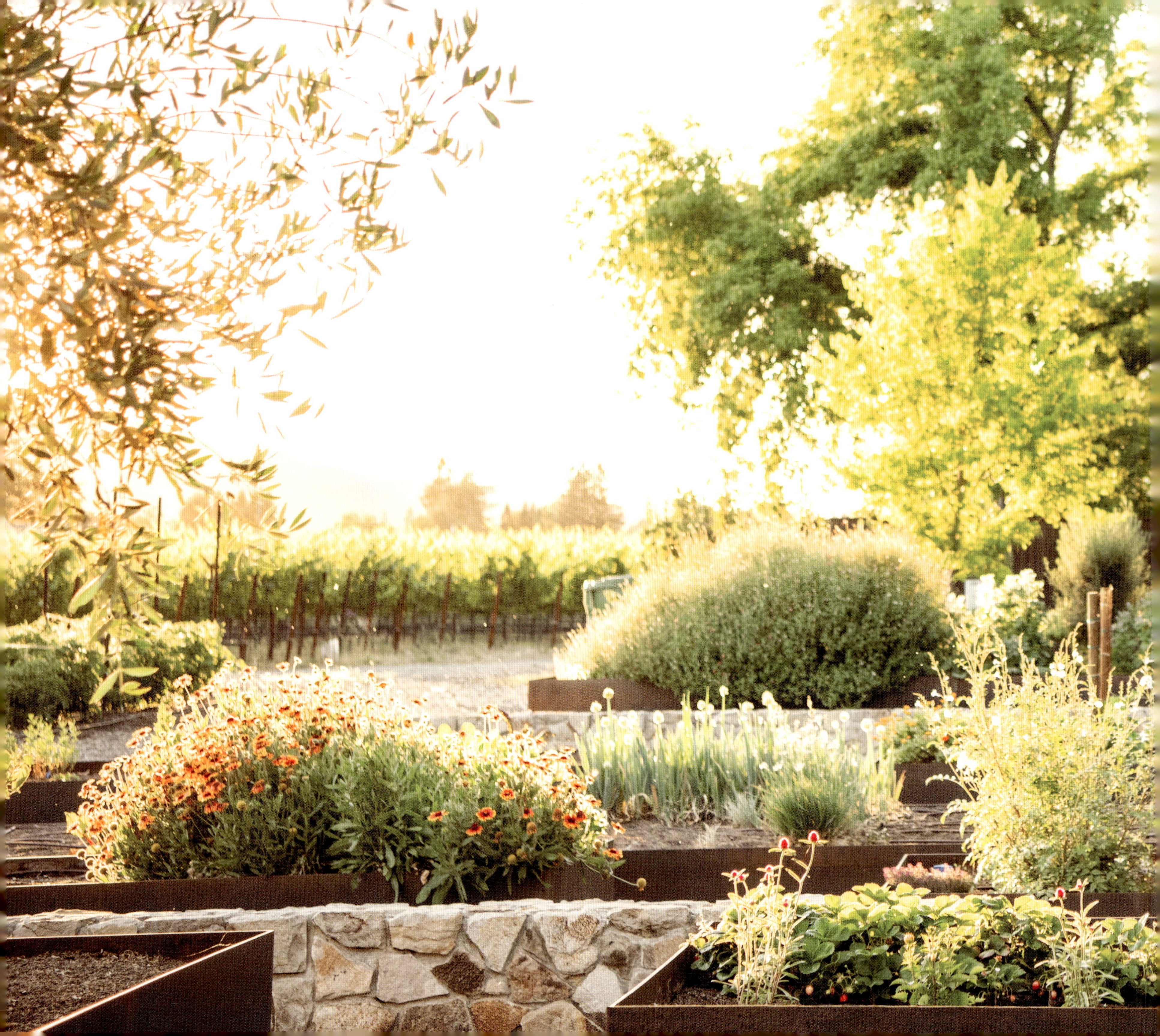

gather

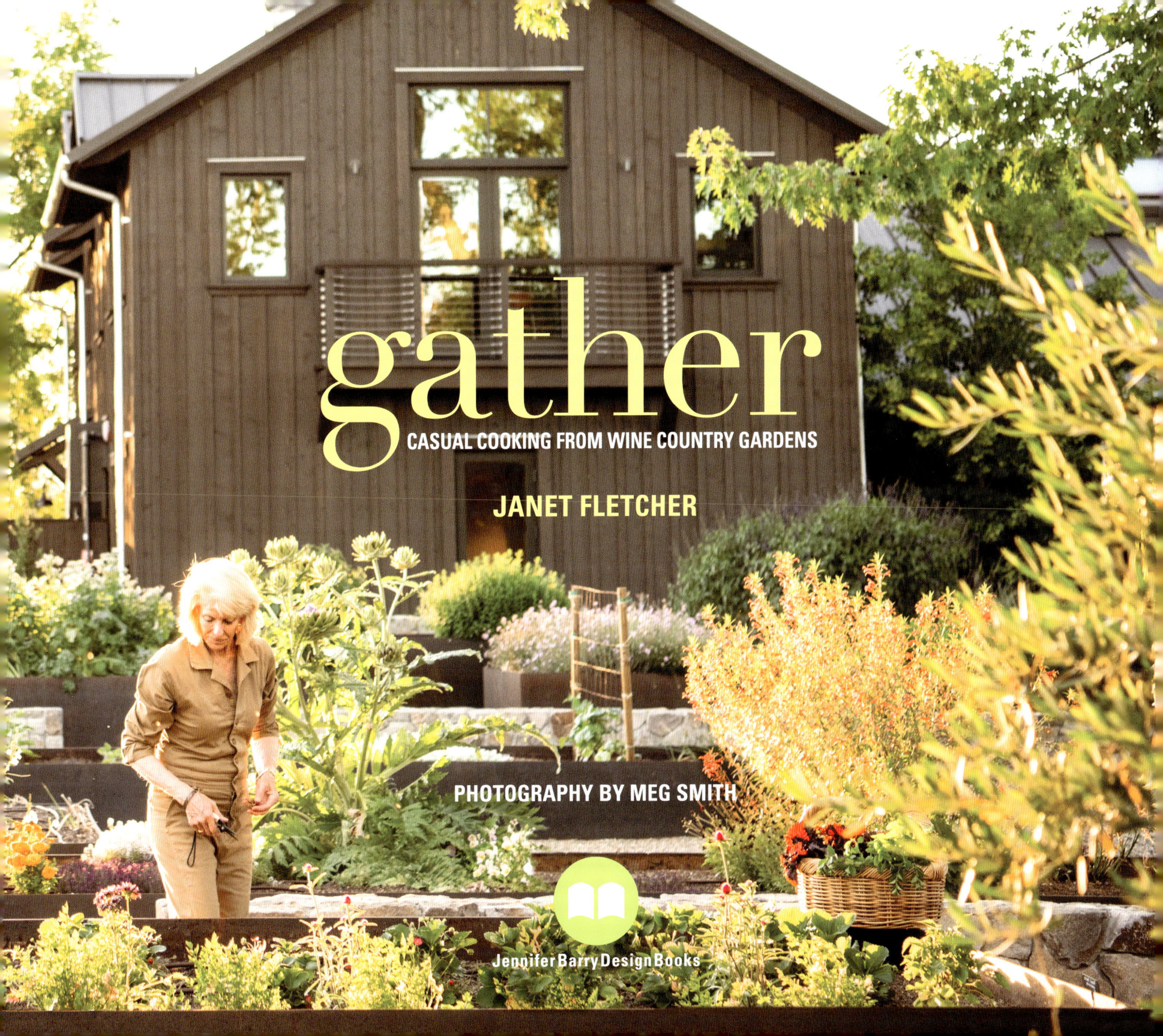

CASUAL COOKING FROM WINE COUNTRY GARDENS

JANET FLETCHER

PHOTOGRAPHY BY MEG SMITH

Jennifer Barry Design Books

Gather: Casual Cooking from Wine Country Gardens copyright © 2020 by Jennifer Barry Design Books, LLC and Janet Fletcher
Photographs copyright © 2020 by Meg Smith Photography

All rights reserved. No part of this book may be used or reproduced in any manner whatsoever without written permission from the book producer or author except in the case of reprints in the context of reviews.

For information, write to
Jennifer Barry Design Books, LLC
229 Tamalpais Road, Fairfax, CA 94930, USA

First Edition

ISBN: 978-0-578-75194-8

Library of Congress Control Number: 2020916129

Produced and designed by Jennifer Barry Design, Fairfax, CA
Text by Janet Fletcher
Photography by Meg Smith
Food Styling by Abby Stolfo
Prop Styling by Thea Chalmers
Copy Editing by Sharon Silva

www.jenniferbarrydesign.com
www.janetfletcher.com
www.megsmith.com

Printed in China

Preceding pages: *Young fava beans at Wheeler Farms; Wheeler Farms co-owner Daphne Araujo in the winery's culinary garden*

Above and right: *Ha'ogen melon, a prized Israeli variety, at Cakebread Cellars; thriving stand of corn soaks up the Napa Valley sun at Regusci Winery*

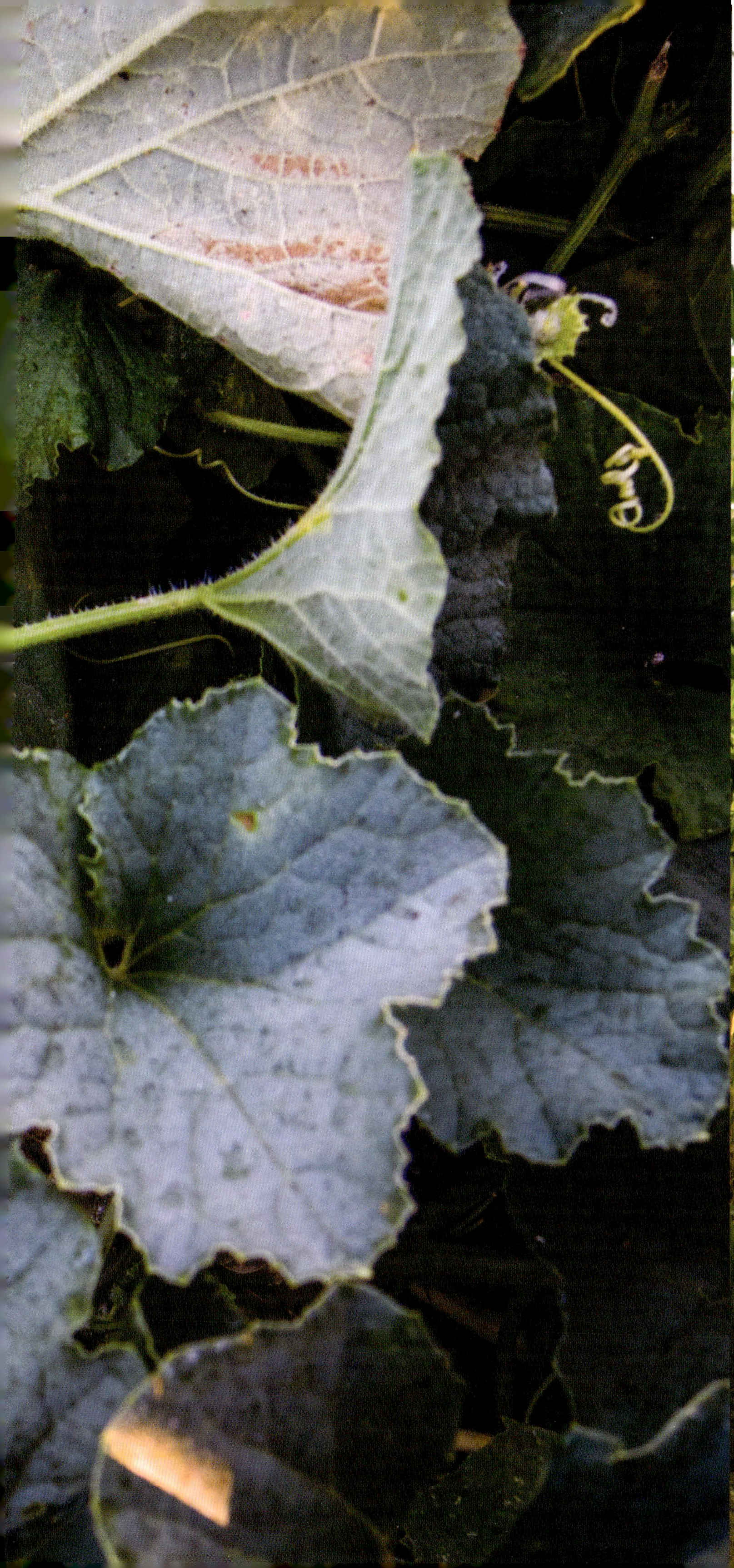
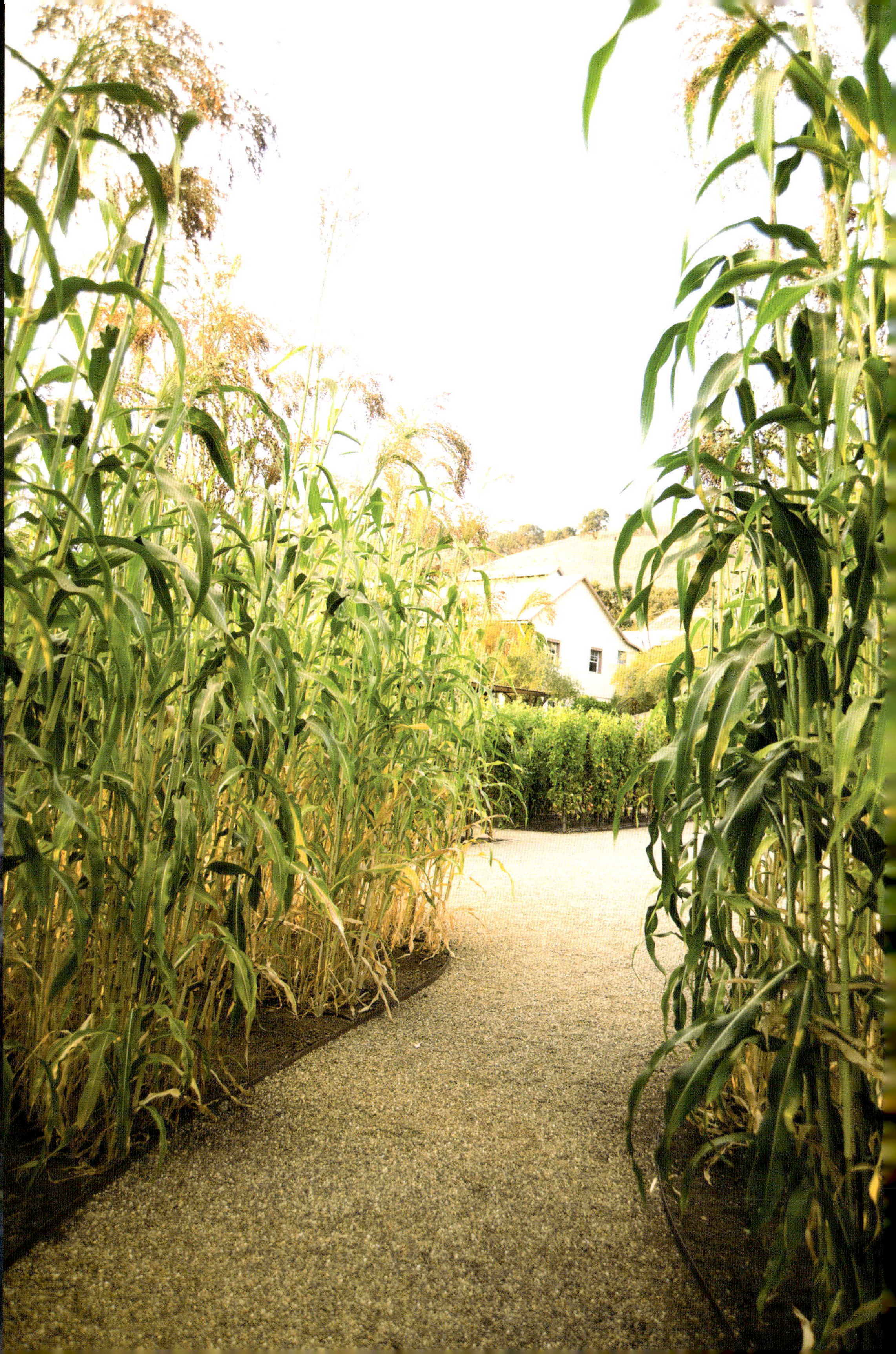

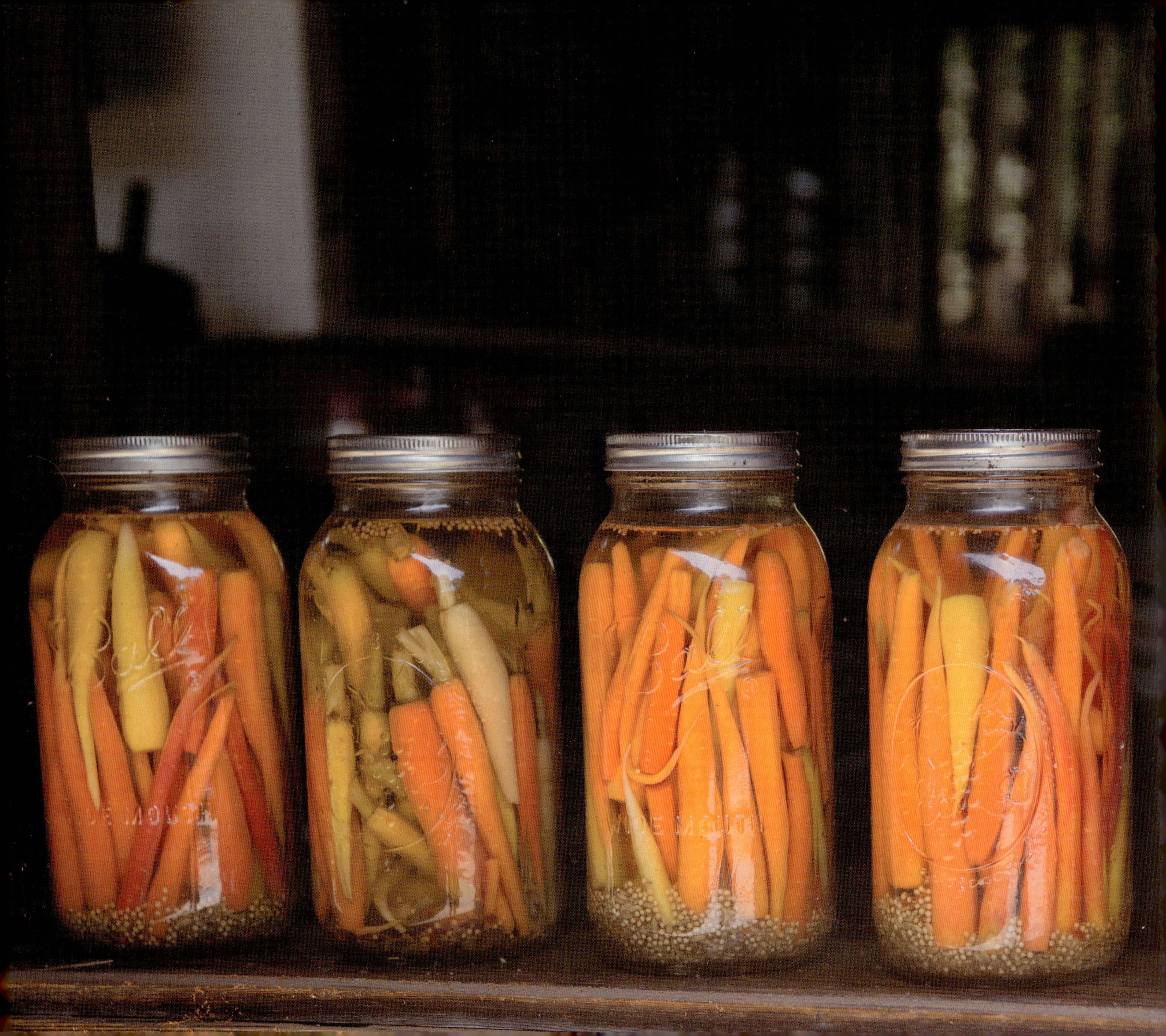

contents

Introduction: *An Invitation to Gather* — 8

Alexander Valley Vineyards: *Farmers' Market Favorite* — 15
B Cellars: *New Ways to Engage* — 31
Beringer Vineyards: *A Sensory Teaching Garden* — 49
Cakebread Cellars: *Farm-to-Table Pioneers* — 65
Clif Family Winery: *Farm to Truck to Table* — 81
HALL Wines: *Art of the Garden* — 99
The Prisoner Wine Company: *A Courtyard Garden* — 117
Regusci Winery: *Italian-American Abbondanza* — 133
Robert Mondavi Winery: *Garden Carved from a Vineyard* — 151
Skipstone: *A Mediterranean Tribute* — 169
Trefethen Family Vineyards: *A Joyful Jumble* — 187
Wente Vineyards: *Deep Roots in One Place* — 205
Wheeler Farms: *Restoring Diversity* — 221

Visitor Guide — 236
Acknowledgments — 237
Index — 238

Left: *Pickled carrots in the kitchen at Alexander Valley Vineyards; Dolores Cakebread with Cakebread Cellars chef Brian Streeter*

introduction *An Invitation to Gather*

Northern California is wine country, among the most acclaimed viticultural regions on earth. Not coincidentally, this paradise for Pinot Noir and Chardonnay is also a sublime place to garden. The same mild Mediterranean climate that wine grapes love is what many herbs, fruits, and vegetables appreciate, too. Fertile soil, abundant sun, and moderate temperatures allow edible gardens to thrive year-round in the area's scenic wine valleys. To the surprise of many wine country visitors, some of the most delightful of these culinary gardens reside at wineries. *Gather: Casual Cooking from Wine Country Gardens* takes you on a tour of these picturesque plots and into the kitchens of those fortunate cooks who reap the harvest.

What beautiful food comes out of these gardens! And vintners want you to taste it. Most of them make wine, after all, because they relish sharing it with others. They believe that many of life's most pleasurable moments happen around the table, with friends and well-prepared food. Like gardeners, they embrace the rhythms of nature: the calm of winter, the optimism of spring, the adrenaline rush of harvest. They love creating a product that encourages hospitality and contributes to a healthy lifestyle. For many vintners, an abundant garden is essential to the life they want to lead and the zest for living they want to convey.

Gather: Casual Cooking from Wine Country Gardens showcases thirteen Northern California wineries with inspiring edible gardens. These enterprises differ in many ways, but they share the belief that

Above: *(clockwise from left) Laura Regusci in the Regusci garden; Trefethen Vineyards tomatoes and dried chile powders; Cakebread Cellars melon; Trefethen chef Chris Kennedy; apples at Wente Vineyards*

fresh, seasonal, garden-to-table meals are the most satisfying and flattering companions for their wines.

These charming gardens serve many ends. They provide some of the produce used in meals served to visitors, as at Cakebread Cellars, where Dolores Cakebread's marvelous garden has delighted and fed guests for almost fifty years. Wente Vineyards' large organic garden has long supported its restaurant and robust visitor events, while the mountain garden maintained by Clif Family Winery keeps its popular Bruschetteria food truck supplied daily.

At other wineries, the garden inspires handmade gifts for guests, such as chef Sarah Heller's edible flower cookies at Wheeler Farms, or the southern-style pickled okra that chef Angel Perez puts up every summer at Regusci Winery, a nod to vintner Laura Regusci's Kentucky roots. At Beringer Vineyards, winery hosts use the sensory garden as a teaching tool for guests, a way to make wine aromas more discernible by connecting them to more familiar scents in nature.

A culinary garden makes a scenic backdrop for many winery events and receptions. At The Prisoner Wine Company, private events often begin in the garden, giving guests a chance to congregate casually outdoors with a glass of wine and explore the unusual culinary

Wine country culinary gardens make a scenic backdrop for many winery events and receptions.

herbs that fill the deep raised beds. A garden tour is one of the opportunities that Robert Mondavi Winery offers guests, who get to cook with what they harvest and enjoy a family-style lunch in the garden.

Some wineries, such as Trefethen Family Vineyards, view the garden primarily as a staff perk, a creative way of investing in employee health and wellness by encouraging staffers to take home what the winery chef doesn't use. The garden at Alexander Valley Vineyards feeds many families. The winery operates a farm stand at the nearby farmers' market, so locals can enjoy fresh eggs from the winery's pastured hens and the tomatoes and peppers that winery co-owner Hank Wetzel delights in growing.

Skipstone owner Fahri Diner grew up in rural Cyprus surrounded by fruit trees and free-range hens, and he and his wife, Constance, want their young children to have a similar experience. At B Cellars and HALL Wines, the garden reflects a deep-rooted commitment to sustainability and a belief that diversity creates a healthier ecosystem.

In this book, so stunningly photographed by Meg Smith, you will visit thirteen magical gardens—some of them open to the public, some not. I hope you will gather ideas for your own culinary garden, tips on what to plant, and techniques for keeping the garden healthy and productive. You will, I hope, gather inspiration for your own cooking and make time to re-create some of these mouthwatering meals. Above all, I hope this book will compel you to gather friends and family around the table, open a bottle of California wine, and celebrate the unending generosity of the earth.

Right: *Napa Valley chef Sarah Scott prepares garden tomato sauce; a vineyard view for an alfresco meal*

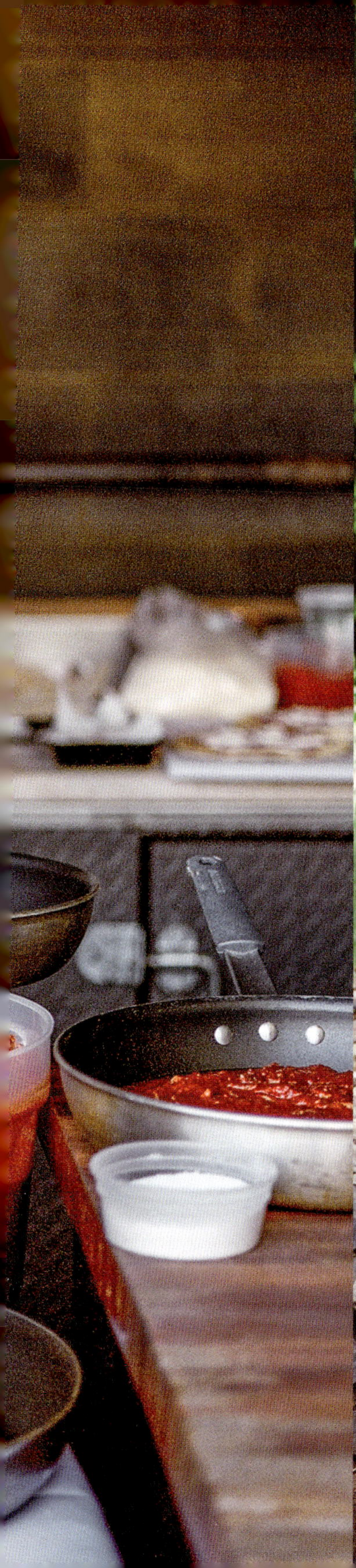
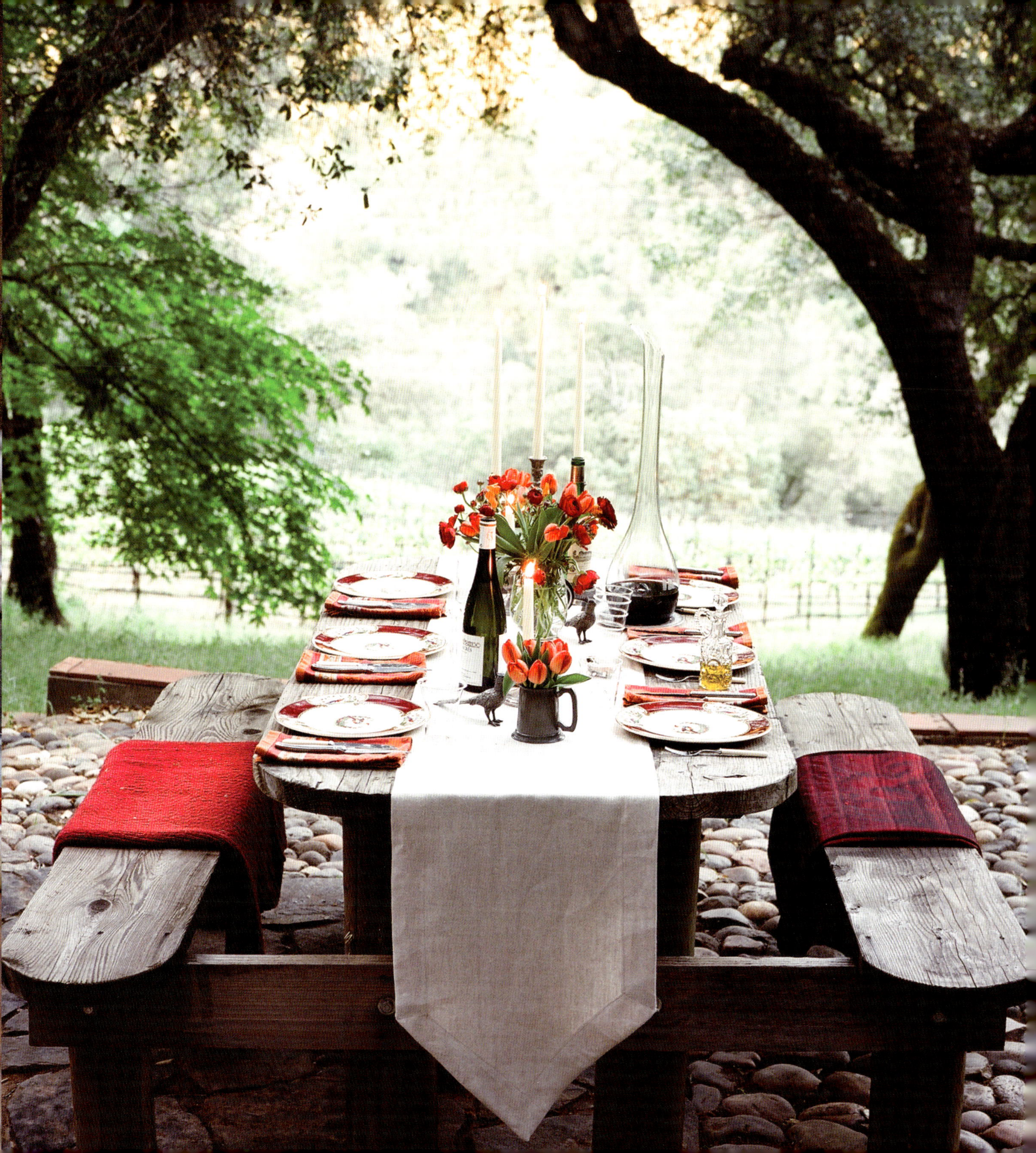

Above and right: *Kikinda gourds dangle from a trellis at Cakebread Cellars; Katie Wetzel Murphy prepares garden citrus for marmalade.*

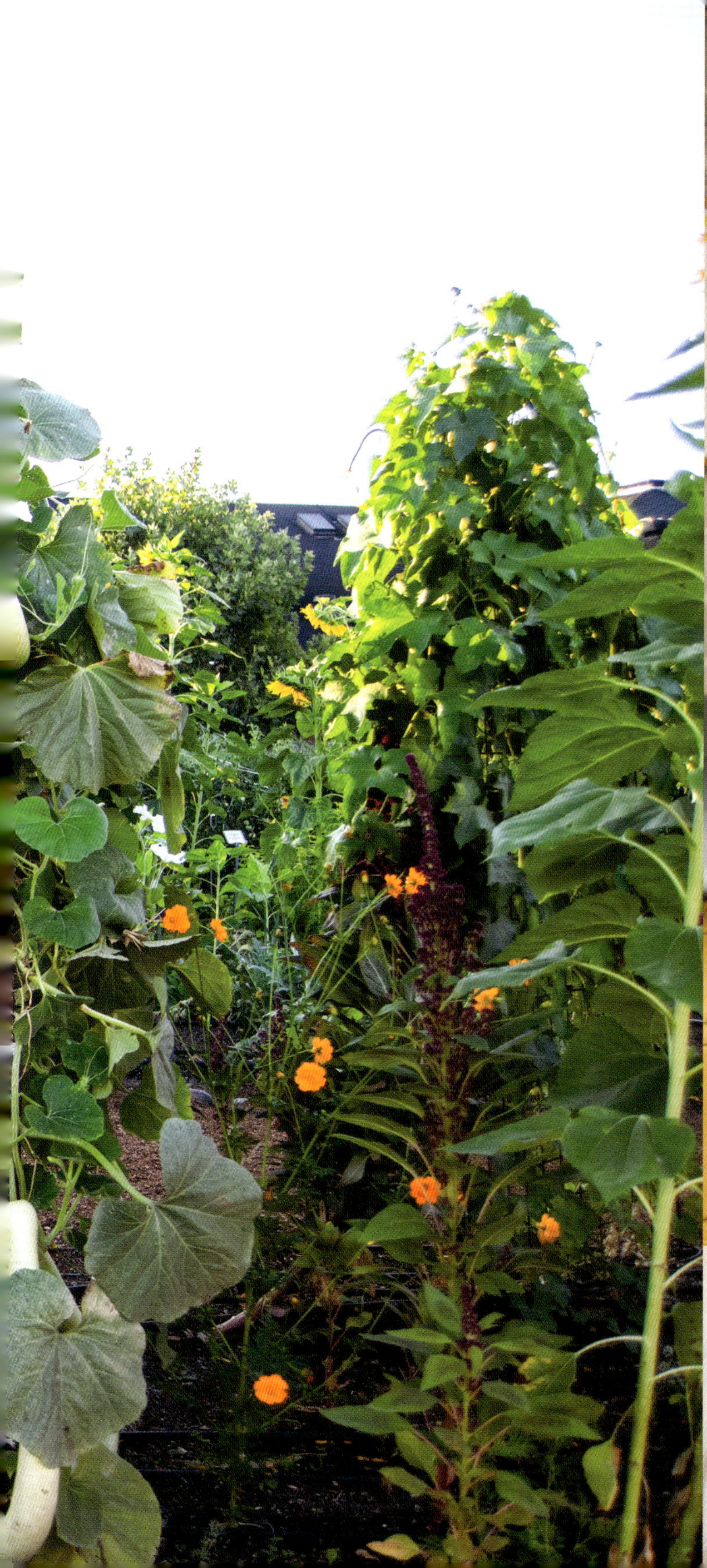

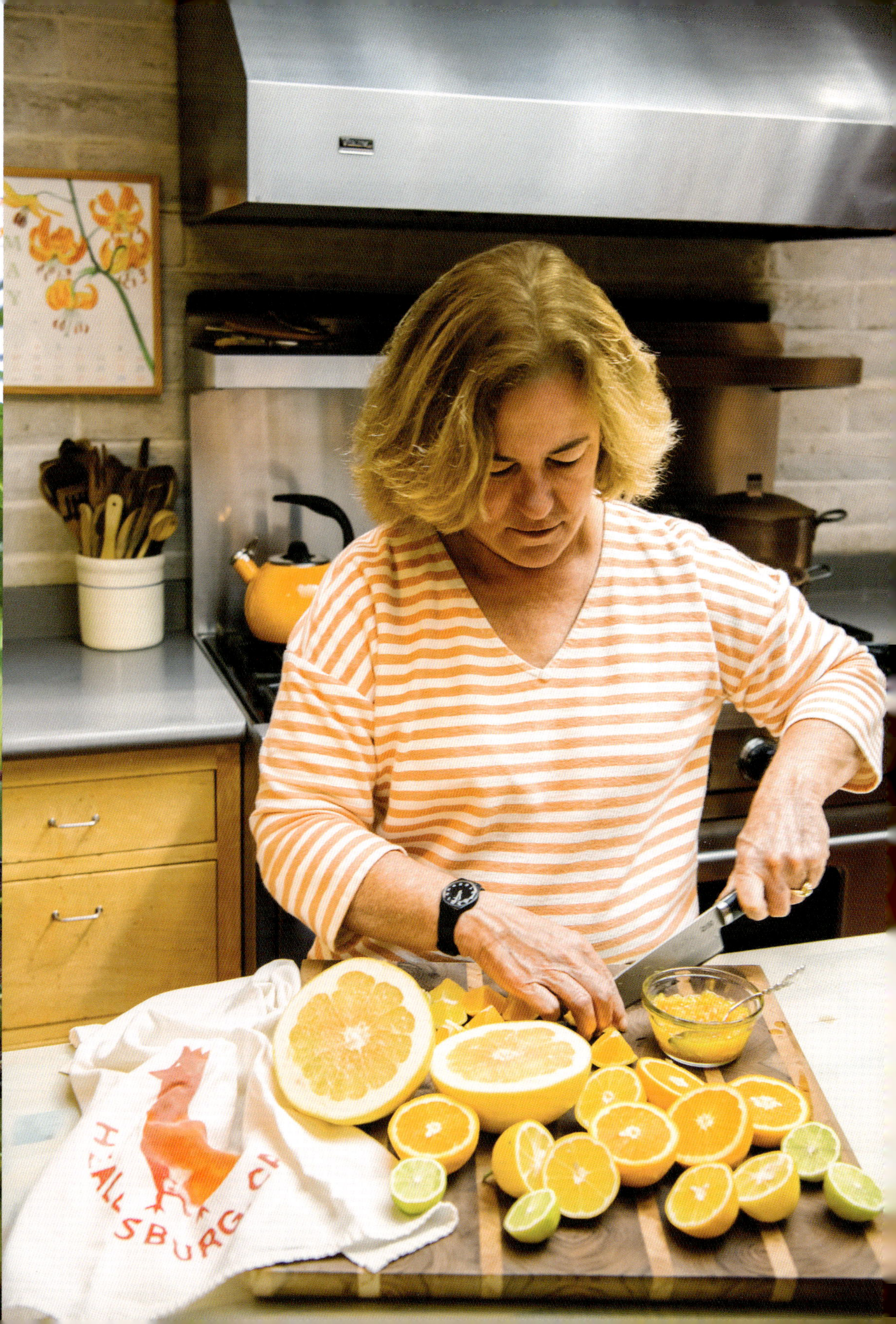

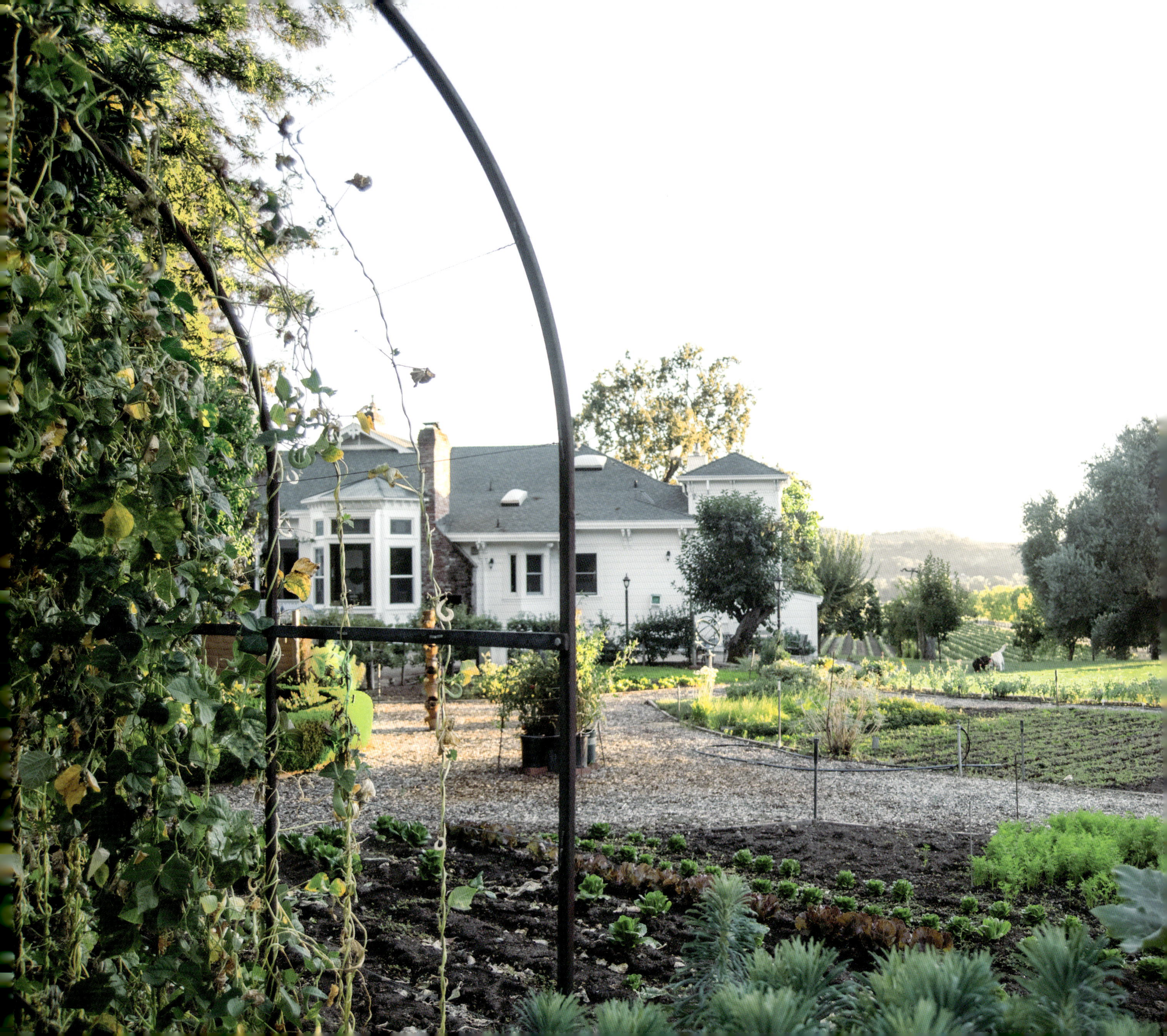

Alexander Valley Vineyards: *Farmers' Market Favorite*

Healdsburg

For the Wetzel family, Cyrus Alexander is ever present, a hovering spirit who perpetually reminds them of their property's storied past. Family members live, garden, and make wine on the historic Alexander estate, the long-ago home of the pioneering settler who gave Alexander Valley its name. This landmark property's roots plunge deep, like those of its massive olive and oak trees.

"We think Alexander parked himself here because the soil is great," says Katie Wetzel Murphy, whose father purchased the heritage acreage in 1962 from Alexander's heirs. The site is a half mile from the Russian River but not in the floodplain, an ideal spot for fruit trees and other food crops, which Alexander planted. A teetotaler, he left it to later generations to plant the first wine grapes in what became one of California's most esteemed wine appellations.

Ironically, Alexander was scouting ranchland, not vineyard, when he traveled north from San Diego in the late 1830s. He found a suitable tract near the future town of Healdsburg, and for four years he managed the vast Rancho Sotoyome for his patron. His reward was a fertile parcel of his own where he started a family and, in 1842, built an adobe home. The old adobe still stands, gently restored and used for winery events, adjacent to the Victorian-style home where Katie's brother Hank and his wife, Linda, live now.

Today, Hank, Katie, and their families oversee Alexander Valley Vineyards, the enterprise their parents started after purchasing the Sonoma County estate sight unseen. Gradually, Maggie Wetzel, their mother, transformed the neglected landscape with rose gardens, dahlias, and espaliered pears. She planted citrus trees around the swimming pool and asparagus beds that still produce, but she was really more of an ornamental gardener, says Hank.

The five acres of edible gardens that make Alexander Valley Vineyards such a draw for visitors today are largely Hank's doing. He has worked in the family vineyards since childhood, but it's the vegetable patch that kindles his sense of awe. "Planting a seed and having it produce something edible feels like a miracle," says Hank, who is something of a celebrity at the Healdsburg Farmers' Market.

Hank has operated a popular stand at this lively local market since 2014, when he decided to test it as a sales venue for the estate's extra virgin olive oil. To make his stall more alluring, he began growing tomatoes and peppers, melons and zucchini, lettuces and lima beans. "I love the phenomenon of farm to table," says the vintner. "I have a regular clientele who would never think of missing the market."

Left and above: *Five acres behind the Wetzel family home yield produce for the Healdsburg Farmers' Market; Hank Wetzel at the market with his sought-after eggs*

With garden manager Javier Patino, Hank oversees the planting and pampering of at least ten different types of cherry tomatoes (Chocolate Cherry is a favorite), sauce tomatoes, and slicers, such as Mortgage Lifter, Brandywine, and Pineapple. In one of several separate garden plots, lemon cucumbers weave their way over decorative wrought-iron trellises, while wire arches cloaked in pole beans create verdant tunnels. Picture-perfect rosettes of Salanova lettuce are farmers' market favorites, but it's the farm's eggs that have the real cult following, especially among local chefs.

"When the chickens have that first flush of green grass to eat, the eggs are fantastic," says Katie. Coyotes are a constant menace, but the eggs have too much of a fan club to let the coyotes prevail. Hank buys baby chicks online, and the post office calls him when the chirping box arrives; he adopts roosters from city folks who want only hens. The birds' mobile coop can be towed from one vineyard block to another so the chickens can do pest control. During the day, they wander freely, feasting on insects and worms and fertilizing as they go; at night, they retreat to the safety of the coop and a dinner of garden scraps.

A separate plot near the winery caves is allocated to employees. Javier oversees this productive patch of tomatillos, chiles, tomatoes, corn, watermelon, and squash. Staffers can take whatever they want, a treasured perk for those who lack the time or space to garden at home.

Despite the energy and resources directed at the garden, it is no profit center. "I have a goal to make money from the garden before I die," sighs Hank, but no one really believes that the bottom line drives him. The winery's business is wine. For the Wetzel clan, the garden is

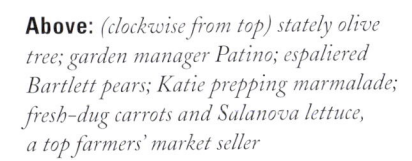

Above: *(clockwise from top) stately olive tree; garden manager Patino; espaliered Bartlett pears; Katie prepping marmalade; fresh-dug carrots and Salanova lettuce, a top farmers' market seller*

The garden tells a story about the Wetzel family's passion for their land and for the Eden that is Sonoma County. "To not have a garden in a place like this would be a crime," says Katie.

a lifestyle choice and a way to honor their parents, who had the foresight to purchase such a fertile parcel. It is also a vehicle for telling stories: about their passion for the land; about the Eden that is Sonoma County; about the pleasures of a life that revolves around home-grown food and good wine.

Or mostly wine. A few tasks require stronger stuff. "We drink bourbon and shell limas on the porch," admits Hank. "That's a favorite habit of mine."

Hank cooks, but Katie cooks better, he says. Among the four siblings, she is the one who accompanied her mother to La Varenne, the Parisian cooking school, and inherited the French copper cookware. She makes the tangerine marmalade that overnight visitors find in the

Alexander Valley Vineyards   17

guesthouse, and she is the family's preserver in chief, responsible for transforming extra produce into pickled green beans, bread-and-butter pickles, spicy ketchup, tomatillo salsa, fruit chutney, preserved lemons, and dried cherry tomatoes for pizza, bruschetta, and spaghetti sauce.

When the Healdsburg Farmers' Market reopens each May, the Alexander Valley Vineyards garden is ready for it with soft spring lettuces, asparagus, radishes, turnips, beets, and, of course, plenty of fresh eggs. Throughout the summer, the evenings are warm enough to eat on the front porch, and the garden brims with tender young vegetables, the only excuse this close family needs to gather for a dinner alfresco.

Above and right: *(clockwise from left) Hank's Victorian home; trellised pear-shaped tomatoes for salad; Alexander Valley Vineyards' farmers' market stand; bean trellis with gopher-deterring euphorbia*

A chilled bottle of Gewürztraminer makes the rounds with Katie's creamy pimiento cheese (made with garden pimientos in season) and a sliced baguette from the local bakery. As the sun sets, a big platter of crudités, boiled eggs, and olives appears with a salsa verde–avocado dip, a favorite family recipe that Katie perfected after encountering it in Mexico. The summer garden yields plenty of dip-worthy vegetables, with radishes, slender scallions, baby carrots, sugar snap peas, green beans, cauliflower, and beets among them. To follow, Katie roasts a quartered chicken the way Maggie often did: with a basting of butter, French mustard, garden tarragon, and honey to brown and crisp the skin. Linda takes charge of the salad, a jumble of lettuces, mild spring onions, early tomatoes, and lemon cucumbers, tossed with the vinaigrette that she perfected and that everyone in the family makes now. A pear and blackberry crisp made with ranch pears and topped with Katie's homemade granola provides the finale.

Surveying this lush landscape, nature seems endlessly generous and benign. But the Wetzels have seen nature's fury, too. In the autumn of 2019, a windstorm-whipped fire tore through this dry valley, causing major damage at neighboring properties. Alexander Valley Vineyards lost some of Maggie's citrus trees, Hank's greenhouse, and other outbuildings, but fortunately the family home and the grandest old trees survived. Hank can still forage for breakfast under the sprawling fig, peach, and apple trees with nothing but a pocketknife. One of the apple trees, an old Russian variety called Red Astrachan, may have been planted in Cyrus Alexander's day.

As fierce preservationists, the Wetzels recognize that they have a treasure to protect and nurture. Fortunately, Hank's sons, Harry and Robert, are involved in the winery, preparing to perpetuate what their grandparents started. Hank's ambitious garden will evolve—gardens always do—but it should still be ripening tomatoes a generation from now. "We have water, sun, and soil," says Katie. "To not have a garden in a place like this would be a crime."

menu

Katie's Pimiento Cheese
Alexander Valley Vineyards Dry Rosé of Sangiovese or Gewürztraminer

Crudités with Avocado Salsa Verde
Alexander Valley Vineyards Dry Rosé of Sangiovese

Summer Garden Salad with Linda's Dressing
Alexander Valley Vineyards Chardonnay

Maggie's Ranch Chicken
Alexander Valley Vineyards Merlot

Pear, Blackberry, and Granola Crisp
Alexander Valley Vineyards Gewürztraminer

Katie's Pimiento Cheese

Makes about 3½ cups

1 small pimiento pepper or red bell pepper, about 4 ounces

½ cup mayonnaise

1 tablespoon fresh lemon juice

1½ teaspoons dry mustard, such as Colman's

½ teaspoon Worcestershire sauce

1 pound sharp Cheddar cheese, coarsely grated

Optional additions: minced scallion, chopped fresh flat-leaf parsley, chopped roasted pecans, chopped green olives, ground cayenne, Tabasco sauce

Wine: Alexander Valley Vineyards Dry Rosé of Sangiovese or Gewürztraminer

katie's tip:

Pack pimiento cheese in a decorative jar for a hostess gift. It's a great appetizer for Thanksgiving or a large dinner party because you can make it well ahead. "It lasts for days if it doesn't get eaten," says Katie.

Katie discovered pimiento cheese on a business trip to Charleston, South Carolina, and fell in love with this classic Southern specialty. She uses sweet pimientos from the garden when they ripen in late summer and fall and grills them over charcoal if she has time. No wonder many of her friends say, "For my birthday, I'd like pimiento cheese." Serve with a sliced baguette.

Roast the pepper until blackened all over by your preferred method: over a charcoal fire, over a gas flame, or under a broiler. Let cool, then peel and remove the stem, seeds, and ribs. Cut the pepper into small dice.

In a bowl, using an electric mixer, combine the pepper, mayonnaise, lemon juice, mustard, and Worcestershire sauce and beat on medium speed until blended. Add the cheese and beat again until blended. Stir in the optional ingredients to your taste.

Crudités with Avocado Salsa Verde

Makes 1⅓ cups salsa

1½ pounds tomatillos, husked and coarsely chopped (about 4 cups)

1 Anaheim or poblano chile, seeded and coarsely chopped

1 jalapeño chile, seeded and coarsely chopped

3 cloves garlic, peeled

½ small white onion, sliced

Sea salt

½ large avocado, peeled

1 small handful arugula

⅓ cup coarsely chopped fresh cilantro leaves and stems

¼ cup extra virgin olive oil

2 tablespoons fresh lime juice

Assorted vegetables, hard-cooked eggs, and olives, for serving (see headnote)

Wine: Alexander Valley Vineyards Dry Rosé of Sangiovese

Preheat the oven to 350°F. Put the tomatillos, Anaheim chile, jalapeño chile, garlic, and onion in a 9-by-13-inch baking dish and stir to mix. Bake, stirring halfway through, for 1 hour. Let cool slightly, then put all the ingredients into a blender, add ½ teaspoon salt, and blend until smooth. Set aside 1 cup of this salsa and refrigerate the remainder for another use.

Return the reserved 1 cup salsa to the blender and add the avocado, arugula, cilantro, oil, 2 tablespoons lime juice, and ¾ teaspoon salt. Blend until smooth, adding a splash of water if the sauce needs thinning. Taste for salt and lime juice. Serve the salsa with the assorted vegetables, hard-cooked eggs, and olives.

This dip, which Katie discovered in Baja, may well become your go-to sauce for crudités, steamed vegetables, or fish. In spring, Katie serves it with steamed artichokes or a platter of fresh radishes, spring onions, lightly steamed baby carrots, sugar snap peas, baby turnips, and roasted beets. In summer, think tomatoes, bell peppers, blanched green beans, and steamed zucchini. Hard-cooked farm eggs and olives round out the platter.

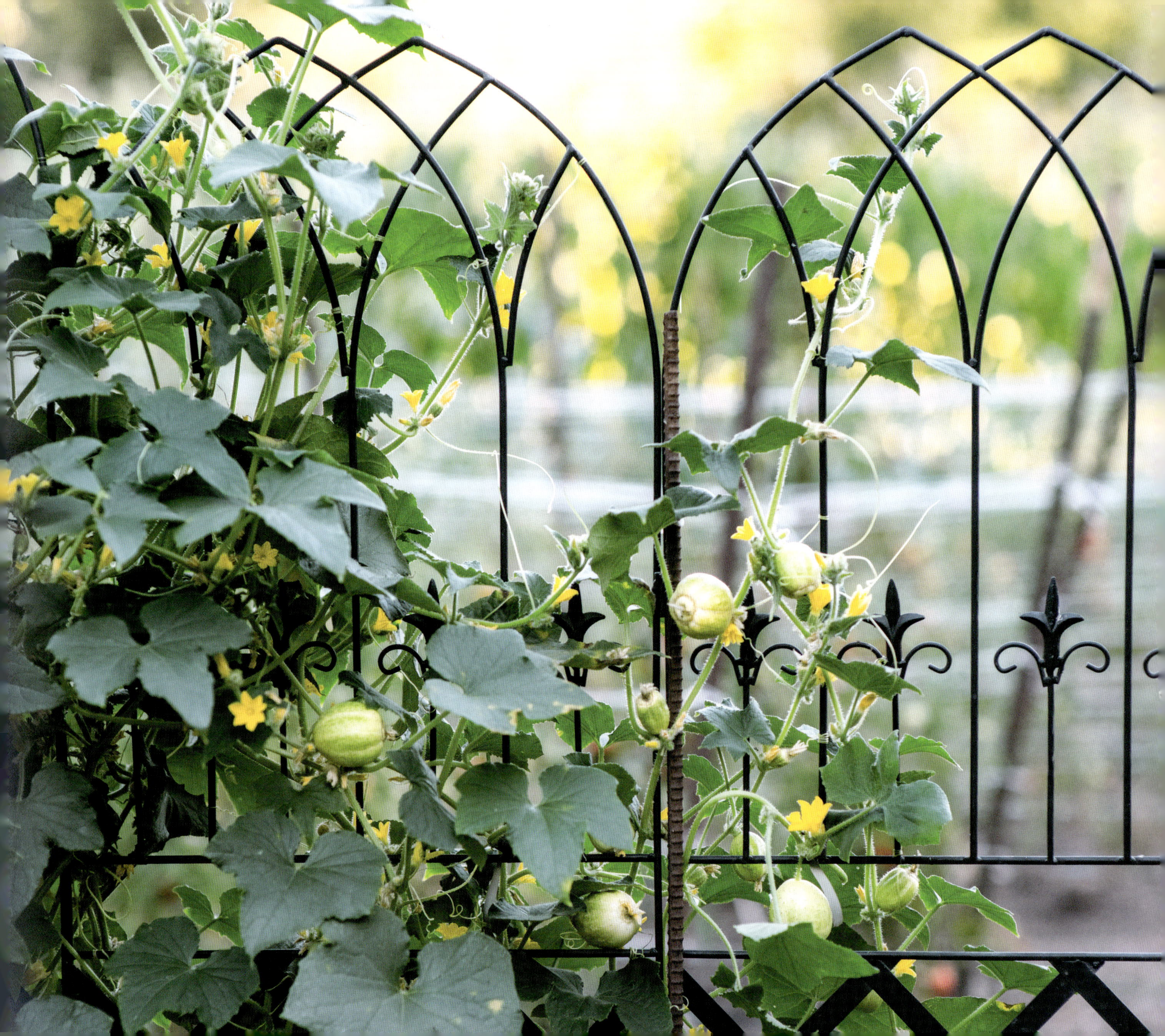

Summer Garden Salad with Linda's Dressing

Makes 1 cup dressing

Linda's Dressing:

1/3 cup extra virgin olive oil

1/3 cup grapeseed oil

1/3 cup red wine vinegar

1 teaspoon sea salt

1 teaspoon dry mustard, such as Colman's

1 heaping teaspoon sugar

1/2 teaspoon freshly ground black pepper

Optional additions: chopped shallot, minced fresh herbs, Worcestershire sauce

Salad ingredients from the garden such as lettuces, cherry tomatoes, sweet peppers, lemon cucumbers

Wine: Alexander Valley Vineyards Chardonnay

Left and right: *Lemon cucumbers climb an ornamental garden trellis; harvest of Little Gem lettuces from the Alexander Valley Vineyards garden*

Everybody in the Wetzel family makes this salad dressing, but they all switch it up a bit. This recipe is Linda's version. (Katie adds a dash of Worcestershire sauce.) It can be kept on the kitchen counter because it doesn't contain anything perishable. The one constant, of course, is Alexander Valley Vineyards extra virgin olive oil. The dressing complements whatever lettuces and vegetables the garden provides, so feel free to improvise.

Prepare the dressing: Combine all the ingredients in a tightly capped glass jar and shake well.

Combine the salad ingredients of your choice in a large bowl. Add just enough dressing to coat the salad lightly and toss. Taste for salt and pepper. Serve immediately.

Alexander Valley Vineyards

Maggie's Ranch Chicken

Serves 4

One whole fresh chicken, 4 to 4½ pounds, backbone removed, quartered

Sea salt and freshly ground black pepper

⅓ cup honey

4 tablespoons salted butter

1 tablespoon Dijon mustard

4 six-inch sprigs fresh tarragon

Wine: Alexander Valley Vineyards Merlot

Ranch chicken has nothing to do with ranch dressing, says Katie. "It's what we called this dish as kids," she recalls. "It seems that my mother only made it when we came to 'The Ranch,' which is what we called the vineyards before we had a winery." Baked with honey, mustard, and tarragon, the quartered chicken emerges with a crisp brown skin, and the sweet aroma draws everyone to the kitchen. "Kids like it and adults like it," says Katie, "and most of the food we make has to be that way."

Preheat an oven to 350°F. Season the chicken all over with salt and pepper.

In a small saucepan, combine the honey, butter, and mustard and stir over low heat until the butter melts.

Put the chicken quarters in a 9- by 13-inch baking dish and pour the honey mixture over them. Place a tarragon sprig on each quarter. Bake for 30 minutes, then remove the dish from the oven, spoon the juices over the chicken, and return to the oven for 30 minutes more. The chicken will be fully cooked, with beautifully browned skin. Let rest at least 15 minutes before serving to allow the juices to settle.

Right: Hank's sons, Robert (left) and Harry Wetzel, enjoy the family's wine in front of the entrance to the winery cave.

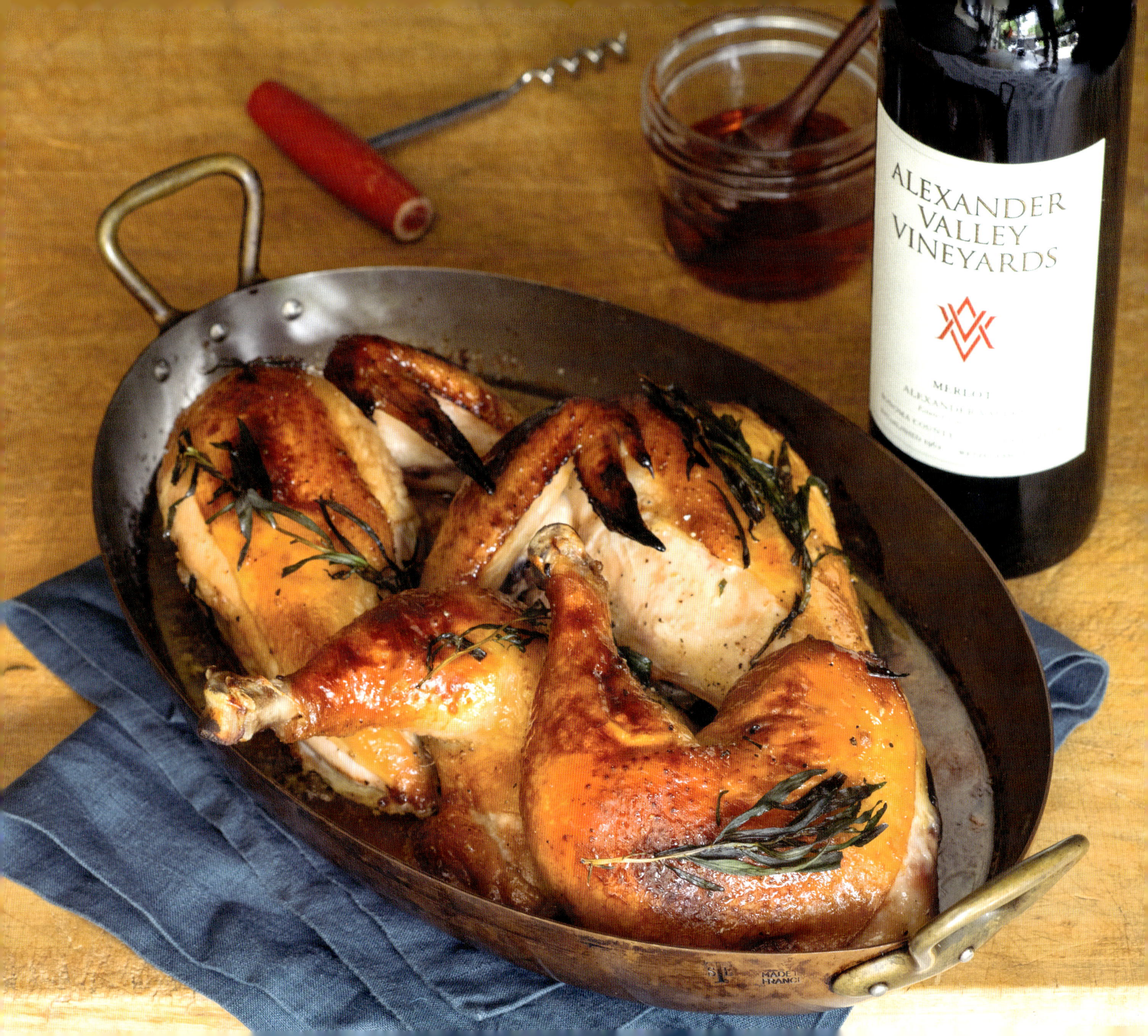
ALEXANDER VALLEY VINEYARDS
MERLOT

Above and right: *Katie checks on the laying hens in the mobile chicken coop; pasture-fed chickens produce eggs with thick, creamy yolks.*

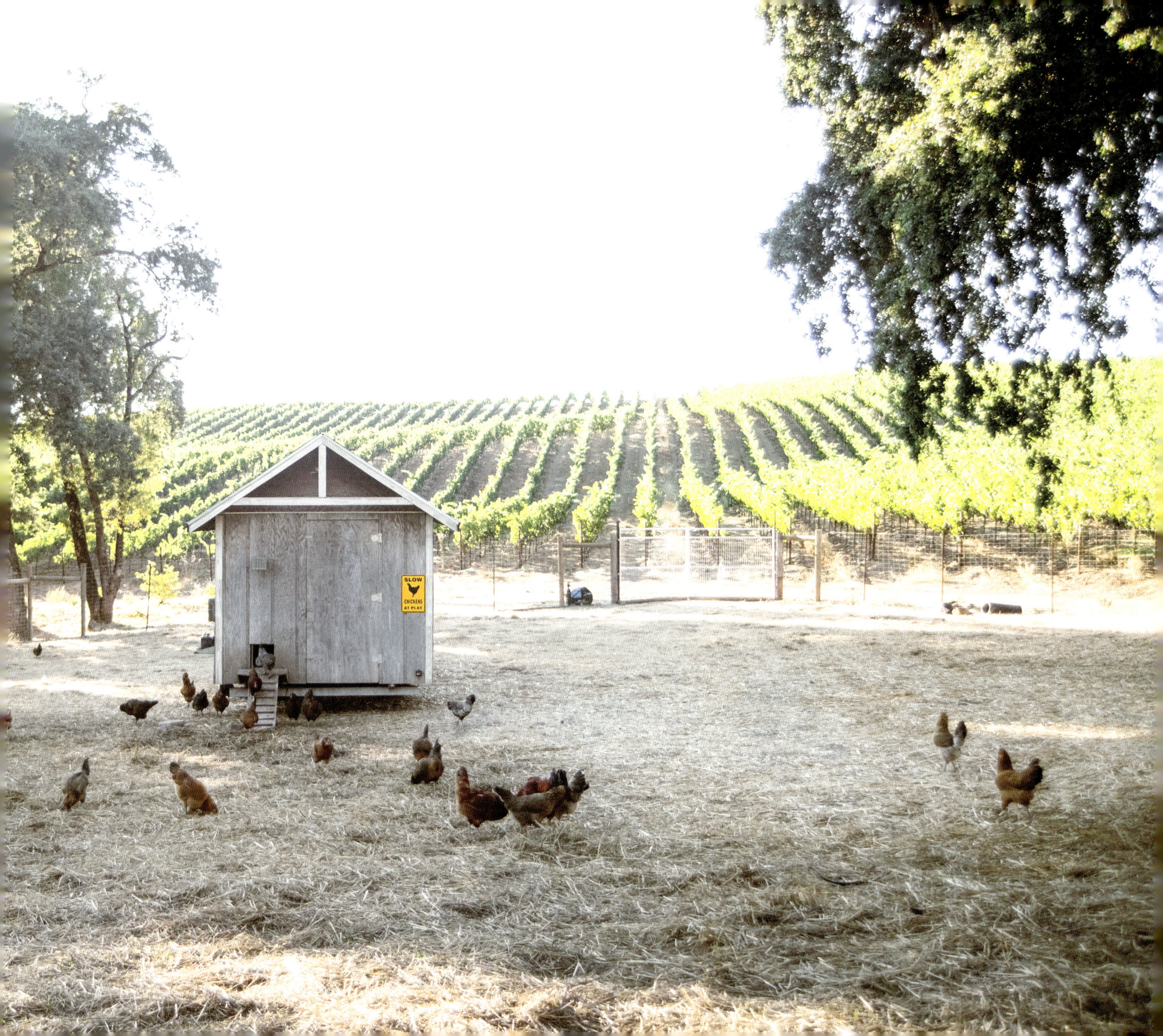
SLOW
CHICKENS
AT PLAY

katie's tip:

Katie makes her own granola for family breakfasts. If you want to include dried fruits, such as raisins, add after baking so the fruit doesn't burn. If you want to substitute store-bought granola, choose one with no dried fruit.

Pear, Blackberry, and Granola Crisp
Serves 6 to 8

This crisp showcases the ranch's abundant late-summer pear crop. The property has many Bartlett pear trees, reminiscent of a time before wine grapes became the primary crop in the Alexander Valley. Unlike most fruits, Bartlett pears are harvested while still green and hard. They will soften and turn yellow in a few days on the kitchen counter.

4 firm but ripe pears, peeled, halved, cored, and sliced

2 cups blackberries

¼ cup Demerara or turbinado sugar

3 cups Katie's Granola (recipe follows)

4 tablespoons unsalted butter, melted

Wine: Alexander Valley Vineyards Gewürztraminer

Preheat the oven to 375°F. In a large bowl, toss the pear slices and blackberries with sugar. Transfer to an 11-by-9-by-3-inch baking dish and spread in an even layer. Top with the granola, patting it into place. Pour the butter evenly over the granola.

Bake the crisp until fruit has softened and the topping has browned and crisped, about 25 minutes. Serve warm (not hot) or at room temperature with whipped cream or ice cream if desired.

Katie's Granola   Makes about 7 cups

⅓ cup pure maple syrup

⅓ cup packed light brown sugar or Demerara sugar

1 tablespoon plus 1 teaspoon pure vanilla extract

½ teaspoon sea salt

1 teaspoon ground cinnamon

½ cup vegetable oil

5 cups old-fashioned rolled oats

2 cups raw walnuts, broken into chunks

Position an oven rack in the upper-middle position. Preheat the oven to 325°F. Line a 12-by-17-inch baking sheet with parchment paper.

In a large bowl, whisk together the maple syrup, sugar, vanilla, salt, and cinnamon. Whisk in the oil. Fold in the oats and walnuts until thoroughly coated.

Transfer the mixture to the prepared pan and spread into an even layer. Using a stiff metal spatula, compress the mixture until very compact. Bake the granola, rotating the pan back to front halfway through, until lightly browned, 40 to 45 minutes. Place the pan on a rack and let the granola cool to room temperature. Break into pieces or crumble. Store in an airtight container at room temperature.

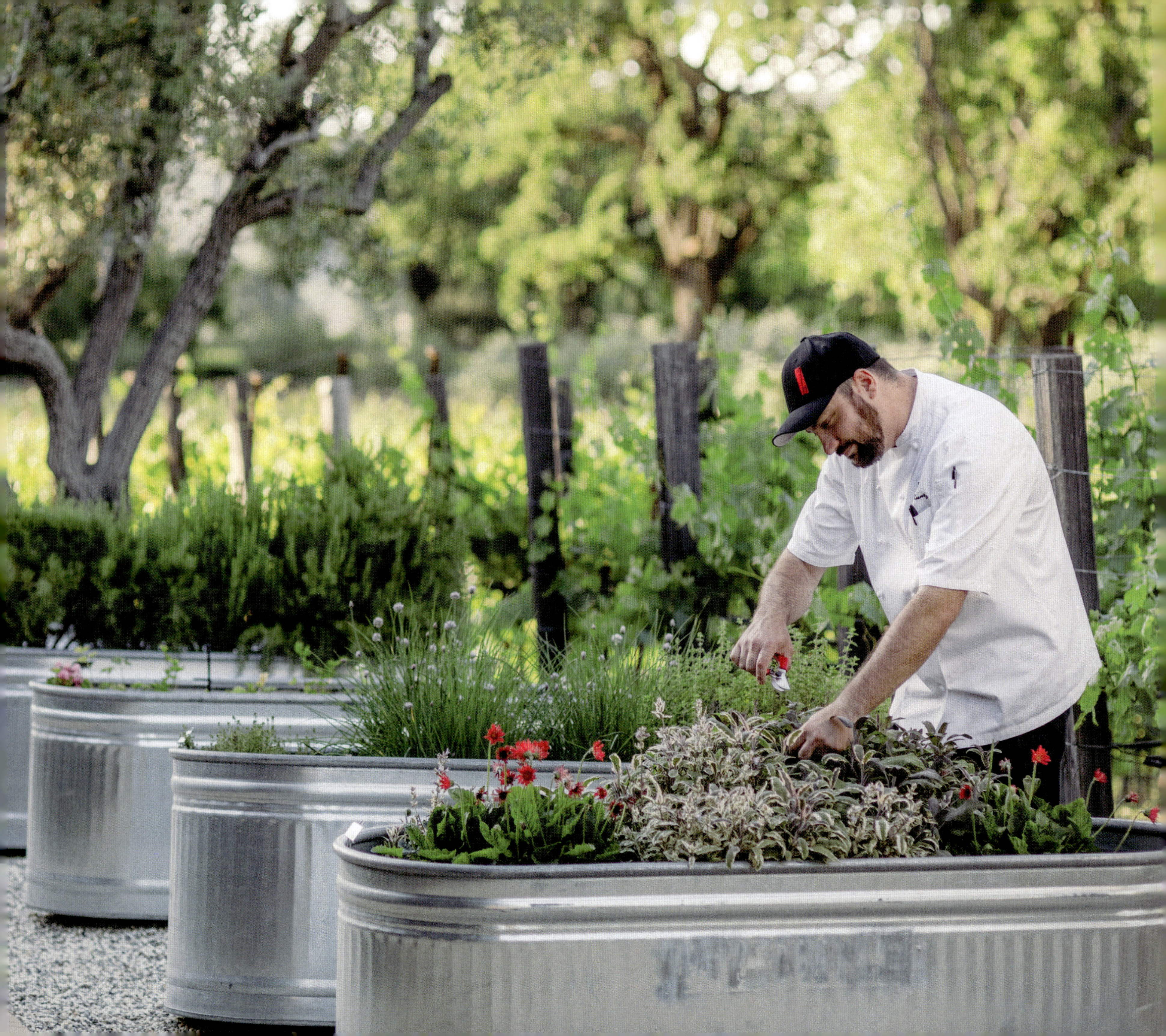

B Cellars: *New Ways to Engage*

Napa

When Jim Borsack and Duffy Keys envisioned the winery they intended to build, they knew B Cellars would need to deliver a unique visitor experience. Napa Valley already had plenty of wineries with welcoming tasting rooms and friendly staff. How does a new venture break out of that pack? How do you connect with guests in a way that they won't soon forget?

"For the most part, the Napa Valley wine-tasting experience seemed pedestrian to me," says Duffy, a longtime luxury-hotel executive. "We wanted to change the way visitors engage with a winery; we wanted to go beyond the expected."

Mission accomplished. Opened in 2014, B Cellars quickly became a top destination for wine country travelers, a winery that other wineries recommend to their guests. Five years in, more than a third of B Cellars guests are repeat visitors, people who clearly feel a rapport with the place and the people.

Who wouldn't want to return to this stylish and inviting venue, with its strollable edible gardens and shady terraces? The outdoor armchairs look so comfy, it's a wonder guests don't curl up and stay all day. The tasting room, christened the Hospitality House, is equally hard to leave, with multiple seating areas and a stunning open kitchen with a wood-burning hearth. First-timers may wonder if they took the wrong driveway and mistakenly landed at a chic boutique hotel.

Left and above: *Galvanized-steel troughs make handsome planters for the winery herb garden; chef Derick Kuntz (left) can snip chives, sage, or tarragon as needed for the creative "B bites" served to visitors.*

"We wanted to create an environment where all your senses were engaged the moment you came in the door," says Duffy. "That's why we put the kitchen and the living room together in our Hospitality House."

The seduction starts as soon as guests gather in the arrival courtyard. Within moments, they have wine in hand, perhaps the plush B Cellars Dutton Ranch Chardonnay. After a sip or two, and a welcome from their guide, an elegant one-bite appetizer arrives, maybe featherlight pumpkin gnocchi in a porcelain spoon.

Chef Derick Kuntz oversees the kitchen, henhouse, apiary, and culinary garden; he's the mastermind behind these petite and pretty "B bites"—more than sixty different ones every year to showcase B Cellars wines. "The garden is part and parcel of the kitchen," says general manager Curtis Strohl. "The experience wouldn't be the same without it. Guests are seeing vegetables and flowers on their plate that thirty minutes ago they saw in the garden."

With glass in hand, visitors take a guided stroll that leads them past the culinary herb garden, a series of deep aluminum troughs filled with rosemary, mint, nasturtiums, chives, and sage. Around the corner, the edible garden is an orderly grid of rectangular beds separated by gravel walkways. In late summer, tall spires of feathery red amaranth tower above rows of peppers, both sweet and hot (the chiles are for the daily staff meals); heirloom tomatoes; yard-long beans; cucumbers; and sunchokes. A dormant asparagus bed promises a tasty crop the following spring, when the garden will also be flush with Kalette (a kale–Brussels sprout cross), kohlrabi, Chioggia beets, baby zucchini, arugula, Nantes carrots, spring garlic, young basil, and salad greens.

"I like growing things that others don't typically try," says the chef, pointing to the finger limes whose tart, caviar-like "pearls" he uses for garnishes, the huckleberries he adds to sauces and house-made sausage, a caper bush, and a leafy horseradish plant. His treasured Espelette peppers, a rare variety from France's Basque region, ripen to red in early fall. After drying them, Derick will grind them for a fragrant, gently spicy, pumpkin-colored seasoning he uses all year. Pineapple guava, an attractive shrub with deep-pink blossoms and gray-green leaves, provides fuzzy egg-shaped fruits, while cherry, apple, peach, pear, Asian pear, Meyer lemon, and blood orange trees are just getting settled into this young landscape.

"What I love most about the garden is that people will come lean against the fence while I'm working," says Michael Christophel, a professional gardener who helps with the plant sourcing and maintenance. "I get to meet people from all over the world, and they get to

Above: *(clockwise from left) The winery garden is at the base of a hillside blanketed with ancient walnut trees that the owners spared from vineyard development; onion patch; plaque commemorating the vineyard planting date; a carrot bouquet; Tuscan kale; a home for the winery's hens*

"It's rewarding to see our vineyards in harmony with barn owls, hawks, falcons, and wild turkeys," says Duffy. "There's diversity here, and that's what we like."

taste something right out of the garden." Michael plants lemon verbena, cherry tomatoes, and strawberries in the corners, so even guests who don't venture into the garden can snatch a taste as they pass.

A scheduled visit to B Cellars typically includes a barrel tasting—a privilege reserved for VIPs at most wineries—before guests return to the Hospitality House for a sit-down wine sampling. The winery produces small lots of many types—single-varietal and single-vineyard bottlings as well as complex blends—so Derick has a relentless creative challenge. Every wine has its own precise accompaniment, a fully realized mini dish designed to enhance it. "We set our wines up for success," says Curtis, and the property's fruits, vegetables, and herbs provide a big assist, subtly echoing wine aromas and textures.

In late spring, the release of the winery's lively rosé coincides with the start of California salmon season. To highlight the pink wine's freshness and brisk acidity, Derick pairs it with salmon tartare, adding finely diced garden strawberries and cucumbers to lighten and brighten the rich, fatty fish. It's a surprising, even shocking, combination, but it works, complemented by the wine's youthful fruitiness.

Above and right: *(clockwise from left) Renowned for its ambitious hospitality program, the winery entices visitors with creative food offerings, such as handmade beet tortellini with elk* sugo *and kale chips; B Cellars Rosé; outdoor tastings have a vineyard view.*

34 Gather

Summer is the garden's peak moment, of course, when the estate's stone fruits and tomatoes grow ripe and sweet. For B Cellars Blend 23—a marriage of Sauvignon Blanc, Chardonnay, and Viognier—Derick composes a salad of tomatoes, watermelon radishes, burrata, and peaches in vivid summer hues. The tomatoes and spicy radishes connect with the Sauvignon Blanc, the creamy burrata speaks to the Chardonnay, and the peach echoes the aromatics in the Viognier.

By late autumn, the cool-weather-loving root vegetables in the garden are sizing up. Derick showcases the season's first parsnips with seared scallops, preparing the underappreciated vegetable two ways: a silky puree for the dish's foundation and fried ribbons for crunch on top.

In winter, to match the winery's Blend 24 and to nudge guests out of their comfort zone, the chef often looks to farm-raised game, such as ostrich and elk. "You should get a little nervous about one of the bites, I think," says Derick. Certainly, any guests uneasy about the chef's elk *sugo* will quickly be won over. The meaty braise, like the Super Tuscan–style Blend 24, is concentrated and rich, with a mirepoix of garden vegetables adding sweetness. The winery's heirloom chickens contribute the eggs for the tortellini dough (and for the staff's Saturday buffet breakfast), but Derick fills and shapes every dumpling by hand.

"One club member told me, 'My husband never eats vegetables except when he's here,'" says Curtis.

Jim's retailing background schooled him in creating experiences that make an impression—that aren't quite what guests expected when they got out of the car. "We have a shared vision of excellence," says Duffy about his business partner. "We take pride in our wine, in the warmth of our employees, in the beauty of our surroundings. And it's rewarding to see our guests appreciate them, too."

From the beginning, Jim and Duffy imagined an integrated estate, with gardens, orchards, grapevines, and honeybees in symbiosis with the native landscape. "There's diversity here," says Duffy, "and that's what we like."

menu

Strawberry Salmon Tartare
B Cellars Rosé

Heirloom Tomato and Peach Salad with Burrata
B Cellars Blend 23

Seared Sea Scallops with Parsnips Two Ways
B Cellars Chardonnay

Elk Sugo with Herb Cheese Tortellini and Kale Chips
B Cellars Blend 24

Dijon-Crusted Lamb Chops with Pistachio Puree, Chard, and Huckleberry Gastrique
B Cellars Cabernet Sauvignon

Strawberry Salmon Tartare

Serves 6

Pickled Peppers:

3 baby bell sweet peppers, preferably a mix of colors

1 jalapeño chile, halved lengthwise

¼ cup white wine vinegar

¼ cup sugar

¼ cup water

5 to 6 ounces skinless salmon fillet, pin bones removed, in small, neat dice

3 large strawberries, hulled, in small, neat dice

1½ teaspoons extra virgin olive oil

Finely grated zest of 1 lemon

Sea salt

1 small lemon cucumber or 2-inch chunk English cucumber, peeled if desired, halved lengthwise, and very thinly sliced crosswise (12 half-moons)

12 fresh chive batons, each 1 to 2 inches long, for garnish

Wine: B Cellars Rosé

"When I taste our rosé, the two flavors that come to mind are salmon and strawberries," says Derick. "The wine is tart, so the fat of the salmon helps. And the rosé can stand up to a lot of spice." The combination of ingredients is unusual, but the recipe is among the most requested at B Cellars. If you can't find Baby Bell sweet peppers, choose a long, narrow sweet pepper, such as Corno di Toro or Anaheim, so the rings are small.

Make the pickled peppers: Cut off the tip of each pepper, then slice thinly crosswise with a vegetable slicer. Put the pepper slices and jalapeño in a heatproof bowl. In a small saucepan, combine the vinegar, sugar, and water and bring to a simmer over medium heat, stirring to dissolve the sugar. Pour the hot mixture over the peppers. Let cool, then cover and chill for at least 1 day. The pickled peppers can be made up to 2 weeks ahead.

In a bowl, combine the salmon, strawberries, oil, and lemon zest, season with salt, and toss gently. Taste for salt.

Divide the salmon mixture evenly among twelve Chinese porcelain soupspoons. (Derick uses two small spoons to shape the salmon mixture into neat quenelles, but that's optional.) Top each portion with a cucumber half-moon and a sweet pepper ring. Garnish each with a chive baton. Serve immediately.

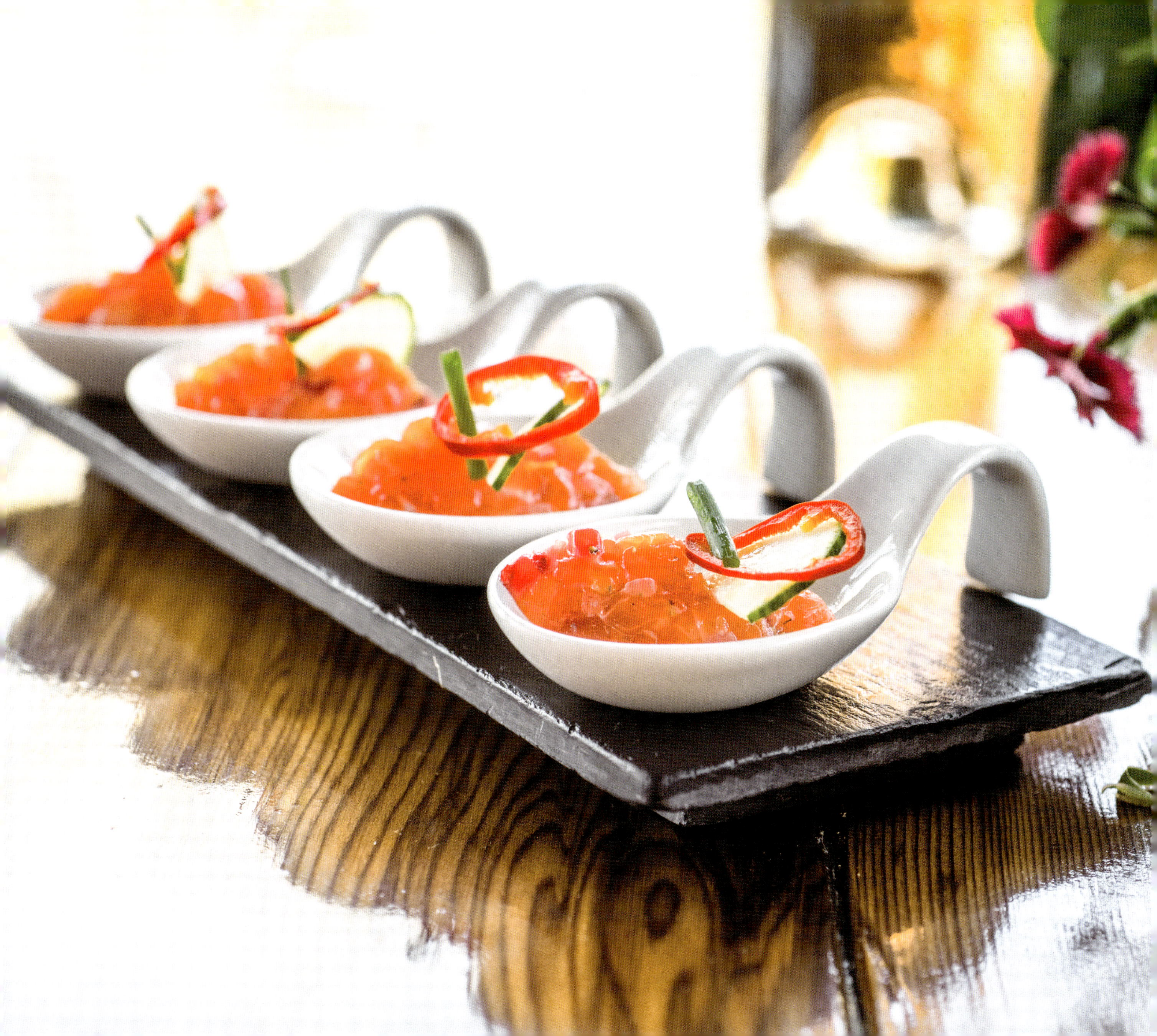

chef's tips:

Immersing shaved watermelon radishes in ice water helps them stay crisp.

For long keeping, wrap fresh herbs in a moist paper towel and refrigerate in a lidded container.

Heirloom Tomato and Peach Salad with Burrata

Serves 6

This gorgeous summer salad is always a riot of color but never exactly the same, says Derick. Depending on what's coming out of the garden, he may change up the tomatoes, or the type of cucumber, or the way he arranges the components. Sometimes he uses microgreens in place of the cress or adds Spanish black radishes from the garden. "I have fifty pictures of these salads and no two are identical," says the chef.

Pickled Red Onion:

½ cup sugar

½ cup white wine vinegar

½ cup water

½ red onion, ends removed, thinly sliced from stem to root end

2 large or 3 small yellow peaches, halved, pitted, and cut into wedges

3 tomatoes, preferably a mix of colors, cut into wedges

1 tablespoon extra virgin olive oil, plus more for the cheese

Sea salt and freshly ground black pepper

1 small watermelon radish, thickly peeled, then halved and thinly shaved

½ pound burrata cheese, drained, at room temperature

1 lemon cucumber or Persian cucumber, peeled if desired, then thinly shaved

Carr's Ciderhouse Cider Syrup, for drizzling

1 bunch watercress, upland cress, or peppercress, thick stems removed

Wine: B Cellars Blend 23

Make the pickled red onion: In a small saucepan, combine the sugar, vinegar, and water and bring to a simmer over medium-high heat, swirling the pan to dissolve the sugar. When the sugar has dissolved, remove from the heat and let cool completely. Put the onion slices into a bowl and pour the cooled liquid over them. Cover and refrigerate for at least 24 hours.

Put the peach and tomato wedges on a platter. Drizzle with the oil and season with salt and pepper. Let stand for 30 to 45 minutes to absorb the seasonings.

Put the shaved radish into a bowl with ice water to cover and let stand for about 30 minutes to crisp.

Divide the burrata into 6 equal slices and put 1 slice on the center of each of six salad plates. Season each slice with salt and pepper and a few drops of olive oil. Surround with the peach and tomato wedges and the cucumber. Drain the radishes, pat dry, and add them to the plates, scattering them attractively. Place slivers of pickled onion here and there. Drizzle each portion with about ½ teaspoon cider syrup. (A squeeze bottle is helpful.) Garnish each serving with tufts of cress. Serve immediately.

Seared Sea Scallops with Parsnips Two Ways

Serves 6

6 small Chioggia beets, greens removed
½ cup sugar
½ cup white wine vinegar
½ cup water
2 parsnips, about ¾ pound total, peeled
Sea salt
Canola oil, for deep-frying

Vinaigrette:
1 small navel orange
1 lemon
1 lime
¼ cup apple cider vinegar
1 teaspoon sea salt
1 tablespoon honey
1 vanilla bean
1 cup extra virgin olive oil
1 cup canola oil

½ cup raw hazelnuts
2 small navel oranges
12 sea scallops, feet removed
1 tablespoon B Cellars Blend 7 (see Note)
2 tablespoons extra virgin olive oil
3 small heads frisée, pale inner hearts only

Wine: B Cellars Chardonnay

This complex dish demonstrates how Derick approaches the challenge of creating "bites" that heighten the wine experience. Buttery scallops and hazelnuts are classic with Chardonnay, but B Cellars' Chardonnay shows more bright citrus fruit and acidity than many. Weaving citrus into the dish helps highlight those qualities. The fruit, beets, and parsnips all come from the property, and this dish always makes new fans for the humble parsnip.

Put the beets into a saucepan with lightly salted water to cover and bring to a simmer over medium heat. Adjust the heat to maintain a simmer and cook uncovered until the beets can be pierced easily, about 30 minutes. Drain. When cool enough to handle, peel the beets and put them into a small, heatproof bowl.

In a small saucepan, combine the sugar, vinegar, and water and bring to a simmer over medium-high heat, swirling the pan to dissolve the sugar. When the sugar has dissolved, remove from the heat and pour over the beets. Let cool to room temperature, then cover and refrigerate for 24 hours.

With a vegetable peeler, shave the parsnips lengthwise into ribbons. Stop when you have used about half of each parsnip and set the ribbons aside. Cut the remaining half of each parsnip into ¾-inch pieces and put them into a saucepan with lightly salted water to cover. Bring to a simmer over medium heat, then adjust the heat to maintain a simmer and cook until the parsnips are tender when pierced, about 15 minutes. Drain, reserving the cooking liquid. In a blender, puree the parsnips with enough of the reserved cooking liquid to make a silky puree. Season with salt.

Pour canola oil to a depth of 3 inches into a heavy saucepan and heat to 340°F. Add the parsnip ribbons and fry, agitating them constantly, until golden, about 2 minutes. With a wire-mesh skimmer, lift them out and drain on paper towels. Season with salt.

Make the vinaigrette: With a rasp grater, remove the zest from the orange, lemon, and lime. Cut all the citrus in half, then squeeze the juice and strain. Combine the juices and zests in the blender with the vinegar and add the salt and honey. Halve the vanilla bean lengthwise and, with the tip of a small knife, scrape the seeds into the blender. Blend briefly. With the blender running, add the oils slowly. Taste for salt.

Preheat the oven to 350°F. Toast the hazelnuts on a baking sheet until fragrant and lightly colored, about 10 minutes. Let cool, then chop coarsely.

Cut a thin slice off both ends of 1 orange so it will stand upright. Stand the orange on a cutting surface and, using a sharp knife, remove all the peel and white pith by slicing from top to bottom all the way around the orange, following the contour of the fruit. Cut along the membranes to release the individual segments and place them in a bowl. Repeat with the second orange.

Season the scallops on both sides with the Blend 7. Heat two large skillets over medium-high heat. Add 1 tablespoon of the olive oil to each skillet. When the oil is hot, add the scallops and sear until lightly browned on the bottom, about 1 minute. Turn and cook the other flat side until nicely colored, about 1 minute, then reduce the heat and continue cooking until the scallops are just barely cooked at the center, about 2 minutes longer.

Spoon about 1½ tablespoons of the parsnip puree onto each of six salad plates and spread it thinly. Scatter the hazelnuts around the rim of each plate. Toss the frisée with just enough of the vinaigrette to coat it lightly. Arrange a tuft of frisée on the parsnip puree on each plate, then nestle 2 scallops alongside the frisée. Quarter the beets and scatter them and the orange segments attractively around each salad. Place the fried parsnips on top and serve immediately.

Note: *B Cellars Blend 7 is a proprietary spice mix that includes dried thyme, orange peel, onion, lemon verbena, Espelette pepper, sugar, and salt. It is available for purchase in the winery's tasting room. Alternatively, use salt and pepper only or create your own blend using some or all of the listed spices to your taste.*

Elk Sugo with Herb Cheese Tortellini and Kale Chips

Serves 6

Elk Sugo:

2 pounds boneless elk sirloin, in ¾-inch dice

2 tablespoons B Cellars Blend 8 (see Note)

¼ cup extra virgin olive oil

1 large yellow onion, in ½-inch dice

1 large carrot, in ½-inch dice

3 large celery ribs, in ½-inch dice

1 medium fennel bulb, in ½-inch dice

10 cloves garlic, chopped

1 cup dry red wine

4 cups diced Roma tomatoes (no need to peel)

1 bay leaf

½ teaspoon chile flakes, or to taste

1 cup chicken broth or water

Sea salt and freshly ground black pepper

Tortellini Dough:

2 large whole eggs plus 4 large egg yolks

1 tablespoon extra virgin olive oil

1 tablespoon water

2 cups Italian "00" flour

¾ teaspoon sea salt

Tortellini Filling:

½ pound whole-milk ricotta cheese (about 1 cup)

¼ cup grated Parmigiano-Reggiano cheese

2 tablespoons chopped fresh flat-leaf parsley

1 tablespoon chopped fresh sage

¼ teaspoon freshly ground black pepper

Sea salt

Derick buys elk from a Montana farm, but you can order it from a good butcher. The meat is dark, deeply flavorful, and lean. Substitute beef top or bottom round or lamb shoulder, if you prefer. For sugo *(Italian for "meat sauce"), the elk is always braised slowly with diced garden vegetables, and the flavor improves overnight. If making tortellini seems daunting, substitute store-bought* pappardelle.

Fine semolina, for dusting

1 whole egg beaten with 1 teaspoon water, for egg wash

Kale Chips:

Canola oil, for deep-frying

¼ pound Tuscan kale (½ bunch), ribs removed

Sea salt

Extra virgin olive oil, for drizzling

Wine: B Cellars Blend 24

Make the elk *sugo*: Season the elk all over with the Blend 8. Let stand at room temperature for 1 hour.

In a large, heavy pot, heat the olive oil over high heat. Add the elk and sear without stirring for about 2 minutes. Stir briefly and continue searing the meat on all sides, stirring as little as possible to avoid drawing out the meat juices. It will take 5 to 10 minutes to sear the elk properly. Reduce the heat as needed to prevent burning.

Add the onion, carrot, celery, and fennel and cook over medium heat, stirring, for about 5 minutes to soften the vegetables. Add the garlic and cook, stirring, until fragrant, about 2 minutes. Add the wine and simmer until reduced by half. Add the tomatoes, bay leaf, chile flakes, and broth, then season with salt and pepper. Bring to a simmer, adjust the heat to maintain a gentle simmer, and cook uncovered until the meat is tender, about 1 hour. Remove the bay leaf. Taste for seasoning. You can prepare the *sugo* up to 1 day ahead and refrigerate.

Make the tortellini dough: In a bowl, whisk together the eggs, egg yolks, olive oil, and water.

In another bowl, whisk together the flour and salt. Transfer the flour to a work surface and make a well in the center large enough to contain the eggs. Make sure the flour "walls" are high enough to keep the eggs from escaping. Pour the egg mixture into the well. With a fork, begin drawing in the flour from the sides and whisking it with the eggs. Take care not to let the runny eggs breach the flour walls. When the dough becomes too stiff to mix with the fork, continue with your hands, kneading until you have incorporated all the flour and the dough is smooth and elastic. Divide the dough into 4 equal portions, shape each portion into a ball, flatten slightly, and wrap in plastic wrap. Let rest for 1 hour at room temperature.

Make the tortellini filling: In a bowl, combine the cheeses, parsley, sage, and pepper and mix with a wooden spoon until blended. Season to taste with salt.

To shape the tortellini, line a baking sheet with parchment paper and dust the parchment with semolina. Set up a pasta machine. Work with 1 dough portion at a time and keep the others covered with plastic wrap or a dish towel to prevent drying.

With a rolling pin, flatten the dough into a rectangle thin enough to pass through the pasta machine set at the widest setting. Pass the dough through the rollers twice at the widest setting, then continue passing it through the rollers, tightening the rollers by one setting each time, until the dough is as thin as you can manage. (Derick flattens the dough through setting #7 on his machine.)

Lay the flattened dough sheet on a work surface and cut into rounds with a 3¾-inch cutter. Put 1 rounded tablespoon of the filling on the center of each round. Brush the edge of a round lightly with egg wash, then fold the round into a half-moon, pressing the edges to seal. With the straight edge facing you, grasp the two ends, bring them together, and pinch to secure, brushing with a little egg wash if needed to help them seal. Place the tortellino on the prepared pan and repeat with the remaining filling-topped rounds and then the remaining dough and filling. You should have 18 to 20 tortellini. Let them dry uncovered at room temperature for about 30 minutes before cooking them.

While the tortellini rest, make the kale chips: Pour canola oil to a depth of 3 inches in a deep saucepan and heat to 340°F. Cut the kale crosswise into 2-inch-wide pieces. Dry thoroughly. Working in small batches, add the kale to the hot oil (be careful, as the oil can pop) and fry, agitating constantly, until the kale crisps, about 2 minutes. With a wire-mesh skimmer, lift out the chips and drain on paper towels. Sprinkle with salt while warm.

At serving time, reheat the elk *sugo* if necessary. Bring a large pot of salted water to a boil over high heat. Add the tortellini and cook at a gentle simmer, until they float and the pasta is fully cooked, about 2 minutes. (Lift one out and taste a bit of the pasta to be sure.) With the skimmer, lift them out into a bowl and drizzle lightly with olive oil.

Divide the *sugo* among six pasta bowls. Arrange 3 tortellini around the *sugo* in each bowl. Perch kale chips on top of the *sugo* to garnish. Serve immediately.

Note: *B Cellars Blend 8 is a proprietary spice mix that includes salt, ginger, onion, garlic, black pepper, rosemary, oregano, and chile. It is available for purchase in the winery's tasting room. Alternatively, use salt and pepper only or create your own blend using some or all of the listed spices to your taste.*

Dijon-Crusted Lamb Chops with Pistachio Puree, Chard, and Huckleberry Gastrique

Serves 6

Huckleberries are one of Derick's favorite crops from the B Cellars estate. They ripen in late summer but freeze well. He often uses them in dishes to complement the winery's Cabernet Sauvignon, which typically has a huckleberry scent. The tiny marble potatoes, chard, and garlic for this recipe also come straight from the winery garden. Garlic oil and garlic confit are part of Derick's toolbox at the winery and at home. He spreads the confit on crackers ("it's like candy") and uses the aromatic oil on vegetables.

Garlic Confit:

¼ cup peeled whole garlic cloves

1 cup extra virgin olive oil (or part canola oil, if desired)

Pistachio Puree:

½ cup raw pistachios

½ cup whole milk

½ cup water

¼ cup coarsely chopped fresh flat-leaf parsley

1 tablespoon coarsely chopped fresh tarragon

1 teaspoon Banyuls or sherry vinegar

¼ teaspoon sea salt

Huckleberry Gastrique:

½ cup huckleberries, thawed if frozen

2 cups dry red wine

3 tablespoons sugar

2 tablespoons Banyuls or sherry vinegar

½ teaspoon sea salt

2 tablespoons Dijon mustard

2 tablespoons B Cellars Blend 9 (see Note)

2 tablespoons extra virgin olive oil

12 lamb rib chops, about 1 inch thick

1 pound marble potatoes, about 1 inch in diameter

2 tablespoons extra virgin olive oil

Chard:

2 small bunches chard, ribs removed

1 large shallot, ends removed, then halved lengthwise and thinly julienned lengthwise

1 cup dry red wine

2 tablespoons extra virgin olive oil

Sea salt and freshly ground black pepper

1 cup panko (Japanese-style bread crumbs)

½ cup canola oil

Wine: B Cellars Cabernet Sauvignon

(continued)

44 Gather

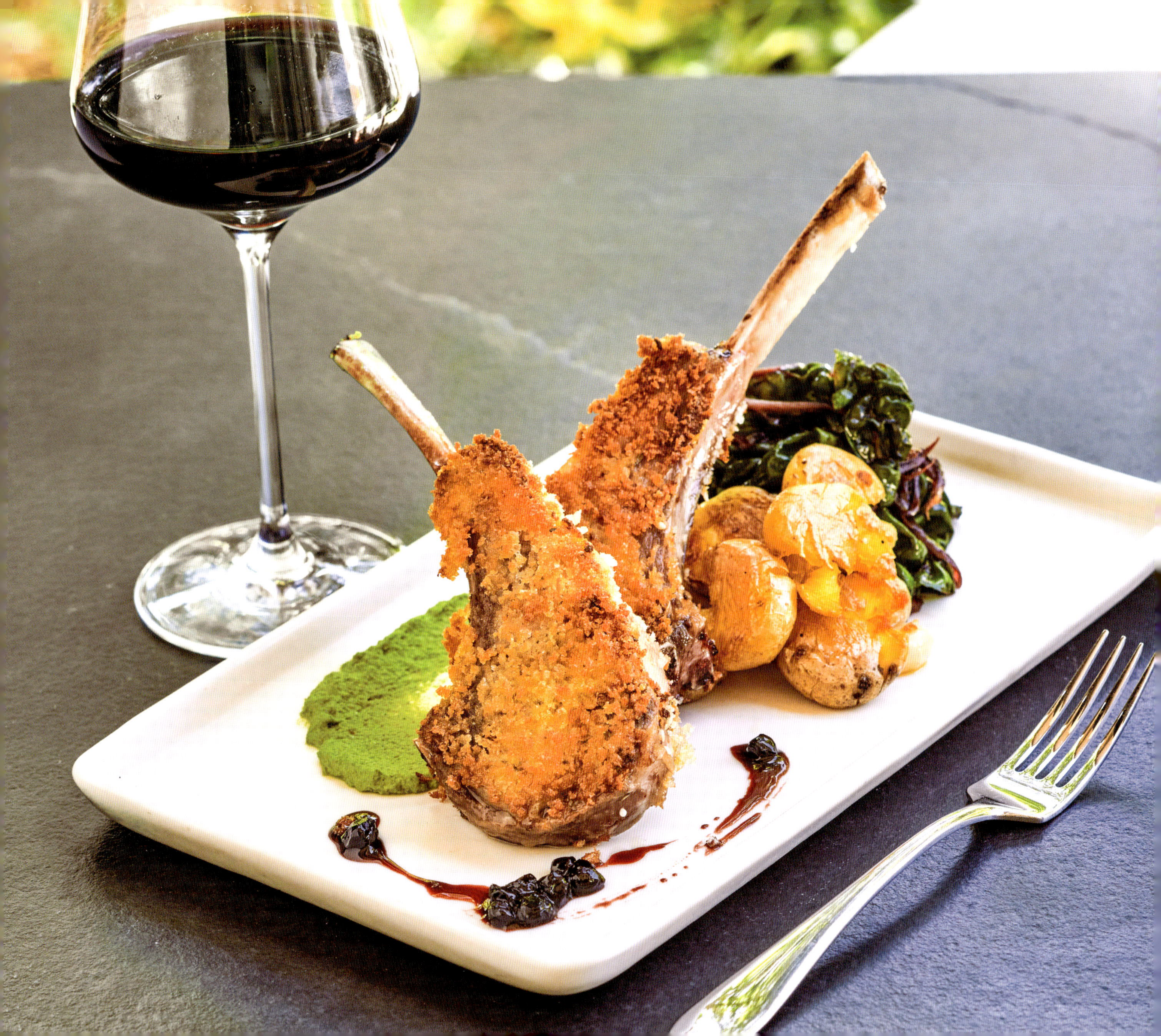

Dijon-Crusted Lamb Chops with Pistachio Puree and Huckleberry Gastrique *(continued)*

Make the garlic confit: In a small saucepan, combine the garlic cloves and olive oil and bring to a simmer over medium-high heat. Reduce the heat to maintain a gentle simmer and cook uncovered until the cloves are tender and just starting to color, 10 to 15 minutes. Drain the garlic, reserving both the cloves and the garlic oil. The oil will keep refrigerated for weeks. The garlic will keep refrigerated for up to 1 week.

Make the pistachio puree: In a small saucepan, combine the pistachios, milk, and water and bring to a simmer over medium-high heat. Reduce the heat to maintain a gentle simmer and cook uncovered until the nuts are tender, about 15 minutes. Let the mixture cool to room temperature.

In a blender, combine the pistachios and any liquid in the pot, the parsley, tarragon, vinegar, and salt and blend until smooth. Taste for salt.

Make the huckleberry gastrique: In a small saucepan, combine the huckleberries, wine, sugar, vinegar, and salt and bring to a simmer over medium heat. Simmer until reduced to a scant 1 cup. Let cool slightly.

In a small bowl, stir together the mustard, Blend 9, and olive oil to make a paste. Slather the paste on both sides of each lamb chop. Set the chops on a platter and let rest at room temperature for 45 minutes.

Preheat the oven to 375°F or 350°F with a convection fan. Put the potatoes on a baking sheet and toss with the olive oil. Bake until tender when pierced, about 15 minutes. Let cool on the pan, then smack the potatoes with your palm or the back of a plate until they split. Season to taste with salt. Drizzle with 1 tablespoon of the garlic oil and toss gently to coat. Scatter the cooked garlic cloves all around the potatoes. Leave the oven on.

Meanwhile, prepare the chard: Stack the chard leaves in batches and cut crosswise into thirds or quarters. You should have about 2 quarts loosely packed. In a small skillet, combine the shallot and wine and bring to a simmer over medium heat. Simmer until the wine has evaporated completely, about 15 minutes.

At serving time: Return the potatoes to the oven until they are lightly crisped, about 10 minutes.

To finish the chard, heat a large skillet over high heat. Add the olive oil, then add the red wine–cooked shallots and stir for about 30 seconds. Add the chard, season with salt and pepper, and cook, tossing with tongs, until the chard has wilted and softened but is not fully tender, about 2 minutes. Keep warm.

Coat the lamb chops on both sides with the panko. Heat two large skillets over medium-high heat until very hot. Add ¼ cup of the canola oil to each skillet. When the oil is hot, add the lamb chops, dividing them evenly between the skillets, and sear on one side until the panko is browned, about 2 minutes. Turn and transfer the skillet to the oven. For medium-rare, cook the chops until they are somewhat firm to the touch but still have some give, about 5 minutes.

To serve, put about 1½ tablespoons pistachio puree on each of six dinner plates and spread it thinly. Divide the chard and potatoes among the plates. Arrange 2 lamb chops artfully on each plate. Drizzle the huckleberry gastrique around the edge of each plate. Serve immediately.

Note: *B Cellars Blend 9 is a proprietary spice mix that includes coriander, cinnamon, cumin, pepper, rosemary, salt, garlic, thyme, and chile. It is available for purchase in the winery's tasting room. Alternatively, use salt and pepper only or create your own blend using some or all of the listed spices to your taste.*

uncommon edibles:

B Cellars chef Derick Kuntz likes to grow produce he can't easily buy. Here are a few top performers in the B Cellars garden.

Espelette pepper: This French red pepper is usually dried and ground for a spice; it resembles hot paprika but is less earthy.

Finger lime: The green-skinned fruit looks like a tiny cucumber. Inside are hundreds of pale, sweet-tart caviar-like beads that pop in the mouth.

Hibiscus: Known as *jamaica* in Spanish, this plant (*Hibiscus sabdariffa*) produces beautiful red blossoms. The petals can be dried and then steeped for a tart tea, served hot or cold.

Huckleberry: Similar to blueberries, huckleberries are crunchier, seedier, and more intense in flavor.

Kalette: A cross between kale and Brussels sprouts, this new hybrid produces leafy green and violet florets.

Pineapple guava: Also known as *feijoa*, this lovely shrub yields egg-shaped fruits with juicy, sweet-tart flesh and a pineapple-like flavor.

Right: *Huckleberries thrive in the B Cellars winery garden.*

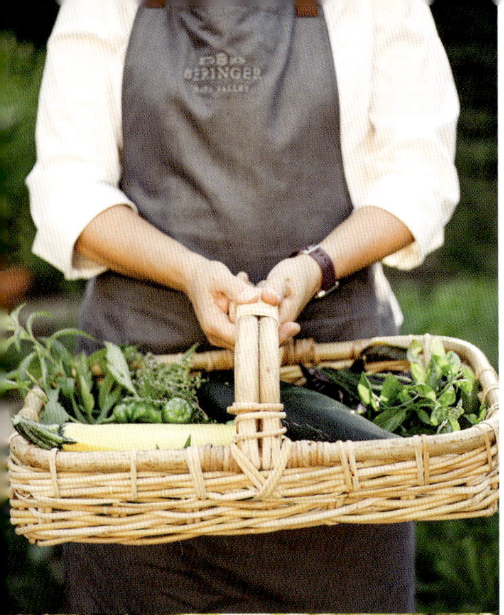
BERINGER

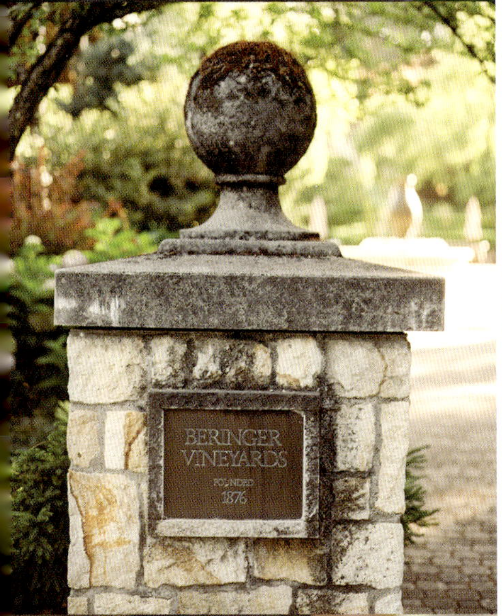
BERINGER
VINEYARDS
1876

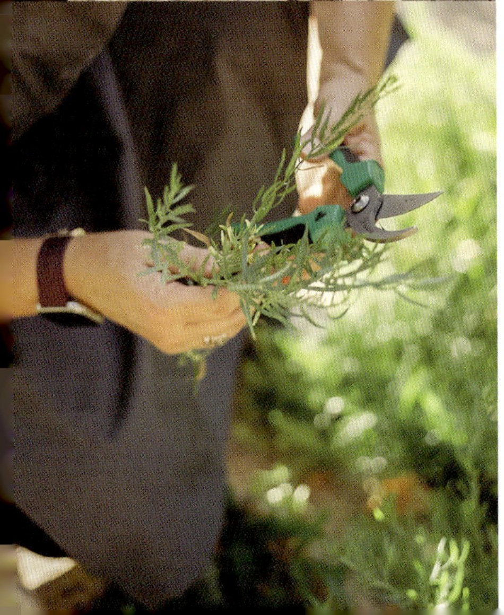

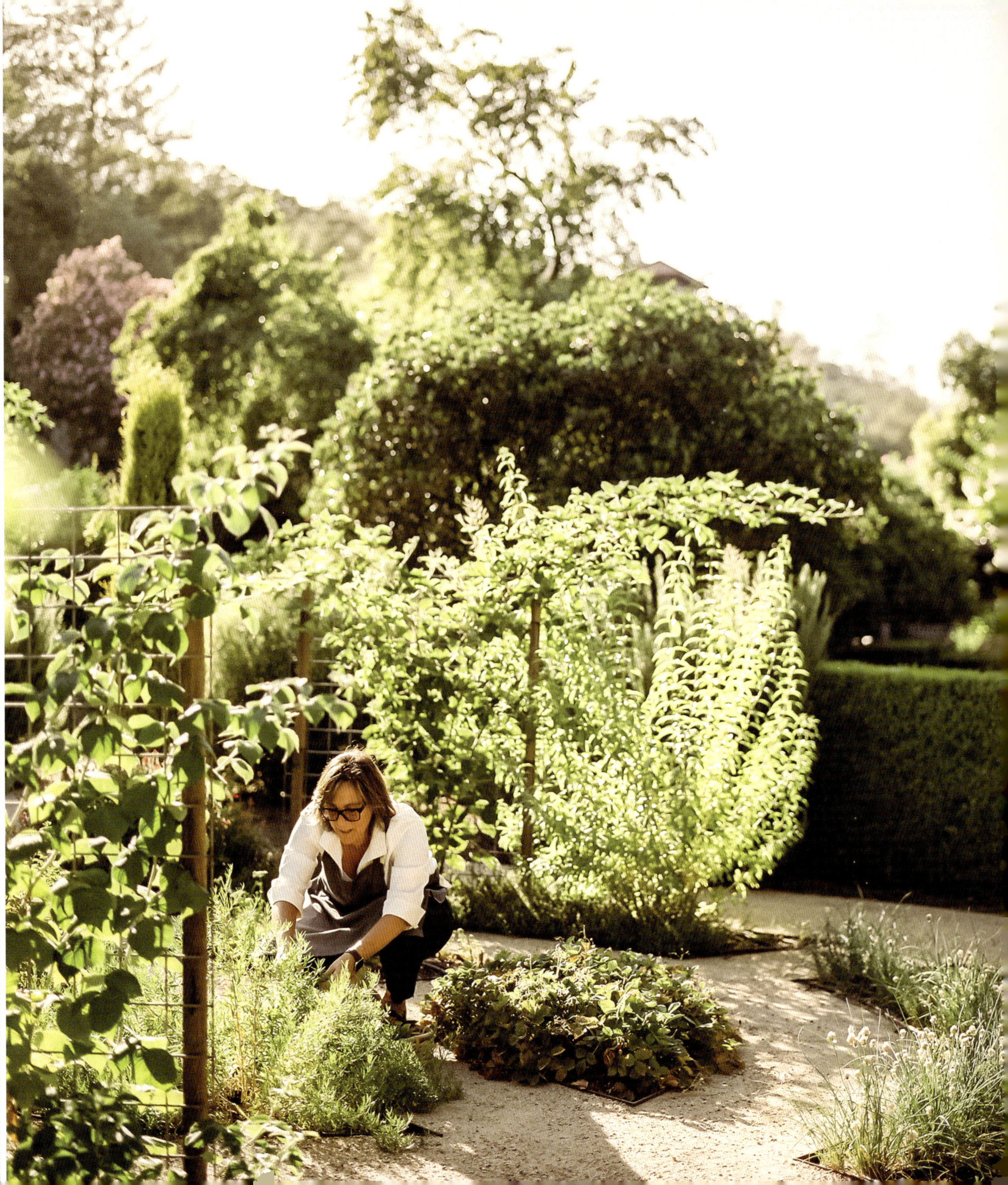

Beringer Vineyards: *A Sensory Teaching Garden*

St. Helena

One of the most visited wineries in Napa Valley, Beringer Vineyards enchants guests with its historic nineteenth-century architecture and expansive, shady grounds. The winery was the first in the valley to offer public tours, laying the foundation for the polished hospitality offerings at Napa Valley wineries today. Yet many who make a beeline for the Beringer tasting room, drawn by the renown of its wines (its Cabernet Sauvignon and Private Reserve Chardonnay are California standard bearers), miss the experience of discovering its handsome landscape and gardens.

People with time for a more leisurely visit can enjoy an hour-long Taste of Beringer tour, which includes a guided stroll through the winery's sensory garden. Located behind the Rhine House, the seventeen-room mansion that is the centerpiece of the property and former home of cofounder Frederick Beringer, the sensory garden is a verdant teaching venue for people who want to deepen their perception of wine. Beringer's wine educators consider it a scratch-and-sniff playground, a compendium of smells and textures that helps them make wine components more vivid for guests.

Devoted primarily to scented and edible plants that echo the aromas and sensations of wine, the garden allows Beringer's wine educators to make sensory connections for visitors that are harder to convey in the tasting room. Tannins in particular can be challenging to explain. A winemaker might describe tannin as bitter or astringent, or contributing a rough, sandpaper texture. Yet Merlot has soft, velvety tannins, similar to the velour-like feel of a sage leaf, a correlation that Beringer's hosts can highlight in the garden.

Strawberries thrive in small, sunny patches in the sensory garden, along with blueberries, kumquats, pomelos, blood oranges, Valencia and navel oranges, Asian pears, and pomegranates. Depending on what's blossoming or bearing fruit, hosts can open an appropriate wine and help guests understand what wine experts mean when they describe a red wine as smelling of red fruits, black fruits, or blue fruits.

Many of Beringer's white wines have vibrant citrus notes. In the garden, guides can parse that scent more finely, pointing out the subtle differences between lemon verbena, lemon pith, lemon blossom, or Meyer lemon with its sweetness. Beringer's ambition for the sensory garden was to help guests connect more easily with the aromas in wine given that the senses of taste and smell are so closely linked.

The sensory garden's plantings of rosemary, mint, lavender, and fennel provide other opportunities for Beringer wine educators to help guests plumb the depths of aromas in their wineglass. Cabernet Sauvignon, especially from mountain-grown fruit, often exhibits the anise scent of fresh fennel. For many visitors, a whiff of fresh rosemary warmed by the summer sun elicits memories of grilled meat, an association that clears a path to Cabernet Sauvignon or Cabernet Franc. Chocolate mint speaks to the richer red wines in the Beringer portfolio, such as the Merlot, which has deep mocha notes.

Left and above: *(clockwise from bottom left) Fresh tarragon; winery entrance; garden haul; Beringer's sensory garden plantings replicate some of the aromas found in wine; the property's 19th-century Rhine House is a Napa Valley historic landmark.*

These exercises in aromatic discernment help guests become more comfortable with describing fine wine and, perhaps, more confident about wine and food pairing. Beringer patrons fortunate enough to dine at the winery's Hudson House—a special-event venue—can experience these principles put into practice by the culinary team.

The gracious Hudson House, the historic home of Jacob Beringer, Frederick's younger brother and winery cofounder, dates from about 1850. Originally, it stood where the Rhine House is today. But Frederick coveted that site for his own home, so he had the Hudson House moved two hundred feet north in 1883. For a decade, beginning in 1990, the Hudson House hosted the School for American Chefs, a rigorous two-week training session for professional chefs overseen by the eminent French cooking teacher Madeleine Kamman. Today, the updated Hudson House hosts many VIP guests for lunch and dinner, with the culinary team drawing ingredients and inspiration from a small culinary garden at the rear of the house.

This almost-secret nook consists of several curved beds arranged in a circular pattern around a central fountain. Tuteurs and wire trellises for pole beans and tomatoes give the design some verticality, while large terra-cotta pots filled with rosemary topiary, bushy mint, and silvery curry leaf add texture. Clusters of marigolds provide pest protection, lavender chive blossoms dance in the breeze, and lush, burgundy-hued opal basil tempts visitors to snitch a fragrant sprig. Paths of decomposed granite separate the planting beds, the coarse material crunching underfoot as cooks harvest zucchini, cucumbers, eggplants, and sweet peppers and snip culinary herbs.

Above: *(clockwise from left) Culinary program manager Gina Baldridge harvests vegetables; magnificent walnut tree; classical garden statue; harvesting navel oranges from the winery citrus grove; ripening tomatoes; snipping fragrant lemon verbena*

Beringer's wine educators view the sensory garden as a scratch-and-sniff playground, a compendium of smells and textures that help them make wine components more vivid for guests.

The adjacent outdoor kitchen sees action in good weather, but the primary kitchen, inside the Hudson House, produces most of the wine-driven, garden-based cooking that defines Beringer's entertaining. In spring, when the first few fava beans land in the kitchen, a meal at the Hudson House might begin with a glass of steely Sauvignon Blanc and crostini topped with white beans and fava bean pesto—a clever way to celebrate favas when the garden has delivered only a handful. The winery's navel oranges peak in sweetness in spring, prompting the kitchen to prepare a gazpacho of golden beets, olive oil, and orange juice. Edible spring flowers make a delicate garnish.

An elaborate salad of roasted carrots, sugar snap peas, baby greens, and garden herbs features two creamy dressings, a composition

Beringer Vineyards 51

Above and right: *(clockwise from lower left) Garden blueberries work well in dishes paired with Beringer Vineyards Merlot; Hudson House; Hudson House interior; Beringer's wines echo the aromas and flavors found in its gardens; garden stairway*

that welcomes the lushness of the Private Reserve Chardonnay. With pomegranate-glazed lamb chops, a slam-dunk choice for Beringer's concentrated Cabernet Sauvignon, the kitchen pairs couscous sweetened with finely diced garden vegetables.

Dessert can be a challenging course at wineries that don't produce sweet wines, but Beringer has no such problem. Its much-admired Nightingale, a Sauternes-inspired dessert wine from Sémillon and Sauvignon Blanc, brings meals to a memorable close all by itself, but the culinary team has developed a German honey-spice cake to match it and honor the winery's German heritage. Served with oranges from the estate and orange-scented mascarpone, the dessert heightens the honey and tangerine notes in this luscious wine.

"Scent is associated with our deepest memories," says Ryan Chernick, Beringer's premium experiences manager. "In the garden, and in our wines, we help people reconnect with scent and the long-ago experiences we still carry with us."

pairing help from the garden:

Many of the flavors in garden produce can create a bridge between a dish and a wine or amplify the character of a wine, creating a pairing that soars. Beringer's Wine Education Team has a few favorite affinities.

Sauvignon Blanc: Consider adding peaches, apricots, or citrus, especially pomelo, to the dish. Chervil is a compatible herb, and this variety is the go-to wine for asparagus.

Chardonnay: If the wine has been through malolactic fermentation, it will have a rounder, creamier mouthfeel, compatible with buttery apples and pears. Barrel-fermented or barrel-aged Chardonnay will have toasty notes; look to grilled onions or shallots for a flavor bridge. Lemon, lemon basil, citrus blossoms, and tarragon are other complementary scents with this variety.

Pinot Noir: Raspberries, strawberries, and pomegranates speak to the red fruit in Pinot Noir. Consider a pairing with roast duck and raspberries, or roast lamb with a pomegranate glaze. Thyme and lavender are also compatible with this variety.

Merlot: Blueberries can find an aromatic echo in Merlot. Add blueberries to a pan sauce for roast chicken or to a garden greens salad with shredded rotisserie chicken.

Cabernet Sauvignon: Rosemary, fennel, and chocolate mint hint at aromas found in this variety. Top a rib-eye steak with rosemary butter.

Zinfandel: Beringer's fig trees also create pairing opportunities for the winery's culinary team, as several of the winery's red wines exhibit hints of fig. Consider serving Zinfandel with a main course of grilled pork and figs.

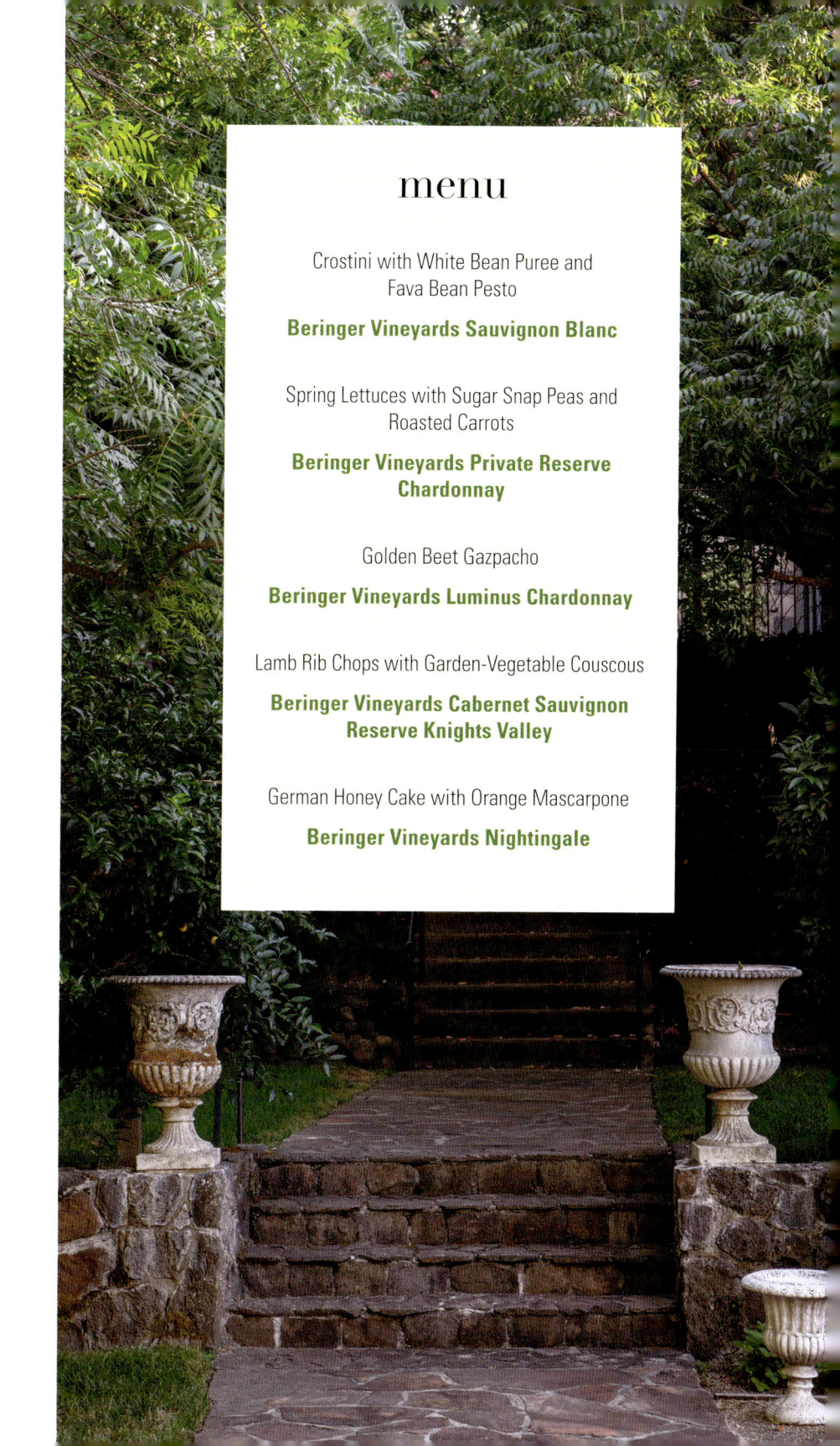

menu

Crostini with White Bean Puree and Fava Bean Pesto

Beringer Vineyards Sauvignon Blanc

Spring Lettuces with Sugar Snap Peas and Roasted Carrots

Beringer Vineyards Private Reserve Chardonnay

Golden Beet Gazpacho

Beringer Vineyards Luminus Chardonnay

Lamb Rib Chops with Garden-Vegetable Couscous

Beringer Vineyards Cabernet Sauvignon Reserve Knights Valley

German Honey Cake with Orange Mascarpone

Beringer Vineyards Nightingale

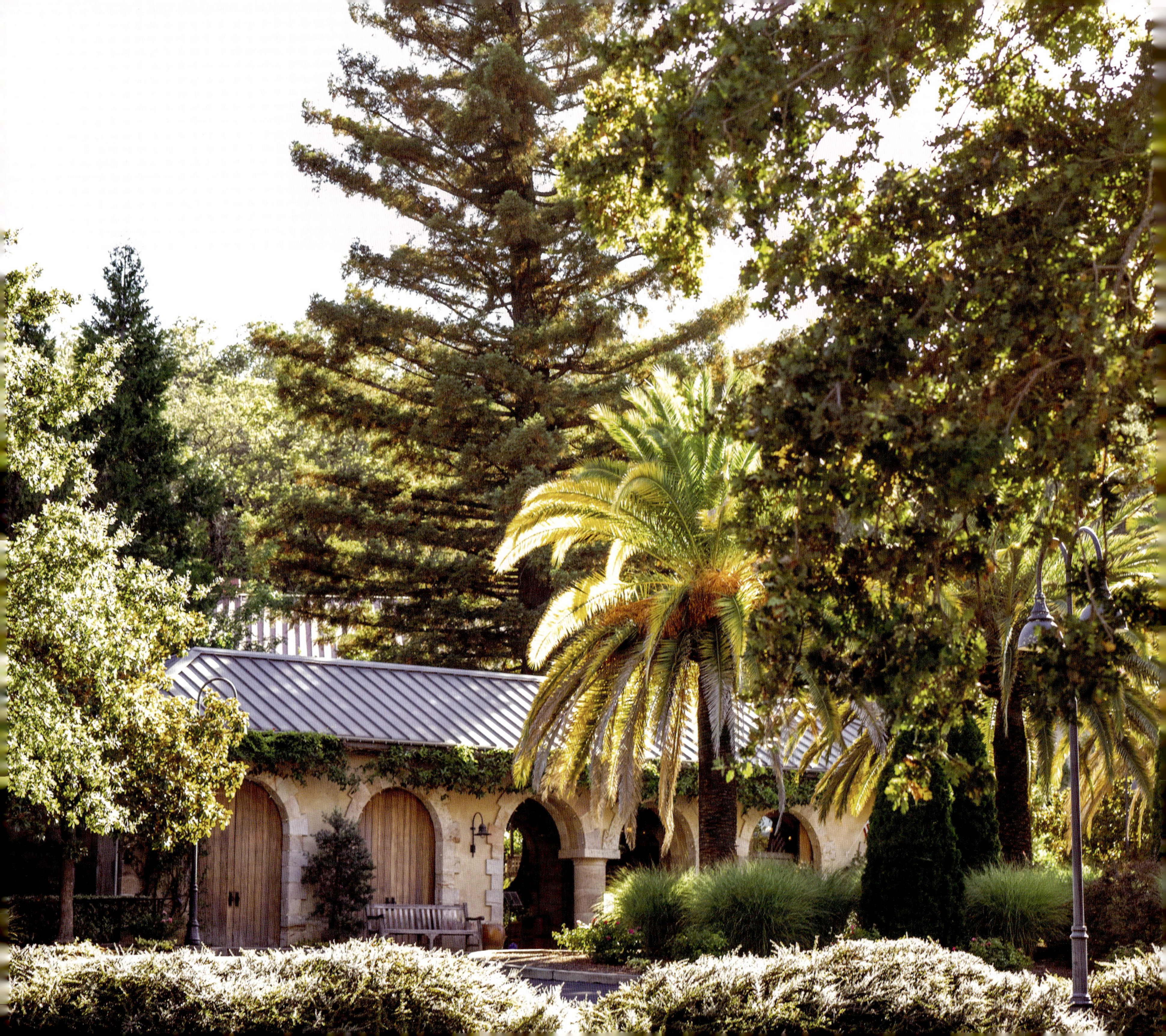

Crostini with White Bean Puree and Fava Bean Pesto Serves 4

This recipe yields more bean puree and fava bean pesto than you need, but you'll be glad for that. Serve the white bean puree with roast leg of lamb or salmon or as a sandwich spread. Use the pesto on pasta or pizza.

White Bean Puree:

1 cup dried cannellini or other white beans, soaked overnight in water to cover

2 cups chicken broth

2 garlic cloves, peeled

¼ yellow onion

2 fresh thyme sprigs

2 fresh flat-leaf parsley sprigs

2 bay leaves

1 teaspoon black peppercorns

1 cup pure olive oil (not extra virgin)

Sea salt

Fava Bean Pesto:

½ cup fully cooked peeled fava beans

¼ cup freshly grated Parmigiano-Reggiano cheese

20 large fresh basil leaves

1 tablespoon fresh oregano leaves

2 tablespoons pine nuts

¼ cup pure olive oil (not extra virgin)

Sea salt

8 baguette slices, each cut on the diagonal ¼ inch thick

Extra virgin olive oil, for brushing

Fleur de sel

Fresh fava bean blossoms or rosemary blossoms, for garnish

Wine: Beringer Vineyards Sauvignon Blanc

Make the white bean puree: Drain the soaked beans. Put them into a small saucepan with the broth, garlic, and onion. Tie the herbs and peppercorns in a cheesecloth bag and add to the pan. Bring to a simmer over medium-low heat, adjust the heat to maintain a gentle simmer, and cook, uncovered, until the beans are just tender and have absorbed most of the liquid, 30 minutes or more, depending on their age.

Remove the cheesecloth bag. Transfer the contents of the pan to a food processor and puree until smooth. With the motor running, add the oil slowly through the feed tube, then continue to puree until the mixture is completely smooth, about 5 minutes. Press the puree through a fine-mesh sieve to remove any bean skins. The puree will be fairly thin. Season well with sea salt. You should have about 3 cups. Set aside ¼ cup for the crostini. Pour the remainder into an airtight container, press plastic wrap against the surface of the puree to prevent browning, cover tightly, and refrigerate for up to several days.

Make the fava bean pesto: Put the beans, cheese, basil, oregano, and pine nuts into a food processor and process until nearly smooth. With the motor running, add the oil slowly through the feed tube and process until smooth. Season with sea salt. You will have about ½ cup. Set aside 2 tablespoons plus 2 teaspoons for the crostini. Put the remainder into an airtight container, press plastic wrap against the surface of the puree to prevent browning, cover tightly, and refrigerate for up to 1 day.

Preheat the oven to 350°F. Brush the baguette slices on both sides with oil and season lightly with salt. Arrange in a single layer on a baking sheet and toast until golden brown, 10 to 15 minutes. Let cool.

Top each toast with about 1½ teaspoons bean puree, spreading it to cover most of the toast. Top the bean puree with about 1 teaspoon fava bean pesto. Sprinkle a little fleur de sel on each toast, then garnish with blossoms.

Spring Lettuces with Sugar Snap Peas and Roasted Carrots Serves 4

Pickled Onions:

2 yellow onions, halved and sliced

2 cups water

1 cup raspberry vinegar

Quince Raspberry Dressing:

1 cup raspberries

¼ cup quince paste

2 tablespoons raspberry or apple cider vinegar

1½ teaspoons whole-grain Dijon mustard

½ cup canola or grapeseed oil

Yogurt Tahini Sauce:

½ cup full-fat plain Greek yogurt

¼ cup tahini

Grated zest of ½ lemon

8 slender, young carrots, preferably a mix of colors, peeled

Canola oil, for coating

1 tablespoon za'atar

Sea salt

12 sugar snap peas, trimmed

1 small handful microgreens

12 fresh tarragon or chervil leaves

¼ pound mixed baby salad greens

12 raspberries

4 teaspoons minced fresh herbs (mint, basil, and flat-leaf parsley)

Pansies or other edible flowers, for garnish

Wine: Beringer Vineyards Private Reserve Chardonnay

In spring, the Beringer garden yields big harvests of leafy greens, tender herbs, sugar snap peas, and sweet baby carrots. The winery's culinary team unites them in this pretty salad with two different dressings. Note that you need to pickle the onions at least 1 day ahead.

Make the pickled onions: Put the onions into a heatproof bowl. In a saucepan, combine the water and vinegar and bring to a boil over high heat. Pour the hot liquid over the onions. Let cool, then cover and refrigerate overnight before using. The onions will keep for weeks.

Make the quince raspberry dressing: In a food processor, combine the raspberries, quince paste, vinegar, and mustard and blend until smooth. With the motor running, add the oil through the feed tube. Blend until smooth.

Make the yogurt tahini sauce: In a small bowl, whisk together all the ingredients until smooth.

Preheat the oven to 350°F. Put the carrots into a small baking dish and toss with just enough oil to coat them. Add the za'atar, season with salt, and turn to coat with the seasonings. Cover and bake until tender, about 10 minutes. Let cool.

Bring a small pot of salted water to a boil over high heat and prepare a bowl of ice water. Add the sugar snap peas to the boiling water and blanch for about 30 seconds, then drain and immediately transfer to the ice water. When cool, drain, pat dry, and halve crosswise.

To serve, put about 2 tablespoons yogurt tahini sauce on half of each of four salad plates. Spread the sauce into a thin layer with the back of a spoon but keep it confined to half of the plate. Top the sauce on each plate with 2 carrots, a tuft of microgreens, and 3 tarragon or chervil leaves.

Lift about one-fourth of the pickled onions out of the pickling liquid and place them in a bowl. Add the salad greens and just enough of the quince raspberry dressing to coat them lightly. Toss gently, then season with salt. Divide among the four plates, placing the greens on the uncovered half of the plate. Top with the sugar snap peas and raspberries. Put 1 teaspoon minced herbs on top of each salad. Garnish each plate with pansies.

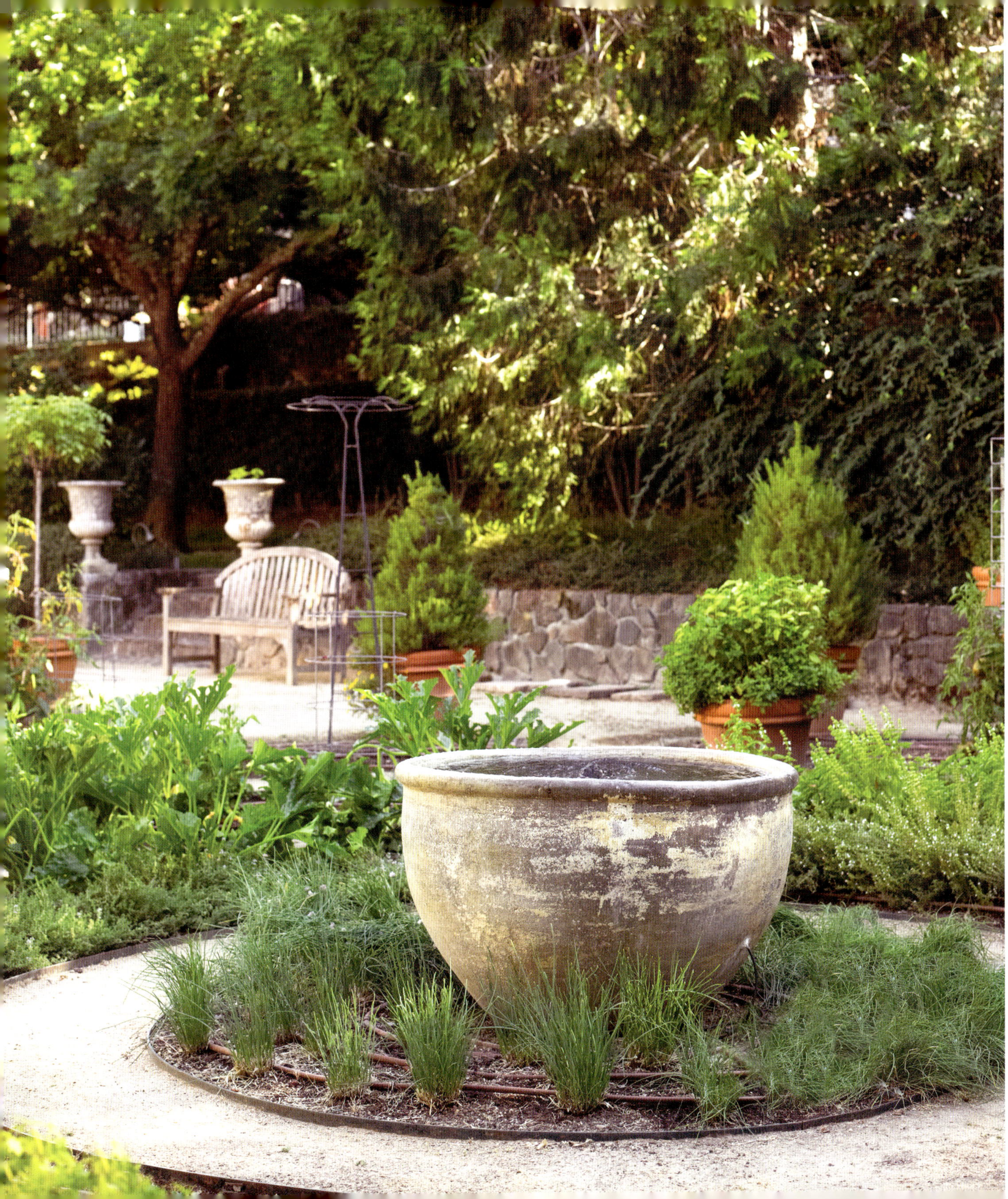

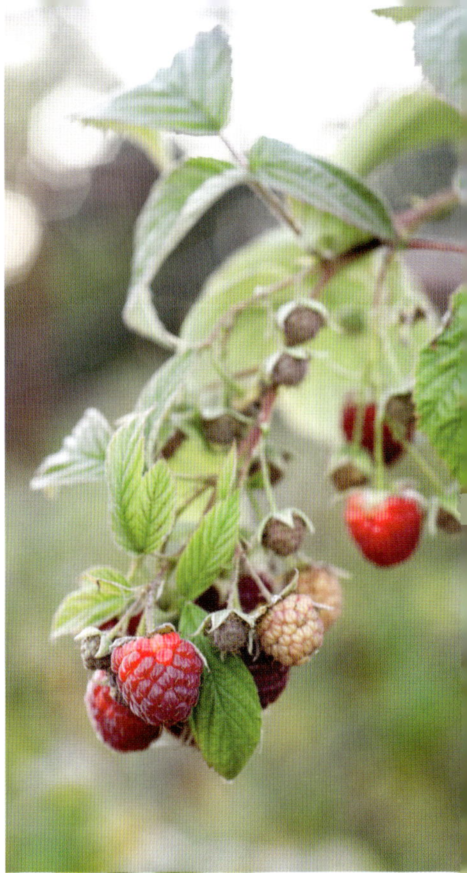

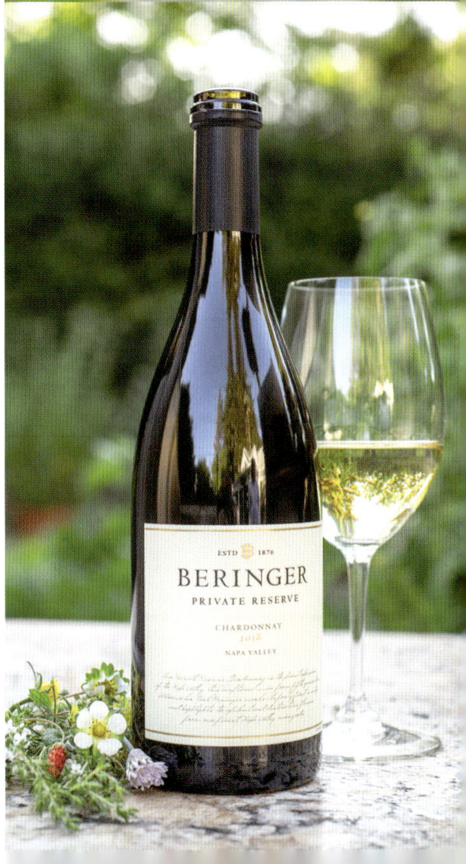
BERINGER
PRIVATE RESERVE
CHARDONNAY
NAPA VALLEY

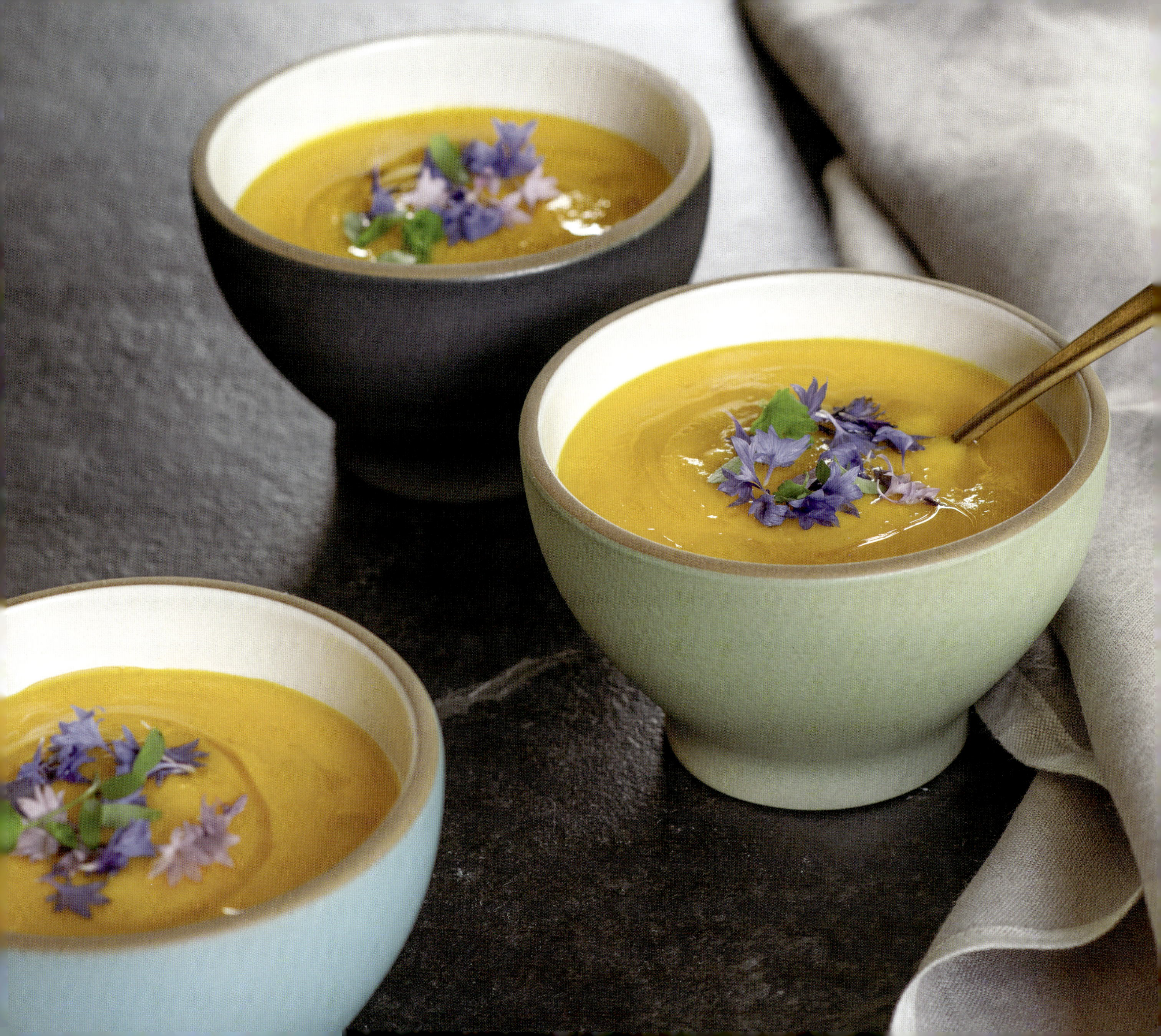

Golden Beet Gazpacho

Serves 6

3 extra-large golden beets, greens and any roots removed

1 cup extra virgin olive oil, plus more for coating beets and garnish

½ yellow onion, in 2 pieces

2 bay leaves

4 cloves garlic, peeled

Stems from 1 bunch fresh flat-leaf parsley

½ bunch fresh thyme

1 tablespoon black peppercorns

Sea salt

1½ cups water

2 navel oranges

Fleur de sel

Fresh micro cilantro or finely sliced cilantro, for garnish

Pansies, violas, or other edible flowers, for garnish

Wine: Beringer Vineyards Luminus Chardonnay

chef's tip:

Save the nutrient-packed beet greens and boil or steam them, then cool and squeeze dry. Reheat with olive oil and minced garlic and serve with feta.

Citrus trees of several types grace the grounds at Beringer Vineyards. When the navel oranges and golden beets overlap in spring, Beringer's culinary team uses them both in this silky, sunflower-colored soup. You can serve the soup chilled or at room temperature.

Preheat the oven to 350°F. Coat the beets lightly with oil, then put them into a baking dish with the onion, bay leaves, garlic, parsley, thyme, peppercorns, 1 teaspoon sea salt, and ½ cup of the water. Cover tightly and bake until the beets are tender when pierced, 45 minutes or more, depending on size. Peel the beets while warm and cut into quarters. Strain the juices in the baking dish and reserve.

Cut a slice off both ends of each orange. Stand each orange on a cutting surface and remove all the peel and white pith by slicing from top to bottom all the way around the orange, following the contour of the fruit. Quarter each peeled orange.

Put the beets, oranges, and strained juices into a blender and blend well. With the blender running, add the oil and the remaining 1 cup water through the opening in the blender lid and blend until smooth. Strain through a fine-mesh sieve, then season with sea salt.

Divide the soup among six bowls. Top each serving with a pinch of fleur de sel and a drizzle of oil. Garnish with cilantro and flowers.

Lamb Rib Chops with Garden-Vegetable Couscous

Serves 4

Lamb Chops:

1 tablespoon plus 1 teaspoon extra virgin olive oil

1 tablespoon plus 1 teaspoon canola oil

1 tablespoon plus 1 teaspoon pomegranate molasses

1 yellow onion, halved and sliced

4 cloves garlic, thinly sliced

Leaves from 3 fresh thyme sprigs

Leaves from 3 fresh flat-leaf parsley sprigs

1 teaspoon sea salt

½ teaspoon sumac

½ teaspoon ras el hanout

½ teaspoon za'atar

8 lamb rib chops, preferably not frenched

Couscous:

2½ tablespoons extra virgin olive oil

1 yellow onion, chopped

1 red onion, chopped

½ teaspoons ras el hanout

1 tablespoon Garlic Confit (recipe follows), mashed to a paste

½ cup golden raisins

1 cup pearl couscous

1⅓ cups chicken broth, heated

1 small carrot, peeled, in ¼-inch dice

1 parsnip, peeled, in ¼-inch dice

1 small zucchini, in ¼-inch dice

1 small crookneck yellow squash, in ¼-inch dice

1 medium Yukon Gold potato, peeled, in ¼-inch dice

1 teaspoon pomegranate molasses

1 tablespoon finely minced mixed fresh herbs (mint, basil, and flat-leaf parsley)

Sea salt

¼ cup sliced almonds, toasted

In late spring, Beringer's culinary team harvests tender baby vegetables from the winery garden for this refined version of couscous. The recipe uses pearl couscous (sometimes called Israeli couscous), which is larger than the familiar North African pasta, and the kitchen team cooks it separately from the lamb. Pomegranate molasses in the marinade gives the lamb chops a subtle sweetness and a beautiful sheen.

Wine: Beringer Vineyards Cabernet Sauvignon Reserve Knights Valley

Marinate the lamb: In a large bowl, mix together the oils, pomegranate molasses, onion, garlic, thyme, parsley, salt, sumac, ras el hanout, and za'atar. Add the lamb and toss to coat evenly with the seasonings. Cover and refrigerate for at least 2 hours or up to 24 hours, turning occasionally to redistribute the seasonings. Bring to room temperature before cooking.

Prepare the couscous: Heat 1 tablespoon of the oil in a saucepan over medium heat. Add half each of the yellow onion and red onion and all the ras el hanout and sauté until the onions soften, about 5 minutes. Add the garlic and raisins and sauté, stirring, for about 1 minute. Add the couscous and cook, stirring, for about 2 minutes to toast it. Pour in the broth, bring to a simmer, cover, reduce the heat to low, and cook until the liquid is absorbed, about 15 minutes. Set aside to rest.

Bring a small pot of salted water to a boil over high heat and prepare a bowl of ice water. Add the carrot to the boiling water and cook for 30 seconds, then drain and immediately transfer to the ice water. When cool, drain again.

Warm the remaining 1½ tablespoons oil in a skillet over medium heat. Add the remaining yellow and red onion and sauté until softened, about 5 minutes. Add the parsnip, zucchini, yellow squash, and potato and sauté until the vegetables are tender and almost caramelized, about 10 minutes. Stir in the carrots and cook until they are hot, about 1 minute. Keep warm.

Preheat the oven to 325°F. Heat a heavy ovenproof skillet large enough to hold all the chops and warm it over medium-high heat. (Use two skillets if necessary.) When hot, add the chops and sear on both sides, about 1 minute per side, adjusting the heat to prevent smoking or burning. Transfer the skillet to the oven and roast until the lamb is done to your taste, about 5 minutes for medium.

Transfer the couscous to a bowl and fluff with a fork. Add the sautéed vegetables, pomegranate molasses, and mixed herbs and fluff with a fork. Season with salt.

Divide the couscous among four plates. Scatter the almonds over the couscous then top each portion with 2 chops.

Garlic Confit

Makes about ½ cup

12 large garlic cloves, peeled
½ cup vegetable oil

In a small saucepan, combine the garlic cloves with vegetable oil to cover. Cook over low heat until the cloves are soft but not colored, about 20 minutes. (Use a flame tamer if necessary to keep the cloves from browning.) Let cool, then refrigerate in a covered container for up to 1 week.

German Honey Cake with Orange Mascarpone

Serves 12

To honor Jacob Beringer, the winery's German cofounder, the winery's culinary team developed this cake from an old German recipe. Richly spiced, it contains no fat, so it is almost more like bread than cake. Sweet oranges from the winery's garden moisten the cake, and orange blossom water scents the creamy topping. Beringer's much-admired dessert wine makes the perfect accompaniment.

Nonstick cooking spray, for the pan

2 cups all-purpose flour

2 teaspoons baking powder

2 teaspoons sea salt

1 teaspoon ground cloves

1 teaspoon ground allspice

1 teaspoon ground ginger

2 oranges

4 large eggs

1 cup honey, plus more for drizzling

½ teaspoon orange blossom water

Orange Mascarpone:

½ cup heavy cream

½ cup powdered sugar

¼ teaspoon orange blossom water

1 cup mascarpone

Wine: Beringer Vineyards Nightingale

Preheat the oven to 325°F. Spray an 8-inch round cake pan generously with cooking spray. Line the bottom of the pan with parchment and spray the parchment.

Sift together the flour, baking powder, salt, cloves, allspice, and ginger into a bowl.

Grate the zest of 1 of the oranges directly into the bowl of a stand mixer. Place the bowl on the mixer and fit the mixer with the whisk attachment. Add the eggs and beat on medium speed until well blended. Add the honey and orange blossom water and beat until light. Switch to the paddle attachment and, on low speed, add the flour mixture and mix just until blended. Do not overmix.

Transfer the batter to the prepared pan and spread it evenly. Bake until a cake tester inserted into the center comes out clean, about 45 minutes. Let cool in the pan on a rack for 10 minutes, then invert onto another rack. Lift off the pan, turn the cake right side up, and let cool completely.

Cut a slice off both ends of the zest-free orange so it will stand upright. Stand the orange on a cutting surface and, using a sharp knife, remove all the remaining peel and the white pith by slicing from top to bottom all the way around the orange, following the contour of the fruit. With the knife, cut along both sides of each orange segment to free the segment from its membrane. Put the segments into a small bowl. Repeat with the second orange.

Make the orange mascarpone: In a bowl, whisk together the cream and sugar until soft peaks form. Whisk in the orange blossom water, then whisk in the mascarpone until blended.

To serve, cut the cake into 12 wedges. Transfer to dessert plates and top each slice with a generous dollop of orange mascarpone, 2 orange segments, and a generous drizzle of honey.

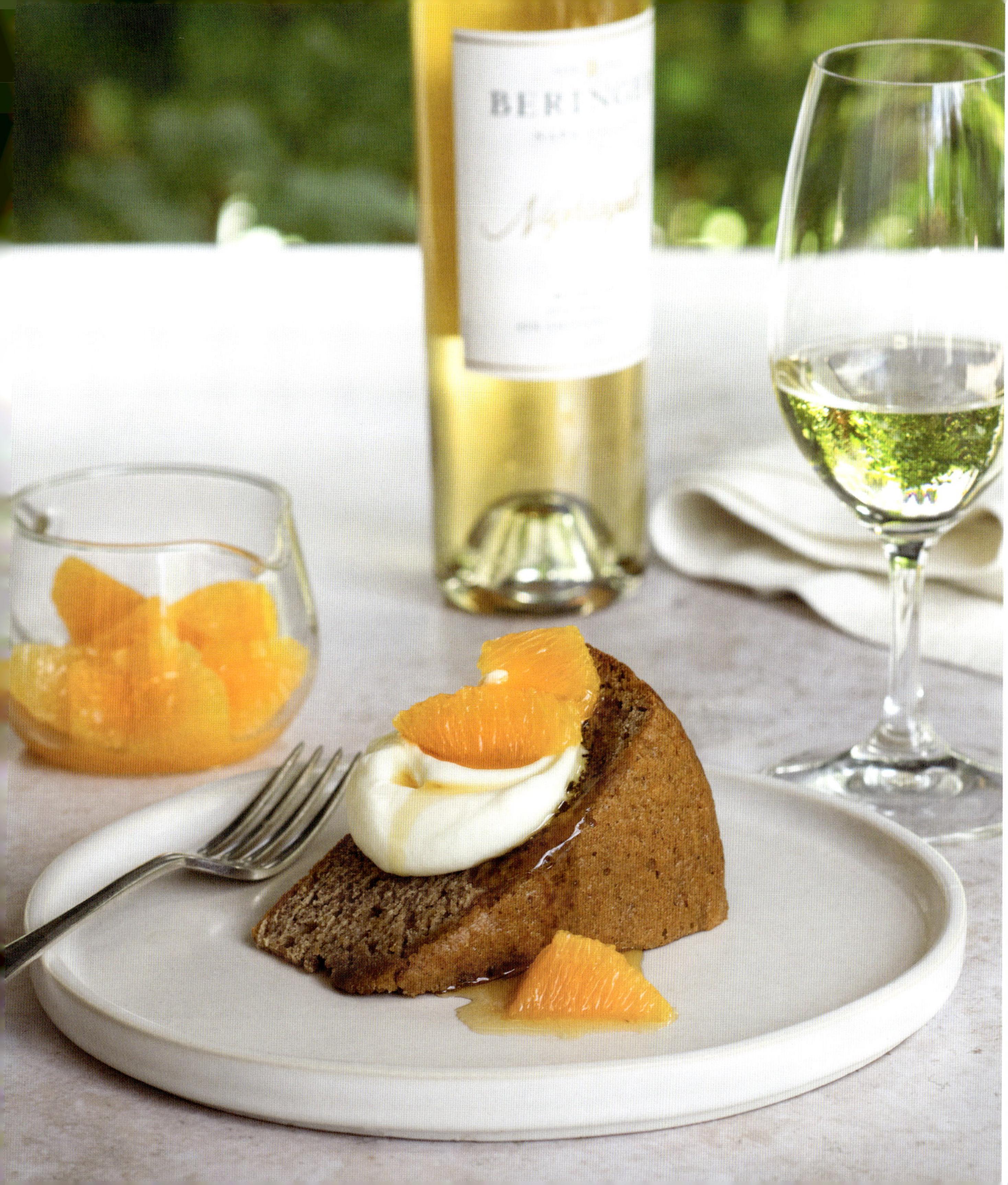

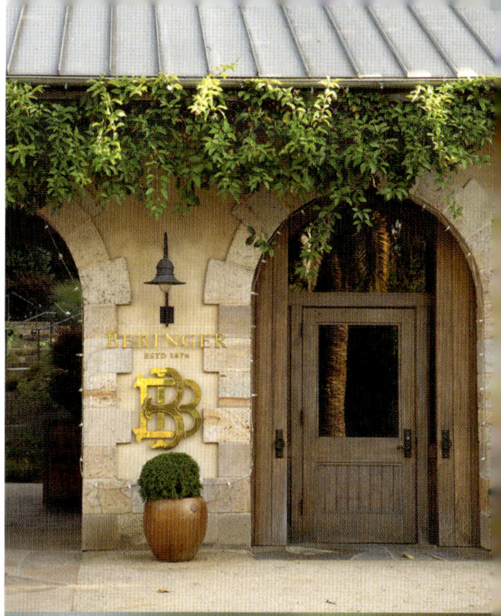
BERINGER

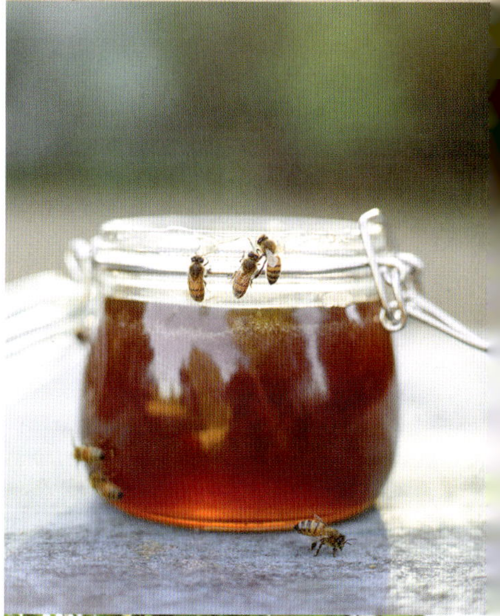

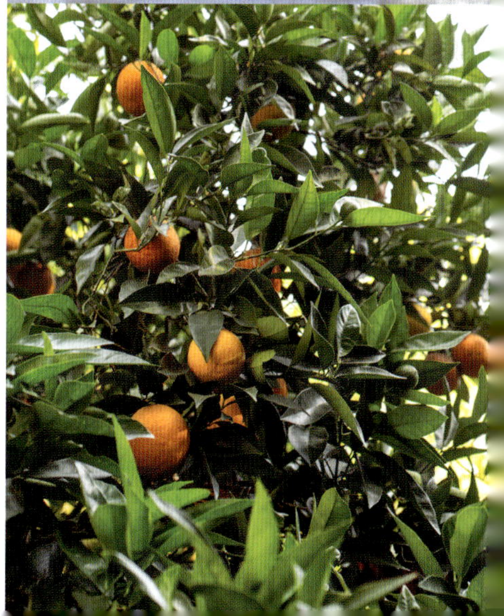

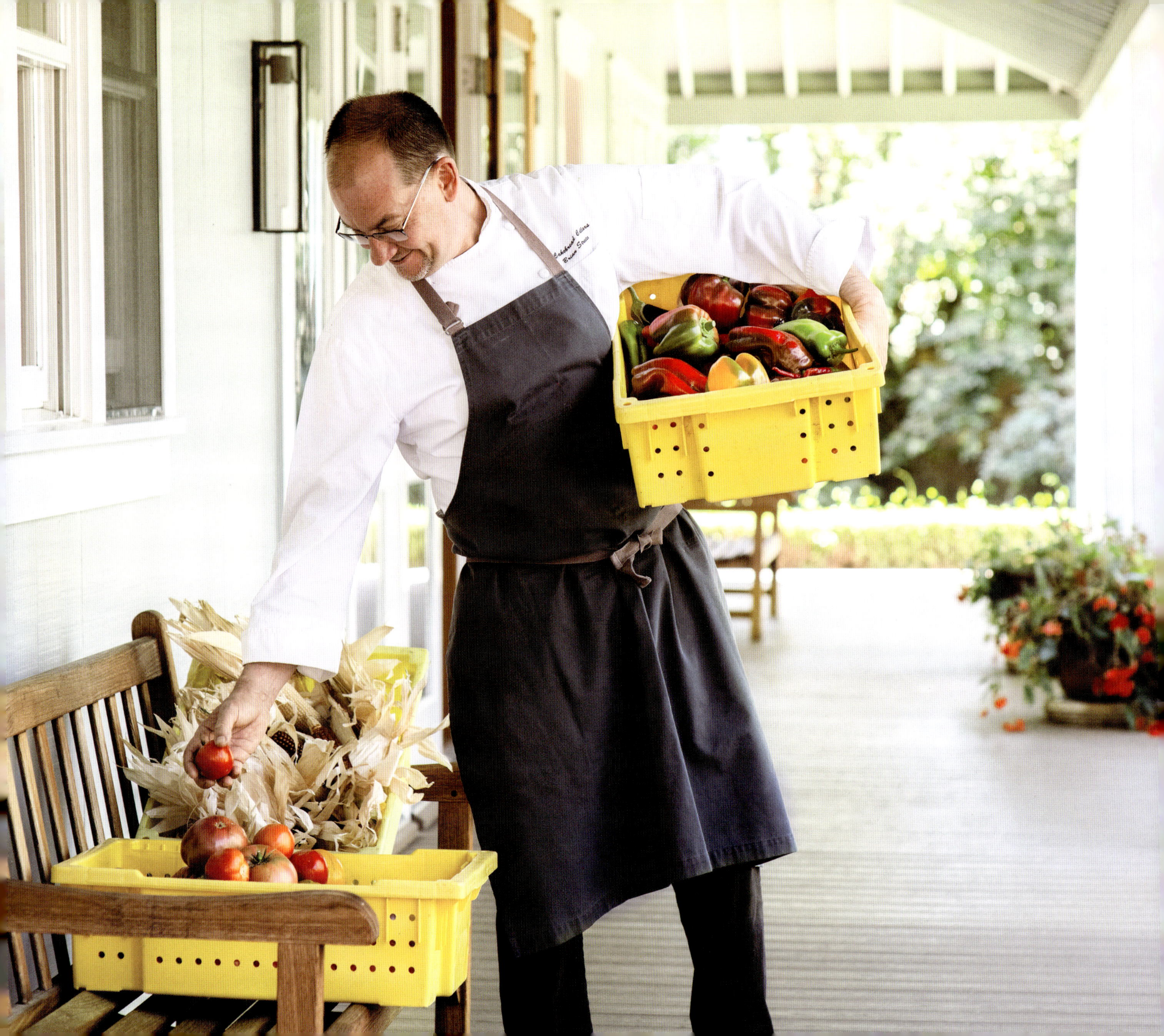
Cakebread Cellars

Cakebread Cellars: *Farm-to-Table Pioneers*

Rutherford

In 1972, Jack and Dolores Cakebread impulsively bought twenty-two acres of cow pasture in the heart of Napa Valley. They were excited about having a place in the country, a weekend respite from their Oakland home and auto-repair business. They figured they would develop a vineyard and sell the grapes, but one of the first things Dolores did was plant a vegetable garden. An enormous one.

Predictably the two-and-a-half-acre plot produced far more than the Cakebreads and their three boys could manage. Every available family member was recruited to help harvest the Rutherford garden and haul produce back to Oakland in lug boxes. Faced with a deluge of tomatoes and beans, Dolores carved out a pantry under the stairs of their Oakland home. She put her elderly father to work washing and peeling vegetables, and soon the pantry was stocked with enough jars to carry the family through the winter.

"Then we learned that in Napa Valley you can grow a winter garden," recalled Dolores. "So we didn't need any of the canned food."

When the fertile land just kept churning out produce, Dolores converted the property's small pump house into an honor-system farm stand. Soon enough, locals and Napa Valley tourists—there weren't many of either in those days—were veering off the highway to stock up on fresh fruits and vegetables. The property's caretaker teased Dolores that if she and Jack didn't make it in the wine business, he would move the farm stand to the highway and she could make apple pies.

Left and above: *Winery chef Brian Streeter returns from the garden with heaped bins of sweet peppers and tomatoes; a tasting plate at the ready for a Cakebread Cellars guest*

Decades later, Cakebread Cellars is a Napa Valley landmark, its redwood-clad compound—expanded several times—a favorite stop for wine tourists. The vegetable garden has moved a few times to accommodate vineyard development and now measures a sensible three-quarters of an acre, but it remains a key element of the visitor experience and of the family's legendary hospitality.

"The garden is part of our DNA and one of the great perks of working here," says Cakebread Cellars culinary director Brian Streeter, who started in the winery kitchen in 1989, straight out of cooking school, and has never left. A restaurant chef may be tied to the same menu for weeks or months, notes Streeter. His own menu making for Cakebread visitors starts fresh every day, responding to what gardener Marcy Snow has to offer.

For many years, the garden was Dolores's domain. A certified Master Gardener, she decided what to plant every year and doggedly promoted the garden as part of the winery's identity. Today, under Marcy's management, it is colorful, prolific, and welcoming, with neat fir-bark paths and signage to educate unaccompanied guests. "We have small beds and lots of variety so our guests can smell and taste things," says Brian.

Whenever Brian conducts a cooking class or prepares a meal for winery guests, they tour the garden first. "It hits home when people sit down for lunch and find vegetables on the plate they just saw," says the chef. Many have never seen the lacy foliage of an asparagus bed or the garnet-red hibiscus flowers that Mexicans dry, then steep for a sweet-tart tea.

Brian now works closely with Marcy to select the seeds for each season's plantings. Marcy loves the visual showstoppers, such as climbing purple hyacinth beans, towering sunflowers, and the gourds that dangle like baseball bats from an arbor. Brian, of course, wants the basics that define the California kitchen: heirloom tomatoes, purple basil, lemon cucumbers, Tuscan kale. But he also peruses seed catalogs for novelties to jazz up his plates, such as yellow romano beans, toadskin melons, Italian flint corn for polenta, and Mexican gherkins. The collaboration produces a year-round harvest that evolves a bit every year to keep both gardener and chef energized.

Feeling the physical demands of the job, Marcy tried to retire in 2018 but failed. "After six months away, I was so sad," she admits. The

Above: *(clockwise from left) The garden in autumn; dangling kikinda gourds and purple amaranth; red hibiscus for tea; sign designates a Certified Bee Friendly garden; Marcy Snow with purple asparagus; hyacinth beans*

"The garden is part of our DNA and one of the great perks of working here," says culinary director Brian Streeter. "Our menu making for visitors starts fresh every day."

winery welcomed her back part-time, with an assistant to do the heavy lifting, and the indefatigable gardener is once again staking corn, outsmarting voles, and nurturing the lush borders of zinnias, marigolds, and borage that keep bees and beneficial insects on the job. "I'm so happy to be here, you wouldn't believe it," says Marcy. She regularly makes bouquets for employees to brighten their day; when her beds yield more than the kitchen can use, staffers take home the bounty.

With the garden only a short walk from the kitchen, Brian's cooking can be hyper-seasonal, reflecting not just the month but the moment. If Marcy has pulled some perfect baby turnips or radishes, they will find their way onto the plate.

Cakebread Cellars

Above: *(clockwise from lower left) Dolores Cakebread harvests sunflowers and purple basil for a colorful arrangement; Brian and Dolores discuss menu ideas; butternut squash are ready for harvest.*

A vegetable garden enables, but it also challenges, demanding flexibility. A supermarket shopper can choose carrots that are all the same size, but at Cakebread, the day's harvest may include a few baby carrots and some bigger ones, a handful of early fava beans and asparagus spears, the first spring garlic, a bunch of tarragon, and a few pounds of peas. Brian's answer to this delivery is likely to be a vivid vegetable medley, merging all these ingredients into a succulent side dish for spring salmon or lamb.

Many vintners ask chefs to steer clear of asparagus and artichokes, two vegetables notorious for challenging wine, but "we're not that kind," said Dolores, who passed away in late 2020. "We can drink wine with almost anything." Roasting artichokes or combining them with other vegetables mitigates their wine-altering impact, says Brian, and

Cakebread's steely Sauvignon Blanc can manage asparagus. When you appreciate vegetables and wine as much as the Cakebreads do, any pairing "don'ts" are easy to sweep aside.

For more than two decades, Brian has volunteered monthly in an elementary school classroom, introducing Napa fourth graders to the pleasures of garden-based cooking. They make tortillas with fresh salsa and learn the cultural origins of different foods. Once a year, the kids come to the winery for a garden tour and lunch. "You'll never see kids as excited about carrots as when they pick them," says Brian.

For a menu designed to showcase the Cakebread garden in full autumn glory, Brian turned to carrots for his opening salvo. Heirloom varieties in multiple colors are sliced and briefly sautéed, then piled on crostini spread with local goat cheese, a delightful match for the winery's Sauvignon Blanc. Cranberry beans—one of the chef's favorite crops—anchor a classic minestrone topped with Tuscan kale pesto, a cool-weather alternative when the basil starts to fade. The orchard at Cakebread's River Ranch vineyard provides buttery pears for a chicory salad with cubes of sweet delicata squash, a composition of contrasting flavors and textures that blossoms with a lush Chardonnay. Thanks to Napa Valley's mild fall weather, Brian can prepare the main course outdoors, first grilling salmon fillets on a cedar plank, then glossing them with a roasted-tomato butter. Red wine with fish? Absolutely. A French prune tree in the orchard contributes fruit for the meal's finale. Brian dries the fresh prunes, plumps them in brandy, and then folds them into homemade coffee ice cream. Sublime.

Cakebread Cellars' eventual success did save Dolores from the pie business, but she still dreamed of relaunching the farm stand. Stocked with fruits and vegetables from the orchard and garden, it would reinforce what the Cakebreads have always advocated: simple cooking, shared meals, good wine. From the beginning, the family's wine country adventure was never just about the wine. "We had to grow vegetables," said Dolores. "You wouldn't buy vegetables when you had this wonderful land to grow them on."

menu

Crostini with Garden Carrots, Goat Cheese, and Dukkah
Cakebread Cellars Sauvignon Blanc

Autumn Squash, Pear, and Arugula Salad
Cakebread Cellars Chardonnay Reserve

Winter Vegetable and Bean Soup with Tuscan Kale Pesto
Cakebread Cellars Chardonnay

Cedar Plank Salmon with Roasted-Tomato Butter
Cakebread Cellars Two Creeks Pinor Noir, Anderson Valley

Profiteroles with Coffee Ice Cream, Armagnac-Soaked Prunes, and Chocolate-Caramel Sauce

Crostini with Garden Carrots, Goat Cheese, and Dukkah

Serves 6

12 baguette slices, each cut ¼ inch thick on the diagonal

Extra virgin olive oil

Dukkah:

¼ cup chopped raw pecans or raw whole pistachios

1 tablespoon sesame seeds

1 tablespoon coriander seeds

1½ teaspoon cumin seeds

½ teaspoon sea salt

Freshly ground black pepper

¼ pound small carrots, preferably a mix of colors, scrubbed but not peeled

1 tablespoon extra virgin olive oil

¾ cup fresh rindless goat cheese, at room temperature

1 tablespoon thinly sliced fresh chives

Honey, warmed enough to drizzle

Wine: Cakebread Cellars Sauvignon Blanc

Rainbow carrots from the Cakebread garden—purple, red, orange, and yellow—display their stunning colors atop these crostini. Dukkah, *an Egyptian nut-and-spice blend, is the captivating seasoning that keeps you coming back for just one more toast. You will have leftover* dukkah, *but that's no problem. Store it in an airtight container and enjoy it later in the classic way, dipping bread first in extra virgin olive oil and then in* dukkah. *On another occasion, substitute sliced roasted beets or butternut squash for the sautéed carrots.*

Preheat the oven to 375°F. Brush the baguette slices lightly on both sides with oil. Arrange in a single layer on a baking sheet and toast until golden brown, about 15 minutes. Set aside to cool. Leave the oven on.

Prepare the *dukkah*: Put the pecans or pistachios into a pie pan and toast in the oven until fragrant and lightly colored, 5 to 10 minutes. If using pistachios, chop roughly. Toast the sesame seeds in a dry skillet over high heat, stirring constantly, until lightly colored and fragrant, 1 to 2 minutes. Let cool. Add the coriander and cumin seeds to the skillet and toast, stirring, until fragrant and starting to darken. With a mortar and pestle, coarsely grind the coriander and cumin seeds. Transfer to a small bowl and stir in the pecans or pistachios, sesame seeds, salt, and a few grinds of pepper.

Slice the carrots into ⅛-inch-thick rounds. Heat a large skillet over high heat. Add the oil and carrots, season with salt and pepper, and sauté, stirring, until the carrots are tender and starting to brown, about 5 minutes. Transfer to a plate and let cool to room temperature.

In a bowl, mash together the goat cheese and chives with the back of a spoon until smooth and spreadable.

To assemble the crostini, spread 1 tablespoon of the goat cheese on each toast and arrange on a platter. Top each toast with a few rounds of carrots, using a mix of colors on each, and a generous pinch of *dukkah*. Drizzle the toasts with honey, using a total of about 2 teaspoons. Serve immediately.

Autumn Squash, Pear, and Arugula Salad

Serves 6

Some people think wine doesn't go with salad, but that has never been the thinking at Cakebread Cellars. The family loves salads of every kind, in every season, and Brian finds ways to make his salads wine friendly. In autumn, juicy pears and sweet roasted squashes balance the bitterness of chicories, with toasted pumpkin seeds and Vella Dry Jack for nutty richness. Brian goes easy on the vinegar to make the salad more compatible with wine.

5 tablespoons extra virgin olive oil

2 cups peeled and diced butternut squash (½-inch dice)

Sea salt and freshly ground black pepper

½ delicata squash, about ½ pound, seeded, ends removed, and sliced crosswise about ¼ inch thick

1 tablespoon pure maple syrup

¼ cup raw green pumpkin seeds (pepitas)

Vinaigrette:

1 small shallot, minced

1 teaspoon Dijon mustard

1½ tablespoons sherry vinegar or golden balsamic vinegar

½ cup extra virgin olive oil

2 handfuls arugula (about 2 ounces total)

2 Belgian endives, chopped

½ head radicchio, chopped

1 Bartlett pear, halved and cored (no need to peel)

Vella Dry Jack cheese, for shaving

Wine: Cakebread Cellars Chardonnay Reserve

Heat a large nonstick skillet over medium heat and add 2 tablespoons of the oil. When hot, add the butternut squash and season with salt and pepper. Sauté, stirring occasionally, until the squash is lightly browned and tender, about 7 minutes. Transfer to a plate.

Return the skillet to medium heat and add 2 tablespoons of the oil. When hot, add the delicata squash and season with salt and pepper. Cook, stirring occasionally, until lightly browned and almost tender, about 5 minutes. Add the maple syrup and cook for about 1 minute longer to glaze the squash slices. Transfer to the plate with the butternut squash.

In a small skillet, heat the remaining 1 tablespoon oil over medium-high heat. Add the pumpkin seeds and sauté, stirring almost constantly, until they darken, about 2 minutes. Season with salt and scoop out onto paper towels to drain.

Prepare the vinaigrette: In a small bowl, stir together the shallot, mustard, and vinegar. Whisk in the oil, then season with salt and pepper.

In a large salad bowl, combine the arugula, endives, and radicchio. Slice the pear lengthwise and add to the bowl along with the sautéed squashes. Add enough vinaigrette to coat the salad lightly (you may not need all of it) and toss gently. Taste for salt and pepper.

Divide the salad among six salad plates. Top with the pumpkin seeds, dividing them evenly. With a vegetable peeler, shave a few ribbons of Dry Jack over each salad. Serve immediately.

BAKER CREEK HEIRLOOM SEEDS

Cakebread
Cellars
2018
NAPA VALLEY

Winter Vegetable and Bean Soup with Tuscan Kale Pesto

Makes 3½ quarts; serves 8 generously

Beans:
½ pound dried cranberry (borlotti) beans (1 rounded cup)
½ yellow onion
1 carrot, in large chunks
1 celery rib, cut into large chunks
1 fresh sage sprig
Sea salt

Tuscan Kale Pesto:
¼ cup pine nuts
1 bunch Tuscan kale (about ½ pound), ribs removed
1 large clove garlic, chopped
3 tablespoons grated Parmigiano-Reggiano cheese
½ cup plus 2 tablespoons extra virgin olive oil

3 tablespoons extra virgin olive oil
1 yellow onion, minced
2 carrots, neatly diced
2 celery ribs, neatly diced
2 cloves garlic, minced
¼ pound prosciutto, neatly diced
½ cup chopped fresh flat-leaf parsley
One 28-ounce can Italian tomatoes, crushed by hand, with juice
4 cups chicken broth, plus more if needed
2 small zucchini, preferably 1 green and 1 yellow, diced
1½ cups small dried pasta, such as tubettini or small elbows
Grated Parmigiano-Reggiano cheese, for garnishing

Wine: Cakebread Cellars Chardonnay

Almost any type of dried bean, from cannellini to lima to chickpea, will work in this hearty minestrone. Marcy grows several types in the Cakebread Cellars garden: cranberry beans, the heirloom Good Mother Stallard, and French Tarbais beans that Brian uses in an annual cassoulet cooking class at the winery. Tuscan kale is a winter staple in the garden, and it makes a great cold-weather stand-in for basil in pesto.

Prepare the beans: Soak the beans overnight in water to cover. The next day, drain, transfer to a deep saucepan, and add water to cover by 1 inch. Add the onion, carrot, celery, and sage and bring to a simmer over medium heat, skimming off any foam. Cook uncovered at a simmer until the beans are tender, about 1 hour, adding water as needed to keep the beans covered. Remove from the heat, season with salt, and let cool in the liquid. With tongs, remove the onion, carrot, celery, and sage.

Prepare the pesto: Preheat the oven to 350°F. Put the pine nuts into a pan and toast until lightly colored and fragrant, about 5 minutes. Let cool. Bring a large pot of salted water to a boil over high heat. Add the kale and cook until just wilted, about 1 minute. Drain and cool under cold running water. Squeeze dry and chop coarsely. Put the kale into a food processor with the garlic, cheese, and pine nuts and pulse until blended. With the motor running, add the oil through the feed tube, pureeing until smooth. Transfer to a bowl and season with salt.

Heat the oil in a large soup pot over medium heat. Add the onion, carrots, celery, garlic, prosciutto, and parsley and sauté until the vegetables have softened, about 10 minutes. Add the tomatoes with their juice and simmer briskly for 5 to 10 minutes. Add the broth, the beans and their cooking liquid, and the zucchini and simmer gently until the zucchini are almost tender, about 10 minutes.

Bring a pot of salted water to a boil over high heat. Add the pasta and cook until just al dente, according to package directions. Drain and add to the soup. Thin the soup with broth or water if necessary. Taste for salt. Ladle the soup into bowls. Spoon a dollop of kale pesto on top of each serving and garnish with Parmigiano-Reggiano. Serve immediately.

Cedar Plank Salmon with Roasted-Tomato Butter

Serves 6

Roasted-Tomato Butter:

½ pound San Marzano or Roma tomatoes, halved lengthwise

Sea salt and freshly ground black pepper

1 tablespoon extra virgin olive oil

1 teaspoon coarsely chopped fresh thyme leaves

2 cloves garlic, unpeeled

1 cup unsalted butter, at room temperature

2 tablespoons coarsely chopped fresh basil

1 teaspoon fresh lemon juice

Pinch of ground Espelette or cayenne pepper

2 pounds skin-on salmon fillets, pin bones removed

Extra virgin olive oil

Wine: Cakebread Cellars Two Creeks Pinot Noir, Anderson Valley

---

For this recipe, you will need an untreated 1 by 6 cedar plank, available at most lumber stores. The smoke it generates when placed on the grill will infuse the salmon, a much easier approach than grappling with a complicated smoker. The recipe makes more butter than you need, but you can freeze what you don't use. It's nice to have on hand for use on steamed clams, grilled lobster, or swordfish. Accompany the salmon with fresh-dug potatoes, greens beans, or corn on the cob.

Soak a 1 by 6 cedar plank (see headnote) in cold water to cover for at least 2 hours.

Prepare the roasted-tomato butter: Preheat the oven to 400°F. Turn on the convection fan, if available. Line a baking sheet with aluminum foil and place the tomatoes, cut side up, on the pan. Season the tomatoes with salt and pepper, then drizzle with the oil and sprinkle with the thyme. Put the garlic cloves on the baking sheet as well. Bake the tomatoes until they are tender and starting to color and shrink, about 45 minutes.

Let the tomatoes cool, then remove the skins and put the flesh into a food processor with any juices from the pan. Squeeze the garlic flesh out of it skins into the food processor, then add the butter and pulse until smooth and creamy. Add the basil, lemon juice, and Espelette pepper and pulse to blend. Taste for salt. Scoop into a bowl and set aside.

Prepare a hot fire in a charcoal grill or preheat a gas grill to high. Brush the fish lightly all over with oil and season with salt and pepper. Place the fillets, skin side down, on the plank and set the plank on the grill directly over the fire. Watch carefully and have the grill lid ready with vents open. The smoldering plank will generate a lot of smoke. When the edges of the plank start to flame, cover the grill and cook the salmon until you can easily slide a metal offset spatula between the skin and the flesh, 8 to 10 minutes, depending on the thickness of the fillets.

With the spatula, transfer the fillets to dinner plates, leaving the skin behind. Top each portion with 1 tablespoon of the tomato butter. Serve immediately.

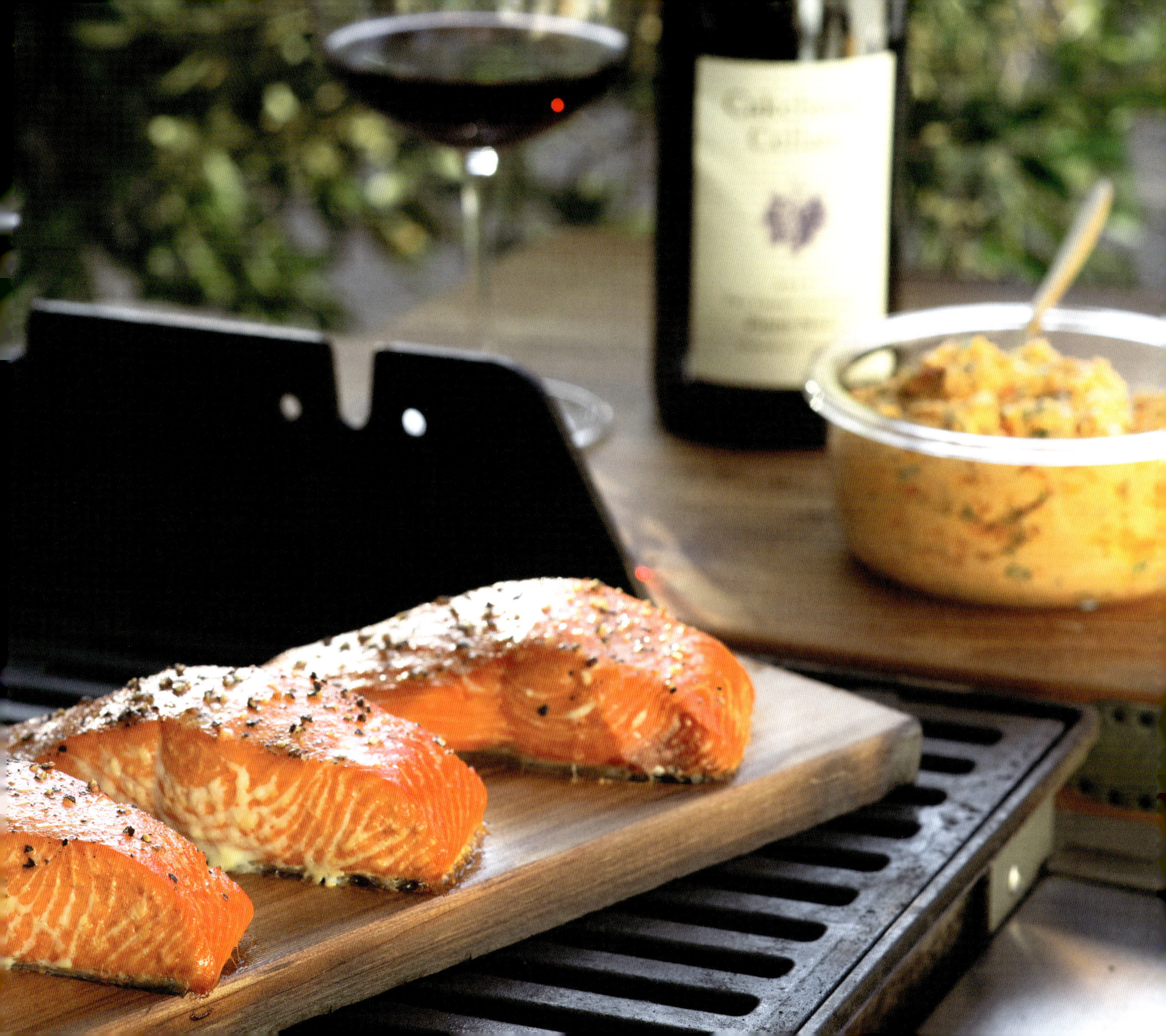

Profiteroles with Coffee Ice Cream, Armagnac-Soaked Prunes, and Chocolate-Caramel Sauce **Serves 6**

An adult version of an ice-cream sandwich, this luscious finale showcases the winery's succulent French prunes. Brian dries them, then steeps them in Armagnac (French brandy) before folding them into coffee ice cream. The prune recipe is adapted from A New Way to Cook *by Sally Schneider and must be made at least 1 week before you plan to serve the profiteroles. If you're pressed for time, substitute store-bought ice cream.*

Ice Cream:

2 cups whole milk

2 cups heavy cream

1 tablespoon instant coffee (not instant espresso)

¾ cup granulated sugar

6 large egg yolks

1 cup diced Armagnac-Soaked Prunes (recipe follows)

Profiteroles:

1 cup water

½ cup unsalted butter, diced

¼ teaspoon sea salt

1 cup all-purpose flour

4 large eggs

Chocolate-Caramel Sauce:

¾ cup granulated sugar

Pinch of cream of tartar

¼ cup water

½ cup heavy cream

½ cup crème fraîche

3 ounces bittersweet chocolate, chopped

Powdered sugar, for dusting

Prepare the ice cream: In a saucepan, combine the milk, cream, and instant coffee and bring to a simmer over medium heat, whisking to dissolve the coffee. Remove from the heat.

In a large heatproof bowl, whisk together the granulated sugar and egg yolks until pale yellow. Slowly add half of the hot milk mixture while whisking constantly. Add the remaining milk mixture and whisk to blend. Return the mixture to the saucepan over low heat and cook, stirring with a wooden spoon, until the mixture visibly thickens and reaches 178°F on an instant-read thermometer; do not let it boil or it will curdle. The mixture has cooked sufficiently when a finger drawn across the back of the spoon leaves a trail that does not fill immediately.

Strain the custard through a fine-mesh sieve into a heatproof bowl. Nest the bowl in an ice bath, stir the custard occasionally until cold, then refrigerate until well chilled. Freeze in an ice-cream maker according to the manufacturer's directions. Stir in the prunes by hand, transfer to a lidded container, and place in the freezer to harden.

Prepare the profiteroles: Preheat the oven to 400°F. Line a baking sheet with parchment paper or a silicone mat. Combine the water, butter, and salt in a saucepan and bring to a simmer over medium heat. When the butter melts, remove the pan from the heat, add the flour all at once, and stir it in vigorously with a wooden spoon. Return the saucepan to medium heat and cook, stirring constantly, until the batter pulls away from the sides of the pan, about 1 minute.

Transfer the batter to a stand mixer fitted with the paddle attachment. Turn on the mixer to medium speed and add the eggs one at a time, waiting for each egg to be incorporated before adding another. When all the eggs are well blended, transfer the batter to a pastry bag fitted with a large straight ½-inch tip. Pipe 1-inch mounds of dough about 1 inch apart on the prepared pan. You should have enough batter to make 24 mounds. With a moistened finger, flatten the peak of each mound.

Bake the profiteroles until golden brown and firm, 25 to 35 minutes. Turn the oven off and let the profiteroles dry in the oven for about 15 minutes before removing.

Prepare the chocolate-caramel sauce: Put the granulated sugar, cream of tartar, and water into a small, heavy saucepan and bring to a boil over medium heat. Cook without stirring until the sugar begins to caramelize and turn golden brown, about 5 minutes, swirling the pan so the sugar colors evenly. (Be very careful to avoid burning yourself with spattering caramel; for extra safety, don a hand mitt.) Remove the pan from the heat and carefully whisk in the cream; it will hiss and boil vigorously. Whisk in the crème fraîche and then the chocolate, whisking until the chocolate melts. Keep the sauce warm over low heat.

To serve, cut each profiterole in half horizontally with a serrated knife. Place 3 bottom halves on each of eight dessert plates. Put a small scoop of ice cream in each half. Top with the upper halves of the profiteroles. Spoon the warm chocolate-caramel sauce over the profiteroles, dust with powdered sugar, and serve immediately.

Armagnac-Soaked Prunes
Makes about 3 cups

1½ cups water
2 tablespoons sugar
1 vanilla bean
¾ pound large dried pitted prunes
½ cup Armagnac, or more to taste

Combine the water and sugar in a small saucepan. Halve the vanilla bean lengthwise and, with the tip of a small knife, scrape the seeds into the saucepan. Add the pod as well. Bring to a simmer over medium-high heat, stirring until the sugar dissolves. Remove from the heat.

Put the prunes into a clean heatproof glass jar or crock. Pour the hot syrup, including the vanilla bean, over the prunes, let cool, and then stir in the Armagnac. Cover and refrigerate for at least 1 week before using. The prunes will keep in the refrigerator indefinitely.

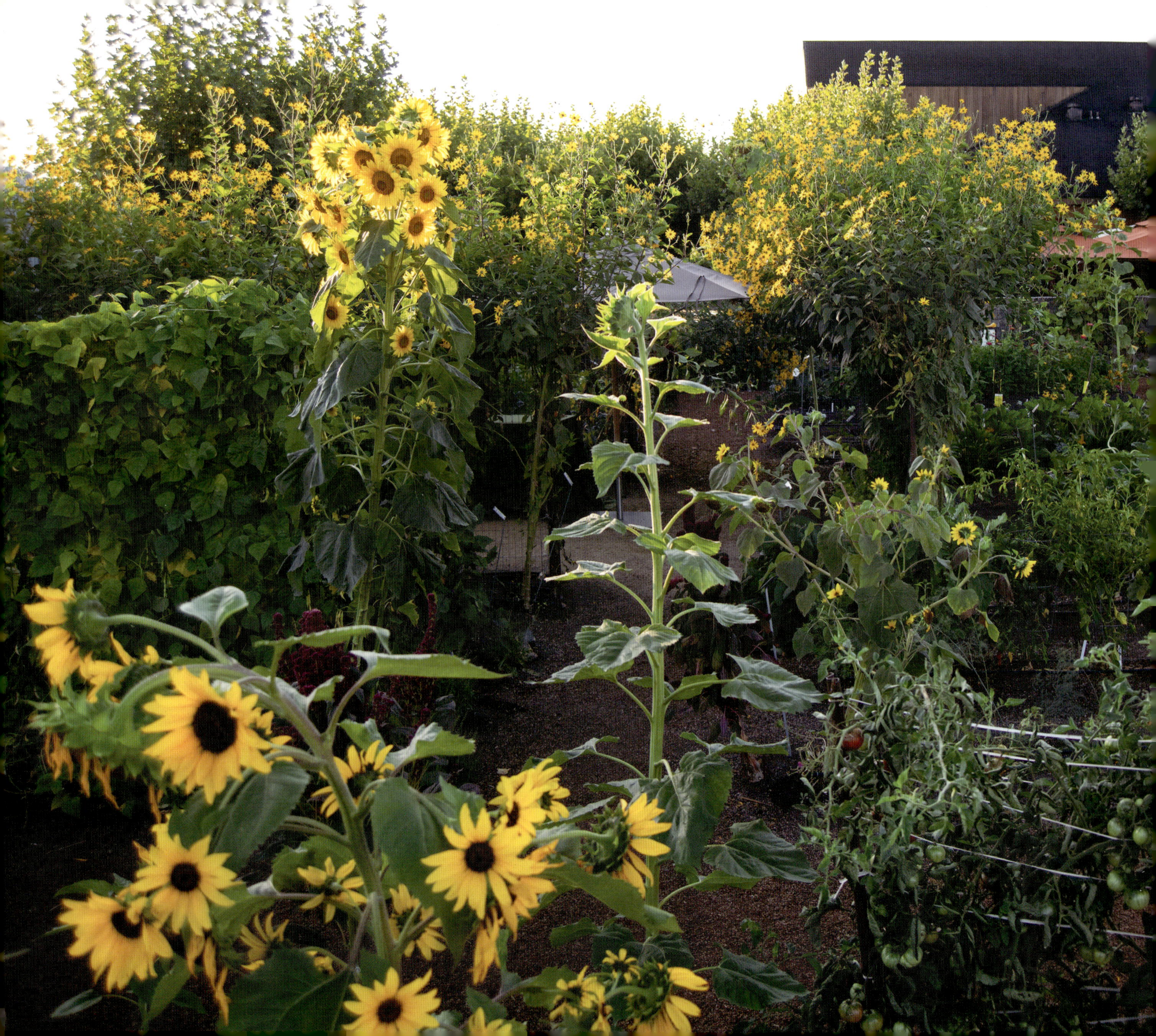

marcy's garden tips:

Take advantage of verticality. Use towering sunflowers and bean trellises to shade lettuces from summer heat. But be mindful that tall plants can also block sun from plants that need it.

Control invasive vegetables like sunchokes by planting in pots or halved wine barrels.

Keep detailed maps of garden beds so you can plan crop rotations. Plants in the Solanaceae family (eggplants, tomatoes, peppers, potatoes) should not be grown in the same location two years in a row or soil diseases may get established.

Plant a blanket of Blue Spice basil around the base of tomatoes to deter nighttime predators, such as raccoons.

Plant marigolds lavishly. Their roots repel root-knot nematodes, soil-dwelling pests that can damage beets, chard, and spinach.

Marcy often starts a second planting of squash, melons, or basil after most gardeners think the window for success has passed. If good weather holds, she gets a crop. If not, she has lost nothing but seeds.

Above and right: *Towering sunflowers create vertical interest and shade more delicate plantings from the summer sun; gardener Marcy Snow inspects Floriani Red Flint corn, an heirloom variety prized for polenta.*

ORDER
PICK UP
fresh
FROM
our
FAMILY
FARM
to you
farm to truck
PUBLIC

Clif Family Winery: *Farm to Truck to Table*

St. Helena

Napa Valley has fine restaurants galore, but some of the freshest, most engaging fare in this famous wine region comes from a food truck. Parked most days outside Clif Family Winery's tasting room, the kelly-green vehicle draws a lunchtime crowd for bruschette with inventive toppings and pristine salads that taste like the lettuces were still growing that morning.

Clif Family Bruschetteria—the truck's official name—is a business on a mission. Encouraging healthy communities, organic farming, outdoor activity, shared food and wine—these are the notions that inspire Kit Crawford and Gary Erickson, the truck's married owners who are also proprietors of the Clif Family Winery and creators of the energy-bar pioneer Clif Bar.

"When we decided to get into winemaking, we didn't want to plant only vineyards," says Kit. "We wanted to create biodiversity."

In the late 1990s, the couple purchased a remote parcel overlooking Pope Valley, on the east side of Napa Valley. Surrounded by a forest of oak and fir, the secluded Howell Mountain location provided just what they sought: trails for cycling and horseback riding and enough sunny acreage for a small vineyard, ambitious vegetable garden, and chicken coop. Kit and her brother planted olive and fruit trees, and over time the vegetable plot evolved into a five-acre farm, a productive paradise of peppers, tomatoes, melons, citrus, herbs, and asparagus.

Left and above: *Avid cyclists and Clif Family owners Gary Erickson and Kit Crawford bike to Bruschetteria, their food truck adjacent to the winery tasting room and a local favorite for lunch.*

By the time the couple opened the St. Helena tasting room to showcase their wines, the farm's output had surpassed the needs of its weekly produce-box subscribers. The Clif Family Bruschetteria, as a companion to the tasting room, would allow them to share their organic-farming philosophy and the bounty of their property, whose residents had grown to include 180 free-range chickens. Inspired by the bruschette they had enjoyed on cycling vacations in northern Italy, the couple hired chef John McConnell and let him loose to devise a flexible menu that would showcase the fruits, vegetables, herbs, and eggs from their farm.

Bruschette, as it turns out, make the perfect neutral stage for presenting whatever farm manager Tessa Henry has in abundance. Using *pain au levain* from a nearby bakery, John can devise tantalizing toast from virtually anything Tessa grows, from Brussels sprouts, kale, and spinach to persimmons and peaches.

Every week, Tessa sends John a harvest list, and they meet at the farm biweekly. "That helps me determine what's high priority," says John. "Instead of writing the menu first, the farm dictates the menu."

This type of cooking in the moment produces flashes of genius, like the truck's Mater Melon Salad, an inspired composition of ripe tomatoes, muskmelon, and watermelon that helped utilize a bumper melon crop. (Clif Family's vibrant extra virgin olive oil, pressed from the farm's Greek and Italian olive varieties, is often the unsung hero on these composed salad plates.) John's no-waste mentality means that whatever Tessa sends his way will find a home. "You have to see opportunity in everything that's coming through the door," says the chef, but that's a talent that can frustrate diners who don't always appreciate that the bruschetta they enjoyed the week before is not repeatable. Nature has moved on.

A farm visitor senses immediately that Kit and Gary's Howell Mountain endeavor is a hybrid: not quite a production farm managed for yield but far more than a hobby garden. Managing the so-called Lower Garden, a large basin surrounded by digger pines and Douglas fir, "feels more like farming," says Tessa. This broad, flat parcel yields close to a ton of tomatoes each summer, many destined for the organic tomato sauce that wine-club members sometimes receive in their shipments. Chile peppers in brilliant hues—some the color of egg yolks, others the size of a cherry—soak up the midday sun, auditioning for their role in single-variety hot sauces for the Clif Family brand. Tessa also grows Floriani Red Flint corn here, an heirloom Italian

Above: *(clockwise from far left) Chef John McConnell; farm box; orchard peaches; lower garden; sauce from estate tomatoes; red flint corn for polenta; cherry peppers; greenhouse-started seedlings*

"We want to educate and inspire others," says Kit. "Sustainably farmed grapes, fruits, and vegetables are so important to the health of our community and our planet."

variety that John dries and grinds by hand for polenta.

The upper area is more relaxed, with raised beds and smaller plots. It could be the fruit and vegetable garden of a large and very hungry family, with a hoop house for seed starting and a tidy storage shed where red onions, garlic, and peppers hang to dry. Fruit trees surround the hoop house but only one or two of each type: Arkansas Black apples, Asian pears, pomegranates, peaches, persimmons, plums, figs, and citrus. A nearby property, which became part of the Clif Family Farm later, hosts a more intensive orchard and supplies the blueberries, blackberries, citrus, and stone fruits for the Clif Family's small-batch marmalades, jams, and preserves.

Clif Family Winery

Whatever the season, both properties will be blanketed in blooms. The IPM (integrated pest management) techniques that Tessa employs rely on California native plants and colorful blossoms to lure beneficial insects, and many of these plants do double duty as plate garnishes. Zinnias, marigolds, amaranth, borage, pineapple sage, pincushion flowers, snapdragons, white salvia, and verbena thrive in thick stands, and Tessa lets parsley, cilantro, and fennel mature until they flower and set seed. John occasionally sends his cooks to the farm to work for a day—"It connects the dots for them," he says—and they

Above and right: *(clockwise from left) Yellow ground cherries; farm manager Tessa Henry delivers a farm box to the chef; red onions dry in the potting shed; sunflowers brighten the lower garden in late summer*

84 Gather

come back to the restaurant's prep kitchen with trays of painstakingly gathered marigold petals or dill pollen.

Working with John has helped Tessa realize how many parts of a plant may be edible. He harvests fennel pollen—a tedious task—to season the truck's popular *porchetta* and uses the leaves from citrus prunings to flavor his pork brine. The delicate blossoms of chives, parsley, and nepitella add beauty and freshness to the Clif Family Bruschetteria plates. In spring, the chef serves young, tender fava beans, pod and all, like green beans. Sometimes, Tessa will tell John she's thinking of turning over a tired bed, and he'll say, "But there's still something usable out there."

Hospitality at Clif Family often centers around John's juicy *porchetta*, a simplified version of the rosemary- and garlic-scented pork roast of Tuscany. Polenta is its usual sidekick, made with the farm's freshly ground dried corn. "It tastes miraculously different from what you can buy," says John. "There are so many nuances in whole-grain polenta."

To launch a late-spring *porchetta* dinner, John looks to the farm's last, lingering brassicas—cauliflower, kale, broccoli—and roasts them to top a bruschetta with the season's first peas. The hardy winter chicories are also about to bow out, so they're celebrated in a colorful salad with spring radishes. Fresh-dug potatoes get an unusual two-part treatment that makes them extra crisp. Accompanied by olives, boiled farm eggs, and a dressing thick with spring herbs, they're about as enticing as potatoes can get. For a sweet finale, John concocts a dreamy parfait, alternating layers of Meyer lemon curd, poppy seed shortbread, and sugared farm blueberries steeped in Clif Family red wine.

Today, Kit and Gary own ninety acres of Napa Valley vineyards, all certified organic, and have helped other grape growers transition to organic production. Leading by example is, fundamentally, what their Clif Family project is about. "We want to educate and inspire others," says Kit. "Sustainably farmed grapes, fruits, and vegetables are so important to the health of our community and our planet."

menu

Bruschetta with Brassicas, Peas, and Burrata

Clif Family Oak Knoll Sauvignon Blanc or Rosé of Grenache

Mixed Chicory Caesar with "Cacio e Pepe" Croutons

Clif Family Chardonnay or Grenache

Fingerling Potato "Tostones" with Olive Salsa Verde and Farm Eggs

Clif Family Rosé of Grenache or Viognier

Clif Family Porchetta with Creamy Polenta

Clif Family Grenache or Chardonnay

Meyer Lemon Curd Parfait with Poppy Seed Crust and Red Wine–Macerated Blueberries

Clif Family Arriva Petite Sirah Dessert Wine

uncommon edibles:

Shake up your edible garden with these unusual plants, all star performers on the Clif Family farm.

Ground cherries: Also known as Cape gooseberries, ground cherries look like miniature gold tomatillos and taste like a cross between a tomato and mango. John halves them and scatters them on tomato bruschetta.

Nepitella: *(Calamintha nepeta)* Sometimes called Tuscan mint or calamint, nepitella has oregano-like leaves and an aroma that mingles mint, oregano, and licorice. John especially likes it with watermelon.

Greek dwarf basil: This delicate herb grows in small, compact mounds and has tiny leaves. "You can use the leaves whole, so they don't oxidize like cut basil," says John, who uses this variety in Clif Family tomato sauce.

Cabernet red onions: The name is a plus, but more important, the variety is useful at multiple stages: as a mild spring onion, a mature summer onion, and a dry storage crop.

Flavor King and Dapple Dandy pluots: These two varieties thrive in Kit and Gary's orchard and are among the sweetest examples of this plum-apricot cross.

Above and right: *Cabernet red onions hanging in the garden shed; upper garden at the Clif Family farm*

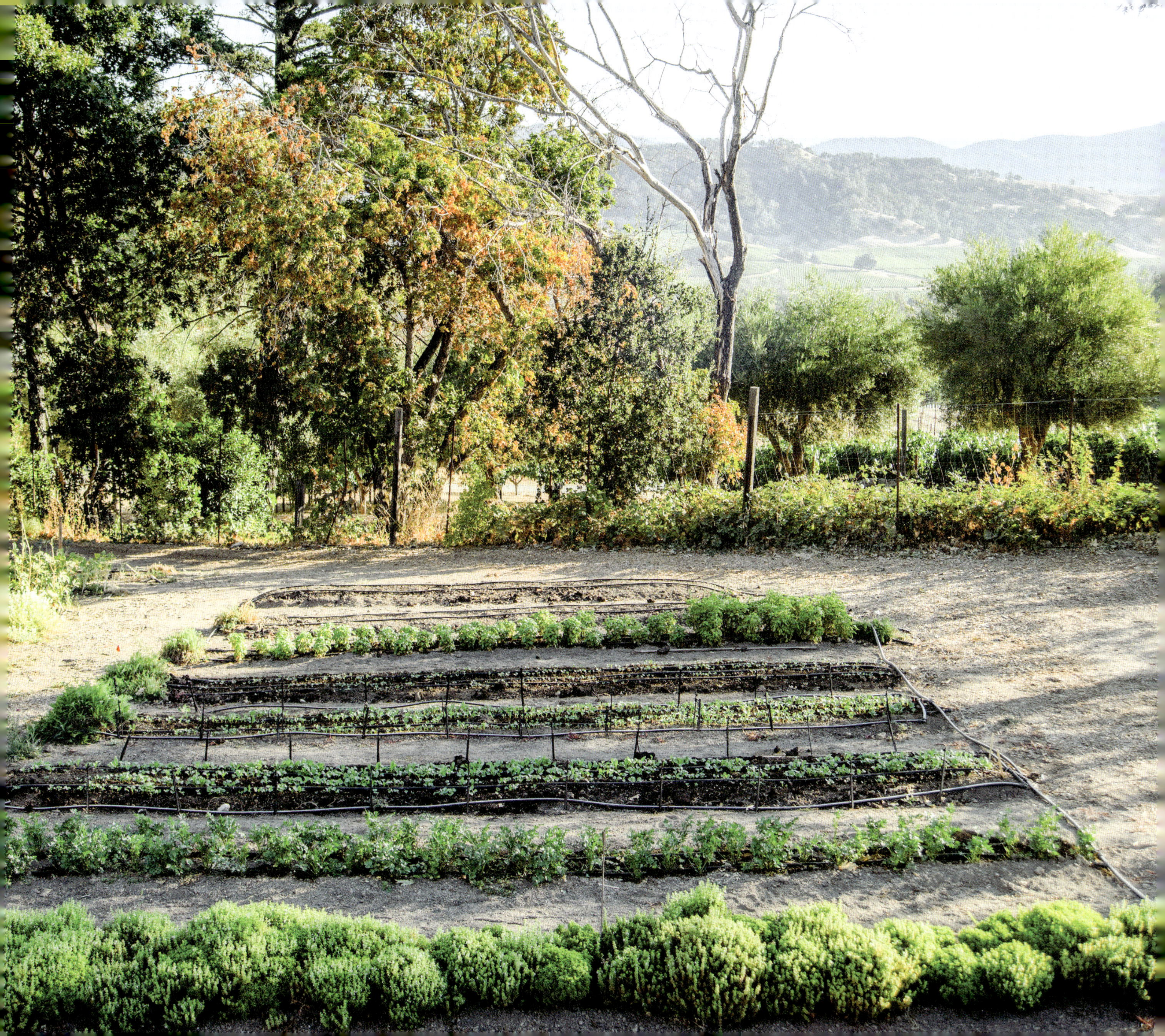

PICK UP

CLIF FAMILY
WINERY
SAUVIGNON BLANC
Napa Valley

BRUSCHETTERIA

Bruschetta with Brassicas, Peas, and Burrata **Makes 6 toasts**

John likes to use the leaves and tender pared stems of broccoli and cauliflower, parts that less resourceful cooks discard. "I love the taste and the contrast," says the chef. "Instead of just roasted florets, you have the crisp, golden-brown leaf tips as well." For this springtime bruschetta, he spreads creamy burrata on hot, crunchy toast, then tops it with roasted brassicas (such as broccoli, Romanesco broccoli, and cauliflower) and sweet English peas, all from the Clif Family farm.

Vinaigrette:

½ cup extra virgin olive oil

¼ cup plus 1½ teaspoons fresh lemon juice

⅛ teaspoon freshly cracked black pepper

4 tablespoons Thai or Vietnamese fish sauce, or to taste

1½ quarts small florets, tender leaves, and coarsely chopped stems of mixed brassicas, such as cauliflower, broccoli, and broccoli Romanesco

2 tablespoons extra virgin olive oil, plus more for brushing the toasts

Kosher or sea salt

¾ to 1 cup shelled English peas

6 slices day-old pain au levain or other sourdough loaf, about 4 inches by 2 inches and ½ inch thick

1 large clove garlic, halved

½ pound burrata cheese

Torn fresh mint leaves, for garnish

Wine: Clif Family Oak Knoll Sauvignon Blanc or Rosé of Grenache

Make the vinaigrette: In a small bowl, whisk together the oil, lemon juice, and pepper. Whisk in the fish sauce 1 tablespoon at a time until the flavor is strong enough for your taste. Depending on the brand of fish sauce, you may need less than 4 tablespoons.

Preheat the oven to 375°F with a convection fan or 400°F without a fan. Line a baking sheet with parchment paper. In a bowl, toss the brassicas with the oil and with salt to taste. Arrange the brassicas on the prepared pan and bake until lightly browned in spots, about 10 minutes.

Have ready a bowl of salted ice water. Bring a small pot of unsalted water to a boil over high heat. Add the peas and blanch for about 1 minute, then drain and plunge immediately into the ice water to stop the cooking. Drain again and pat dry.

Toast the bread on both sides by your preferred method—on a stove-top grill pan, in a toaster oven, under a broiler, or on a grill—brushing each side with oil partway through toasting. The bread should be crusty on the outside but still soft inside. While hot, rub one side of each slice with the garlic.

Slice the burrata into 6 roughly equal pieces. Put a piece of burrata on the garlic-rubbed side of each slice of hot toast and smash the cheese with the back of a spoon so it covers most of the toast.

Put the roasted brassicas into a bowl and toss them with just enough of the vinaigrette to coat lightly. Top each toast with the roasted brassicas and the peas, dividing them evenly. Scatter mint on top and drizzle with a little more vinaigrette. Serve immediately.

Mixed Chicory Caesar with "Cacio e Pepe" Croutons Serves 6

Creamy Anchovy Dressing:

½ cup mayonnaise

1½ teaspoons fresh lemon juice

1½ teaspoons Thai or Vietnamese fish sauce

½ teaspoon Dijon mustard

⅛ teaspoon freshly ground black pepper

"Cacio e Pepe" Croutons:

½ sourdough baguette, torn into rough ½-inch pieces

1 tablespoon extra virgin olive oil

¼ teaspoon freshly cracked black pepper

¼ cup freshly grated Parmigiano-Reggiano cheese

3 quarts torn mixed chicories and other bitter greens, such as radicchio, escarole, frisée, dandelion, puntarella, and arugula

1 cup thinly sliced mixed radishes, including small daikon and watermelon radishes if available

Chunk of Parmigiano-Reggiano cheese, for shaving

Wine: Clif Family Chardonnay or Grenache

Inspired by the Roman pasta dish spaghetti cacio e pepe, *John got the idea to toss hot toasted croutons with grated cheese and black pepper. The cheese melts on contact. Instead of slicing the baguette for the croutons, he tears it into rough chunks. It's more rustic and creates more crevices to trap the seasonings. The croutons are best warm, so if you've made them ahead, reheat them before adding them to the salad. Leftover dressing is great with steamed artichokes, cauliflower, or other steamed vegetables.*

Make the creamy anchovy dressing: In a small bowl, whisk together all the dressing ingredients. Taste and adjust the seasoning.

Make the "cacio e pepe" croutons: Preheat the oven to 375°F or 350°F with a convection fan. Line a baking sheet with parchment paper. In a bowl, toss the baguette pieces with the oil and pepper, then arrange them in a single layer on the prepared pan. Bake until lightly browned in spots, about 8 minutes. Immediately transfer them to a bowl and, while they are hot, toss them with the cheese.

Toss the chicories and radishes with enough of the dressing to coat lightly. Arrange attractively on a serving platter, then scatter the warm croutons on top. Using a vegetable peeler, shave a little Parmigiano-Reggiano over the top. Serve immediately.

chef's tips:

After washing the chicories, soak them in ice water for 30 minutes, changing the water once. The ice water helps crisp them. Spin dry and, if not using them immediately, layer them with paper towels and refrigerate in a plastic bag.

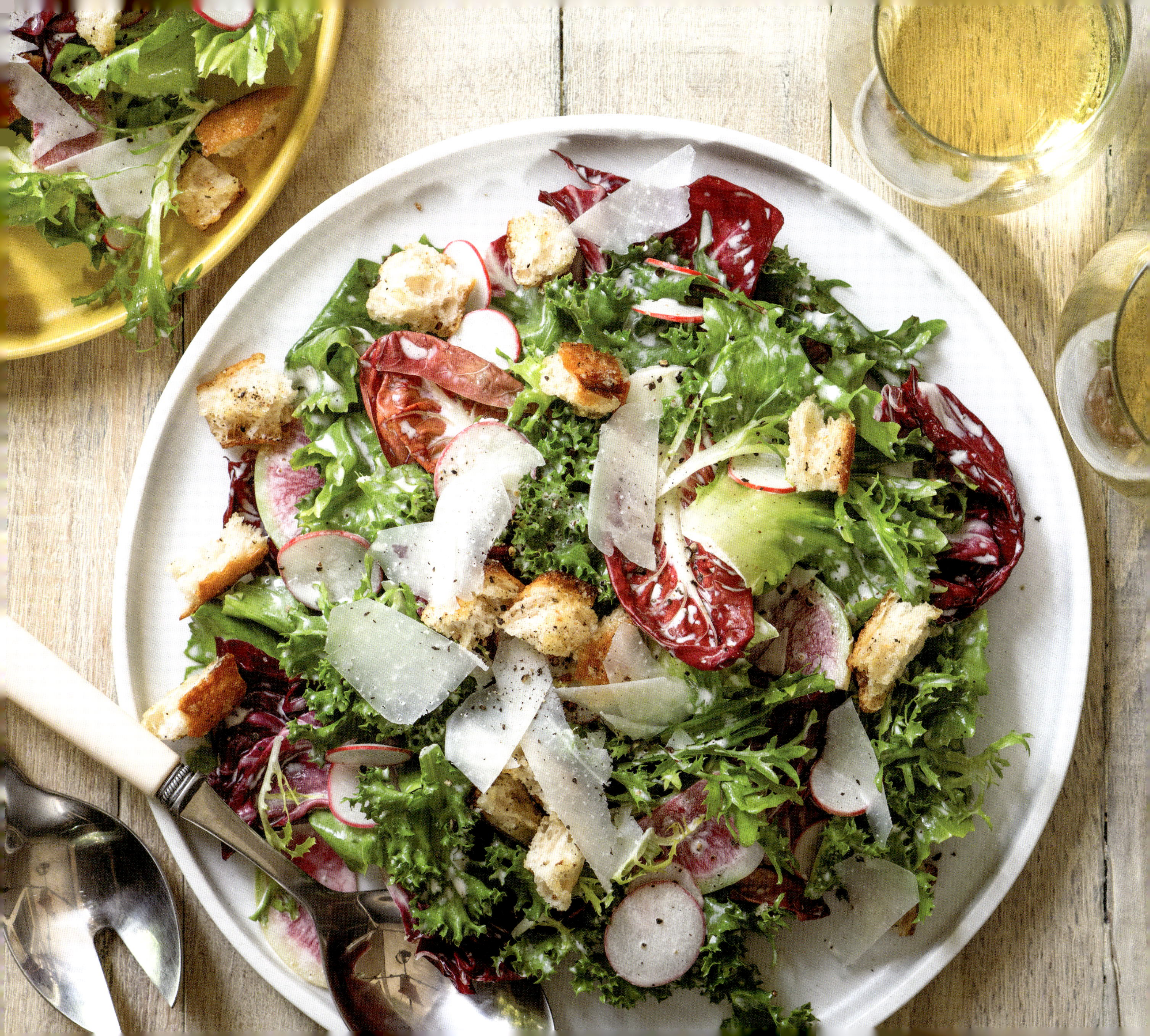

wine for all seasons:

Working daily with the fruits and vegetables from the farm has shaped John's ideas about pairing fresh produce with Clif Family winemaker Laura Barrett's wine.

Spring: "Peas and fava beans from the farm are tender, sweet, and delicate. I can't help but associate that flavor with freshness and white wines with heightened acidity, like our Sauvignon Blanc. Laura's style is exuberant and expressive."

Summer: "A really crisp, cold glass of Clif Family Rosé of Grenache goes hand in hand with what's coming from the garden— herbs, zucchini, eggplants, tomatoes—and the Provençal-type dishes we're making."

Autumn: "We're getting winter squashes, potatoes, beets, and Brussels sprouts from the garden, and we're doing more braising. Our Grenache is lovely with those earthier flavors."

Winter: "I'm roasting root vegetables and cooking the garden chicories in duck fat. Those bold flavors marry with a full-bodied red wine, like Gary's Improv Zinfandel."

Fingerling Potato "Tostones" with Olive Salsa Verde and Farm Eggs Serves 6

Faced with a deluge of spring herbs, fingerling potatoes, and fresh eggs from Clif Family's farm, John devised this dish to showcase them. It weaves together many influences—the tostones *(fried plantain chips) of Puerto Rico, the* chimichurri *of Argentina, Italy's salsa verde, the South American pairing of olives and eggs. The result seems like a dish that was always meant to be: crusty potatoes under a zippy dressing, with the creamy complement of perfectly boiled eggs.*

12 fingerling potatoes, about 1½ pounds total

Olive Salsa Verde:

1 cup loosely packed fresh flat-leaf parsley leaves, plus more whole leaves for garnish

½ cup loosely packed fresh dill leaves

⅓ cup loosely packed fresh tarragon leaves

5 or 6 large green olives, such as Picholine or Castelvetrano, pitted

4 whole cornichons

1 tablespoon brine-packed capers, rinsed

1½ teaspoons Thai or Vietnamese fish sauce

1½ teaspoons sherry vinegar

½ teaspoon kosher or sea salt

½ cup extra virgin olive oil

3 large eggs, at room temperature

¼ cup extra virgin olive oil

½ teaspoon kosher or sea salt

Wine: Clif Family Rosé of Grenache or Viognier

Preheat the oven to 400°F or 375°F with a convection fan.

Put the potatoes into a saucepan with salted water to cover by 1 inch. Bring to a boil over high heat, then lower the heat to maintain a simmer. Cook until you can pierce the potatoes with a skewer or small knife, about 20 minutes. Drain well, then put the potatoes back into the warm saucepan and cover with a lid. Set aside for about 10 minutes to cool slightly.

Make the olive salsa verde: In a food processor, combine the parsley, dill, tarragon, olives, cornichons, capers, fish sauce, vinegar, and salt and pulse until well chopped. Add the oil and puree until smooth, stopping to scrape down the work bowl once or twice. You should have a generous 1 cup.

Have ready a bowl of ice water. Put the eggs into a small saucepan and add water to cover by an inch or so. Remove the eggs. Bring the water to a boil over high heat, then lower the heat to avoid jostling the eggs when you add them. With a spoon, carefully lower the eggs, one at a time, into the simmering water, then adjust the heat to maintain a gentle simmer. Cook for exactly 8½ minutes. With a slotted spoon, transfer the eggs into the ice water. When cool, drain and peel, then cut each egg lengthwise into 8 wedges.

Put a potato between two sheets of parchment paper and flatten the potato with the bottom of a skillet. The potato should be crushed flat but still mostly in one piece. Repeat with the remaining potatoes.

Put the flattened potatoes in a shallow bowl with any scraps. Drizzle with the oil and sprinkle with the salt. Toss gently, then spread the potatoes out on a baking sheet, minimizing any overlap. Bake until crusty, about 12 minutes.

With an offset spatula, transfer the potatoes to a serving platter. Drizzle with 4 to 5 tablespoons of the salsa verde and surround with the egg wedges. Scatter parsley leaves on top. Serve hot.

Clif Family Porchetta with Creamy Polenta Serves 12

Spice Rub:

½ cup whole fresh rosemary leaves

¼ cup whole peeled garlic cloves (about 12)

¼ cup ground fennel seed

½ teaspoon sea salt

¼ cup extra virgin olive oil

One 4-pound piece skinless pork belly

2½ pounds boneless center-cut pork loin, chain attached, silverskin removed

2½ tablespoons sea salt

Polenta:

3 cups polenta

½ cup heavy cream

4 tablespoons unsalted butter

1 cup coarsely grated Fontina Val d'Aosta cheese

⅓ cup freshly grated pecorino romano cheese

Sea salt

Wine: Clif Family Grenache or Chardonnay

Make the spice rub: Put the rosemary, garlic, fennel, salt, and oil into a food processor or blender and process until smooth. You should have about ½ cup.

Customers of Clif Family's popular Bruschetteria food truck would riot if the porchetta *ever left the menu. Modeled on the famous Tuscan preparation of pork loin wrapped in pork belly, chef John's* porchetta *makes a dramatic party dish, a juicy, garlicky, crusty roast scented with rosemary and fennel. If the total weight of your* porchetta *is heavier or lighter than the assembled 6½-pound* porchetta *in this recipe, adjust the quantity of spice rub accordingly. You need about 1½ tablespoons rub per pound of meat.*

Pork belly is typically sold with the skin attached. Ask the butcher to remove the skin for you, leaving all the fat on the belly. You can also choose to have the butcher butterfly the belly for you, or you can follow the method described here. The short sides of the rectangular pork belly should be the same length as the pork loin so the belly will encase the loin completely.

To butterfly the pork belly, put it skinned side down on a work surface with a longer side nearest you. With a sharp boning knife, make a vertical cut down the center of the belly, slicing only halfway through. Starting from that center cut, slice horizontally through the belly from the center to the left end without cutting all the way through. Make a similar horizontal cut from the center to the right end without cutting all the way through. You will have two flaps that you can open like a book and lay flat. The belly is now twice as long and half as thick as it was before.

Season the pork belly and the loin all over with the salt. Then spread the spice rub over the belly and loin, using all of it and slathering it evenly over all the surfaces.

Wrap the pork loin in the butterflied pork belly, jelly-roll style. Tie tightly with butcher's twine in five to seven equidistant places, starting from the center and working out toward the ends. Line a roasting pan or a baking sheet with aluminum foil and place a flat rack on it. Set the tied roast, seam side down, on the rack and refrigerate uncovered for 24 hours.

Two hours before cooking, remove the *porchetta* from the refrigerator. Preheat the oven to 500°F or 450°F with a convection fan.

Roast the pork, rotating the pan back to front after 10 minutes, until the exterior begins to brown, about 20 minutes. Reduce the oven temperature to 325°F or 300°F with a convection fan. Continue cooking, rotating the pan occasionally, until an instant-read thermometer inserted into the center of the roast registers 130°F to 135°F, about 2 hours. Transfer the pork, still on the rack, to a baking sheet that can collect any drippings. The internal temperature will rise about 10°F as the meat rests. Let rest for at least 1 hour before carving.

While the *porchetta* rests, make the polenta: In a large pot, bring 4 quarts lightly salted water to a boil over high heat. Add the polenta gradually, whisking constantly. When the polenta begins to thicken, lower the heat to maintain a gentle bubble. Cook, whisking often and occasionally scraping down the sides of the pan with a heat-resistant rubber spatula, until the polenta is creamy and no longer gritty, about 45 minutes. Whisk in the cream and butter, then remove from the heat and whisk in the cheeses. Taste for salt.

Transfer the *porchetta* to a cutting board. Remove the twine and slice about ½ inch thick. Divide the slices among twelve dinner plates. Pour any collected juices from the board and pan over the sliced pork. Spoon the polenta alongside. Serve immediately.

Meyer Lemon Curd Parfait with Poppy Seed Crust and Red Wine–Macerated Blueberries

Serves 6 to 8

Marmalade made with Meyer lemons from the Clif Family farm is a favorite souvenir for visitors to the winery's tasting room. (It's also available online.) John often uses the marmalade in a lemon curd filling for tarts. In a genius moment, he got the idea to deconstruct the tart, breaking up the shortbread-like crust into shards and layering the pieces with the lemon curd and macerated berries. Serve the parfait shortly after assembly, but you can prepare all the components a day ahead.

Poppy Seed Crust:

1¼ cups unbleached all-purpose flour, plus more for the work surface

2 tablespoons granulated sugar

1 tablespoon poppy seeds

⅛ teaspoon kosher or sea salt

½ cup cold unsalted butter, in small pieces

1 large egg yolk

2 to 3 tablespoons cold heavy cream

Meyer Lemon Curd:

¾ cup Clif Family Meyer Lemon Marmalade or other marmalade

½ cup granulated sugar

6 tablespoons fresh lemon juice

3 large eggs, at room temperature

3 large egg yolks, at room temperature

¼ teaspoon kosher or sea salt

½ cup plus 2 tablespoons unsalted butter, at room temperature, in small pieces

Macerated Berries:

2 pints blueberries or blackberries

¼ cup powdered sugar

2 tablespoons red wine

1 teaspoon fresh lemon juice

6 to 8 fresh mint sprigs, for garnish

Wine: Clif Family Arriva Petite Sirah Dessert Wine

Make the poppy seed crust: In a food processor, combine the flour, sugar, poppy seeds, and salt and pulse to blend. Add the butter and pulse just until the mixture resembles coarse meal. Whisk together the egg yolk and 2 tablespoons of the cream, then drizzle them evenly over the dry mixture. Pulse just until the dough begins to come together, adding another 1 tablespoon cream if the dough seems dry. Handling the dough as lightly as possible, shape it into a flattened disk, wrap in plastic wrap, and refrigerate for at least 1 hour or up to 1 day.

    Preheat the oven to 350°F. Remove the dough from the refrigerator about 15 minutes before rolling to soften it slightly. On a lightly floured work surface, roll the dough out ¼ inch thick. The shape doesn't matter as long as it will fit on your pan. Transfer the rolled dough to a baking sheet. Pierce the dough in several places with a fork.

Bake until golden brown, 20 to 30 minutes. Let cool on a wire rack to room temperature. Gently break the crust into pieces small enough to fit in your serving glasses. Store in an airtight container at room temperature until you are ready to assemble the parfaits.

Make the Meyer lemon curd: Put a bowl into the refrigerator to chill. Put all the ingredients into a blender and puree until completely smooth. Pour the mixture into the top of a double boiler and set over (but not touching) simmering water. Cook, whisking almost constantly and scraping down the sides of the bowl or pan occasionally, until the mixture visibly thickens and registers 178°F to 180°F on an instant-read thermometer. Do not allow the curd to boil or it will curdle. Immediately remove from the heat and whisk the curd for a minute or so to cool it. Transfer it to the chilled bowl and cover with plastic wrap, pressing it directly onto the surface of the curd to prevent a skin from forming. Let cool to room temperature, then refrigerate until chilled. You can make the curd a day ahead and refrigerate it.

Make the macerated berries: In a bowl, gently stir together all the ingredients until the sugar dissolves. Let macerate at room temperature for about 30 minutes to draw some juices out of the berries.

Assemble the parfaits: Set aside a few blueberries to garnish each serving. Put a scoop of lemon curd in each of six to eight clear glass cups or parfait glasses, using about one-third of the curd. Top the curd with poppy seed crust pieces, using about half of the pieces. Spoon macerated berries and juices on top, using about half of the berry mixture. Repeat the layering of lemon curd, crust, and berries. Top with the remaining lemon curd and garnish with the reserved berries and a mint sprig. Serve immediately so the crust stays crisp.

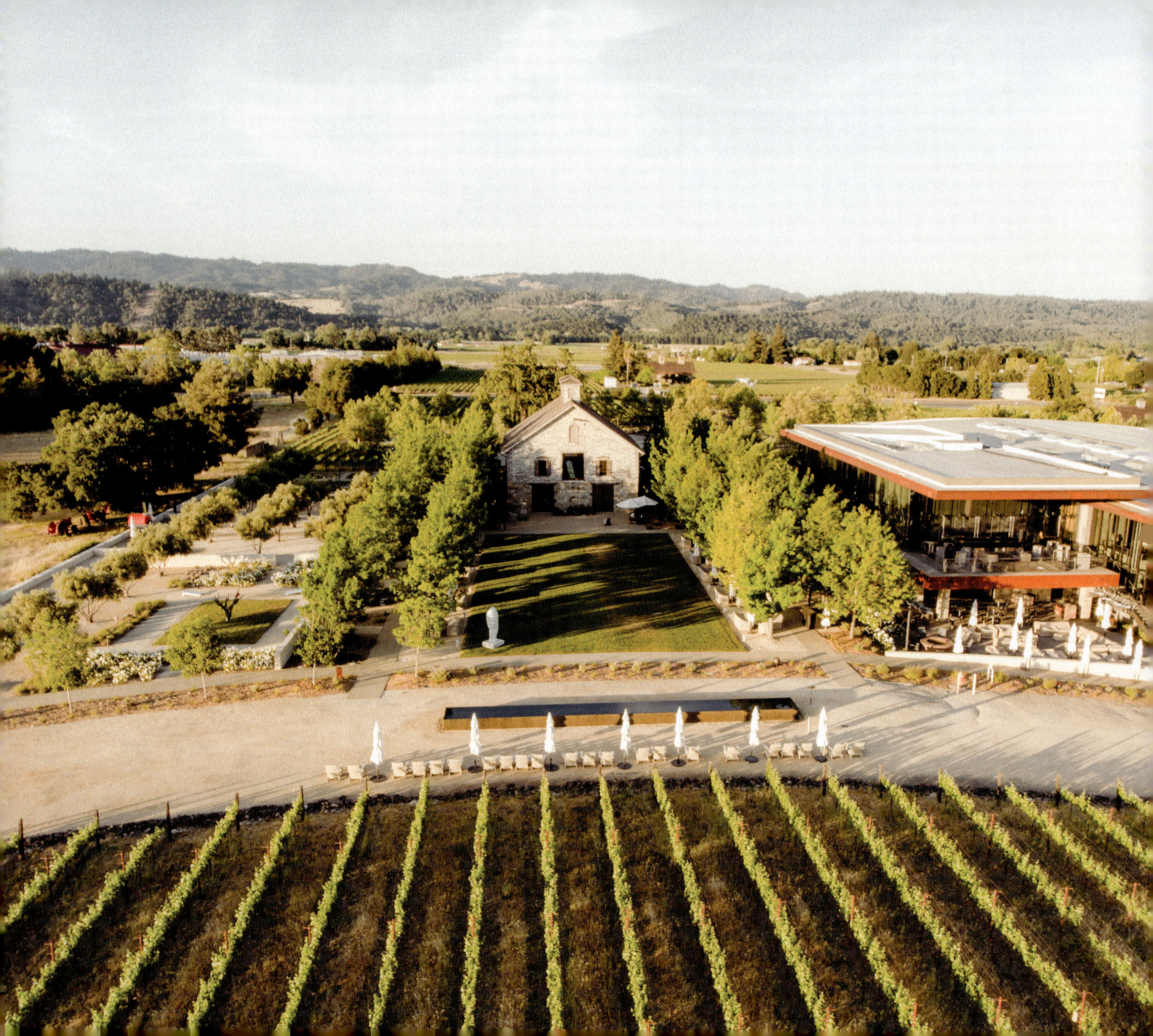

HALL Wines: *Solutions in Nature*

St. Helena

Kathryn and Craig Hall are such enthusiastic consumers of fresh, seasonal produce that they have not one garden, but two. A vegetable plot, herb garden, and fruit trees at their hilltop Napa Valley home supply their table when this busy couple is in residence. But the larger garden, at HALL Wines, is even more ambitious: twenty-six long, sunny beds overseen by an energetic manager whose devotion to organic and sustainable methods is as deep as the Halls'.

"Being organic and sustainable is who we are in our vineyards, so it makes sense to carry that through to the garden," says Kathryn, a former attorney and US ambassador to Austria who founded the winery with her husband in 2003. "It's heartening to see how much our team loves the garden and how proud they are of it. Shelley has taken it to another level."

Shelley Kusch, a longtime Napa Valley professional gardener, keeps both gardens prolific and producing food and flowers year-round. "This is a 365-day garden," says Kusch of the winery's edible landscape. "It needs to always look beautiful."

The winery often hosts visiting chefs for charitable events, and Kusch gives them free rein to forage in the garden. Employees also take home a lot of the harvest, and many of the flowers go into lush bouquets for the tasting room and for events. And, of course, winery visitors are encouraged to stroll the garden, wineglass in hand, and enjoy the dahlias and zinnias, sniff the roses, and admire the sculptures—some of them, like the cast-bronze apple tree, commissioned by the Halls for the garden site.

Left and above: *HALL Wines in St. Helena includes both a contemporary tasting room and gallery and the restored 1885 Bergfeld Winery, now known as the Founder's Cellar; Kathryn and Craig Hall at home*

"I farm using Amish methods," says Shelley. "The Amish garden for inner peace and for productivity—a big yield from a little space. It involves a lot of companion planting."

With a degree in botany and decades of experience in organic gardening, Shelley has learned to look to nature for solutions. In the HALL garden, many plants provide pest or disease protection to their neighbors. "Chives and tomatoes are best friends," says Shelley; plant them together and the tomatoes will be stronger. Radishes growing around cucumbers deter cucumber beetles. Society garlic repels gophers. For additional gopher protection and disease resistance, Shelley plants garlic around all the fruit trees—a collection that includes Blenheim and Moorpark apricots, Babcock white peach, Harko nectarine, Gala apple, Warren pear, and Lapin cherry. The garlic also helps the fruit grow bigger and sweeter, says this avid naturalist.

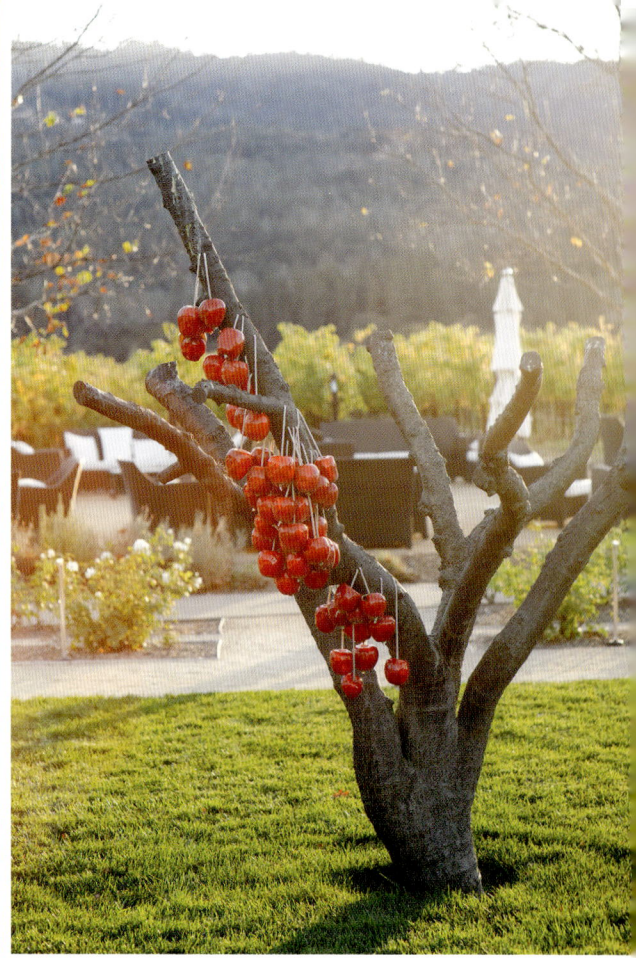

But Shelley reserves her highest praise for borage, a leafy herb with attractive blue flowers. "It's God's gift to the plant world," says the gardener. "It attracts all the good bugs and repels the bad ones." Bees love it, strawberries love it, and chefs appreciate it, too. The leaves have a cucumber-like flavor and make a tasty addition to soups, and the dainty blossoms embellish salads.

"All of my gardens have edible flowers," says Shelley, who manages some restaurant and private gardens as well. "You need them to attract pollinators. The winery staff uses the flowers on cheese plates, and whatever doesn't get used for culinary purposes makes the garden more lovely for visitors." Pansies, alyssum, and sweet Williams in spring give way to marigolds, calendula, and sunflowers, a fall palette that harmonizes with the autumn colors in the winery's adjacent Bergfeld Vineyard. Bulbs are the only nonedibles that Shelley permits in the garden, with irises and calla lilies, ranunculus and daffodils all doing double duty as gopher deterrents.

Shelley starts almost all of her edibles from seed to be sure the seedlings are disease-free. Although she grows heaps of tomatoes, peppers, kale, and green beans, she has a soft spot for the novelties and curiosities that few others grow. Espelette pepper, a mildly spicy red pepper from France's Basque region, is a favorite, as is luffa. The slender, pendulous gourd is a powerful bee attractant and edible when young, with a flavor like summer squash. As it matures, the fleshy interior turns fibrous and can be harvested for sponges. "Everybody thinks luffa comes from the ocean," says Shelley.

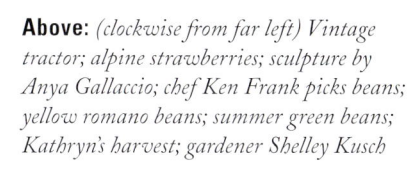

Above: *(clockwise from far left) Vintage tractor; alpine strawberries; sculpture by Anya Gallaccio; chef Ken Frank picks beans; yellow romano beans; summer green beans; Kathryn's harvest; gardener Shelley Kusch*

"Being organic and sustainable is who we are in our vineyards, so it makes sense to carry that through to our garden."

After winter's relative calm, the arrival of spring paints the winery garden in vivid shades of green. Tarragon, chives, and anise hyssop reawaken; green garlic's strappy leaves poke through the earth; and plump artichokes beckon from their silvery fronds. Fava beans quickly spurt to five feet, and the air is heady with the honeyed scent of sweet alyssum.

Summer brings tomatoes in profusion, peppers, potatoes, sweet corn, eggplants, melons, and yellow wax beans. By autumn, when gardeners in other climates might be putting their tools to rest, Shelley is harvesting cranberry beans and sunchokes and making sure the Halls' rock-walled vegetable bed is churning out alpine strawberries, kale, chard, basil, and winter squashes for their home kitchen.

HALL Wines 101

The idea that a fine bottle of red wine needs red meat alongside is not how the Halls approach food and wine pairing. Kathryn is not a meat eater and Craig is a longtime vegan, yet they still find room for red wine every night. "That's never been a problem," laughs Kathryn. "We have at least one glass of red wine with every meal." They certainly have choices: the couple's wine ventures also include WALT, a Pinot Noir and Chardonnay brand, and BACA, which focuses on Zinfandel.

Above and right: *(clockwise from left) Shelley harvests baby shallots; garden bed at the Hall home; companion planting of flowers and edibles; edible flowers for garnish are a fixture in the HALL Wines garden.*

102 Gather

Between their businesses and their philanthropy, the Halls maintain packed schedules, but making time for a relaxed evening meal is a priority. Ken Frank, proprietor of the Michelin-starred La Toque in Napa, is among the chefs they most admire in the Napa Valley, and they occasionally engage him to cook for winery events. Ken is also a celebrity judge in the winery's annual Cabernet Cookoff, a fundraiser that pits teams of prominent chefs against one another to benefit local nonprofits.

Challenged to create a menu using autumn produce from the winery garden, Ken immediately saw the possibilities in the young root vegetables and shelling beans. He prepares a multicourse vegetarian menu nightly at his restaurant, so he is accustomed to putting produce in the spotlight. Ken's recipe for roasted sunchoke soup transforms the humble-looking tubers into a velvety puree fit for guests but easy enough for family meals, too. With carrots and parsnips, he created a light slaw dressed with lemongrass oil—a stand-alone salad that could also accompany grilled shrimp, grilled tofu, or rotisserie chicken. The chef's stunning beet and citrus salad relies on a clever technique—charring citrus—to introduce a subtle burnt-sugar note.

Shelley's harvest of cranberry beans inspired Ken's Pinot Noir–friendly main course, a pan-seared pork chop with garlicky wild mushrooms and a shelling bean ragout. Alpine strawberries, still producing in early fall, prompted Ken to turn to a classic dessert that everyone loves but few people make. Not surprisingly, this French-trained chef produces crêpes that would please a Michelin inspector, with nutty brown butter scenting the warm strawberry filling. Fruit truly does seem to grow better and sweeter at HALL, a testament both to the site and the nature-knows-best gardening practices.

"The garden emphasizes the connection between food and wine, so it seems natural to us to have it," says Kathryn. "In Napa Valley, we take for granted that we can grow fresh produce year-round, but for people from elsewhere, the abundance makes an impression. Touring the garden is part of the enjoyment of visiting HALL."

menu

Roasted Sunchoke Soup
WALT Shea Pinot Noir

Beet and Citrus Salad with Charred Citrus Crème Fraîche
WALT Bob's Ranch Chardonnay

Carrot and Parsnip Slaw with Lemongrass-Ginger Oil
HALL Knights Valley Sauvignon Blanc

Pan-Seared Pork Chops with Shelling Bean and Wild Mushroom Ragout
HALL Jack's Masterpiece Cabernet Sauvignon

Crêpes with Sautéed Strawberries

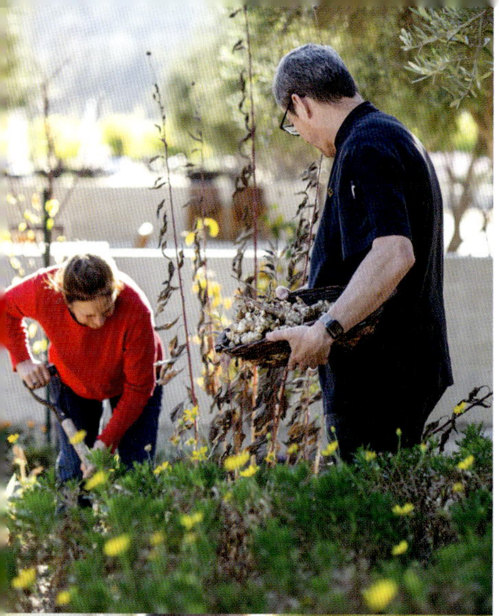
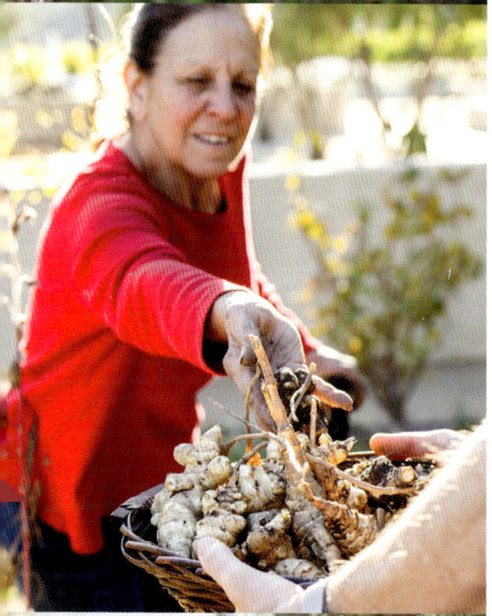
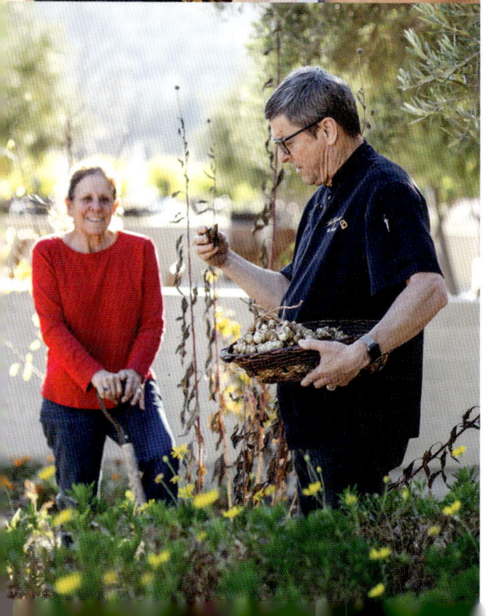
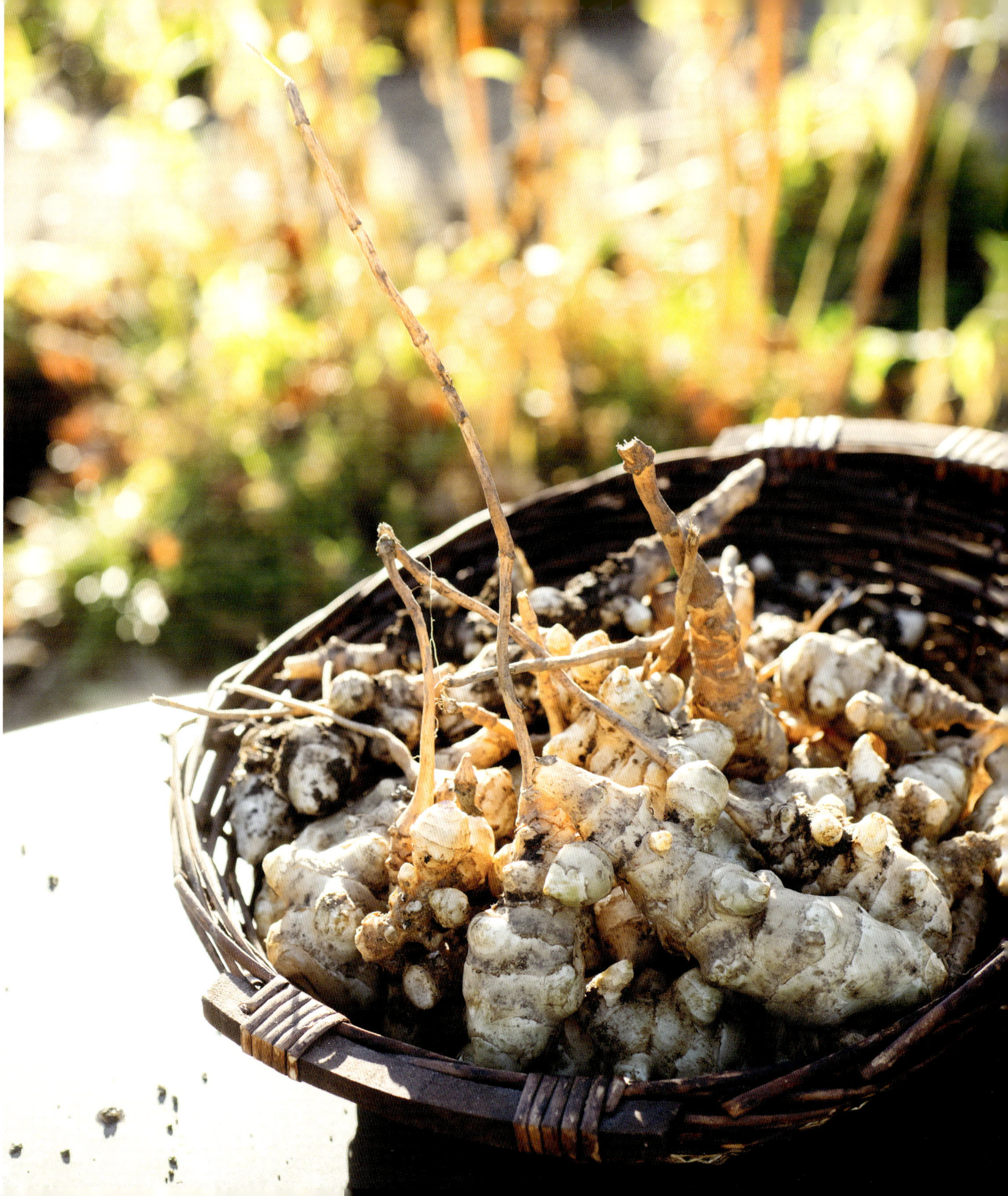

Roasted Sunchoke Soup

Makes about 6½ cups; serves 8

Oven roasting caramelizes the abundant natural sugar in sunchokes and helps develop their nuttiness. They make a surprisingly velvety soup blended with roasted shallots and garlic, with cream supplying richness and white wine brightening the flavor. The porcini powder that Ken uses in the garnish is "like magic," says the chef. "Anything you put it in tastes better." Add it to risotto, to broth, or to pasta in tomato or cream sauce.

1½ pounds sunchokes, scrubbed but not peeled

2 large shallots, peeled

2 tablespoons extra virgin olive oil

2 large cloves garlic, peeled

1 leek, white and pale green part only

4 cups water

¾ cup dry white wine

¾ cup heavy cream

2 teaspoons sea salt

Porcini Crème Fraîche:

3 tablespoons crème fraîche

¼ teaspoon porcini powder (see Note)

Wine: WALT Shea Pinot Noir

Preheat the oven to 400°F. In a bowl, toss the whole sunchokes and shallots in 1 tablespoon of the oil. Arrange the vegetables in a single layer on a baking sheet and roast until they begin to caramelize, about 1 hour, shaking the pan occasionally and turning the sunchokes and shallots if necessary to promote even browning. Add the garlic cloves and roast for an additional 10 minutes. The sunchokes, shallots, and garlic should be completely tender and lightly caramelized in spots.

Halve the leek lengthwise and rinse thoroughly between the leaves; leeks can hide a lot of dirt. Slice crosswise into ½-inch-thick pieces. Heat the remaining 1 tablespoon oil in a large saucepan over medium heat. Add the leek and sauté, stirring, until softened, about 5 minutes. Add the roasted sunchokes, shallots, and garlic, then pour in the water, wine, and cream and add the salt. Bring to a simmer, adjust the heat to maintain a simmer, and cook uncovered for 30 minutes to marry the flavors. Set aside to cool for about 15 minutes, then blend in a blender until completely smooth. Rinse the saucepan and pour in the pureed soup.

Prepare the porcini crème fraîche: In a small bowl, whisk together crème fraîche and porcini powder until smooth.

Reheat the soup gently to serve. Divide among bowls and garnish each serving with a drizzle of the crème fraîche. Serve immediately.

Note: *To make porcini powder, place dried porcini in a spice or coffee grinder and grind to a powder. Store in an airtight container. In spring, garnish the soup with crème fraîche, sliced chives, and chive blossoms.*

Beet and Citrus Salad with Charred Citrus Crème Fraîche

Serves 4

This beautiful composed salad has appeared on the tasting menu at La Toque, Ken's elegant Napa Valley restaurant, but it's easily reproduced at home. Charring the citrus heightens its flavor, enhancing its contribution to the salad dressing. You can replace the kumquats with a halved tangerine, navel orange, or blood orange; grapefruit is too bitter.

¼ cup raw pistachios

12 small beets, preferably a mix of colors (about 1 pound trimmed)

1 tablespoon extra virgin olive oil, plus more for the greens

Dressing:

5 kumquats, halved lengthwise

¼ cup crème fraîche

Pinch of sea salt

¼ teaspoon honey

½ teaspoon grated orange or tangerine zest

1 blood orange, navel orange, or Cara Cara orange

2 tangerines

2 kumquats, thinly sliced crosswise

4 small tufts baby arugula, mâche, or frisée

Wine: WALT Bob's Ranch Chardonnay

Preheat the oven to 400°F. Toast the pistachios on a baking sheet until fragrant and lightly colored, 8 to 10 minutes. Let cool, then chop coarsely.

In a bowl, toss the beets with the oil. Arrange in a single layer on a baking sheet and bake until tender when pierced, 45 to 50 minutes. When the beets are just cool enough to handle, peel them. (They are easier to peel while warm.) Cut into quarters.

Prepare the dressing: Preheat a griddle to high or preheat a cast-iron skillet over high heat. Place the kumquats, cut side down, on the griddle or in the skillet and cook until blackened on the cut side, about 5 minutes. When cool enough to handle, squeeze the pulp, juice, and seeds from the kumquats into a bowl, then add the spent rinds to the bowl. Add the crème fraîche and salt and use the back of a spoon to smash the kumquats even more so their flavor infuses the crème fraîche. Pass the mixture through a sieve into a bowl, pressing on the kumquat solids with a rubber spatula. Whisk in the honey and orange zest and taste for salt.

Cut a slice off both ends of the orange. Stand the orange upright on a cutting board and, using a sharp knife, remove all the peel and white pith by slicing from top to bottom all the way around the orange, following the contour of the fruit. Cut along the membranes to release the individual segments and place them in a bowl. Remove any seeds. Repeat with the tangerines; add them to the same bowl.

To serve, arrange the beets on a platter or individual plates. Scatter the citrus segments and sliced kumquats among the beets. Drizzle with the dressing. In a small bowl, gently toss the arugula with a pinch of salt and just enough oil to gloss it lightly. Top the salad with tufts of the arugula. Scatter the pistachios all around. Serve immediately.

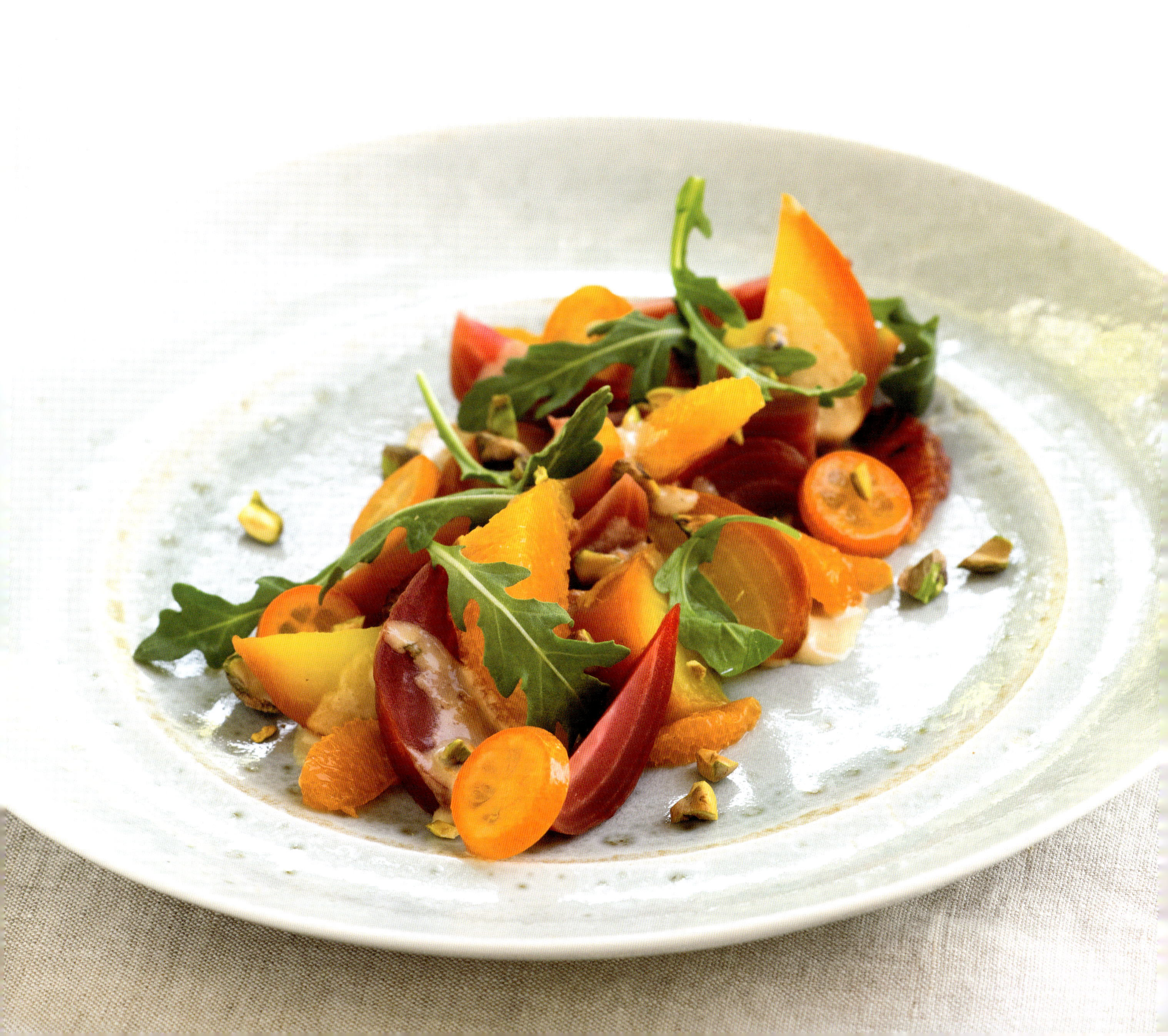

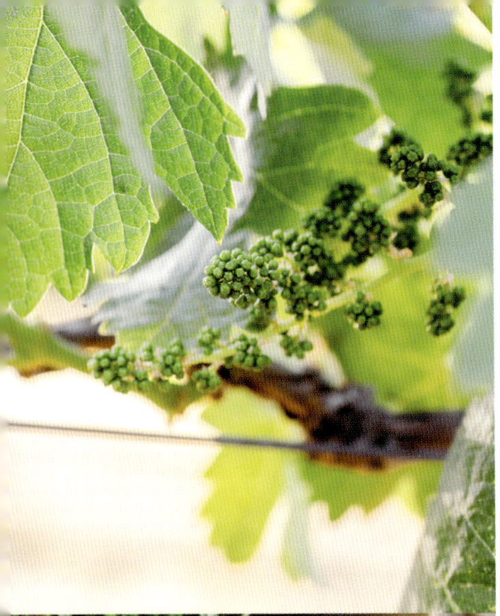

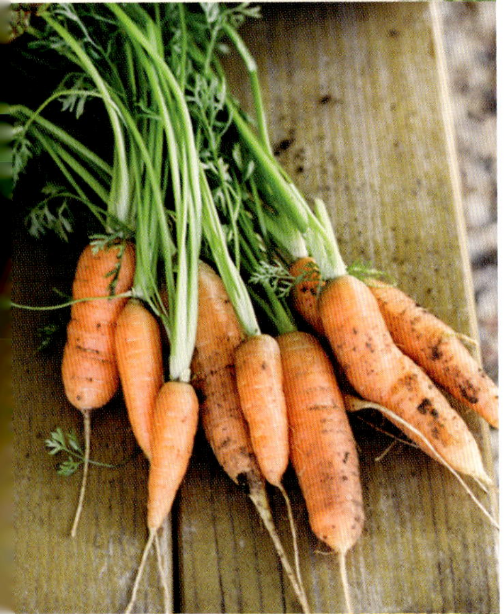

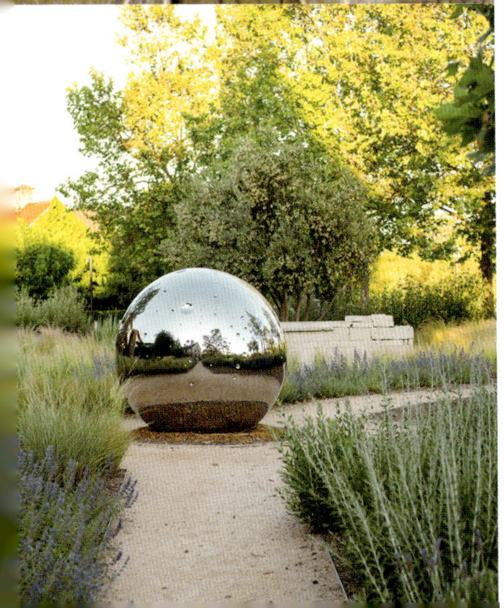

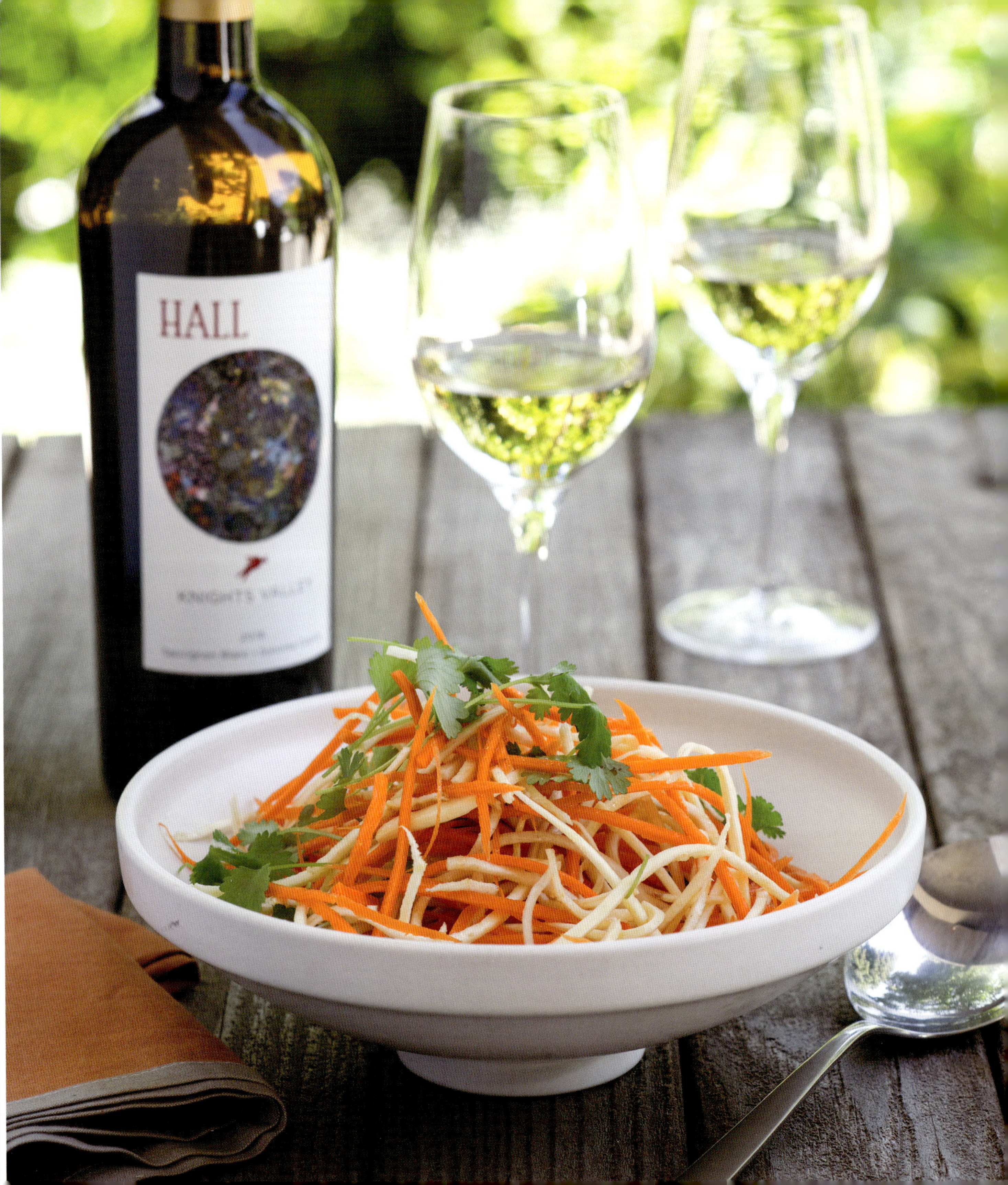
HALL
KNIGHTS VALLEY

Carrot and Parsnip Slaw with Lemongrass-Ginger Oil

Serves 4

Dressing:

1 tablespoon unseasoned rice vinegar

¼ teaspoon tamarind pulp (optional)

Pinch of sea salt

¼ cup Lemongrass-Ginger Oil (recipe follows)

2 large carrots

2 large parsnips

Chopped cilantro leaves or whole microgreens, for garnish

Wine: HALL Knights Valley Sauvignon Blanc

Prepare the dressing: In a small bowl, whisk together the vinegar, tamarind pulp (if using), and salt. Whisk in the lemongrass oil.

Peel the carrots and parsnips and cut them crosswise into 3-inch chunks. With a mandoline or other vegetable slicer, carefully slice the chunks lengthwise into thin slabs about ⅛ inch thick. Stack a few slabs at a time and slice lengthwise as thinly as possible to make a fine julienne. If you don't have a vegetable slicer, grate the chunks lengthwise on the large holes of a box grater to produce long strands. You should have 2 cups each of julienned or grated carrots and parsnips.

Combine the carrots and parsnips in a bowl and add the dressing. Toss with your hands to coat evenly. Taste for salt and vinegar. Let rest for 15 to 30 minutes to soften the slaw slightly.

Divide the slaw among four salad plates. Top each serving with a tuft of cilantro. Serve immediately.

The underappreciated parsnip has many cheerleaders at HALL. Shelley enjoys growing them, the Halls love to eat them, and Ken knows how to prepare them in ways that even skeptics want to try. This lively slaw is scented with lemongrass oil prepared with lemongrass from the winery garden. Make the slaw your own by adding toasted peanuts, chiles, or Asian basil, or add a splash of fish sauce to the dressing.

Lemongrass-Ginger Oil

Makes 1 cup

1 small stalk lemongrass

1 cup canola oil

3 thin slices fresh ginger (no need to peel)

Cut the lemongrass crosswise into thirds. With a mallet, pound the lemongrass pieces to shatter the fibers. Put the lemongrass pieces, oil, and ginger into a small saucepan, place over medium-low heat, and warm until the oil reaches 145°F on an instant-read thermometer. Set aside for 24 to 48 hours, then strain. Store the oil in an airtight container at room temperature if using within a few days or refrigerate for longer keeping.

Pan-Seared Pork Chops with Shelling Bean and Wild Mushroom Ragout **Serves 4**

Fresh cranberry beans from the HALL garden make a creamy bed for thick, succulent pork chops. Sometimes, when he has a night off from the restaurant, Ken will cook cranberry beans, adding chopped tomatoes and cavatelli for an easy pasta e fagioli. *As for cooking pork chops, he has two rules: always brine them and let them rest after cooking. If you follow that advice and don't overcook them, the chops will be tender and juicy.*

Brine:

2 cups water

¼ cup plus 1 tablespoon sea salt

1 tablespoon plus 1 teaspoon sugar

4 bone-in pork loin chops, 10 to 12 ounces each

Beans:

2 slices thick-cut bacon

¼ yellow onion, cut into ¼-inch dice

½ large celery rib, cut into ¼-inch dice

½ carrot, peeled and cut into ¼-inch dice

2 cups fresh cranberry beans, fava beans, or other fresh shelling beans (from about 1½ pounds unshelled)

1 fresh thyme sprig

Sea salt

½ pound mixed wild mushrooms or cultivated maitake or oyster mushrooms, cleaned

Freshly ground black pepper

Canola oil

¼ cup extra virgin olive oil

2 cloves garlic, minced

¼ cup minced mixed fresh herbs, such as flat-leaf parsley, chives, tarragon, and chervil

---

Wine: HALL Jack's Masterpiece Cabernet Sauvignon

(continued)

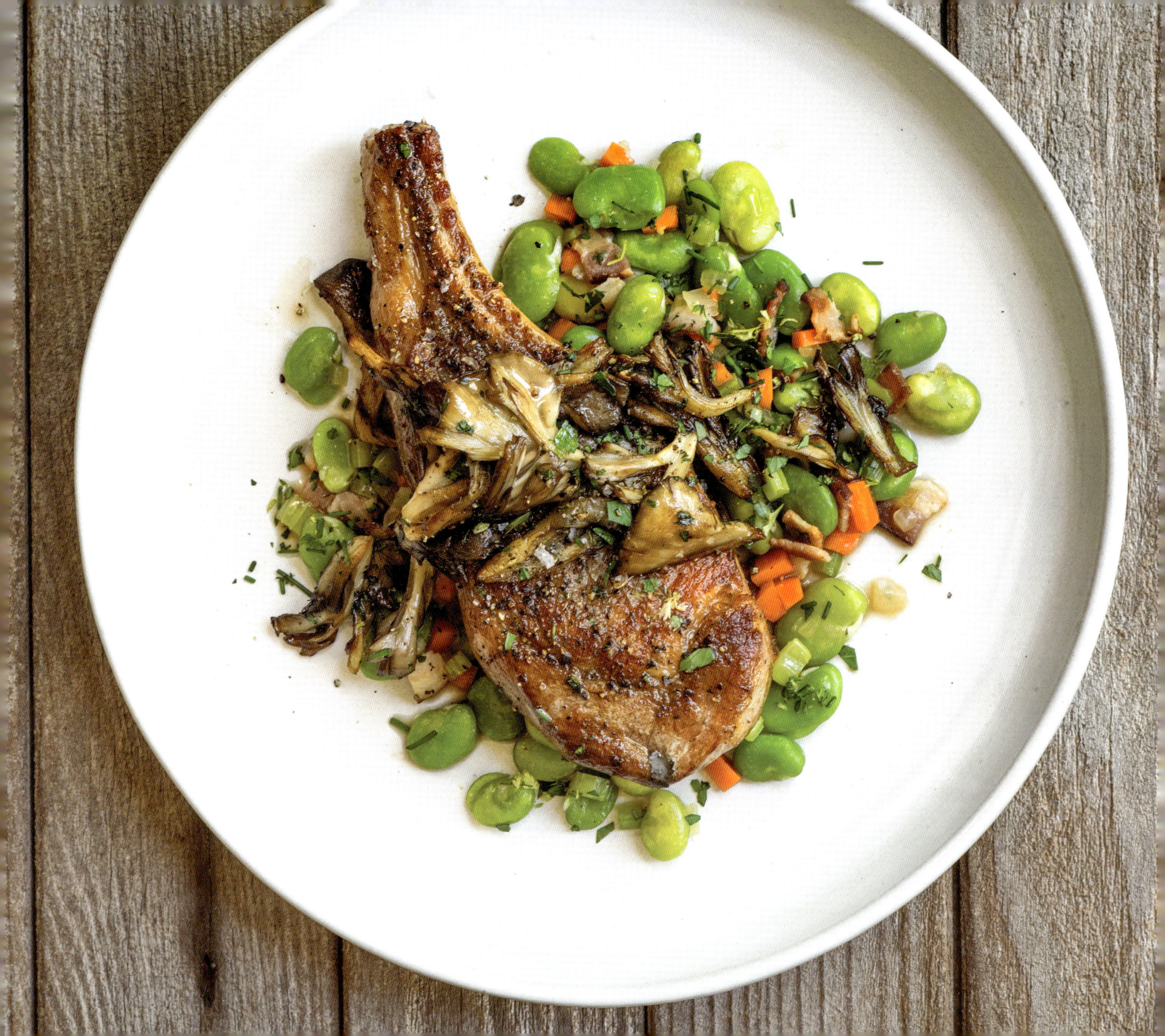

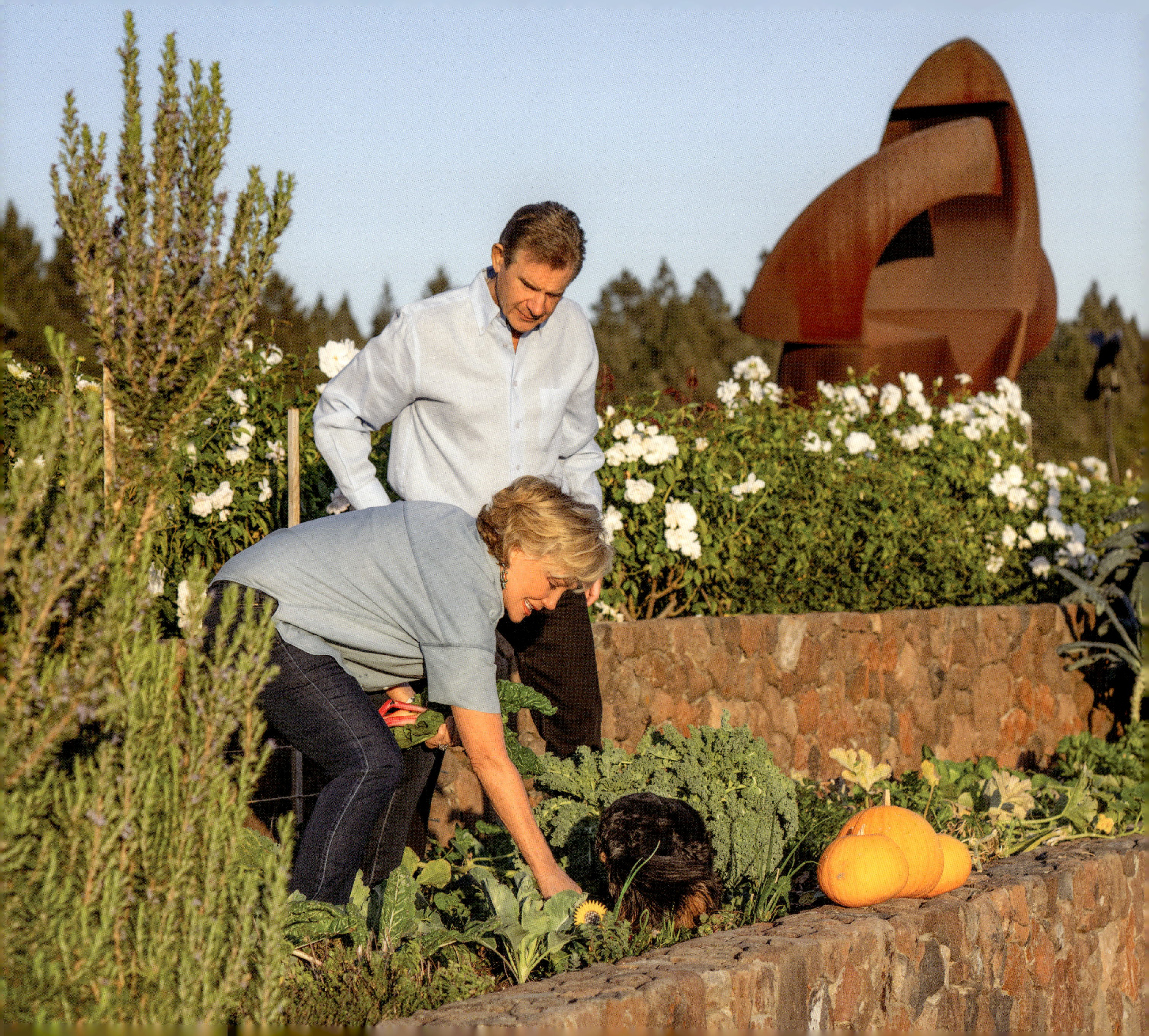

Pan-Seared Pork Chops with Shelling Bean and Wild Mushroom Ragout *(continued)*

Prepare the brine: In a container just large enough to hold the pork chops, combine the water, salt, and sugar and stir to dissolve the salt and sugar. Add the pork chops. They should be submerged. Let stand at room temperature for at least 30 minutes or up to 1 hour, turning them over once halfway through. Remove from the brine and pat dry with paper towels.

Prepare the beans: Halve the bacon slices lengthwise, then cut crosswise into ¼-inch pieces. Place in a saucepan and cook over medium heat until the bacon renders some of its fat and begins to sizzle and color, about 5 minutes. Add the onion, celery, and carrot and cook, stirring, for about 2 minutes. Add the beans, thyme, and enough water just to cover the beans and bring to a simmer. Cover the beans with a round of parchment paper cut just to fit inside the pot and simmer gently until the beans are tender, 20 minutes or more, adding water if needed to keep the original level. Remove from the heat, season to taste with salt, and remove the thyme. Let the beans cool in the liquid if time allows.

Trim the mushrooms of any blemishes or dried ends. Tear them into bite-size pieces if they are tender or slice them with a knife if they are firm.

Heat two 10-inch skillets over medium-high heat. Season the pork chops well on both sides with pepper. (They won't need additional salt.) Add enough canola oil to each skillet to film it generously, about 1½ tablespoons per skillet. Don't skimp on the oil or the pork chops won't sear properly. When the skillets are hot, put 2 chops into each one and sear on the underside until well browned, about 2 minutes. Adjust the heat if needed to prevent scorching. With tongs, turn the chops and continue cooking until the second side is richly browned and the chops are almost done, about 3 minutes; when probed in the center, they should feel neither flabby nor firm. They will continue to cook as they rest. Transfer the chops to a rack to rest while you cook the mushrooms.

Reheat the beans if necessary and keep warm.

Heat a large skillet over medium-high heat. Add the olive oil. When it is almost smoking, add the mushrooms and season with salt and pepper. Cook briskly until they are almost tender, about 4 minutes, then add the garlic and sauté until it is fragrant, about 1 minute. Add half of the mixed herbs, toss well, and remove from the heat.

Make a bed of beans on each of four dinner plates. (You may not use them all.) Top with a pork chop, then spoon the mushrooms on top of the chops, dividing them evenly. Garnish with the remaining herbs and serve immediately.

Left: *The Halls, assisted by Rocky, their Cavalier King Charles Spaniel, harvest Tuscan kale and chard from their stone-walled beds at home on a warm Napa Valley evening.*

Crêpes with Sautéed Strawberries

Serves 6

¾ cup sliced almonds

½ cup heavy cream

2 tablespoons crème fraîche

1 teaspoon powdered sugar

Crêpes:

2 large eggs, at room temperature

⅔ cup unbleached all-purpose flour

¼ teaspoon sea salt

4 tablespoons unsalted butter, melted, plus more for the pan

¾ cup whole milk

Strawberries:

1 pound strawberries, hulled and quartered

4 tablespoons unsalted butter

¼ cup plus 2 tablespoons granulated sugar

Tender crêpes topped with berries are a timeless dessert that never goes out of fashion. Ken's brilliant idea is to cook the HALL garden's fragrant strawberries in brown butter and sugar, adding a caramel note to the sauce that is totally luscious. Serve with whipped cream or ice cream. Peaches or blueberries can replace the strawberries on another occasion.

Preheat the oven to 350°F. Toast the almonds on a baking sheet until fragrant and light brown, about 10 minutes. Let cool.

In a bowl, whisk together the cream, crème fraîche, and powdered sugar to soft peaks. Cover and refrigerate until needed.

Prepare the crêpes: In a bowl, whisk together the eggs, flour, and salt until smooth. Whisk in the warm melted butter, followed by the milk. The mixture should be smooth and thin. Let the batter rest for 15 minutes so any bubbles can dissipate.

Lay a large sheet of parchment paper near the stove top. Heat a well-seasoned crêpe pan or 8-inch nonstick skillet over medium-low heat. When hot, brush with melted butter. Add 1 ounce (2 tablespoons) batter, swirling to coat the pan evenly. (If the batter does not flow readily, thin the batter with a splash of milk.) Cook until the crêpe is golden brown in spots on the bottom and lightly colored around the edge, 30 to 45 seconds, then flip and cook the second side until lightly colored and no longer damp, 30 to 45 seconds. Transfer the crêpe to the parchment and continue with the remaining batter, brushing the pan lightly with butter before cooking each crêpe and adding the finished crêpes to the parchment, overlapping them slightly so you have an edge to grab. You should have enough batter for 12 crêpes.

Prepare the strawberries: Heat a 10-inch skillet over medium-high heat. When hot, add the butter and swirl the pan constantly as the butter melts and sizzles. When the butter turns a deep caramel color, add the strawberries and sugar and cook briskly, stirring, until the berries soften and the mixture becomes almost jam-like, 3 to 4 minutes.

Fold each crêpe into quarters and put 2 crêpes on each of six dessert plates. Spoon the warm strawberries and sauce over the crêpes. Top each serving with almonds and a dollop of whipped cream. Serve immediately.

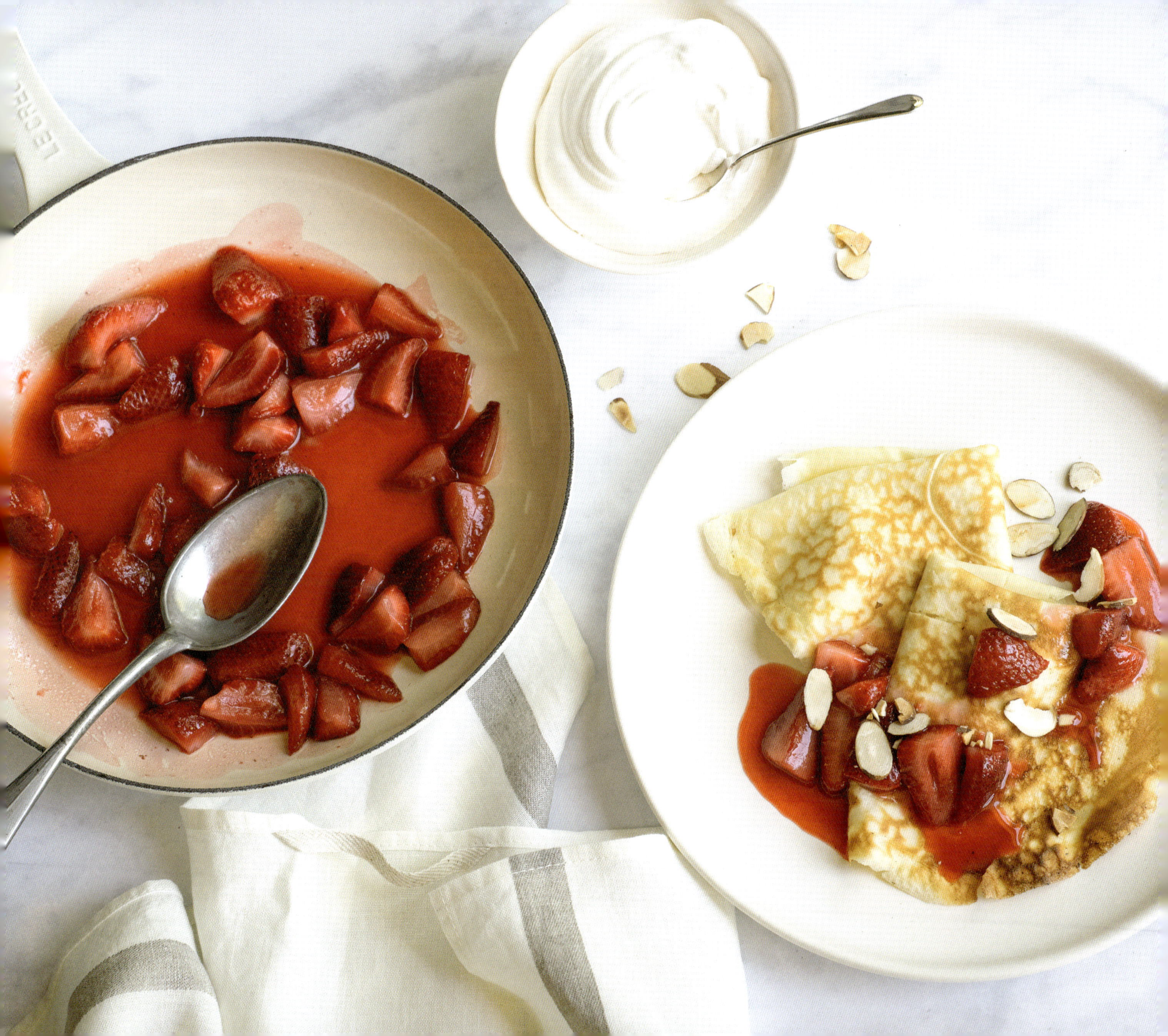

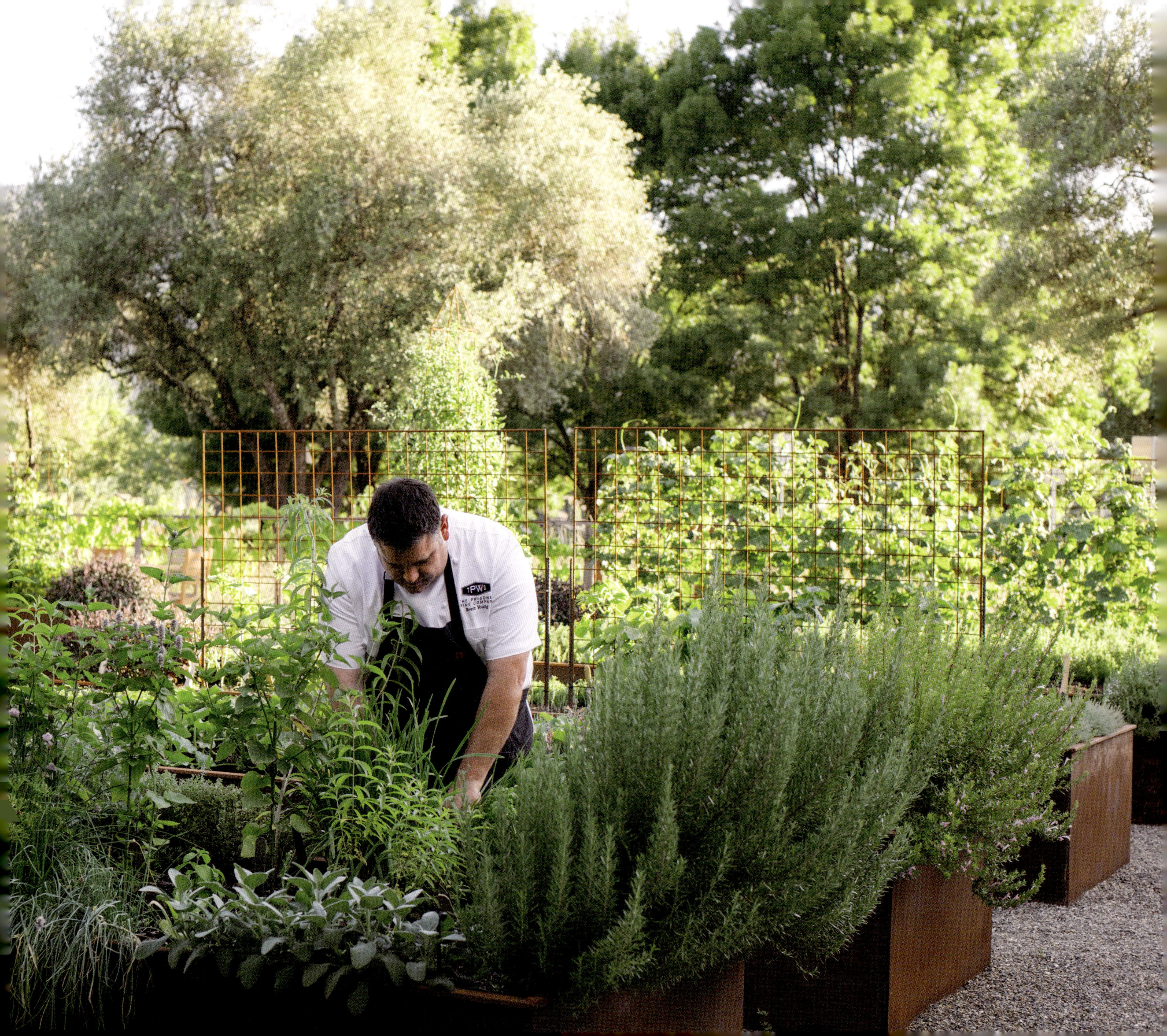
TPW
Brett Young

The Prisoner Wine Company: *A Courtyard Garden*

St. Helena

Many wineries with edible gardens situate the beds out of sight because, truth be told, vegetable plantings can have their unsightly moments. But at The Prisoner Wine Company, the edible garden gets the limelight. Arriving guests can't help but notice the ten handsome, deep corten steel beds in a courtyard adjacent to the winery entrance, their coppery finish glinting in the setting sun. Many after-hours events here begin in the garden, an aromatic alfresco reception room where guests can meander, wineglass in hand, among the rosemary, eggplant, and thyme.

As its many fans know, little about The Prisoner Wine Company is conventional. From its inception, the winery has colored outside the lines, building its reputation on blended wines from purchased grapes at a time when critics reserved their highest marks for single-variety, estate-grown bottlings. Founder David Phinney, who has since sold the company, unknowingly unleashed a movement when he debuted The Prisoner in 2000. Winemaker Chrissy Wittmann enjoys the creative freedom of blending multiple grape varieties from many sources, and wine lovers embrace these bold yet balanced wines.

"Dave is a visionary," says The Prisoner Wine Company's brand manager Euming Lee. "The way he thinks is different from the norm, and we try to embody that spirit in all we do today."

Designed and built in 2018, after new owners purchased The Prisoner Wine Company, the courtyard garden and the petite fruit orchard alongside can't begin to supply all the produce that this winery's busy kitchen needs. But chef Brett Young appreciates every last basil sprig, and the hospitality team uses the garden as a sensory experience for visitors. Touring the garden with a winery host, guests are introduced to scents they might not know, such as lemon verbena, winter savory, and anise hyssop.

"The garden is an extension of the aromatics found in our wines," says Alex Brisoux, one of the winery's managers. "Visiting the garden makes it easier to correlate those aromas."

Even the winemaker finds that the garden has expanded her sensory vocabulary. "It's sometimes hard to pull those descriptors out," says Chrissy, who takes regular strolls around the beds. "The garden helps me describe wine better, and it has been an inspiration for starting a garden at home."

For Brett, the garden provides an endless palette of toppings for the pizzas he prepares for guests. In spring, he scatters delicate thyme and chive blossoms on top of a leek and bacon pizza. In the cooler months, there's almost always wispy rustic arugula, an heirloom variety that he can strew on top of pizzas when they emerge from the oven, and in early summer, baby zucchini and sliced zucchini blossoms make an alluring topping.

Left and above: *Winery chef Brett Young has access to an enviable variety of culinary herbs just steps from his kitchen; situated on Napa Valley's main highway, The Prisoner Wine Company sees many visitors.*

Herbs thrive in these sunny, west-facing beds constructed of food-safe weathering steel and built almost waist-high so they're easy to plant and harvest. Commonplace types, like parsley and mint, play only minor roles in the collection. Instead, the choices seem designed for adventure as unexpected as the winery's uncommon wine blends. Persian basil, Lettuce Leaf basil, and Green Goddess basil jostle for space with Mexican tarragon, German parsley, and caraway thyme. Brett transforms the fragrant lemon verbena leaves into a tangy fermented kombucha—"like a tart lemon tea," says the chef, a pickling and fermenting enthusiast. The kombucha adds citrus-like acidity to his vinaigrettes. "We can't grow enough lemon verbena."

For the colorful plates of pickles that Brett likes to serve tasting-room visitors, the garden always includes a few vegetables that welcome a quick brining, like oblong Badger Flame and Touchstone Gold beets, French Breakfast radishes, Trieste fennel, sweet Tokyo turnips, and the burgundy-skinned, yellow-fleshed Purple Elite carrots. In Napa Valley's mild climate, the beds remain productive year-round, providing winter cabbage and kohlrabi for sauerkraut to utilize Brett's fermentation skills.

Once each season, Brett sits down with edible-garden expert Stefani Bittner of the Bay Area–based Homestead Design Collective to plan the future harvest. What will he want to cook in three months? What herbs and vegetables will help him and his staff create eye-opening matches for the winery's bottlings? Most winery chefs stick with proven pairing tactics so their food doesn't challenge the wines. At The Prisoner Wine Company, it's all about bending the norms. "We expect the chef and our wine educators to put together uncommon pairings,"

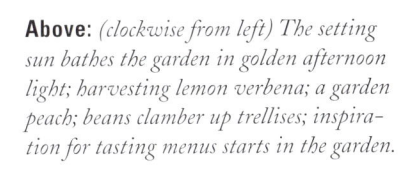

Above: *(clockwise from left) The setting sun bathes the garden in golden afternoon light; harvesting lemon verbena; a garden peach; beans clamber up trellises; inspiration for tasting menus starts in the garden.*

"The garden is an extension of the aromatics found in our wines. Visiting the garden makes it easier to correlate those aromas."

says Alex. "It leads to some interesting debates."

The Prisoner Wine Company garden is a chef's garden first and foremost, but it's also a show garden that has to look groomed all the time. Thoughtful design makes that possible. The dramatic beds and trellises give the garden a pleasing visual structure even when the plantings are in transition. Heights are layered, with tall, vining beans or peas in the center of the beds and cascading or low-growing plants, such as creeping thyme, tarragon, and salad greens, at the edges. Repeating materials also helps, so beds, ornamental tuteurs, and tomato trellises are all made of the same weathering steel. Herbs are planted in large groupings to create a cohesive look, and an allée of ornamental Wild Magic basil hints at a garden entrance.

The Prisoner Wine Company 119

Like any organic garden, the plantings rely on beneficial insects to keep pests in check. Herbs are allowed to bloom to attract desirable bugs and pollinators, and the beds are thickly planted with edible flowers, from violas and lavender in spring to sunflowers, calendulas, and marigolds in summer and fall. Companion planting also helps combat pests and diseases. Signet marigolds, known to deter root-knot nematodes, surround the tomatoes like a fortress. What's more, they are edible. Brett uses the flowers for garnish and the young foliage for microgreens.

Above and right: *(clockwise from left): The winery's handsome open kitchen enhances the guest experience; the winery entrance is steps away from its neat courtyard garden; pizza with leeks and bacon; outdoor mural*

For most of the private events at The Prisoner Wine Company, Brett likes to serve family-style from large bowls and platters. A casual dinner might not follow the flow of a conventional multicourse menu but instead consist of several garden-influenced dishes—a few of them meatless—served more or less at once.

Conjuring a warm spring evening in The Yard, the winery's interior courtyard with its pizza oven, Brett might start the meal with a platter of garden vegetables—some raw, some blanched—and an updated reading of 1970s onion dip with goat cheese and caramelized spring onions. Tender Little Gem lettuces follow, dressed in a fruity vinaigrette that finds echoes in the winery's complex, creamy white wine blend, Blindfold. Brett's pizza mastery elevates a pie topped with bacon, fromage blanc, and caramelized young leeks. A vegetarian fried rice—incorporating whatever the garden provides that day—seduces with its green-garlic fragrance and the season's first peas. And Brett's buttery potato gnocchi prove that, in capable hands, even asparagus—considered a problem vegetable by some wine lovers—can be wine friendly.

With this lush, well-maintained garden just steps from his kitchen, Brett can harvest what he needs *à la minute*. Herbs go from garden to table in minutes—a seize-the-moment approach to cooking that echoes how the winery's staff speaks about the wines. "I often tell people these are wines for the impatient," says Alex. "They are meant to drink sooner rather than later. If you see a bottle of The Prisoner at the store, take it home and drink it."

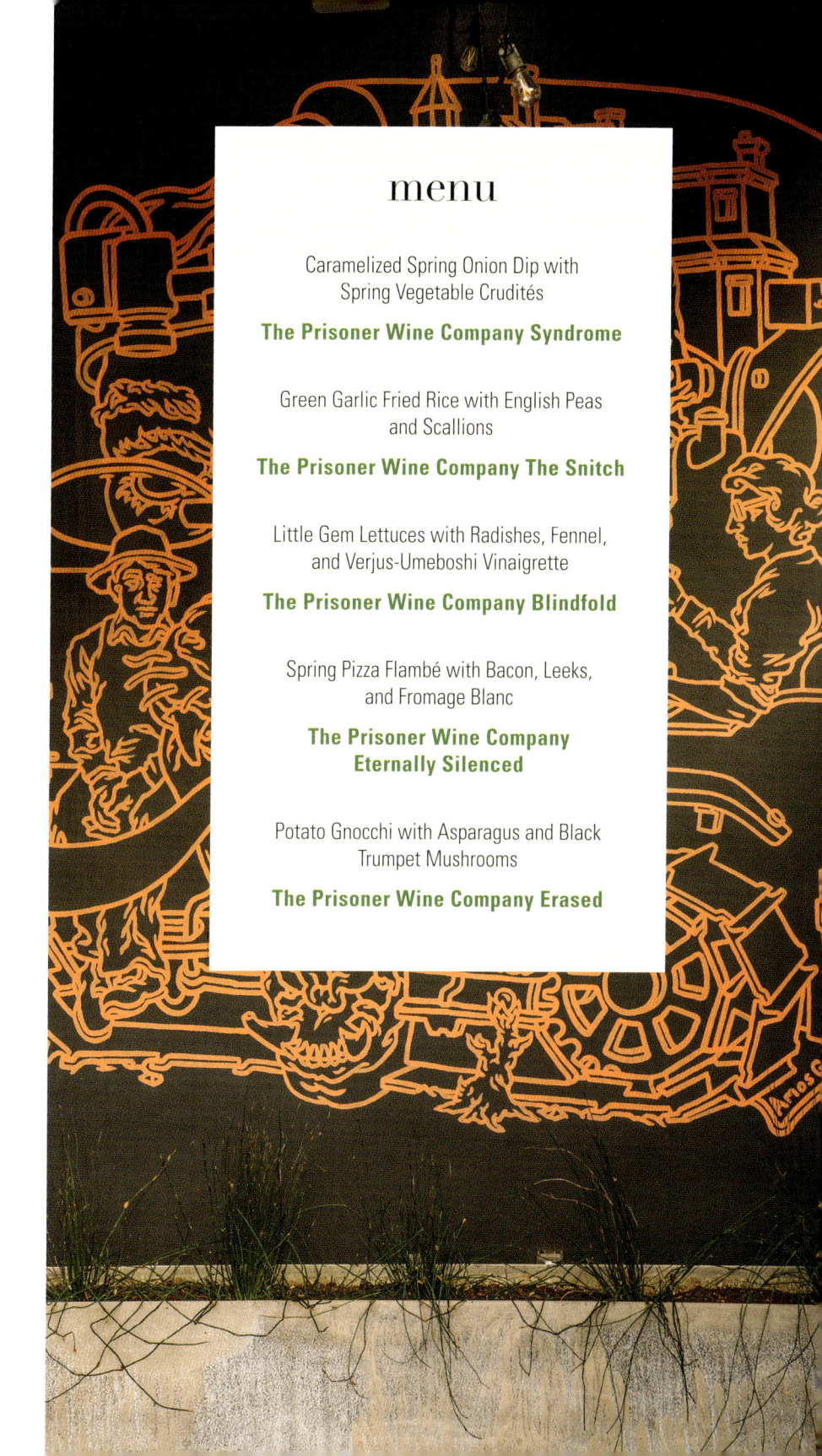

menu

Caramelized Spring Onion Dip with Spring Vegetable Crudités

The Prisoner Wine Company Syndrome

Green Garlic Fried Rice with English Peas and Scallions

The Prisoner Wine Company The Snitch

Little Gem Lettuces with Radishes, Fennel, and Verjus-Umeboshi Vinaigrette

The Prisoner Wine Company Blindfold

Spring Pizza Flambé with Bacon, Leeks, and Fromage Blanc

The Prisoner Wine Company Eternally Silenced

Potato Gnocchi with Asparagus and Black Trumpet Mushrooms

The Prisoner Wine Company Erased

Caramelized Spring Onion Dip with Spring Vegetable Crudités **Makes about 2½ cups**

Every guest who visits The Prisoner for a wine tasting enjoys some small bites along with the wine. Brett has developed a repertoire of dips for this purpose, all of them easy to make in quantity. This caramelized onion dip is understandably a favorite, whether served with potato chips or a cornucopia of garden vegetables. In spring, many of the dippers—like radishes, baby rainbow carrots, and baby fennel—can be served raw, but Brett likes to briefly blanch asparagus, baby zucchini and sugar snap peas, to heighten their color. The dip keeps for 4 days in the fridge.

2 tablespoons canola oil

3 cups chopped spring onions, white and pale green part only

Sea salt and freshly ground black pepper

1 cup fresh rindless goat cheese (about 4 ounces), at room temperature

⅔ cup crème fraîche

¼ cup plus 2 tablespoons buttermilk

2 tablespoons onion powder

1 tablespoon garlic powder

Thinly sliced fresh chives, for garnish

Spring vegetable crudités (see introduction)

Wine: The Prisoner Wine Company Syndrome

Heat the oil in a saucepan over medium-high heat. Add the onions and a pinch of salt, lower the heat to medium, and cook, stirring often and reducing the heat as needed to prevent burning, until the onion is meltingly soft, dark, and sweet, about 35 minutes. Add a splash of water whenever the onions threaten to stick or scorch. Transfer the onions to a bowl or baking sheet and let cool completely.

In a bowl, whisk together the goat cheese, crème fraîche, buttermilk, onion powder, garlic powder, 1 teaspoon salt, and black pepper to taste. Whisk in water as needed to thin to dip consistency. Stir in the caramelized onions. Transfer to a serving bowl and garnish with chives. Surround with crudités and serve.

Green Garlic Fried Rice with English Peas and Scallions Serves 6

Brett makes fried rice often for The Prisoner's family-style guest meals, and he likes to keep it meatless for the winery's many vegetarian visitors. The dish is an accommodating showcase for garden vegetables and herbs. In late spring, the last of the green garlic—mild, immature garlic harvested before the bulb forms—and the first tender English peas overlap, inspiring a particularly fragrant and colorful variation. Note that you need to cook the rice several hours ahead, and preferably a day ahead, so it has time to chill.

2 tablespoons canola oil

2 teaspoons minced garlic

1 teaspoon peeled and minced fresh ginger

1½ cups jasmine rice

1 teaspoon sea salt

2⅔ cups water

¾ cup shelled English peas

1 tablespoon Chinese or Japanese sesame oil

1½ cups very thinly sliced green garlic, white and pale green parts only, sliced on a sharp diagonal, plus more for garnish

½ cup very thinly sliced scallions, white and pale green parts only, sliced on a sharp diagonal, plus more for garnish

2 tablespoons soy sauce

½ preserved lemon, pulp discarded and rind finely julienned

2 large eggs, beaten

Wine: The Prisoner Wine Company The Snitch

Preheat the oven to 375°F or 350°F with a convection fan.

    Heat the canola oil in an ovenproof saucepan over medium heat. Add the garlic and ginger and stir until fragrant, about 30 seconds. Add the rice and salt and cook, stirring, for 1 minute to coat the rice with oil and toast it slightly. Stir in the water and bring to a simmer. Cover the pan, transfer it to the oven, and bake for 20 minutes. Remove from the oven and let rest in the pan for 5 minutes, then spread the rice on a baking sheet to cool quickly. Refrigerate uncovered for at least 4 hours or up to overnight.

    Bring a small pot of salted water to a boil over high heat and prepare a bowl of ice water. Add the peas to the boiling water and blanch until they no longer taste raw, about 2 minutes, then drain and transfer to the ice water. When cool, drain again and pat dry.

    Break up the chilled rice with your hands so there are no clumps. Heat a 12- to 14-inch nonstick skillet over high heat. Add the sesame oil. When it is almost smoking, add the rice and spread it flat with a wooden spoon. Let it cook without stirring for about 2 minutes to allow it to color slightly, then stir. Add the peas and green garlic and stir to combine. Add the scallions and cook, stirring, until they soften slightly, about 30 seconds. Add the soy sauce and preserved lemon and toss well.

    Remove the skillet from the heat and scoot the rice to one side of the pan, leaving half the pan bare. Add the beaten eggs to the bare area, then return the skillet to high heat and scramble the eggs with a wooden spoon until barely set, about 1 minute. Toss the eggs and rice together and taste for salt. Transfer to a serving dish and garnish with a few shreds of raw green garlic and scallion. Serve immediately.

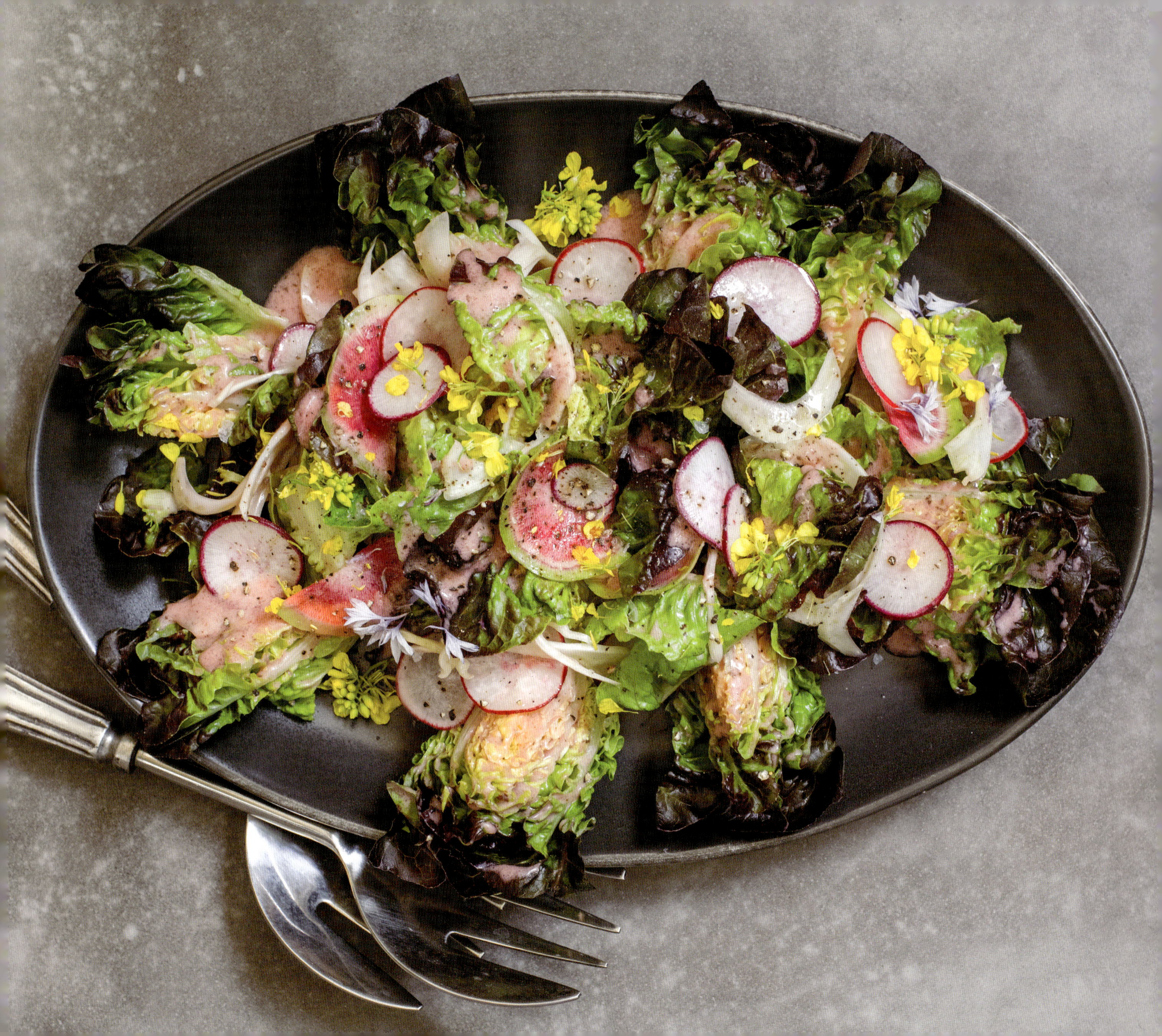

Little Gem Lettuces with Radishes, Fennel, and Verjus-Umeboshi Vinaigrette

Serves 4 to 6

This pretty salad might be on the table when guests visit The Prisoner in spring for a family-style lunch. It adapts to what's in the garden, but the unusual vinaigrette remains unchanged. Like a lot of Brett's food, the vinaigrette merges wine country flavors, such as verjus, the sweet-tart juice from underripe wine grapes, with international ingredients, such as umeboshi paste, an intense fermented seasoning derived from dried Japanese plums. It's difficult to make the dressing in a small volume, so you will have some left over for dressing other salads or saucing grilled fish. It has a fruity, strawberry-like taste.

Verjus-Umeboshi Vinaigrette:

1¼ cups red verjus

6 tablespoons canola oil

2 tablespoons pure olive oil (not extra virgin)

2 tablespoons umeboshi paste

2 tablespoons fresh lemon juice

¾ teaspoon xanthan gum (see Chef's Tip)

Sea salt

½ fennel bulb, stalks removed

4 radishes, preferably a mix of colors, leaves removed

5 Little Gem lettuces

Sea salt and freshly ground black pepper

Edible flowers, for garnish

Wine: The Prisoner Wine Company Blindfold

Make the vinaigrette: In a blender, combine the verjus, both oils, umeboshi paste, lemon juice, and xanthan gum and blend until smooth. Transfer to a bowl and whisk in salt to taste.

Have ready two bowls of ice water. With a mandoline or other vegetable slicer, slice the fennel and the radishes paper-thin. Put each into its own bowl of ice water. Refrigerate for 1 hour to crisp, then drain and pat dry.

Quarter 2 of the Little Gem lettuces through the core. With a pastry brush, lightly brush the quartered lettuces all over with the vinaigrette. Sprinkle with salt and pepper, then arrange the quarters around the edge of a shallow salad bowl.

Chop the remaining 3 lettuces into bite-size pieces and put them into a bowl. Add the fennel and half of the radishes, then drizzle with enough of the vinaigrette to coat the salad lightly and toss well. Season to taste with salt and pepper. Transfer to the salad bowl, heaping it in the middle. Garnish with the remaining radish slices and with edible flowers. Serve immediately.

chef's tip:

Xanthan gum, a powder available at some supermarkets, creates an emulsified vinaigrette that does not separate. It has no flavor. Brett uses it in almost all his salad dressings.

Spring Pizza Flambé with Bacon, Leeks, and Fromage Blanc

Makes two 11-inch pizzas

The Prisoner Wine Company's outdoor pizza oven gets a workout in good weather, when the winery hosts many groups for alfresco events. The garden always provides something enticing for the topping—in spring, tender leeks to caramelize and bake with clumps of fresh cheese and tiny herb blossoms to scatter on after baking for a burst of fragrance.

Pizza Dough:
2½ cups pizza flour or all-purpose flour
¾ cup plus 2 tablespoons cold water
¼ teaspoon instant dry yeast
1 tablespoon warm water
3 tablespoons sourdough starter
1 teaspoon olive oil, plus more for the bowls
2 teaspoons sea salt

Topping:
1 tablespoon canola oil
2 cups leeks, white and pale green part, in ½-inch-thick slices
¼ pound thick-sliced bacon, diced
½ cup fromage blanc
1 tablespoon crème fraîche
Grated zest of 1 lemon
¼ teaspoon sea salt
2 teaspoons fresh herb flowers, such as thyme and chervil blossoms, or 2 teaspoons minced fresh thyme
All-purpose flour, for dusting

Wine: The Prisoner Wine Company Eternally Silenced

Make the pizza dough: In a large bowl, combine the flour and cold water and stir with a wooden spoon until the mixture forms a shaggy mass. Knead lightly until it comes together, cover, and let rest for 30 minutes.

In a small bowl, dissolve the yeast in the warm water. Add to the dough along with the sourdough starter and olive oil. Knead for 1 minute, then add the salt and continue kneading until the dough is smooth and elastic, about 10 minutes. The dough will seem very wet and sticky at first, but the flour will eventually absorb the liquid and the dough will become more manageable. Transfer the dough to an oiled bowl. Cover and refrigerate for at least 12 hours or up to overnight.

Divide the dough in half and shape each half into a ball. Place the balls in an oiled bowl or tub, cover, and refrigerate for at least 24 hours or up to 5 days. On baking day, take the balls out of the refrigerator. Set them on a floured surface, cover with a clean kitchen towel, and let rise at room temperature until doubled.

Make the topping: Heat the canola oil in a skillet over medium-high heat. Add the leeks and cook, stirring almost constantly, until they caramelize and darken, about 5 minutes, adding splashes of water if they threaten to stick or burn. Set aside to cool.

Put the bacon into a cast-iron skillet and set over medium heat. Cook, stirring often, until the bacon crisps, about 10 minutes. Transfer to paper towels to drain and cool.

In a bowl, whisk together the fromage blanc, crème fraîche, lemon zest, and salt.

At least 30 minutes before baking, put a baking stone in the oven and preheat the oven to 550°F or the highest setting.

On a floured surface, flatten 1 dough ball with your hands into a 12-inch round. Transfer it to a well-floured pizza peel. Scatter half of the leeks over the dough, leaving a ½-inch rim. Using half of the fromage blanc mixture, place 8 or 10 dollops of the mixture on the dough. Top with half of the bacon and half of the herb blossoms. Transfer the pizza to the baking stone and bake, rotating it 180 degrees halfway through baking, until well browned on the bottom and the rim, about 8 minutes. Cut into wedges and serve immediately. Repeat with the remaining dough ball.

chef's tips:

The secrets to Brett's remarkable crust are the blended pizza flour he uses in the dough and the extra-long fermentation. The dough is ready to use after 2 days, but it performs even better after another day or two. Look for King Arthur Pizza Flour Blend or Antimo Caputo Pizzeria Flour.

Potato Gnocchi with Asparagus and Black Trumpet Mushrooms Serves 6

⅓ cup dried black trumpet mushrooms, cleaned

2 russet potatoes, 8 to 10 ounces each

¼ cup plus 2 tablespoons Italian "00" flour (page 196), plus more for dusting

Sea salt and freshly ground black pepper

1 large egg, beaten

2 tablespoons extra virgin olive oil, plus more for garnish

12 large asparagus spears (about 1 pound), ends trimmed and stalks peeled

5 tablespoons unsalted butter

1 cup water

1 cup grated pecorino romano cheese, plus more for garnish

½ lemon

Wine: The Prisoner Wine Company Erased

Brett learned to make gnocchi from a master, and he has since perfected his own technique. His gnocchi are beautiful and light, and he attributes the good outcome to two key practices: he insists on quickly transforming the cooked potatoes into dough, and he uses a bench scraper to mix the ingredients and keep gluten from forming. In spring, he likes to pair the gnocchi with asparagus, pureeing some of the cooked stalks for a buttery sauce and tossing in the tender tips at the end.

Soak the mushrooms in hot water to cover until soft, about 30 minutes, then drain and set aside.

Preheat the oven to 400°F or 375°F with a convection fan. Pierce the potatoes all over with a fork. Place on a baking sheet and bake until tender, about 1 hour. Let them rest for 5 minutes, then cut the potatoes in half lengthwise and scoop the flesh into a food mill fitted with the medium blade. Pass the flesh through the food mill onto a work surface. Measure out 1½ cups lightly packed milled potatoes (9 ounces) and discard the remainder or reserve for another use.

In a small bowl, whisk together the flour and ½ teaspoon salt. Sprinkle ¼ cup plus 1 tablespoon of the flour mixture over the potato and then drizzle with the egg. Working with a metal bench scraper, use a chopping and folding motion to incorporate the ingredients gently. When the flour is largely incorporated, knead lightly and briefly by hand until you have a smooth dough, adding the remaining 1 tablespoon flour mixture if needed.

Cut the dough in half. On a floured work surface, roll each half by hand into a rope about 1 inch thick and 14 inches long. Cut each rope crosswise into 1-inch pieces. Use a dinner fork to form the gnocchi in this manner: Put a piece of dough on the fork and pinch it until it is the same width as the fork. With the side of your thumb, make a shallow crosswise indentation in the middle of the dough. Still using the side of your thumb, roll the dough off the tines of the fork lengthwise so the dough curls like a loose jelly roll. The exterior should have shallow ridges from the tines of the fork.

Bring a large pot of salted water to a boil over high heat and add the oil. Prepare a large bowl of ice water. Working in small batches, boil the gnocchi until they float to the surface; wait for another 20 seconds, then transfer them to the ice water with a wire skimmer. When all the gnocchi are cooked, drain them and place them in a single layer on a clean kitchen towel.

Bring a pot of salted water to a boil and prepare a bowl of ice water. Cut off the top 3 inches of each asparagus spear. Set aside 3 of these tips. Cook the remaining tips until crisp-tender, about 2 minutes, then transfer to the ice water with the wire skimmer. Cook the stalks until tender, about 3 minutes, then transfer to the ice water. Drain both and pat dry. Cut the cooked tips in half lengthwise. With a vegetable peeler, shave the raw tips lengthwise.

Put the cooked stalks into a blender, add enough water (about ½ cup) to make a puree with a sauce consistency, and blend until smooth. Transfer to a saucepan, add 1 tablespoon of the butter, and warm over low heat until the butter melts. Season with salt and pepper and keep warm.

Melt the remaining 4 tablespoons butter in a large skillet over medium-high heat. Add the water and bring to a simmer. Add the gnocchi and the halved asparagus tips and season with salt and pepper. Simmer briskly until the liquid has reduced but is not fully absorbed, about 2 minutes. Add the mushrooms and toss until they are hot. Add the cheese and toss until it melts, adding a splash of water if the mixture looks dry.

Divide the asparagus puree among four shallow bowls, spreading it thinly with the back of a spoon. Top with the gnocchi, dividing them evenly. Garnish each portion with shaved raw asparagus, a few drops of lemon juice, a drizzle of olive oil, and a sprinkle of pecorino. Serve immediately.

must-have herbs:

The garden beds at The Prisoner Wine Company offer an enormous palette of culinary herbs for freshening chef Brett Young's creations. Here are five herbs he can't live without.

Lemon thyme: for flavoring marinades and scattering over a hot pizza

Mexican tarragon: less aggressive in its anise scent than French tarragon; for brightening salads and vinaigrettes

Thai basil: for folding into Asian noodle dishes and stir-fries just before serving

Lemon verbena: for fermenting to make kombucha and for perfuming vinaigrettes

Mexican oregano: for contributing authentic flavor to Mexican-inspired dishes

Above and right: *Unusual varieties of culinary herbs flourish in The Prisoner Wine Company's garden beds; a chef's bouquet of Mexican tarragon, lemon verbena, and rosemary*

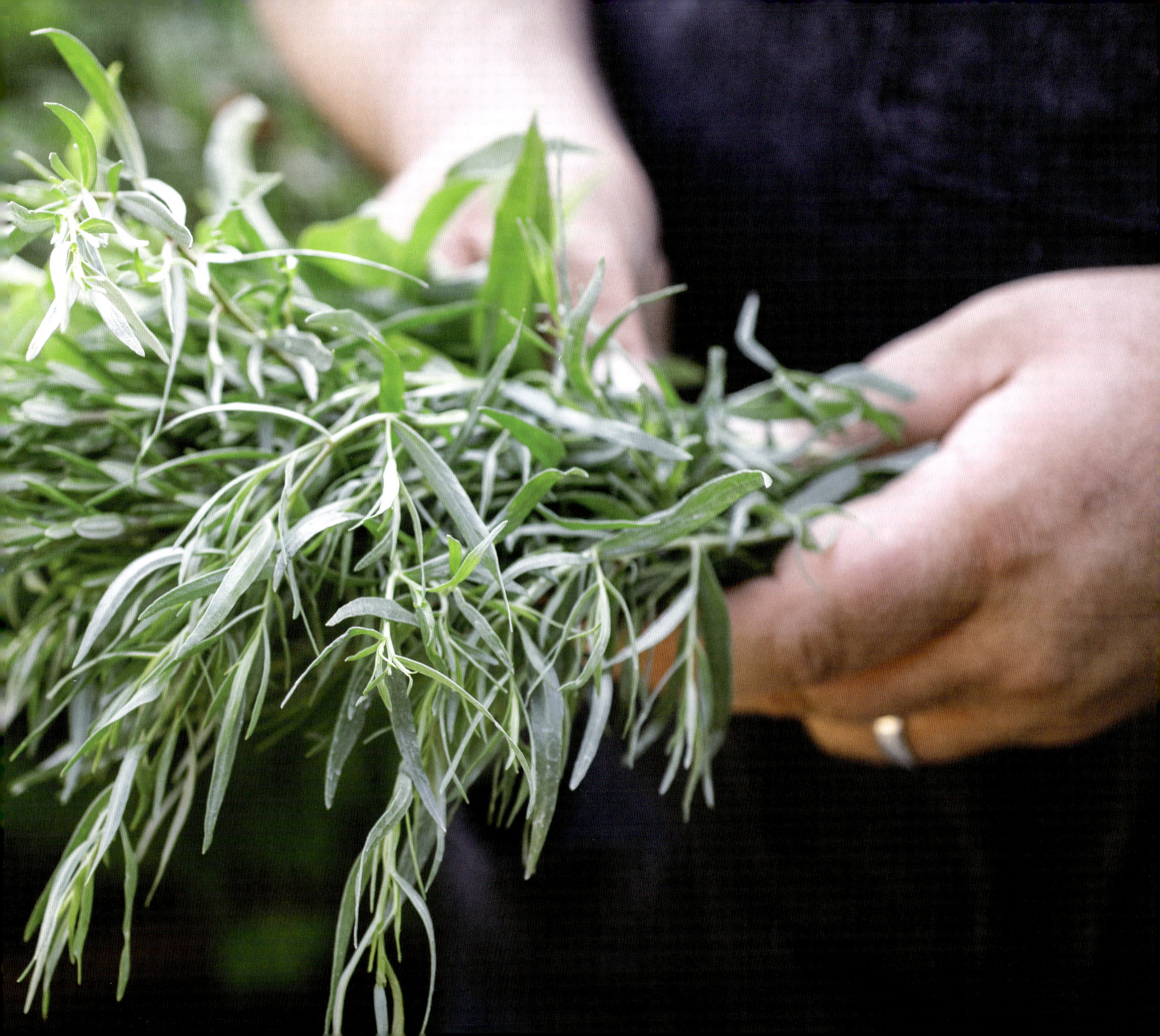

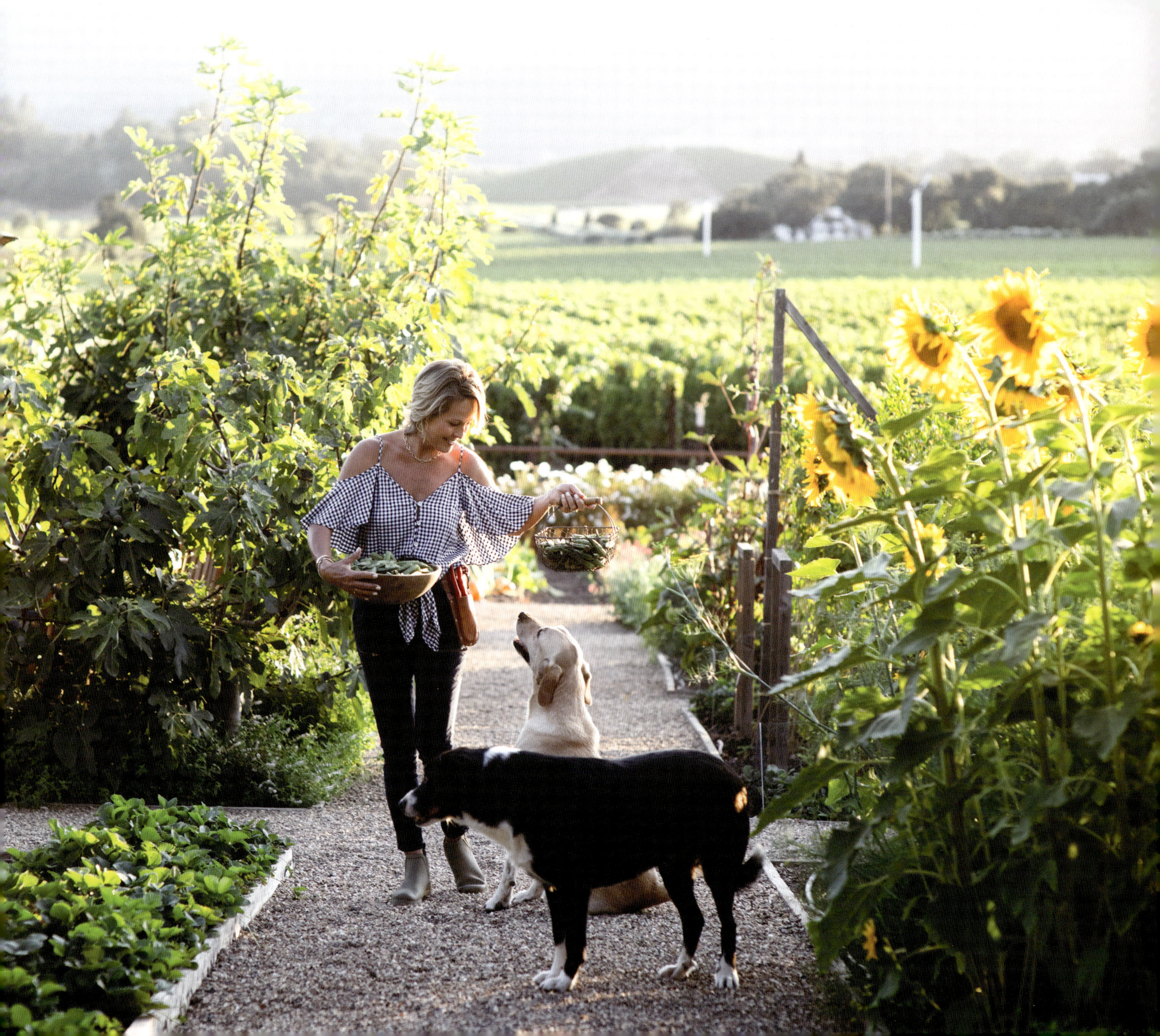

Regusci Winery: *Italian-American Abbondanza*

Napa

Visitors come to Regusci Winery for its celebrated wines, but few leave without a stop at the Garden Wagon to fill their totes with estate-grown fruits and vegetables. "Wine-club members never go home empty-handed," says proprietor Laura Regusci, who makes sure the honor-system farm stand is especially bountiful before winery events.

Neighbor kids bike up the Reguscis' long walnut tree–lined drive to fill their baskets with strawberries and cherry tomatoes. Their parents, many of them internationally known vintners, shop for dinner and fresh flowers at the rustic fruit-and-vegetable wagon. For vintners Laura and Jim Regusci, the expansive garden and produce stand make a personal statement: we are farmers first, on this ranch for more than a century, with Italian roots and an Italian love of *abbondanza.*

Jim's immigrant grandfather purchased the original 286-acre parcel in Napa Valley's prestigious Stags Leap District. Today, Jim's busy farming company, Regusci Vineyard Management, services his own vineyards and those of dozens of other grape growers. In addition, the family raises chickens, turkeys, pigs, goats, sheep, and cattle for its own table and for special events; bottles olive oil; and harvests a cornucopia of orchard fruits and nuts, from apples and plums to persimmons, pomegranates, and walnuts. The family menagerie is missing only a dairy cow, ironic in that the Regusci Dairy, a business Jim's grandfather started in the 1930s, supplied Napa Valley with milk and cream for almost forty years. "Our family has always produced its own food," says Jim, "but now it's chic."

In 2010, when Jim decided that a Cabernet Sauvignon block on the home ranch needed replanting, he asked Laura about its viability as a garden. Laura quickly saw the potential in that idea, believing that an edible garden would create lasting memories for winery guests and distinguish the experience of visiting Regusci. Validation came quickly on social media. "I look at people's images, and they've taken pictures of the vegetable stand," acknowledges Jim.

Raised in Kentucky, Laura fell in love with farming as a way of life while living with farm families in northern Europe during high school. She earned a master's degree in agriculture education, then launched a twenty-year academic career, teaching organic farming and gardening at the junior-college and high-school level and installing edible gardens wherever she went. To bolster youth interest in the local food, wine, and hospitality industries, she helped create California's first high-school viticulture and winemaking curriculum at St. Helena High School, which Jim's children attended.

It wasn't long before Laura and Jim discovered their mutual passions, and soon Laura was sketching garden designs for the former vineyard block. Over time, Laura has softened the beds' angularity with tall, arched trellises for beans and tomatoes and with swaths of

Left and above: *Laura Regusci harvests okra with the help of canine friends; Regusci farm stand, a riot of color, operates on the honor system.*

colorful cosmos and sunflowers. Gardening in a grid is functional, says Laura, making irrigation and planting plans easier.

"This garden is about more than just eating fresh or eating local," says Laura. "For us, growing is a passion." Laura's gardening talents are also evident at the ranch home she shares with Jim, an Eden of olive and avocado trees, strawberry beds, lemon verbena for scenting pitchers of water, and a cutting garden lush with zinnias and sunflowers.

The vegetable garden's annual output could satisfy a dozen Italian grandmothers, with 280 basil plants yielding so heavily that Laura supplies a local juice shop and many of her favorite restaurants in the valley. Pesto and basil oil made in the ranch kitchen find their way into gift baskets for VIP wine-club members, with plenty of basil left to share with employees.

Nine large square beds of perennials and fruit trees—raspberries, pomegranates, figs, strawberries, fennel, asparagus, artichokes, and culinary herbs—form the core of the landscape, so the garden's heart remains largely green year-round. The larger twenty-by-forty-foot beds on the perimeter change with the seasons. In summer, they're home to twenty varieties of tomatoes planted in rows by color; shishito, Padrón, and banana peppers and thick stands of broom corn; Rosa Bianca and Nadia eggplants for estate chef Angel Perez's famous eggplant parmigiana; green beans; cucumbers; mini watermelons; and multiple types of summer squash. Perez is Oaxacan, so this wine country garden always includes an abundance of fiery chiles for salsas and pickles, as well as many of the ingredients that make up his mother's laborious mole.

Above: *(clockwise from left) Napa Valley vista; garden coordinator Jim Bachor (left) harvests with chef Angel Perez; Shooting Stars eggplant; colorful blooms lure beneficial insects; ripening chiles; farm stand bounty*

"In nature, more diversity creates a resilient garden," says Laura, who views the whole Regusci estate as an ecosystem where *"everything feeds everything else."*

Cherry tomato and gourd vines clamber over arches made of hog-wire fencing, creating shady, mysterious tunnels that beckon children.

Autumn weather ripens the butternut squash that Angel uses for one of the family's favorite soups. A vast pumpkin patch bordered with white cosmos has its moment in the spotlight, and the estate's walnut trees deliver their annual treasure.

In winter, the pace is slower compared to summer's marathon. Half the garden will be carpeted with mustard, a cover crop that improves the soil, while the other half will furnish garlic, cabbage, fava beans, leeks, kale, Brussels sprouts, collards, beets, and carrots for the family kitchen and for employees. "The cabbages here are ridiculous," says Jim. "Let's just say they may not go through a basketball hoop."

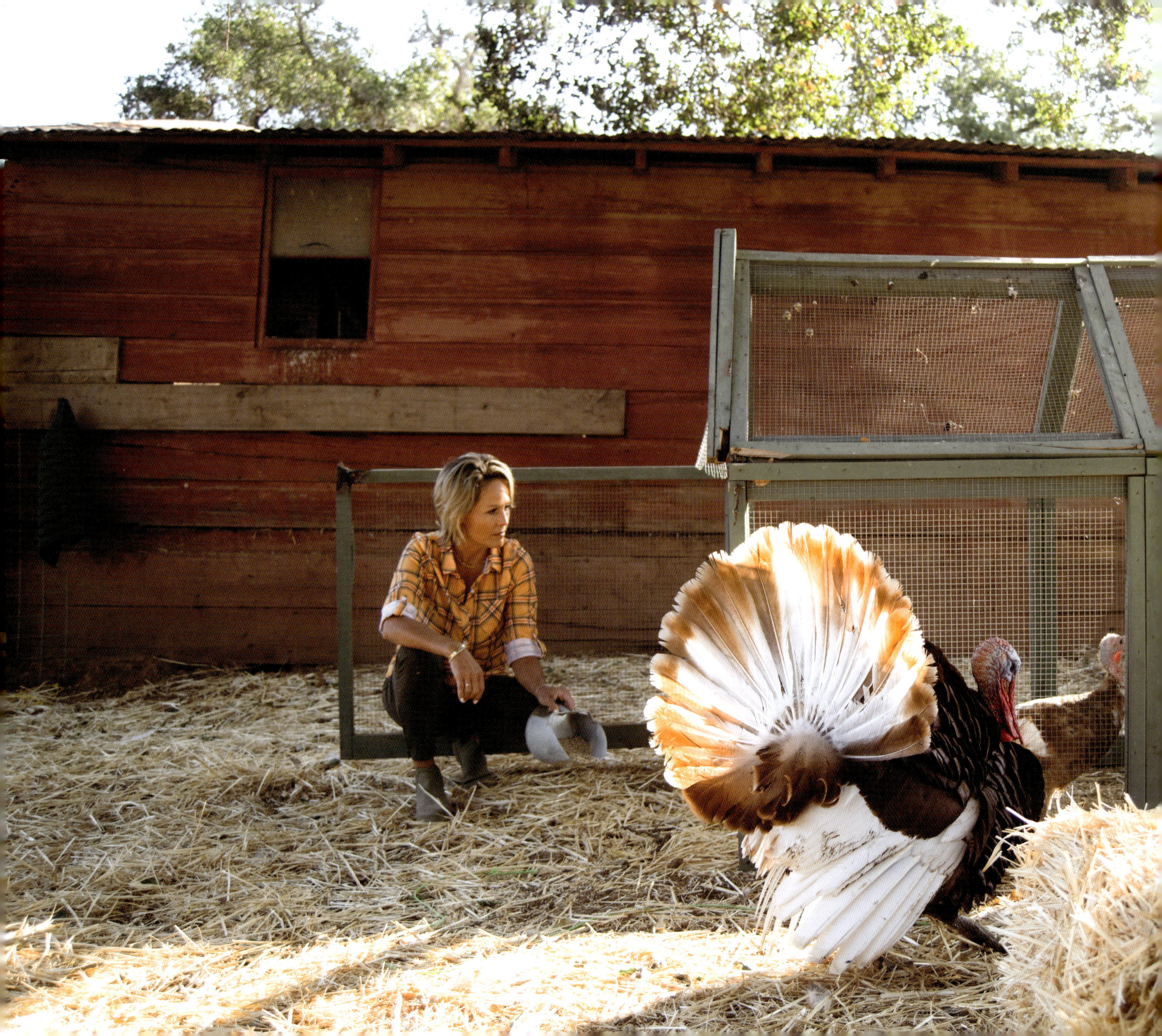

And always, year-round, bees and beneficial insects will find welcoming thickets of blooms: sunflowers, lavender, lemon verbena, zinnias, salvias, scabiosa, and roses, garden residents valued for the habitat they provide and the charming bouquets they inspire.

To create a more integrated and sustainable system, Laura has gradually introduced heritage livestock to the ranch. Now the pasture supports beef cattle, sheep, turkeys, and goats; chickens and ducks provide eggs for the winery kitchen; and squealing litters of piglets grow to maturity on garden scraps. It's an ancient and synergistic approach, with landscape nurturing livestock and vice versa.

Left and above: *Laura enjoys feeding the ranch turkeys; Jim and Laura relax at sunset with a glass of Regusci Winery Block 3 Cabernet Sauvignon.*

Regusci Winery 137

"In nature, more diversity creates a resilient garden," says Laura, who views the estate as an ecosystem where "everything feeds everything else." The animals provide manure that nourishes the soil. The garden provides produce—misshapen or overripe—that nourishes the animals. Strategically planted insectaries keep an army of good bugs on patrol so pests rarely get the upper hand.

"That's the way we garden, by understanding the biological aspects," says Jim Bachor, the garden coordinator and a former student of Laura's.

Above and right: *(clockwise from left) Angel heads for the kitchen with jumbo heirloom tomatoes; farm stand artichokes and avocados; historic Regusci stone winery; sun-ripened cherry tomatoes*

The bonanza of vegetables and fruits from this garden would be daunting without a resourceful cook to manage it. Angel, whose wife, father, sister, and brothers also work at Regusci, has a long résumé with Napa Valley restaurants and an experimental bent that serves him well when the garden delivers a deluge. He makes crackers incorporating oven-dried tomatoes and grissini flavored with pureed artichokes. He puts up numberless jars of fig jam, marinara sauce, pickled jalapeños, spicy *giardiniera*, and—Laura's favorite—pickled okra. He makes spiced walnuts for cakes and cheese boards, pistachio pesto for visitor gifts, and avocado-tomatillo salsa and chips for business meetings.

Angel's talents and the garden bounty merge most impressively at Thanksgiving, when Jim and Laura host a crowd. Italian-American, Mexican, and southern foodways mix and mingle in a feast that always showcases a turkey raised on the ranch and begins with a massive charcuterie board. Pickled okra makes an appearance, as does Angel's butternut squash soup with balsamic reduction, a cornbread dressing with Italian seasonings, Brussels sprouts with apples (estate grown, of course), and a persimmon-walnut pudding that nods to a nut crop that once rivaled grapes in Napa Valley.

If Jim had any doubts about Laura's ability to realize her garden vision, they are long gone. As he has learned in the years since they married, she has an almost supernatural green thumb. Jim likes to tell about the time the couple visited the former World Trade Center site in New York City and Laura spotted a few acorns under the only surviving oak tree. Those forlorn acorns are now thriving young oaks at Regusci Winery.

Jim's vineyard-management business is a dusty world of pickup trucks, tractors, and tool sheds. Now, at its center, is an orderly oasis of greenery and calm. "Laura has softened the ranch with her garden," says Jim, and that's surely a good return on investment.

menu

Antipasto Platter with Southern-Style Pickled Okra
Regusci Winery Rosé

Roasted Butternut Squash Soup with Pomegranate and Pumpkin Seeds
Regusci Winery Merlot

Brussels Sprouts with Bacon, Apples, and Pistachios

Italian Cornbread Dressing
Regusci Winery Zinfandel

Steamed Persimmon and Walnut Pudding
2001 Regusci Winery Cabernet Sauvignon

Est. 1932
REGUSCI
STAGS LEAP DISTRICT
Block 3
CABERNET SAUVIGNON
2016

Antipasto Platter with Southern-Style Pickled Okra

Makes 6 pints

Laura developed a passion for pickling in her grandmother's Kentucky kitchen. The family pastime began as a way to preserve vegetables for winter and share homegrown gifts with neighbors. Today, Laura carries on the tradition, growing okra and other seasonable vegetables in the Regusci estate garden for pickling. Each Thanksgiving, pickled okra adds a southern spirit to the family's antipasto board alongside salumi, figs, grissini, *and marinated artichokes.*

3 pounds small okra
6 cups distilled white vinegar
4 cups water
½ cup kosher or sea salt
¼ cup sugar

For Each Pint Jar:
¼ teaspoon yellow mustard seeds
¼ teaspoon dill seeds
6 black peppercorns
6 cumin seeds
2 cloves garlic, peeled
1 fresh oregano sprig
1 bay leaf
Pinch of ground coriander
Pinch of red chile flakes

Wine: Regusci Winery Rosé

In a saucepan, combine the vinegar, water, salt, and sugar and bring to a simmer over medium-high heat, stirring to dissolve the sugar. Keep hot.

Into each of the six jars, put the mustard seeds, dill seeds, peppercorns, cumin seeds, garlic, oregano, bay leaf, coriander, and chile flakes. Fill the jars with the okra, packing it in upright—alternating the stems up and down if needed—as tightly as possible. Fill the jars with the hot liquid, leaving ¼-inch headspace, and top each jar with a flat lid and screw band. Process the jars in a boiling water bath for 15 minutes, then cool on racks without disturbing.

Refrigerate any jars that failed to seal and use within 2 weeks. Store sealed jars in a cool, dark place for up to 1 year. Wait for at least 1 week before opening a jar to allow the flavor to mellow.

Have ready six sterilized pint canning jars and two-part lids. Trim the okra stems if needed to fit the whole pods upright in the jars. Otherwise, leave the stems intact.

Roasted Butternut Squash Soup with Pomegranate and Pumpkin Seeds Makes 10 cups; serves 10 to 12

1 butternut squash, about 4 pounds

7 tablespoons unsalted butter

1 tablespoon brown sugar

Sea salt and freshly ground black pepper

1 teaspoon extra virgin olive oil

1 large white onion, chopped

2 celery ribs, sliced

1 large carrot, peeled and sliced

2 cloves garlic, minced

½ large shallot, sliced

1 teaspoon peeled and minced fresh ginger

Kosher or sea salt and freshly ground white pepper

1 bay leaf

1 fresh thyme sprig

6 cups water

½ teaspoon ground cumin, toasted in a dry pan

Freshly grated nutmeg

10 to 12 small winter squashes, about 1 pound each, stems attached

For Garnish:

Bottled balsamic vinegar reduction or glaze

Pomegranate arils (seeds)

Roasted and salted pumpkin seeds (pepitas)

Thinly sliced fresh chives

Angel's festive soup is a fixture at the Regusci family's Thanksgiving table and holiday parties. Served in hollowed-out miniature squashes, this creamy soup is topped with pomegranate arils, pepitas, and a drizzle of balsamic vinegar reduction. During the winery's annual wreath-making event, wine club members enjoy this signature soup from mugs. A handsome tureen is another serving option if you can't find mini squashes.

Wine: Regusci Winery Merlot

Preheat the oven to 350°F. Line a baking sheet with parchment paper. With a cleaver or heavy chef's knife, cut off the stem end of the butternut squash, then cut the squash crosswise where the bulbous base meets the straight neck. Cut both pieces in half lengthwise. Remove the seeds and stringy membranes from the cavities. Put the squash halves, skin side down and generously spaced, on the prepared pan. Using 4 tablespoons of the butter, dot the surface and cavities of the squash. Sprinkle with the sugar and season with sea salt and black pepper. Bake until the squash is tender when pierced and lightly caramelized, 50 to 55 minutes. Let cool, then scrape the flesh from the skins.

In a large pot, melt the remaining 3 tablespoons butter with the oil over medium heat. Add the onion, celery, carrot, garlic, shallot, and ginger and season with kosher salt and white pepper. Sauté until the vegetables soften, 7 to 8 minutes; do not allow them to brown. Add the bay leaf, thyme sprig, and 4 cups of the water. Bring to a boil over medium-high heat, adjust the heat to maintain a gentle simmer, and simmer uncovered for 45 minutes.

Remove the bay leaf and thyme sprig, then add the squash flesh, breaking it up with a wooden spoon. Stir in the remaining 2 cups water, the cumin, and a few scrapes of nutmeg and bring the soup back to a boil, stirring often. Let cool, then puree in batches in a blender until completely smooth and pour into a clean saucepan.

(continued)

Gently reheat the soup, stirring often and adding a little more water if it is too thick for your taste. Season to taste with kosher salt and white pepper.

To make the squash bowls, use a heavy chef's knife or cleaver. Working very carefully, slice off the tops just below the stem. The easiest and safest way to do this is to score the squash first, slicing all the way around but not all the way through. Once you have scored the squash, you can more easily slice all the way through and remove the top. With a soupspoon, scoop out the seeds and membranes. You can prepare the bowls several hours ahead.

Just before serving, place the squash bowls on a parchment-lined baking sheet and bake at 350°F until very warm, about 5 minutes.

Set the warm squash bowls on individual plates. Ladle hot soup into the cavities, stopping short of the rim; you should have enough room for about ¾ cup. Drizzle with balsamic vinegar reduction (using a squeeze bottle if you have one). Scatter a few pomegranate arils, pumpkin seeds, and chives on top of each serving and cover each squash bowl with its top. Serve immediately.

Brussels Sprouts with Bacon, Apples, and Pistachios Serves 6

If there's one Thanksgiving dish the Regusci family can't be without, it's this Brussels sprout preparation. Made with young, mild sprouts from the estate garden, this side dish will turn even Brussels sprout skeptics into believers. You can blanch the sprouts 1 day ahead. Pat dry and refrigerate in a plastic bag.

1½ pounds Brussels sprouts, trimmed and halved lengthwise

1 tablespoon canola oil

½ pound thick-sliced bacon, in large dice

½ large white onion, sliced

Sea salt and freshly ground black pepper

½ teaspoon minced fresh thyme

¼ cup apple cider vinegar whisked with 2 teaspoons sugar

1 apple, halved, cored, and sliced about ¼ inch thick

½ cup chopped roasted and salted pistachios

Bring a large pot of salted water to a boil over high heat. Add the Brussels sprouts and blanch for 1½ minutes. Drain into a sieve or colander. Let dry completely, patting dry with paper towels if necessary. They must be completely dry to sear properly.

Heat the oil in a large skillet over medium-high heat. Add the bacon and sauté until it renders most of its fat but is not yet crisp, about 5 minutes; lower the heat if necessary to keep the bacon from burning. With a slotted spoon, transfer the bacon to a bowl. Add the onion to the skillet and sauté just until it softens slightly but does not color, about 1 minute. With a slotted spoon, transfer the onion to the bowl with the bacon. Pour off and reserve the bacon fat and wipe the skillet clean.

Return 2 tablespoons bacon fat to the skillet and set over high heat. When the fat is hot, add the Brussels sprouts and let them sear without stirring for about 3 minutes so they brown well on one side. Season with salt and pepper, then stir briefly to redistribute them and let them again sear without stirring for about 3 minutes. Lower the heat if necessary to keep them from burning and add another 1 tablespoon bacon fat if the pan seems dry.

Remove from the heat and stir in the thyme. Immediately add the cider-sugar mixture, bacon and onion, apple slices, and pistachios and toss to mix. Taste for seasoning, then serve.

Above: *A Regusci family Thanksgiving includes Roasted Butternut Squash Soup, Italian Cornbread Dressing, and Brussels Sprouts with Bacon, Apples, and Pistachios to accompany ranch-raised turkey.*

Italian Cornbread Dressing

Serves 8

The perfect Thanksgiving accompaniment to ranch-raised ham and turkey, the family's cornbread dressing is a recipe that will be shared with generations to come. Angel's wife, Adriana, bakes the cornbread, then Angel and Laura prepare the dressing with sautéed vegetables and herbs.

Jalapeño and Fresh Corn Cornbread:

1 jalapeño chile
1 cup fresh corn kernels (from about 1 ear corn)
1 cup unbleached all-purpose flour
1 cup yellow cornmeal
1 cup sugar
¼ cup cake flour
2 tablespoons baking powder
1½ teaspoons kosher or sea salt
4 large eggs
1 cup whole milk
½ cup buttermilk
¾ cup unsalted butter, melted and cooled
⅓ cup canola oil

6 tablespoons unsalted butter
1 teaspoon extra virgin olive oil
6 carrots, chopped
1½ white onions, chopped
4 large celery ribs, thinly sliced
3 cloves garlic, minced
1 shallot, thinly sliced
Sea salt and freshly ground black pepper
¼ cup dry white wine
3 tablespoons chopped fresh flat-leaf parsley
½ teaspoon finely minced fresh thyme
3 fresh sage leaves, finely minced
½ teaspoon red chile flakes
1 cup chicken broth
1 cup chopped toasted pecans (optional)

Wine: Regusci Winery Zinfandel

Prepare the cornbread: Preheat the oven to 350°F. Line a 12-by-17-inch baking sheet with parchment paper.

Toast the whole jalapeño in a dry small skillet over medium heat, turning it with tongs until it is blistered all over. Immediately wrap the chile in plastic wrap and let steam until cool. Unwrap and discard the skin, stem, and seeds, then finely chop.

Toast the corn in the same dry skillet over medium heat, stirring constantly, until the corn loses its raw taste, about 2 minutes. Let cool.

In a large bowl, whisk together the all-purpose flour, cornmeal, sugar, cake flour, baking powder, and salt. In a medium bowl, whisk together the eggs, milk, buttermilk, butter, and canola oil. Add the liquid ingredients to the dry ingredients and whisk to blend. Stir in the jalapeño and the corn.

Transfer the batter to the prepared pan and bake the cornbread, rotating the pan back to front halfway through, until lightly browned and firm to the touch, 20 to 30 minutes. Transfer the pan to a rack.

Set aside half of the cornbread to enjoy warm and let the other half cool completely. Transfer the cooled half to a cutting board and cut into ½-inch cubes. Leave to dry out at room temperature overnight.

Preheat the oven to 350°F. Put the cornbread cubes on a baking sheet and bake until lightly browned, about 15 minutes. Let cool. Leave the oven on.

In a 12-inch skillet, melt the butter with the olive oil over medium-high heat. Add the carrots, onions, celery, garlic, and shallot, season with salt and pepper, and sauté until lightly colored, about 5 minutes. Add the wine and cook, stirring, until it evaporates, about 1 minute. Add the parsley, thyme, sage, and chile flakes and cook, stirring, for about 1 minute. Add the broth, bring to a simmer, and remove from the heat. Stir in the toasted cornbread and the pecans, if using. Spread the dressing in an 11-by-9-by-2½-inch baking dish. Cover with aluminum foil and bake for 15 minutes. Serve immediately.

Steamed Persimmon and Walnut Pudding Serves 12

Sharing recipes is an honored tradition among Napa Valley agricultural families. This family recipe comes from Regusci garden coordinator and friend Jim Bachor. Walnuts are plentiful on the Regusci Ranch and recall the days before grapes became the valley's mainstay. The pudding calls for Hachiya persimmons, the heart-shaped variety that is harvested firm. Leave them on the kitchen counter until they are squishy, then remove the cap, cut in half, and inspect for seeds before pureeing, skin and all.

⅓ cup unsalted butter, melted, plus more for the mold

1 cup sugar

1 cup all-purpose flour

2 teaspoons baking soda

1 teaspoon ground cinnamon

½ teaspoon sea salt

½ cup raisins

½ cup coarsely chopped toasted walnuts

1 teaspoon pure vanilla extract

½ cup whole milk

1 large egg

1 cup Hachiya persimmon pulp (about 2 ripe persimmons)

Powdered sugar, for dusting (optional)

Whipped cream, for serving (optional)

Wine: 2001 Regusci Winery Cabernet Sauvignon

Place a steamer rack in the bottom of a large pot and add enough water to come to within 1 inch of the top of a 1½-quart pudding mold. Bring the water to a boil over high heat. With melted butter, brush the interior and the underside of the lid of the pudding mold and set aside.

In a large bowl, whisk together the sugar, flour, baking soda, cinnamon, and salt until blended. Stir in the raisins and walnuts. In a medium bowl, whisk together the butter, vanilla, milk, egg, and persimmon. Fold the wet ingredients into the dry ingredients just until blended.

Transfer the batter to the prepared mold and clamp on the lid. Place on the rack in the boiling water, cover the pot, and reduce the heat to maintain a gentle simmer. You should see some steam escaping from the pot throughout the cooking. Cook for 1¼ hours.

Carefully transfer the pudding mold to a rack. Let cool for 30 minutes, then remove the lid and unmold the pudding onto a serving dish. Serve warm or at room temperature. If desired, dust with powdered sugar just before serving and accompany with whipped cream.

chef's tip:

Hachiya persimmon puree freezes well. Freeze in 1-cup containers and use another time to make this moist steamed pudding or fruit smoothies year-round.

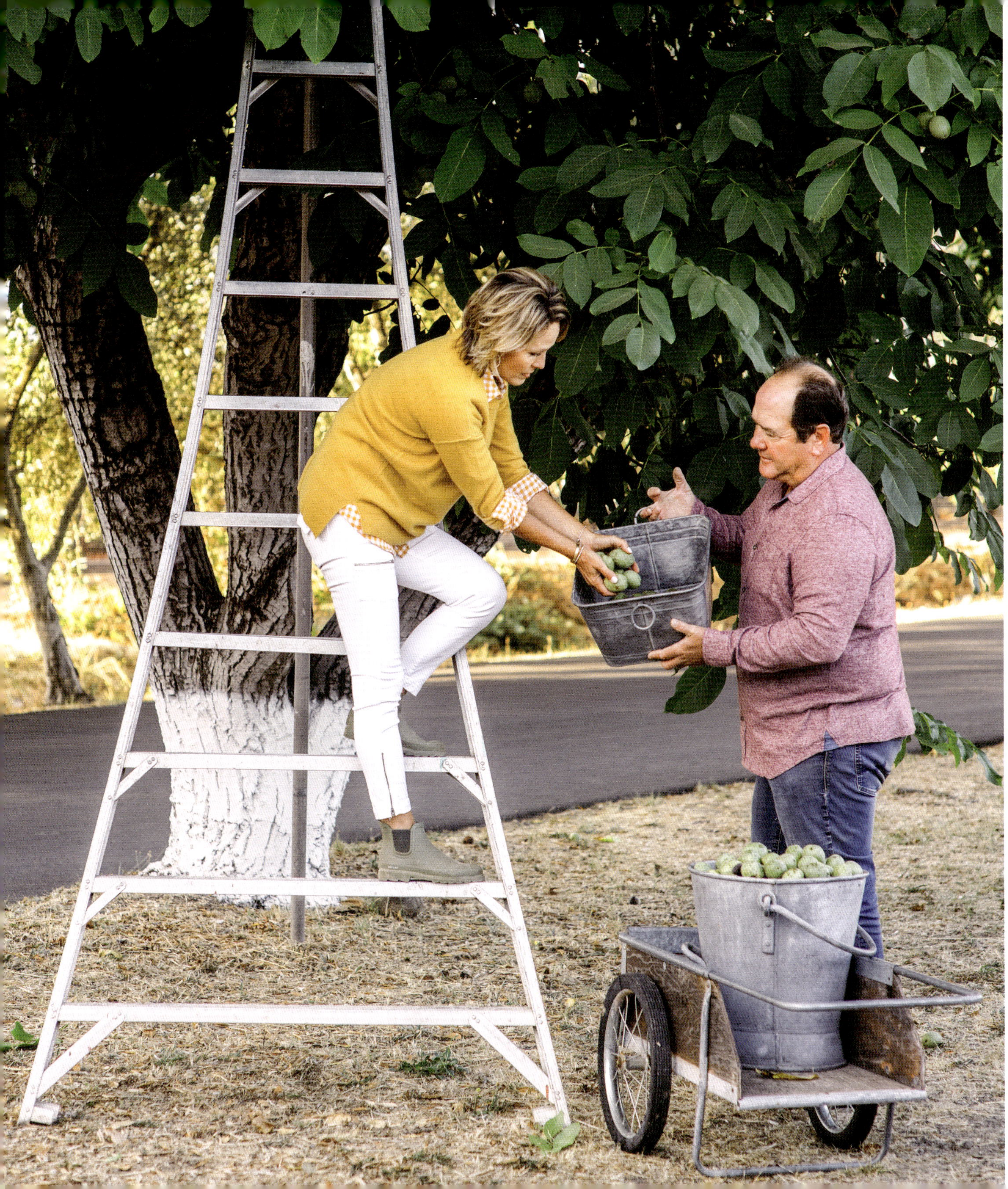

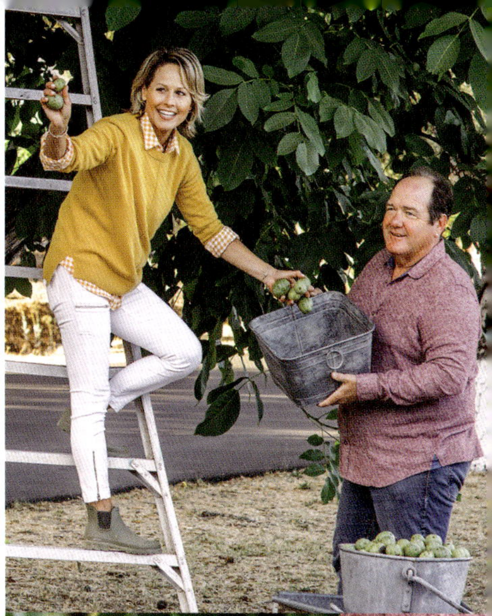

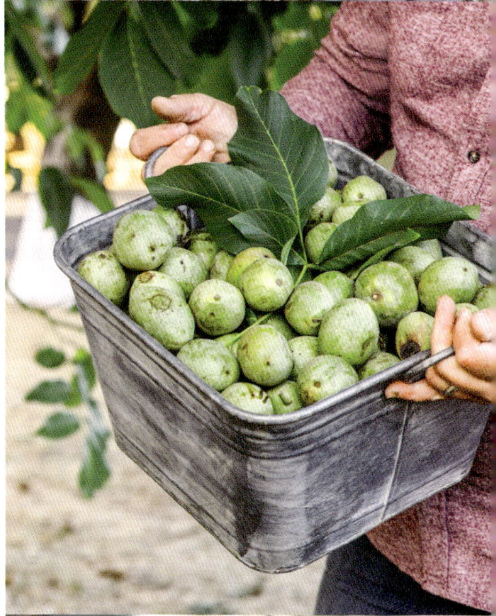

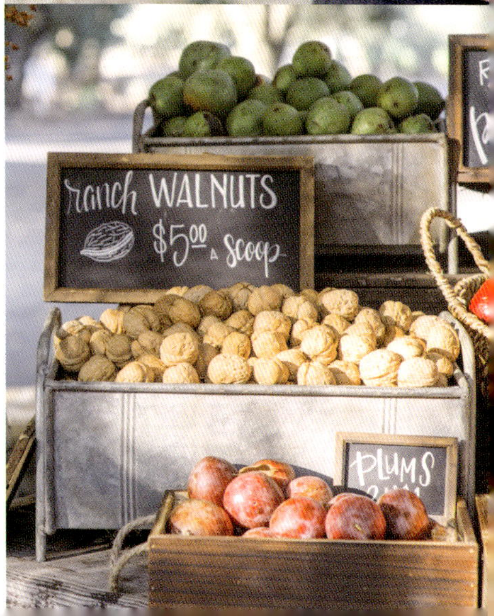
ranch WALNUTS
$5.00 a scoop
PLUMS

Left and above: *Laura gathers dried fava beans to plant for next year's crop; a bed of sunflowers and blooming fennel frames a view of the vineyards and distant Mayacamas Mountains.*

top habitat plants for healthy gardens:

The Regusci garden puts out the welcome mat for bees and beneficial insects. Some of Laura's favorite plants for luring good bugs and butterflies include the following:

Cosmos	Milkweed
Dill	Red Valerian
Echinacea	Salvia
Fennel	Yarrow

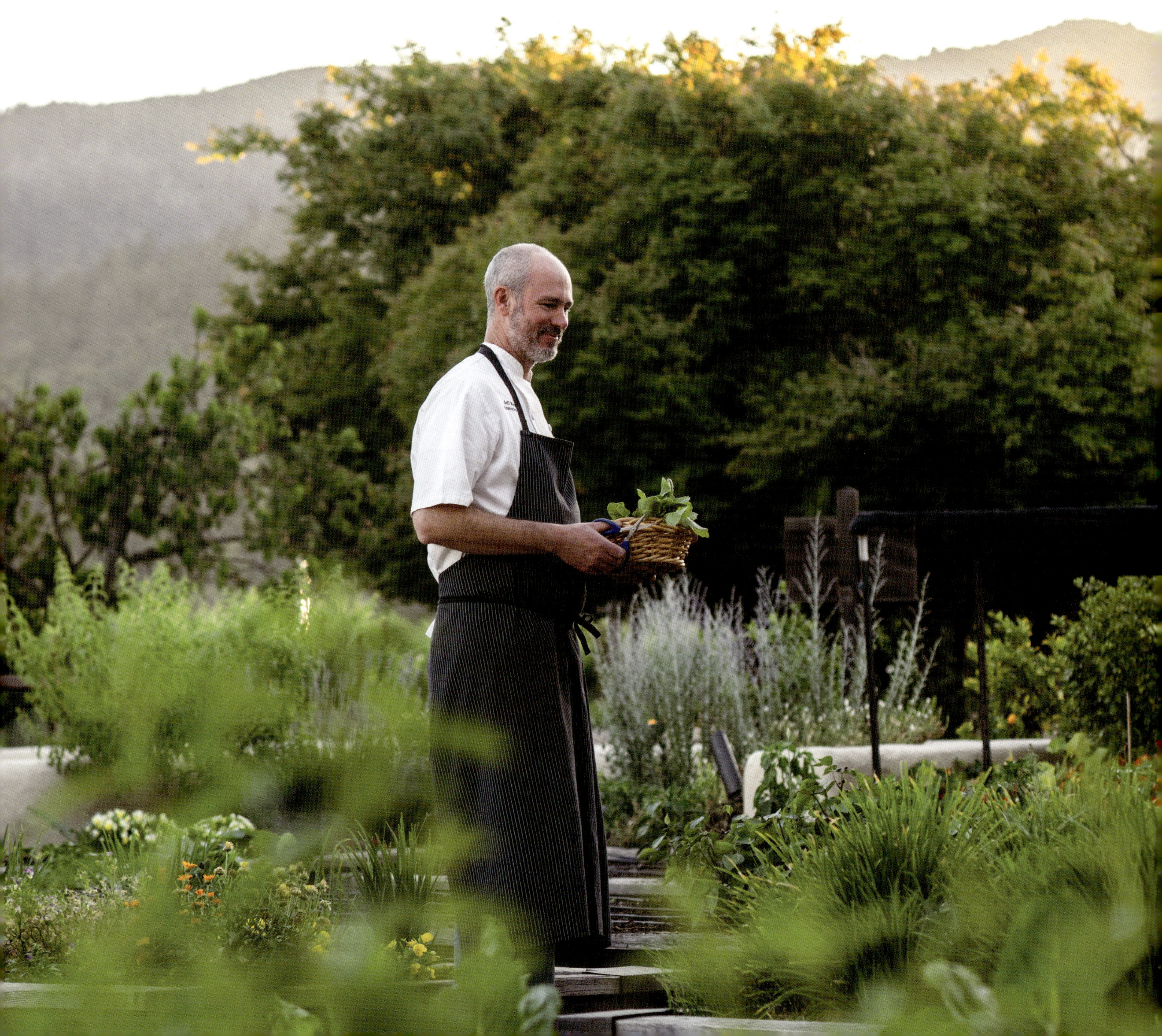

Robert Mondavi Winery: *Garden Carved from a Vineyard*

Oakville

Robert and Margrit Mondavi were legendary hosts whose warm approach to wine country hospitality persists at Robert Mondavi Winery years after the couple's passing. Margrit, especially, was a fresh-air and fresh-food enthusiast who believed that a vegetable garden was as essential to the winery as the prime vineyards alongside it. From its beginning in 1966, the Robert Mondavi Winery, with its mission-style architecture, exemplified the relaxed California way of life. Entertaining visitors with a garden-to-table meal only underscored the message, then as now.

Today, winery executive chef Jeff Mosher manages the edible garden with his culinary team. They plant it and tend it, harvest its bounty and cook what it yields. Christened the "Piccolo" To Kalon Garden, after the adjacent To Kalon Vineyard, source of the winery's finest Cabernet Sauvignon, the garden is a small (*piccolo* in Italian) parcel carved out of a world-renowned vineyard. Given the market value of the wine grapes that this terrain could produce, the garden speaks volumes about the winery's priorities.

"The garden communicates the winery's commitment and connection to the land," says Nova Cadamatre, senior director of winemaking. "It's about following the seasonal cycle, like we do in the vineyard. Jeff's menus are always driven by what is growing right now."

With its low redwood-framed beds and shredded bark paths, the edible garden is as understated as the winery, a compound acclaimed for its tasteful design and lack of ostentation. The garden, a neat, flat grid of raised beds surrounded by fig, olive, and citrus trees, supplies only a small portion of the produce this busy winery—one of Napa Valley's most visited—needs. But it serves as a scenic backdrop for some of the visitor experiences and an educational venue as well.

From late spring until fall, the garden stars in some of the winery's small-group offerings. Guests who opt for these experiences will tour the garden with a winery chef, gather herbs and produce, and then decamp to the winery's nearby kitchen for a hands-on cooking lesson. They'll prepare a dish or two with the produce they picked, then tour the winery while the culinary staff completes and serves the meal.

With the culinary garden only steps from the kitchen, Jeff and his crew can pop out to snip fresh chives the moment they're needed or gather violas, dianthus, nasturtiums, or calendulas to add vivid color to their plates. "It's hard for us to plant enough onions, but we can plant enough flowers," says the chef.

Left and above: *Winery chef Jeff Mosher harvests spring vegetables at the foot of the Mayacamas Mountains; from the To Kalon Vineyard, a view of the winery's mission architecture*

In spring's gentle light, the culinary garden has a newborn softness and freshness. Trellises and stakes are in place for the vining squashes, tomatoes, and towering sunflowers that will cover them in the weeks to come, but the garden's inhabitants in May are mostly low growing: tufts of chives, fragile lettuces, the tender tops of French breakfast radishes, wisps of arugula. The To Kalon vines, bare all winter, are steadily pushing out their leafy canes against the stately backdrop of the Mayacamas Mountains.

For Jeff and his team, the garden also expands the potential for food and wine pairing and heightening guests' experience of Robert Mondavi wines.

"It's a nice collaboration," says Nova. "I'll take a new wine to him and his team and we'll taste it together. We'll talk about the different flavors in the wine and toss ideas back and forth. Jeff's team does an amazing job of teasing out subtle differences that even my winemaking team doesn't perceive because we're not as familiar with the flavors of fruits and vegetables."

The conventional "red wine with red meat" approach to wine pairing doesn't begin to describe the pairing strategies that emerge when a chef has a culinary garden at arm's reach.

"One of the things Jeff's team has opened my eyes to is how well fennel goes with our Fumé Blanc," says Nova. The wine that Robert Mondavi christened—Fumé Blanc was his poetic rebranding of Sauvignon Blanc—has some of the same fresh, faint licorice or anise scent that fennel contributes to a dish. "Pairing that wine with shaved fennel or candied fennel is always mind-blowing," says Nova.

Above: *(clockwise from left) The winery garden abuts the famous To Kalon Vineyard; Jeff samples spring peas; garden signage; iconic winery entrance; French Breakfast radishes; nasturtium pesto prep*

"The garden communicates the winery's commitment and connection to the land. Jeff's menus are always driven by what is growing right now."

While a grilled steak is a slam-dunk pairing for Robert Mondavi's classic Cabernet Sauvignon, a wine that has long been a standard bearer for California wine around the world, the accompanying vegetables can make the match even more profound. "Jeff does this great braised kale that goes so well with Cabernet Sauvignon," says Nova. "Kale has a strong flavor and crunch, but our Cabernet is strong and structured, so it marries well with that type of vegetable."

With the winery's Chardonnay, the kitchen turns to creamy vegetables that welcome butter, such as potatoes, sweet potatoes, and butternut squash. Even parts of the plant that cooks rarely use, such as nasturtium leaves, become elements of the kitchen's palette, employed to help highlight aspects of a wine. For a composed salad of spring

Robert Mondavi Winery   153

vegetables and ricotta, Jeff adds nasturtium leaves to the accompanying pesto, believing that their peppery, herbal character produces a more intriguing match for the Fumé Blanc Reserve. Nasturtiums thrive in these garden beds, so the peppery pesto makes other appearances, often with grilled bread, burrata, and spring vegetables.

To see such creative, high-level cooking coming from this kitchen is no surprise. Robert and Margrit Mondavi were tireless supporters of the arts, bringing world-renowned chefs, musicians, painters, and performers to the winery to enrich the valley's cultural life. For many years, the Robert Mondavi Winery's Great Chefs

Above and right: *(clockwise from lower left) Ripening blueberries; harvesting radishes; beehives and fruit trees add diversity to the winery garden; sunset and moon over To Kalon Vineyard*

cooking school lured culinary luminaries to Napa Valley, establishing this wine valley as a destination for food enthusiasts, too.

In April and May, the winery garden yields delicate greens, sweet baby carrots, pristine English peas, and a profusion of edible flowers and wispy herbs. The gorgeous dishes that Jeff and crew create from this bounty practically beg for a painter to capture them; Margrit Mondavi, an avid watercolorist, would have relished the chance.

An appetizer tostada topped with avocado, cured yellowtail, and sweet-tart beads of finger lime complements the winery's unoaked Chardonnay, a bright, citrus-forward interpretation of this variety. Fluffy house-made ricotta and a bouquet of spring vegetables pair up for the next course, a ravishing salad, but the showstopper is sous-chef Lisa Moore's edible flower *croccante*, cracker art produced by pressing garden blossoms and leaves into the dough. A pasta course follows, to showcase the garden's first spring peas, fava beans, and sweet onions. Lisa is the crew's pasta specialist, transforming ten egg yolks and a cup of flour into a heap of golden fettuccine.

For the main course, a seared rib-eye steak, Jeff forages in the garden for tender herbs for a salsa verde. Fresh-snipped parsley, chives, and marjoram bring this classic Italian sauce to life, and the accompanying grilled vegetables, still growing that morning, give the composition a California stamp. Like many meals at the Robert Mondavi Winery, this one concludes with Moscato d'Oro, the winery's signature dessert wine from Muscat grapes. Blueberry bushes in the winery garden produce just enough fruit to share occasionally with VIP guests; sous-chef Lissette Garay stretches a few cups of the precious berries into a dessert for a dozen by transforming them into a gelée to top a silky cheesecake.

Napa Valley wineries offer visitors countless ways to explore their properties and products, but a vineyard lunch at the Robert Mondavi Winery is surely among the most pleasant. Dining outside by the edible garden, enjoying the scent of Meyer lemon blossoms and Jeff's exquisite garden-based food, would be a highlight of anyone's valley experience.

menu

Hamachi Crudo Tostada with Finger Limes and Avocado

Robert Mondavi Winery Napa Valley Unoaked Chardonnay

Spring Vegetable Salad with Ricotta, Nasturtium Pesto, and Edible Flower Croccante

Robert Mondavi Winery Napa Valley Fumé Blanc Reserve

Parsley Fettuccine with Fava Beans, Peas, Spring Onions, and Parmesan Cream

Robert Mondavi Winery Napa Valley Carneros Pinot Noir Reserve

Grilled Rib Eye with Grilled Spring Vegetables and Salsa Verde

Robert Mondavi Winery Napa Valley Cabernet Sauvignon Reserve

Cheesecake with Blueberry Gelée

Robert Mondavi Winery Napa Valley Moscato d'Oro

Above and right: *Just-picked edible spring flowers and nasturtium leaves are pressed into a cracker dough with a pasta machine; the baked sheet makes a crisp cracker or croccante.*

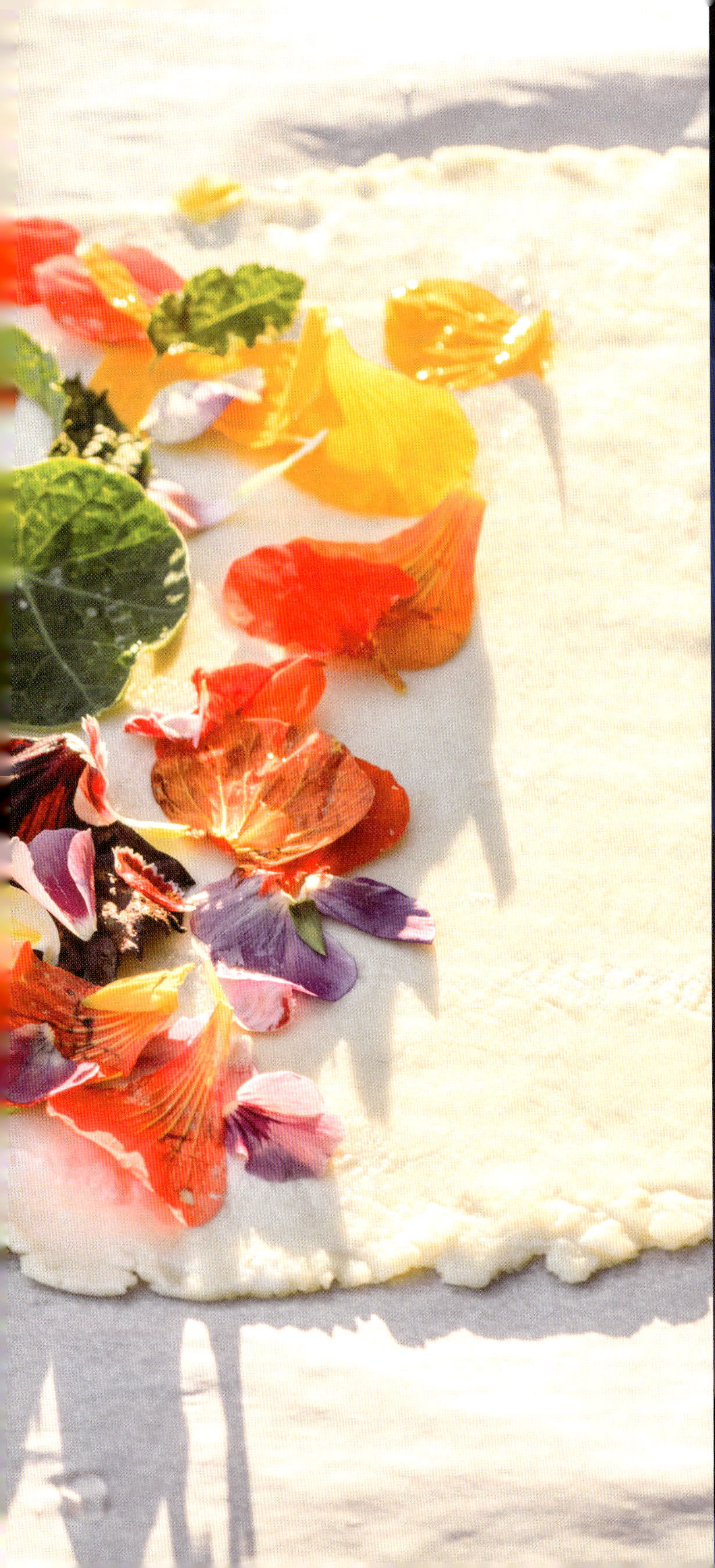
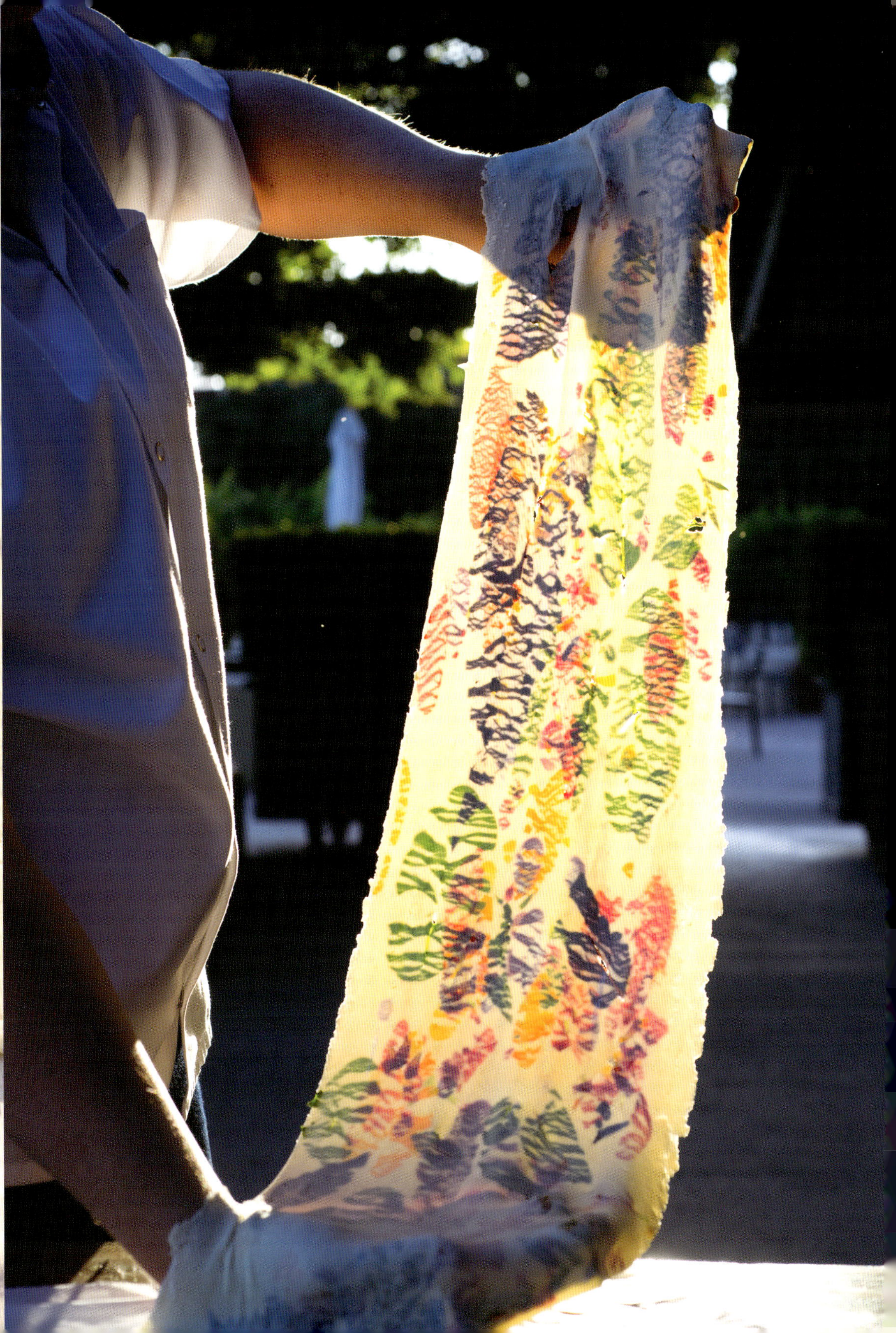

Hamachi Crudo Tostada with Finger Limes and Avocado Serves 4

The winery's lone finger-lime tree (Citrus australasica) *produces an abundant crop of these tiny, tangy fruits. The caviar-like beads inside are crunchy, sweet-tart, and juicy, a refreshing garnish for this lovely tostada. You can make all the components a few hours ahead—even the cured and sliced fish—and then assemble the tostada just before serving.*

Hamachi Crudo:

½ cup kosher salt

½ cup light brown sugar

¼ pound skinless hamachi (yellowtail) fillet

Vegetable oil, for deep-frying

4 corn tortillas

Sea salt

1 large or 2 small ice cubes

1 avocado, halved, pitted, and peeled

½ medium jalapeño chile, seeded

1½ teaspoons extra virgin olive oil

Juice of 1 lime

Garnishes:

4 finger limes, or a few drops of fresh lime juice for each tostada

Fresh edible flowers, baby miner's lettuce, bronze fennel fronds, or chives

---

Wine: Robert Mondavi Winery Napa Valley Unoaked Chardonnay

Prepare the hamachi crudo: In a bowl, combine the kosher salt and sugar and mix with your hands until no lumps remain. Bury the fish in the mixture and let stand at room temperature for 15 to 30 minutes.

Pour vegetable oil to a depth of 2 inches into a heavy saucepan and heat to 350°F. With a 3-inch round cookie cutter, cut out a round from each tortilla. Pierce each round in a few places with the tip of a knife to keep it from curling in the hot oil. Fry the rounds, agitating them almost constantly to keep them submerged in the oil and flipping them halfway through, until lightly colored, about 1½ minutes. Lift them out of the hot oil with tongs or a wire-mesh skimmer and transfer to paper towels to drain. Sprinkle with sea salt while hot.

Put the ice cube into a blender and add the avocado, jalapeño, olive oil, lime juice, and a pinch of sea salt. Blend until smooth. Taste for salt.

Remove the fish from the salt mixture. Rinse well and pat dry on paper towels. Slice against the grain on the diagonal into 12 thin slices.

Top each tostada with about 1 tablespoon of the avocado puree, spreading it evenly with the back of a spoon. (Save leftover avocado puree for another use.) Arrange 3 slices of fish on top of each tostada. Slice the tip off of each finger lime and squeeze the caviar-like seeds directly onto the fish, using 1 lime per tostada. Garnish with flowers and serve immediately.

Spring Vegetable Salad with Ricotta, Nasturtium Pesto, and Edible Flower Croccante **Serves 4**

Whatever is most tender and tempting in the winery's spring garden can find a place in this salad: radishes, baby carrots, fennel, spring onions. Young nasturtium leaves paired with basil produce a lightly spicy pesto that brings even more of the garden to the plate. Jeff makes his own ricotta, but a good store-bought ricotta, such as Calabro, works as well.

Pickled Red Onions:

2 red onions (about 1 pound)
2 cups red wine vinegar
2 cups water
½ cup sugar
1 tablespoon plus 1 teaspoon kosher salt
1 tablespoon black peppercorns
6 fresh thyme sprigs
2 bay leaves
2 whole star anise
2 whole cloves

Edible Flower Croccante:

1¼ cups all-purpose flour, plus more for dusting
¼ cup cornstarch
½ teaspoon sea salt
¼ teaspoon baking powder
2 tablespoons extra virgin olive oil, plus more for brushing
½ cup water, plus more if needed
Nonstick cooking spray, for the parchment
Fresh edible flowers, nasturtium leaves, and fava leaves
Flaky sea salt, such as Maldon

Nasturtium Pesto:

1 tablespoon pine nuts
2 cups lightly packed fresh nasturtium leaves
2 cups lightly packed fresh basil leaves
½ cup grapeseed oil
¾ teaspoon finely minced garlic
1 tablespoon plus 1 teaspoon freshly grated Parmigiano-Reggiano cheese
Pinch of sea salt
1 teaspoon fresh lemon juice

½ large fennel bulb, stalks removed
10 small radishes, leaves removed
1 medium carrot
2 cups sugar snap peas (about ¼ pound)
2 tablespoons plus 2 teaspoons extra virgin olive oil
2 tablespoons plus 2 teaspoons fresh lemon juice
Sea salt
¾ cup whole-milk ricotta cheese
Flaky sea salt, such as Maldon
Small fresh basil and nasturtium leaves, for garnish

Wine: Robert Mondavi Winery Napa Valley Fumé Blanc Reserve

Prepare the pickled red onions: Cut off both ends of each onion, halve through the root end, and then peel. Thinly slice each half from stem to root. Put the onion slices into a nonreactive container.

In a saucepan, combine the vinegar, water, sugar, kosher salt, peppercorns, thyme, bay leaves, star anise, and cloves. Bring to a simmer over medium heat, stirring to dissolve the sugar. Remove from the heat and let steep for 30 minutes, then pour over the onions.

(continued)

chef's tip:

Refrigerate extra pesto in an airtight container, pressing a sheet of plastic wrap directly onto the surface, and use within a day. Or freeze in ice cube trays, then transfer the cubes to a plastic bag and store in the freezer for up to 3 months.

Spring Vegetable Salad *(continued)*

Let cool, then cover and refrigerate for at least 1 day before using. They will keep for up to 2 weeks.

Make the edible flower croccante: In a food processor, combine the flour, cornstarch, salt, and baking powder and pulse to blend. Add the oil and pulse several times until evenly blended. Pour in the ½ cup water and pulse just until the mixture comes together into a dough, adding a little more water if too dry. Gather into a ball, wrap in plastic wrap, and refrigerate until chilled.

Preheat the oven to 425°F or 400°F with a convection fan. Line a heavy baking sheet with parchment paper and spray the parchment with cooking spray.

Set up a pasta machine. On a lightly floured work surface, flatten the dough with a rolling pin into a rectangle thin enough to pass through the pasta machine set on the widest setting. Pass the dough through the rollers twice at the widest setting, then continue passing it through the rollers, tightening the rollers by one setting each time, until you have a 20-inch-long sheet. Lay the sheet on a work surface and lightly brush half the sheet (widthwise not lengthwise) with water. Arrange edible flowers and leaves on the moistened half, placing them close together—even overlapping—until they cover the surface. Fold the other half over to enclose the flowers, pressing with your hands to seal. Lightly flour both sides, then feed the dough sheet through the pasta machine, tightening the rollers by one setting each time, until the sheet is almost as thin as fresh pasta and you can see the flowers easily.

Cut the sheet into lengths that fit the prepared baking sheet. Transfer to the baking sheet (you may need to bake in batches), brush lightly with oil, sprinkle with flaky sea salt, and prick all over with a fork. Bake until lightly browned and crisp, about 8 minutes. Let cool, then break into rough pieces by hand.

Make the nasturtium pesto: Preheat the oven to 350°F. Toast the pine nuts in a pie pan until lightly colored and fragrant, 4 to 5 minutes. Let cool. Bring a large pot of salted water to a boil over high heat and prepare a bowl of ice water. Add the nasturtium leaves, push them under the water, and cook until just tender, about 45 seconds. Lift them out with a wire skimmer and transfer immediately to the ice water. When the water returns to a boil, add the basil, push the leaves under the water, and cook for about 30 seconds, then lift them out with the wire skimmer and transfer immediately to the ice water. When cooled, drain them and squeeze to remove as much water as possible.

Pour the grapeseed oil into a blender and add the greens, breaking them up a bit as they go into the jar. Add the pine nuts, garlic, cheese, and sea salt and blend until very smooth. Transfer to a bowl and taste for salt. You should have about ¾ cup pesto. Set aside ¼ cup pesto (and the 1 teaspoon lemon juice) for the salad and reserve the remainder for another use (see Chef's Tip).

Have ready a bowl of ice water. Halve the fennel bulb through the root. With a mandoline or other vegetable slicer, slice the fennel thinly from top to bottom (not crosswise). Put the fennel slices into the ice water to help them crisp and curl. Slice the radishes thinly with the mandoline or vegetable slicer. Add the radishes to the ice water to keep them crisp. Peel the carrot and, using a vegetable peeler, shave it lengthwise into thin ribbons.

Bring a small pot of salted water to a boil over high heat and prepare a bowl of ice water. Add the sugar snap peas to the boiling water and blanch for about 1 minute, then drain and immediately transfer to the ice water. When cool, drain and pat dry.

To assemble the salad, drain the fennel and radishes and pat dry. Put them into a bowl with the carrot and sugar snap peas. With a fork or slotted spoon, retrieve about one-fourth of the pickled red onions from the pickling liquid and add them to the bowl. (Reserve the remaining pickled onions for another use.) Add the olive oil, lemon juice, and sea salt to taste and toss gently.

Stir the lemon juice into the pesto to brighten the flavor. On each of four salad plates, put 1 tablespoon pesto and spread thinly with the back of a spoon. Put 3 tablespoons of the ricotta in the center of the plate. Mound the dressed vegetables on top of the ricotta, dividing them evenly. Sprinkle with flaky sea salt and garnish with basil and nasturtium leaves. Place 3 or 4 croccante shards around each salad and serve.

Parsley Fettuccine with Fava Beans, Peas, Spring Onions, and Parmesan Cream **Serves 6**

The garden's early fava beans and English peas are so moist and tender they hardly need cooking. Jeff tosses them with handmade fettuccine and a delicate cream sauce with just enough cheesy flavor to make the case for Pinot Noir.

Fettuccine:

1 cup Italian "00" flour (page 196), plus more for dusting

1 tablespoon finely minced fresh flat-leaf parsley

1 teaspoon sea salt

10 large egg yolks

1 teaspoon extra virgin olive oil

2 tablespoons water

Fine semolina, for dusting

Cream Sauce:

4 tablespoons unsalted butter

4 cloves garlic, thinly sliced

2 shallots, thinly sliced

3 cups heavy cream

Two 2-ounce pieces Parmigiano-Reggiano cheese rind

Sea salt and freshly ground white pepper

Grated zest of 1 lemon

1 cup shelled English peas

1 cup shelled and peeled fava beans

2 small spring onions, thinly sliced

Fresh edible flowers, for garnish

Wine: Robert Mondavi Winery Napa Valley Carneros Pinot Noir Reserve

Make the fettuccine: In a bowl, whisk together the flour, parsley, and salt. Make a well in the center. Put the egg yolks, oil, and water into the well. Mix with a fork, incorporating the flour gradually, then turn the dough out onto a work surface and knead until smooth and elastic, dusting lightly with flour as needed. Wrap in plastic wrap and refrigerate to rest for 30 minutes.

Stretch the dough with a pasta machine into a long, thin sheet. Cut into 10-inch lengths, then use the fettuccine attachment to cut noodles or cut by hand about 1/3 inch wide. Put the noodles on a baking sheet lightly dusted with semolina and let dry at room temperature for about 1 hour.

Make the cream sauce: Melt the butter in a saucepan over medium heat. Add the garlic and shallots and sauté until softened, about 3 minutes. Add the cream, cheese rinds, and a pinch each of salt and pepper and simmer gently until slightly thickened, about 20 minutes. Strain and transfer to a wide skillet large enough to hold the pasta. Add the lemon zest and taste for salt. Keep warm.

Bring a large pot of salted water to a boil over high heat and prepare a bowl of ice water. Add the peas and blanch for 1 minute, then transfer with a wire skimmer to the ice water. Drain when cool.

Add the pasta to the boiling water and cook until al dente. While the pasta cooks, add the peas, fava beans, and spring onions to the cream sauce and bring just to a simmer. With tongs, transfer the pasta to the skillet and toss to coat. Divide among six bowls, garnish with flowers, and serve.

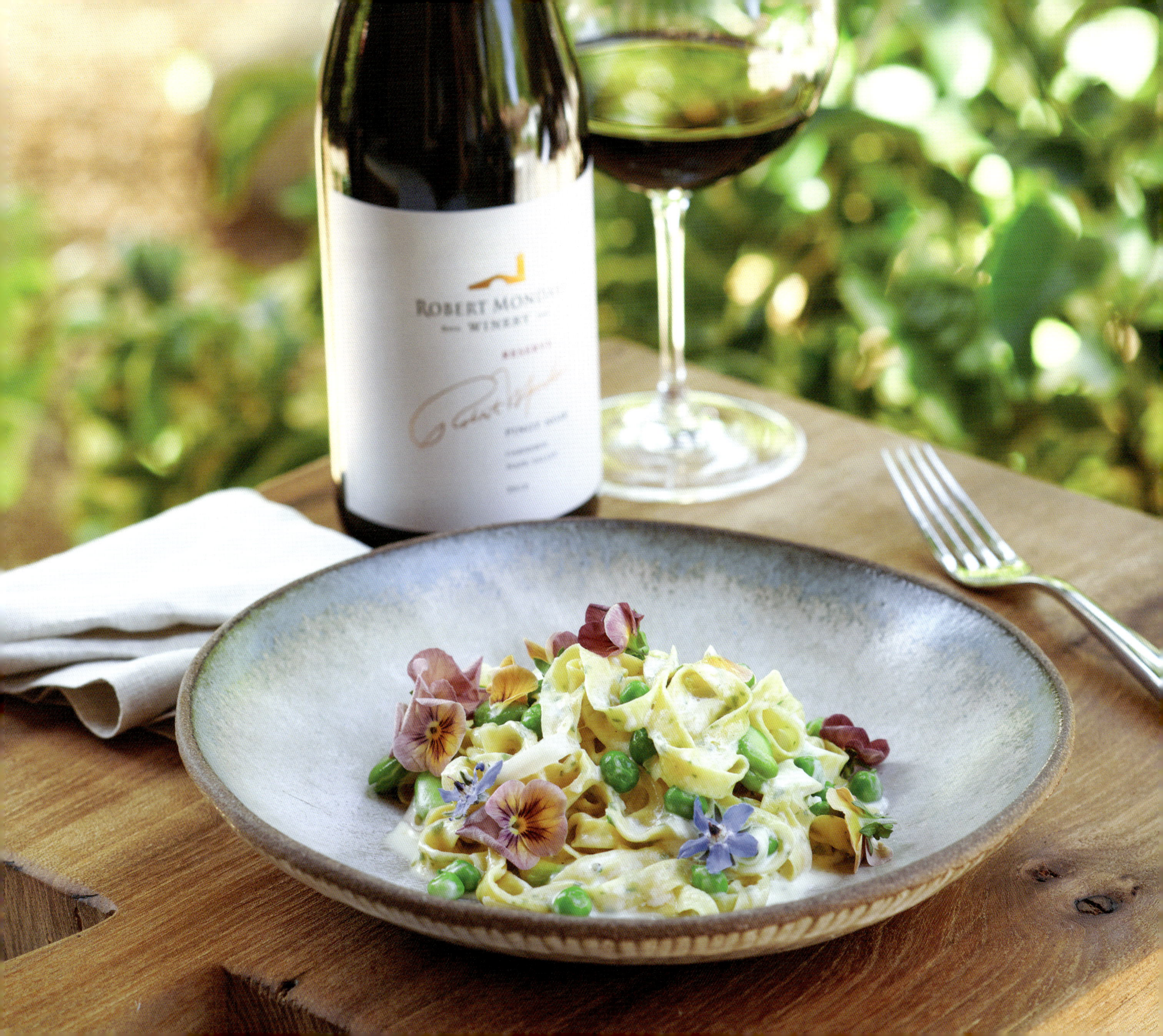
ROBERT
WINERY

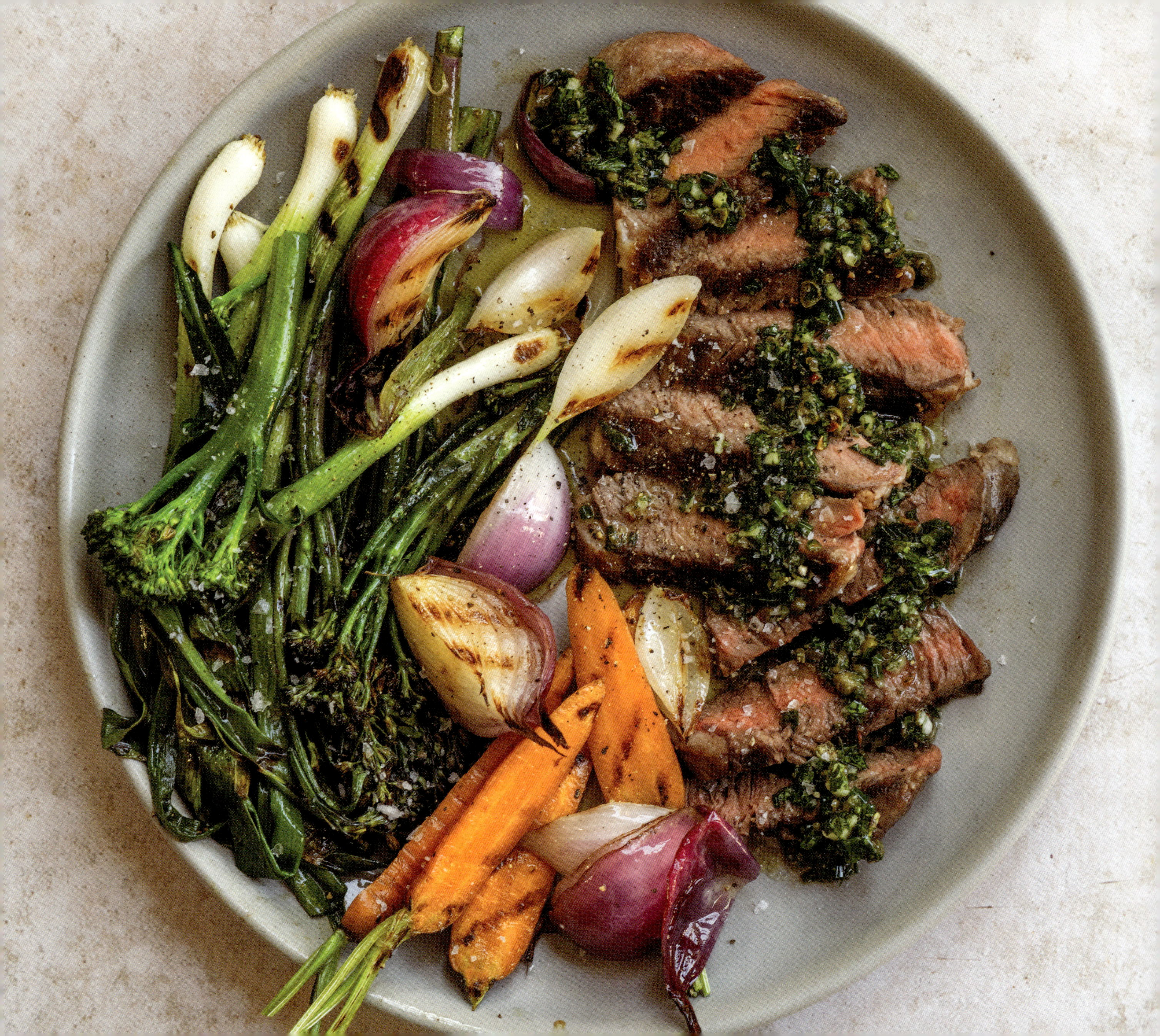

Grilled Rib Eye with Grilled Spring Vegetables and Salsa Verde **Serves 4**

To flatter the winery's signature wine, Cabernet Sauvignon, Jeff often grills thick steaks. A salsa verde with garden herbs makes a brighter, more contemporary accompaniment than a reduction sauce, and the vegetable garnish can change with the seasons. In spring, a bouquet of grilled baby turnips, carrots, spring onions, and sprouting broccoli gives the garden a chance to shine.

Salsa Verde:

½ cup plus 2 tablespoons extra virgin olive oil

¼ cup chopped fresh flat-leaf parsley

2 tablespoons minced fresh chives

1½ tablespoons minced fresh marjoram

1½ teaspoons minced garlic

1½ teaspoons brine-packed capers, well rinsed and coarsely chopped

¼ teaspoon red chile flakes

Grated zest of 1 lemon

Pinch of sea salt

Two ¾-pound boneless rib-eye steaks, at room temperature

Sea salt and freshly ground black pepper

4 small spring onions, ends trimmed

8 baby turnips, peeled and halved

8 baby carrots, peeled

12 broccoli di cicco (sprouting broccoli) florets

¼ pound king trumpet mushrooms, cleaned and halved lengthwise

Extra virgin olive oil

½ lemon

Wine: Robert Mondavi Winery Napa Valley Cabernet Sauvignon Reserve

Make the salsa verde: In a medium bowl, combine all the ingredients and mix well.

Prepare a hot charcoal fire or preheat a gas grill to high. Season the steaks well on both sides with salt and pepper. Grill until well seared on one side, about 5 minutes, then turn and grill until done to your taste, about 4 minutes longer for medium-rare. Set aside to rest while you grill the vegetables.

Coat all the vegetables and mushrooms lightly with oil. Season with salt and pepper. Grill, turning as needed, until just tender. The spring onions will cook the fastest, in about 2 minutes. The turnips and carrots will take the longest, about 5 minutes.

Put the salsa verde into a small saucepan and warm gently over low heat. Do not allow it to boil. Remove from the heat and add a squeeze of lemon juice to brighten the flavor.

Slice the steaks on the diagonal to desired thickness. Divide the steak and the vegetables and mushrooms among four plates. Drizzle the salsa verde over all and serve.

Cheesecake with Blueberry Gelée

Serves 12

Crust:

½ cup unsalted butter, at room temperature, in small cubes

¼ cup granulated sugar

Pinch of sea salt

1 large egg yolk

¾ cup all-purpose flour, measured then sifted

Filling:

1 pound cream cheese, at room temperature

1 cup granulated sugar

4 large eggs

1 teaspoon pure vanilla extract

Pinch of sea salt

Topping:

¾ pound blueberries

⅓ cup loosely packed light brown sugar

Pinch of sea salt

8 sheets leaf gelatin

Garnish:

2 cups blueberries, some halved

24 strawberries, hulled and quartered

Granulated sugar

Fresh edible flowers

Wine: Robert Mondavi Winery Napa Valley Moscato d'Oro

The winery garden yields just enough blueberries to use them judiciously in desserts—as a wine-dark gelée on top of a cheesecake, for example. With this strategy, a dozen people can enjoy a taste of this sweet-tart fruit without wiping out the week's harvest. The winery's fragrant Moscato d'Oro, with its honeysuckle aroma, was a favorite of Margrit Mondavi.

Make the crust: In a stand mixer fitted with the paddle attachment, cream the butter on medium speed until smooth. Gradually add the granulated sugar, stopping to scrape down the sides of the bowl once or twice. Add the salt, then the egg yolk and beat until blended. On low speed, add the flour and beat just until blended. Gather the dough, flatten it into the shape of a hamburger patty, wrap in plastic wrap, and refrigerate for at least 30 minutes or up to 1 day.

Preheat the oven to 350°F. Unwrap the dough and place it between two sheets of parchment paper. With a rolling pin, flatten it into a 9-inch round of even thickness. With scissors, trim the excess parchment. Lift off the top sheet of parchment. If it threatens to stick, return the dough to the refrigerator until chilled, then try again. Invert the dough onto the bottom of a 9-inch springform pan with the sides removed and lift off the parchment. Reattach the sides of the springform pan.

Bake the crust, rotating the pan 180 degrees halfway through baking, until very lightly colored, 8 to 12 minutes. Let cool on a wire rack for 30 minutes.

Make the filling: In a stand mixer fitted with the whisk attachment, whip the cream cheese on medium speed until creamy. Scrape down the sides of the bowl and the whisk. Gradually add the granulated sugar and beat until light and smooth. Add the eggs one at a time, beating well after each addition. Add the vanilla and salt, mixing well.

Pour the filling into the springform pan. Grasping the sides of the pan, tap the pan vigorously two or three times on a work surface to deflate any bubbles. Bake the cake, rotating the pan 180 degrees halfway through baking, until a cake tester inserted into the center comes out clean, about 45 minutes. Let cool on the rack.

Make the topping: In a small saucepan, combine the blueberries, brown sugar, and salt. Cook over medium-low heat, stirring until the sugar dissolves and mashing the blueberries lightly with a wooden spoon to release some of their juices, for 5 to 10 minutes. Transfer to a blender and blend until smooth. For extra smoothness, press the mixture through a fine-mesh sieve into a bowl.

Put the gelatin sheets into a bowl of ice water to cover and let soften until pliable, about 3 minutes. Lift them out and squeeze dry. Put them into a small saucepan over low heat just until they melt, then stir them into the warm blueberry puree. Let the puree cool until it begins to set, about 30 minutes.

Pour the blueberry mixture on top of the cooled cheesecake, spreading it almost to the edge but leaving a narrow rim. You may not need all the blueberry mixture. With an offset spatula, level the topping. Refrigerate the cheesecake until chilled.

To serve, slice the cheesecake into 12 wedges, wiping the knife after every cut. Transfer to individual plates and scatter the blueberries around each slice. Toss the strawberries with sugar to taste. If desired, arrange the sugared berries on a baking sheet and use a kitchen torch to melt and caramelize the sugar. Otherwise, simply scatter the sugared berries around each slice. Garnish with edible flowers.

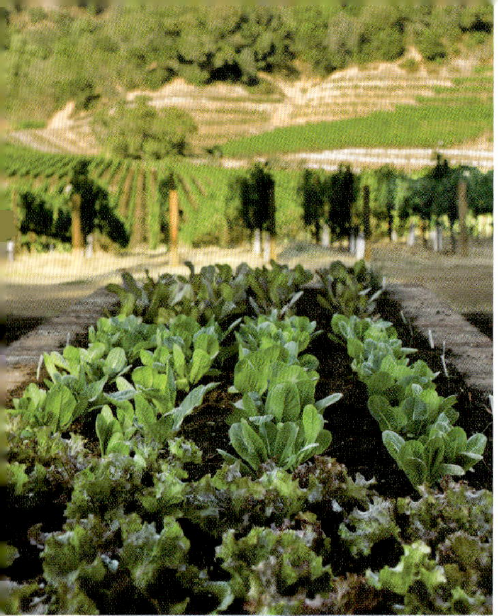

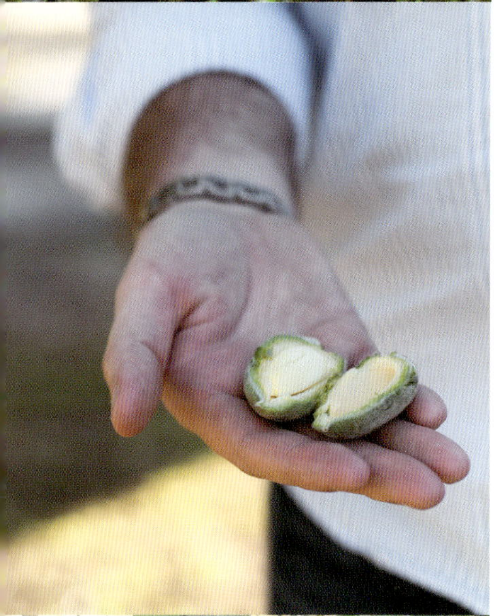

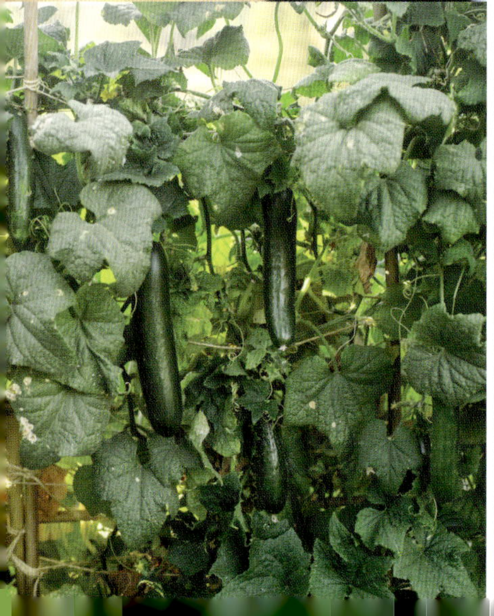

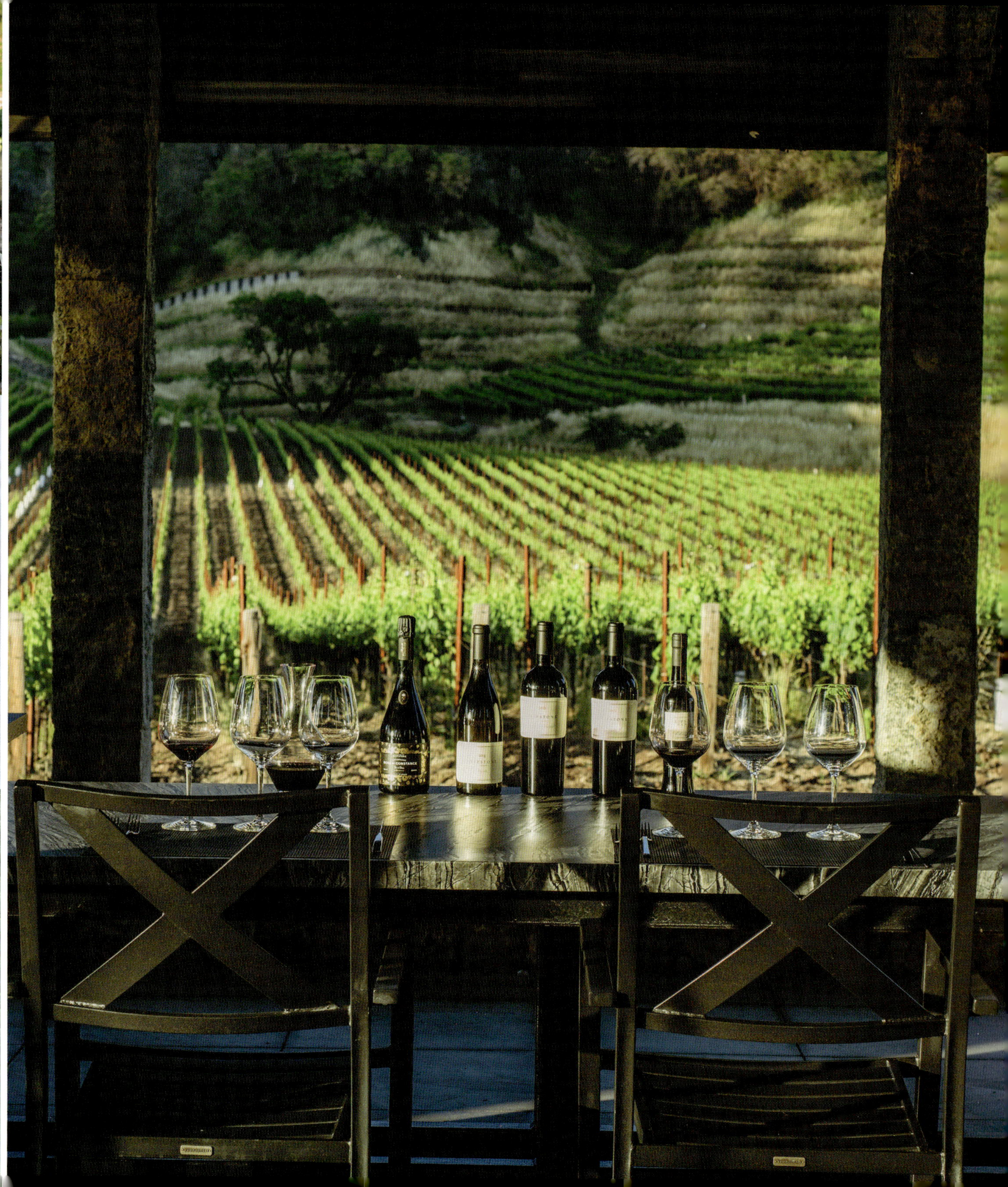

Skipstone: *A Mediterranean Tribute*

Geyserville

Maybe you can't go home again, but Fahri Diner has come close with Skipstone. The hilly, hidden two-hundred-acre property near Healdsburg so closely resembles his native Cyprus that the first sight of it brought him to tears. After a year of searching for a wine country getaway, he had found the one he had to own. A former cattle ranch, the bowl-shaped parcel had grapevine-covered hillsides and a hilltop home with an unparalleled view of the Alexander Valley. The son and grandson of Cypriot olive growers, Fahri had grown up in the Eastern Mediterranean, playing among olive, citrus, and almond trees, and he wanted a similar rural experience for his children.

In 2000, he purchased the parcel and began to transform it. He replanted the vineyards with top-tier wine in mind and established more olive and fruit trees. "Olive oil is in my DNA," says Fahri, a technology entrepreneur and venture capitalist. The Alexander Valley has long been a prime region for apples and plums, but Fahri added to the collection, planting peaches, pears, quinces, figs, pomegranates, persimmons, loquats, and almonds in homage to the island landscape of his childhood.

"Almonds are everywhere in Cyprus," says the vintner. "You can eat them from March to September. In early spring, you can bite into them like a fruit." A spongy green hull surrounds the moist, skinless almond kernel initially. At that early stage, says Fahri, you can pound the soft almonds with water, then strain the mixture to produce sweet fresh almond milk. Over the summer months, the kernel develops its papery brown skin and pockmarked shell, and the hull hardens until it splits open to release the delectable nut.

The Skipstone vegetable garden is a handsome collection of raised beds built from stones gathered on the property, then edged in red brick and surrounded by soft bark paths. Frilly lettuces make a burgundy and emerald-green carpet in some of the beds. In others, cucumbers clamber up a bamboo trellis constructed on a slant so the dangling fruits will be easy to spot. Tomatoes consume much of the real estate in summer, with other produce essential to the Cypriot table—sweet peppers, eggplants, zucchini, potatoes, basil, red onions, and garlic—in supporting roles. Patches of tomatillos, jalapeños, and red hibiscus (dried and used for beverages in the Mexican kitchen) reflect Fahri's insistence that the "family" this family garden serves includes every member of the mostly Hispanic staff. Employees eat from the garden more often than he does.

Left and above: *(clockwise from bottom left) Trellised cucumbers; spring's green (unripe) almonds are moist and tasty; flourishing lettuces; Skipstone's outdoor tasting pavilion; winery owners Fahri and Constance Diner*

Fahri and his own family—his wife, Constance, and four children—live on the property only part time, but those days are treasured ones. The two younger children love to gather strawberries from the raised beds and fresh eggs from the chicken coop, a pristine two-level residence for several pampered free-range hens. The youngsters are "always out there," says their father, "and that's important to me. I think it's part of their whole education, playing in the dirt and picking olives. I want them to learn respect for the soil."

Fahri and Constance, a former luxury-brands marketer, travel widely and sample the local specialties with enthusiasm, but the Mediterranean way of eating appeals to them most—a diet driven by what's in the garden, prepared with minimal manipulation.

"My philosophy of cooking is salt, pepper, and olive oil," jokes Fahri. "I'm very simple. I run in the morning, and when I come back for breakfast, I have cucumbers, tomatoes, and fried eggs."

His tastes may be humble but Fahri loves to cook, and his outdoor kitchen—designed with large gatherings in mind—has the capabilities any serious chef would want: a wood-burning oven, built-in grill, huge cast-iron skillets, and vast granite countertops. Just steps from the garden, the cooking pavilion is the stage in this peaceful natural amphitheater, embraced by hills cloaked in grapevines and oaks.

Several times during the year, Fahri and Constance host alfresco dinners for fans of their wines. As Fahri had hoped, the site has proven to be a world-class vineyard, and Skipstone wines—a Viognier and three red bottlings from Bordeaux varieties, all crafted by acclaimed

Above: *(clockwise from far left) Vineyard at the base of the hills; Fahri and Constance inspect the fall garden; newly planted stone beds; sheep control vineyard weeds; hillside vines; drying garlic; salad greens*

Skipstone's garden evokes the sweetest moments from Fahri's Cyprus childhood, and he and Constance hope to create similar memories for their own children.

winemaker Philippe Melka—are prized by collectors. The annual harvest party in September gives enthusiasts a chance to savor these superb wines in the setting that birthed them, with food prepared by Laura and Sayat Ozyilmaz, young San Francisco chefs who help Fahri bring his Mediterranean heritage to the table. Lamb raised on the property is typically the centerpiece (Skipstone relies on sheep for organic weed control), and the chefs have the run of the garden.

Sayat is Turkish and Laura is Mexican, a culinary marriage that, unlikely as it might seem, results in some delightfully original food. Collaborating with the Diners on an autumn menu to showcase Skipstone wines, the chefs devised a first course that plays cleverly with color. The painterly composition pairs Fuyu persimmons from

Skipstone 171

Skipstone trees with sashimi-style salmon, lightly salt cured and garnished with coral-colored pearls of salmon roe. Small dollops of *zhug*, an Egyptian herb paste, are the genius touch that shakes everything up. The plating is lovely, the combination inspired. What's more, it goes with Rose de Constance, a brut Champagne that Fahri commissioned to honor his wife.

Skipstone's Viognier is bright and fresh, with lively aromas of citrus blossom and stone fruit, a refreshing complement to a dish rich in olive oil. To match this graceful white, the menu looks next to

Above and right: *(clockwise from left) Signature Skipstone wines and estate olive oil; green almonds are a delicacy in Cyprus, Fahri's native country; Alexander Valley sunset view; estate vineyards in the setting sun*

zeytinyağli, a classic Turkish cooking method for slowly poaching vegetables—in this case, flat romano beans simmered gently in Skipstone extra virgin olive oil with tomato and garlic. The beans become silky and heightened in flavor, and they improve in the fridge overnight. Skipstone's wood-burning oven is fired up for the accompanying *pide*, or flatbread, spread with mellow Turkish red pepper paste and olives.

Skipstone's powerful red wines welcome bigger flavors from the garden: smoky eggplant, concentrated tomato, roasted garlic, well-browned potatoes. For Faultline Vineyard, the winery's blend of Cabernet Franc and Merlot, a modern *imam bayildi* reimagines the beloved Turkish home-style recipe of braised eggplant, tomato, and onions. In this deconstructed version, the dish is a sophisticated eggplant carpaccio on a bed of saffron-scented tomato sauce.

To showcase Oliver's Blend, Skipstone's Cabernet Sauvignon–dominated bottling, thick lamb shoulder chops are seasoned with an herb-and-spice mixture as complex as the wine. Seared on the outdoor grill and served with crusty creamer potatoes, the lamb demonstrates how compelling a sizzling, simply cooked chop can be with a profound red wine.

The almond trees at Skipstone don't produce enough crop to sell but plenty for snacking and the occasional dessert. Fahri's fondness for the nuts determined the meal's finale, an almond and semolina cake perfumed with grated citrus zest. After baking, the warm cake is brushed repeatedly with citrus syrup, a reference to the syrup-drenched semolina cakes of Turkey and Greece. Fruit from the garden almost always accompanies it: poached quinces or pears in autumn; citrus in winter; loquats in late spring; *fraises des bois* or sugared peaches in summer.

For Fahri, Skipstone calls to mind the sweetest scenes and sounds from his childhood: walks with his grandfather, fields of sunflowers, grazing sheep, squawking chickens. Hoping to create a similar highlight reel for his own children, he and Constance have fashioned a wine country escape that others can enjoy as well.

menu

Lightly Cured Salmon with Salmon Roe, Zhug, and Persimmons

Skipstone Rose de Constance Champagne

Eggplant Bayildi with Tomato, Saffron, and Pine Nut Sauce

Skipstone Faultline Vineyard

Zeytinyagli Green Beans with Olive Flatbread

Skipstone Viognier

Grilled Lamb Shoulder Chops with Cyprus Potatoes

Skipstone Oliver's Blend

Almond and Semolina Cake with Quince Spoon Sweet

Skipstone Rose de Constance Champagne

Lightly Cured Salmon with Salmon Roe, Zhug, and Persimmons Serves 6

¾ pound sushi-grade fresh skinless salmon fillet, pin bones removed

½ teaspoon sea salt

2 tablespoons Zhug (recipe follows)

2 tablespoons extra virgin olive oil

1 tablespoon fresh lemon juice

1 large or 2 small Fuyu persimmons

6 tablespoons salmon roe (about 3 ounces)

Wine: Skipstone Rose de Constance Champagne

Season the salmon all over with the salt. Put the salmon on a parchment-lined plate, cover with plastic wrap, and refrigerate for 1 hour to firm the flesh.

In a small bowl, mix together the *zhug*, oil, and lemon juice to make a paste.

Remove the persimmon cap. Cut the persimmon in half through the stem. Lay cut side down and slice paper-thin by hand or with a mandoline. You will need a total of 30 half-moon slices.

Slice the salmon in half down the center, then slice crosswise about ⅛ inch thick. You will need a total of 30 slices.

On six serving plates, alternate slices of salmon and persimmon, using 5 slices of each for each serving. Dot each serving with 1 teaspoon of the *zhug* paste, then spoon 1 tablespoon salmon roe over each serving.

The Fuyu persimmon trees at Skipstone inspired this dish, which plays on the visual similarity between the fruit and the fish. Nectarines, peaches, or even pears can replace the persimmons when they are out of season.

Classic zhug, the Egyptian hot sauce, relies primarily on cilantro and parsley, but Laura and Sayat often incorporate other herbs from the Skipstone garden, such as tarragon, chives, and chervil. Zhug will last for up to 1 month, refrigerated, if you add the lemon juice just before using; with the lemon juice, it will last up to 5 days.

Zhug Makes about 1 cup

½ cup extra virgin olive oil

¼ cup chopped fresh cilantro

¼ cup chopped fresh flat-leaf parsley

2 teaspoons sea salt

1 teaspoon Garlic Confit (recipe below)

½ teaspoon ground cardamom

¼ teaspoon ground cloves

¼ teaspoon ground cumin

¼ teaspoon ground fenugreek

¼ teaspoon Aleppo pepper

Fresh Meyer lemon juice

In a bowl, whisk together all the ingredients, adding the lemon juice to taste.

Garlic Confit: In a small saucepan, combine 12 peeled large garlic cloves and vegetable oil to cover (about ½ cup). Cook over low heat until the cloves are soft but not colored, about 20 minutes. (Use a flame tamer if necessary to keep the cloves from browning.) Let cool, then scoop out the garlic cloves, reserving the flavorful oil for another use. Puree the garlic in a small food processor or spice grinder or pound to a paste in a mortar. Makes about 2 tablespoons.

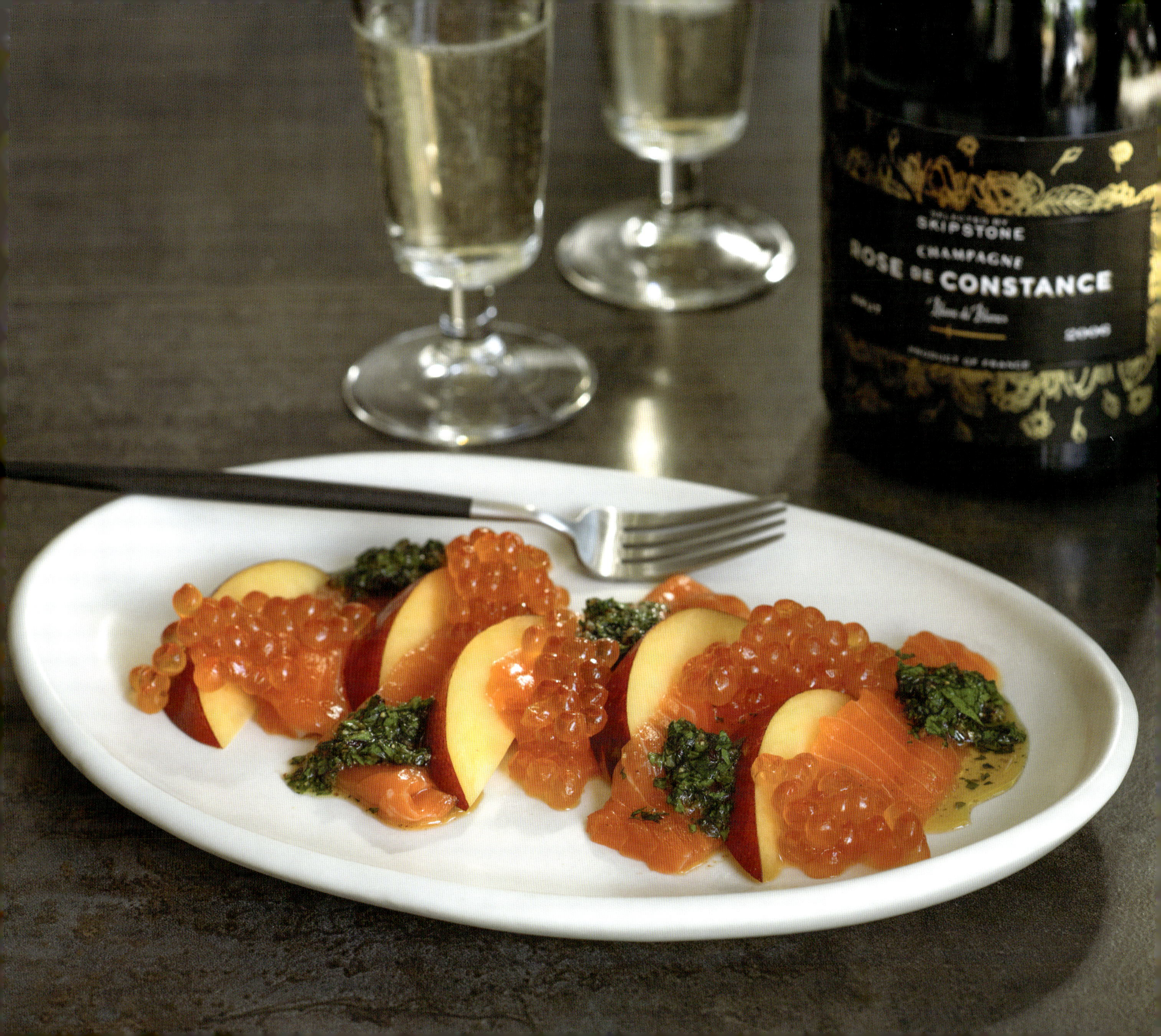
SKIPSTONE
CHAMPAGNE
CONSTANCE

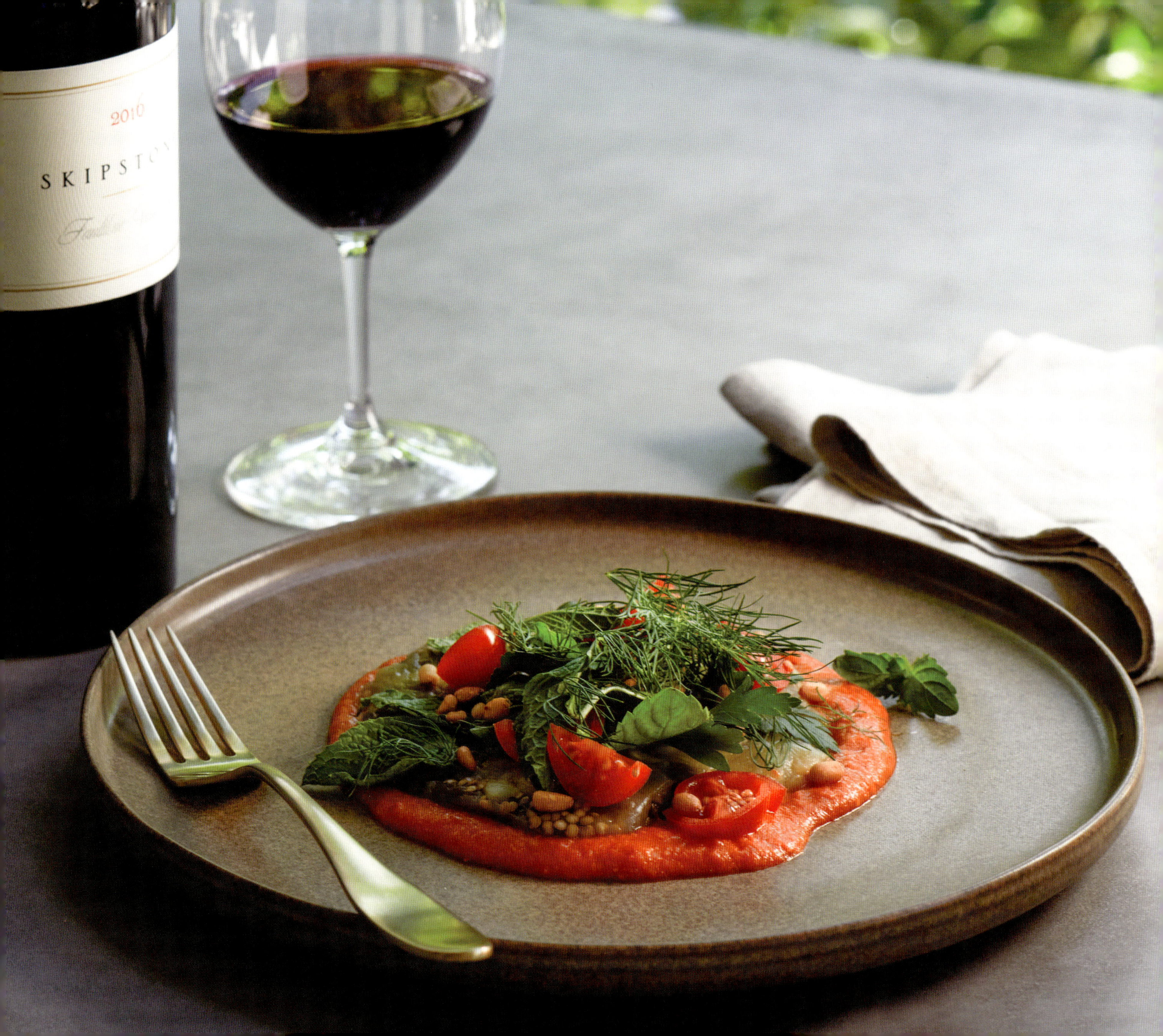
2010
SKIPSTON

Eggplant Bayildi with Tomato, Saffron, and Pine Nut Sauce

Serves 6

This dish is an updated interpretation of imam bayildi—*"the priest fainted"—the classic Turkish stuffed-eggplant recipe. Supposedly, he fainted with pleasure. Who knows what might have happened had he encountered this magnificent version? Laura and Sayat deconstruct the original dish, arranging smoky eggplant "carpaccio" on a bed of tomato and pine nut sauce. A whole-leaf herb salad on top adds a burst of freshness.*

1 large globe eggplant, 1¼ to 1½ pounds

Sea salt

¼ cup plus 3 tablespoons extra virgin olive oil, plus more for drizzling

1 large yellow onion, diced

5 large cloves garlic, thinly sliced

2 tablespoons mild Turkish red pepper paste

Pinch of saffron threads

1 cup diced Roma tomatoes (no need to peel)

⅓ cup untoasted pine nuts, plus toasted pine nuts for garnish

½ cup water

Mixed fresh whole herb leaves, such as dill, cilantro, flat-leaf parsley, thyme, and mint, for serving

18 cherry tomatoes, quartered

Wine: Skipstone Faultline Vineyard

Over a gas flame or charcoal fire, roast the eggplant, turning it often, until it is blackened all over and completely soft, 10 to 20 minutes. The stem area is the last part to soften, so be sure to check there. Transfer the eggplant to a bowl and cover the bowl tightly with plastic wrap; let the eggplant steam until cool, then peel carefully, removing all traces of burnt skin. Break up any large pieces with your hands, season with salt, and then drain the eggplant flesh in a sieve for 30 minutes.

While the eggplant drains, heat 3 tablespoons of the oil in a saucepan over medium heat. Add the onion and garlic and sauté until soft and sweet, about 10 minutes. Add the pepper paste and saffron and sauté, stirring, for about 2 minutes, then add the Roma tomatoes and cook, stirring often, until the tomatoes have broken down and the mixture is thick, about 10 minutes. Add the pine nuts, 1½ teaspoons salt, and ¼ cup of the water, reduce the heat to low, and cook, stirring occasionally, until the mixture is very thick, about 15 minutes.

Transfer the contents of the saucepan to a blender, add the remaining ¼ cup water, and blend well. With the blender running, add the remaining ¼ cup olive oil, blending until smooth.

Return the sauce to the saucepan and cook over low heat, stirring often, until it darkens, about 15 minutes, adding a splash of water to thin if needed. Taste for salt. Keep warm.

Put ¼ cup of the roasted eggplant between two sheets of plastic wrap and flatten gently with the bottom of a 1-cup measuring cup into a 6-inch circle of even thickness. Repeat to make 5 more rounds.

Put about 3 tablespoons of the warm tomato sauce on each of six salad plates. Spread the sauce thinly with the back of a soupspoon. Working with 1 eggplant round at a time, remove the top sheet of plastic wrap and invert the eggplant round onto one of the prepared salad plates. Carefully peel off the second sheet of plastic. Repeat with the remaining eggplant rounds.

Put a tuft of mixed herbs on each eggplant round. Scatter the cherry tomatoes and toasted pine nuts on top, dividing them both evenly. Sprinkle with a little sea salt and drizzle with oil. Serve immediately.

Zeytinyagli Green Beans with Olive Flatbread Serves 6

Zeytinyağli is the Turkish name for vegetables cooked slowly in olive oil until tender. Many vegetables are prepared this way—green beans, carrots, artichokes, potatoes, celery root, red peppers—and they last for several days in the fridge. Typically, they are served at room temperature as part of an assortment of appetizers, or meze. For this contemporary presentation, the soft green beans are topped with crunchy fried capers and served with an olive-topped flatbread to soak up the juices.

1 pound green beans, preferably romano type, ends trimmed

⅓ pound cherry tomatoes

1 large yellow onion, very coarsely chopped

3 cloves garlic, peeled

2 cups extra virgin olive oil

Juice of 1 lemon

2½ tablespoons sea salt

2 cups water

Vegetable oil, for deep-frying

¼ cup plus 2 tablespoons brine-packed capers, rinsed and patted thoroughly dry

Fresh thyme or lemon thyme sprigs, for garnish

Olive Flatbread (recipe follows)

Wine: Skipstone Viognier

In a heavy pot, combine the green beans, tomatoes, onion, garlic, olive oil, lemon juice, salt, and water. The liquid will not cover the beans. Cover the beans with a round of parchment paper cut just to fit inside the pot.

Bring the liquid to a bare simmer over medium heat and adjust the heat to maintain a bare simmer. Cook until the beans are almost tender, about 25 minutes. Remove from the heat and let the beans cool in the liquid to room temperature. They will continue to cook as they cool and should be tender after cooling.

In a small, heavy saucepan, pour vegetable oil to a depth of 2 inches and heat to 375°F. Add the capers and fry until crisp, about 2 minutes. Transfer them with a wire-mesh skimmer to paper towels to drain.

With a slotted spoon, transfer the green beans and tomatoes to a platter or individual plates. Garnish with the fried capers and a few sprigs of thyme. Drizzle with some of the olive oil from the pot. Serve immediately with the flatbread.

chef's tip:

Don't be put off by the amount of olive oil required. The oil picks up flavor from the green beans and seasonings, and you can use it for salad dressings or on fish or steamed vegetables.

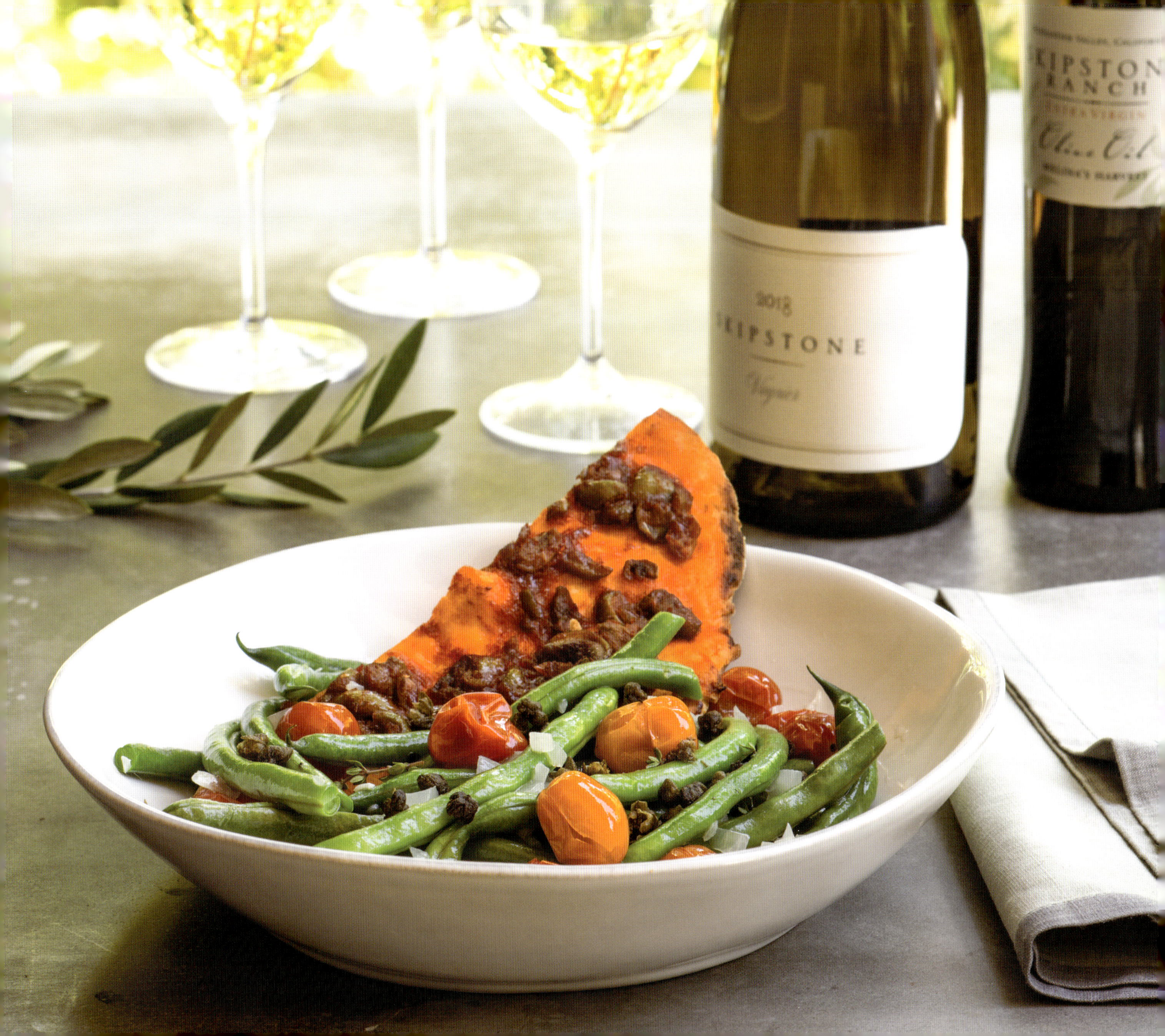
2018

Olive Flatbread

Makes 3 flatbreads; serves 6

Dough:

¾ cup plus 2 tablespoons warm water (105°F to 115°F)

1½ teaspoons active dry yeast

1 cup plus 1 tablespoon unbleached all-purpose flour, plus more for dusting

1 cup plus 1 tablespoon bread flour

2 teaspoons sugar

1½ teaspoons sea salt

1½ tablespoons extra virgin olive oil

Topping:

1 cup coarsely chopped green olives, such as Castelvetrano, Lucques, or Picholine

6 tablespoons mild Turkish red pepper paste

3 tablespoons extra virgin olive oil

The chopped-olive topping on this flatbread is a tribute to Fahri and his upbringing as the son of an olive grower. Add chopped walnuts to the topping, if you like.

Prepare the dough: Combine the water and yeast in the bowl of a stand mixer and whisk to dissolve the yeast. In a bowl, whisk together both flours and the sugar to blend. Add to the yeast mixture, fit the mixer with the dough hook, and mix on low speed until a shaggy mass forms, about 1 minute. Let stand for 20 to 30 minutes.

Add the salt and mix on low speed for 2 minutes. Increase the speed to medium and mix for 5 minutes. Turn off the mixer, add the oil, and then mix on low speed until blended. If the mixer does not readily incorporate the oil, remove the bowl from the mixer, knead the dough by hand until the oil is incorporated, and then return the bowl to the mixer. Increase the speed to medium and mix for 2 minutes.

Remove the dough hook, cover the bowl, and let the dough rise at room temperature for 1 hour. Transfer the dough to a work surface and fold in thirds, then place in a lightly oiled bowl or tub, cover, and refrigerate for at least 8 hours or up to 24 hours. Remove the dough from the refrigerator 1 hour before shaping it. Divide the dough into 3 equal balls. Put the balls on a lightly floured work surface and cover lightly with a clean kitchen towel. Let rest for 20 minutes.

Put a pizza stone in the oven and preheat the oven to 500°F for at least 30 minutes. If the oven has a convection fan, turn it on.

Prepare the topping: In a bowl, mix together the olives, pepper paste, and oil.

On a large sheet of parchment paper lightly dusted with flour, roll 1 ball of dough into an oval roughly 12 inches long and 7 inches wide. Cover with one-third of the topping, spreading it evenly to the edges. Trim any excess parchment with scissors.

Slide a rimless baking sheet or pizza peel under the parchment, then slide the flatbread, still on the parchment, onto the preheated pizza stone. Bake until golden brown, 7 to 8 minutes. Transfer to a cutting board and cut into 6 equal pieces. Repeat with remaining 2 dough balls. Serve hot or warm.

Grilled Lamb Shoulder Chops with Cyprus Potatoes Serves 4

Lamb Marinade:

¼ cup extra virgin olive oil

1½ teaspoons honey

Grated zest of 1 small orange

1½ teaspoons sea salt

½ teaspoon dry mustard

½ teaspoon minced fresh rosemary

½ teaspoon dried lavender flowers

½ teaspoon dried oregano

½ teaspoon Sichuan peppercorns

¼ teaspoon cumin seeds

¼ teaspoon caraway seeds

4 lamb shoulder blade chops, about ½ pound each

Cyprus Potatoes:

1½ pounds Yukon Gold potatoes, 1½ inches in diameter

3 ounces cherry tomatoes (about 15)

2 large cloves garlic, peeled

1 Meyer lemon, sliced

1½ cups extra virgin olive oil

1½ tablespoons sea salt

4 cups water

1 tablespoon Garlic Confit (page 174)

Grated zest of 1 Meyer lemon

¼ cup thinly sliced fresh chives

Wine: Skipstone Oliver's Blend

The rosemary and lavender that grow so profusely at Skipstone are go-to seasonings for the ranch's lamb. The crusty potatoes that accompany the chops are first poached in olive oil, then crisped in a hot oven just before serving. Lemon zest and garlic confit take them over the top. Small waxy creamer potatoes are ideal. Save the flavorful poaching oil and use it in vinaigrettes or on steamed vegetables or fish.

Prepare the marinade: In a small bowl, combine the oil, honey, and orange zest. In a spice grinder or in a mortar, combine the salt, mustard, rosemary, lavender, oregano, Sichuan peppercorns, cumin seeds, and caraway seeds and grind finely. Whisk into the oil mixture. Coat the lamb with the marinade, then put the lamb into a heavy-duty resealable plastic bag and refrigerate for 24 hours. Bring to room temperature before grilling.

Prepare the potatoes: In a saucepan, combine the potatoes, tomatoes, garlic, sliced lemon, oil, salt, and water and bring to a simmer over medium heat. Adjust the heat to maintain a bare simmer and cook until the potatoes are just tender when pierced, 20 to 40 minutes, depending on size. Let cool in the liquid.

Prepare a hot charcoal fire or preheat a gas grill to high. Also preheat the oven to 475°F or 450°F with a convection fan. Line a baking sheet with parchment paper.

Grill the chops to desired doneness, about 5 minutes per side for medium, depending on thickness. (Shoulder chops are best when cooked to at least medium.) Set aside to rest for 5 minutes.

While the chops are on the grill, lift the potatoes out of the cooking liquid with a slotted spoon (leaving the tomatoes behind) and transfer to a bowl. Add the garlic confit and salt to taste and toss well to coat the potatoes evenly with the garlic. Arrange the potatoes on the prepared baking sheet and bake until crisp and sizzling, about 10 minutes. Transfer to a serving bowl, add the lemon zest and chives, and toss well. If desired, add 1 to 2 tablespoons oil from the cooking liquid—just enough to make the potatoes glisten—and toss again.

Divide the chops among four dinner plates and spoon some of the hot potatoes alongside. Serve immediately.

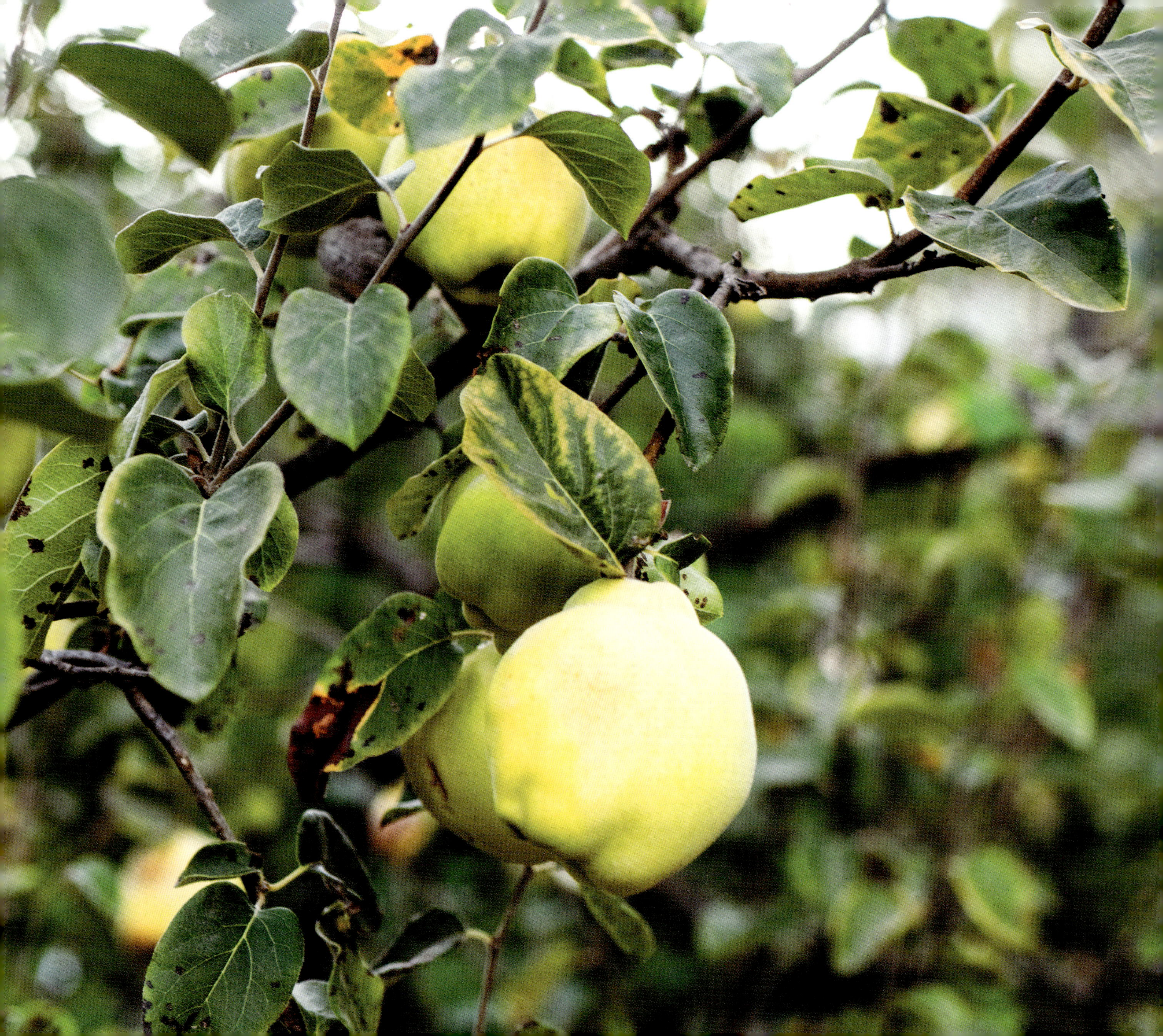

Almond and Semolina Cake with Quince Spoon Sweet

Serves 12

2¼ cups almond flour

1¼ cups fine semolina

2 teaspoons baking powder

Pinch of sea salt

4 large eggs, at room temperature

1 cup plus 2 tablespoons sugar

1 teaspoon pure vanilla extract

1 tablespoon fresh lemon juice

1 tablespoon fresh orange juice

Grated zest of 1 lemon

Grated zest of 1 orange

1 cup extra virgin olive oil

1 cup whole milk

Syrup:

⅓ cup fresh orange juice

⅓ cup sugar

⅓ cup water

2 tablespoons honey

Quince Spoon Sweet:

2 cups sugar

2 cups water

3 pineapple quinces, peeled, each cut into 8 wedges, and cored (reserve peels and core)

Fresh lemon juice

Wine: Skipstone Rose de Constance Champagne

Made with extra virgin olive oil, this moist cake speaks to Fahri's childhood among the olive groves his father and grandfather tended. It welcomes a fruit accompaniment, such as berries or poached quince. These hard, knobby fruits are beloved in Cyprus, and Fahri made sure to plant some at Skipstone. When simmered for several hours in light syrup, they turn a gorgeous ruby color and resemble the preserve-like "spoon sweets" enjoyed in Greece.

Preheat the oven to 350°F. Butter the bottom and sides of a 10-by-3-inch round cake pan. Line the bottom with a round of parchment paper, then flour the pan sides, shaking out any excess.

In a bowl, whisk together the almond flour, semolina, baking powder, and salt. In a stand mixer fitted with the whisk attachment, whip together the eggs, sugar, and vanilla on medium speed until very light, about 5 minutes. Add the lemon and orange juices and zests and whip until blended.

Reduce the speed to medium-low, add the oil, and beat until blended. Then gradually add the dry ingredients, beating just until blended. Scrape down the sides of the bowl, reduce the mixer speed to low, add the milk, and beat just until blended. The batter will be thin. Pour the batter into the prepared pan. Bake the cake until the top is golden brown and a cake tester inserted into the middle comes out clean, about 55 minutes. Let rest in the pan on a rack for 20 minutes. Run a paring knife around the perimeter of the pan to loosen the cake. Invert the cake onto the rack, remove the pan, peel off the parchment, and then invert again onto another rack to finish cooling.

Prepare the syrup: In a small saucepan, combine the orange juice, sugar, water, and honey and bring to a simmer over medium-low heat, stirring to dissolve the sugar. Let cool. Brush the top of the cooled cake generously with the syrup. Wait for 5 minutes, then brush again. Repeat until you have used all the syrup.

Prepare the spoon sweet: In a heavy saucepan large enough to hold the quince, bring the sugar and water to a boil over high heat, stirring to dissolve the sugar. Add the quince wedges, peels, and cores and return to a simmer. Cook uncovered until the fruit turns a deep burgundy, which may take as long as 3 hours. Transfer the quince wedges to a heatproof bowl. Using a fine-mesh sieve, strain the syrup over the wedges and discard the peels and cores. Add lemon juice to taste to the syrup. Let cool, then chill.

Cut the cake into 12 equal portions. Accompany each portion with 2 quince wedges and some of the quince syrup.

Above and right: *Estate-grown olives ripening; olive trees line the road to the top of the hill, where the sweeping view encompasses much of the Alexander Valley.*

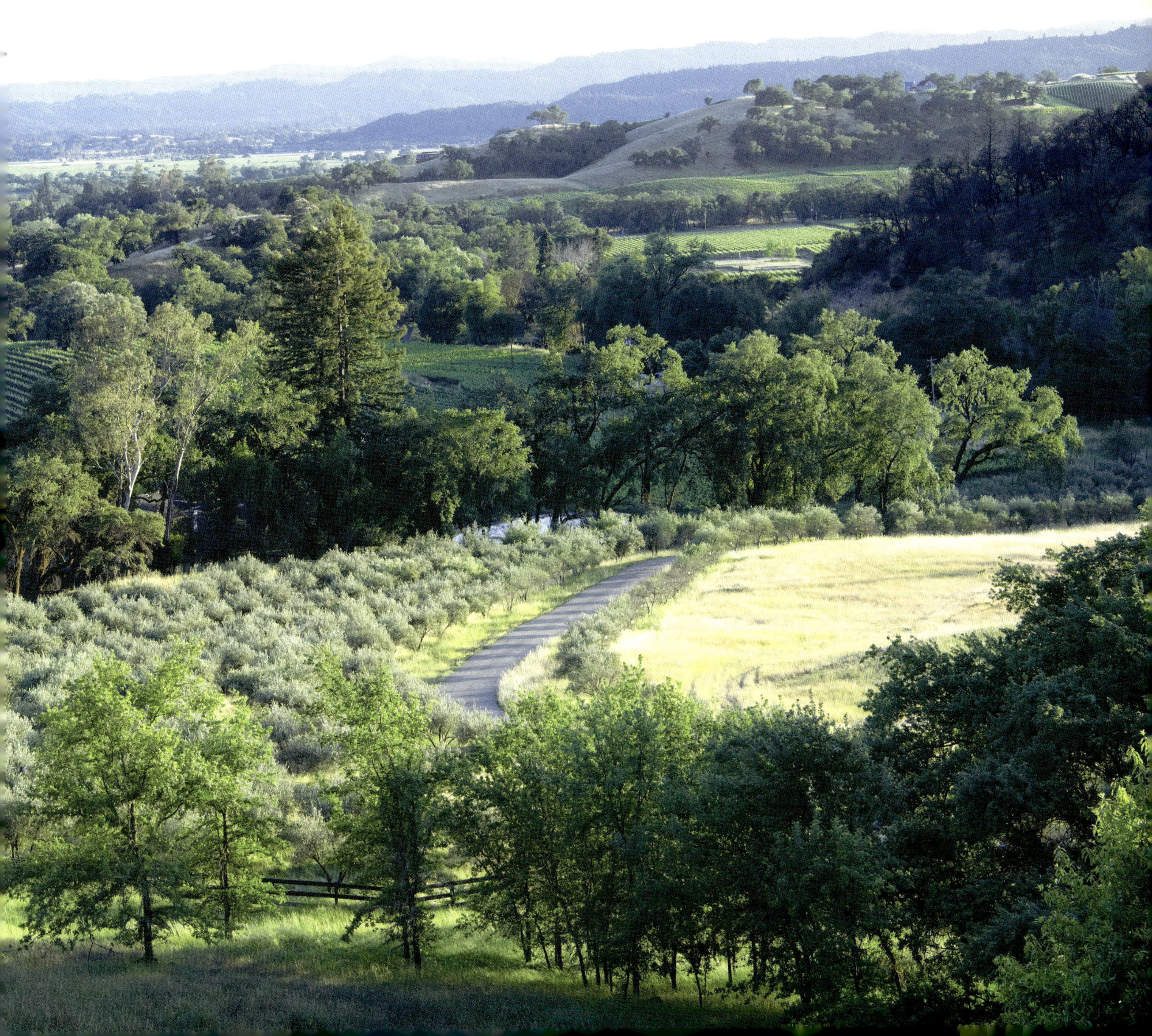

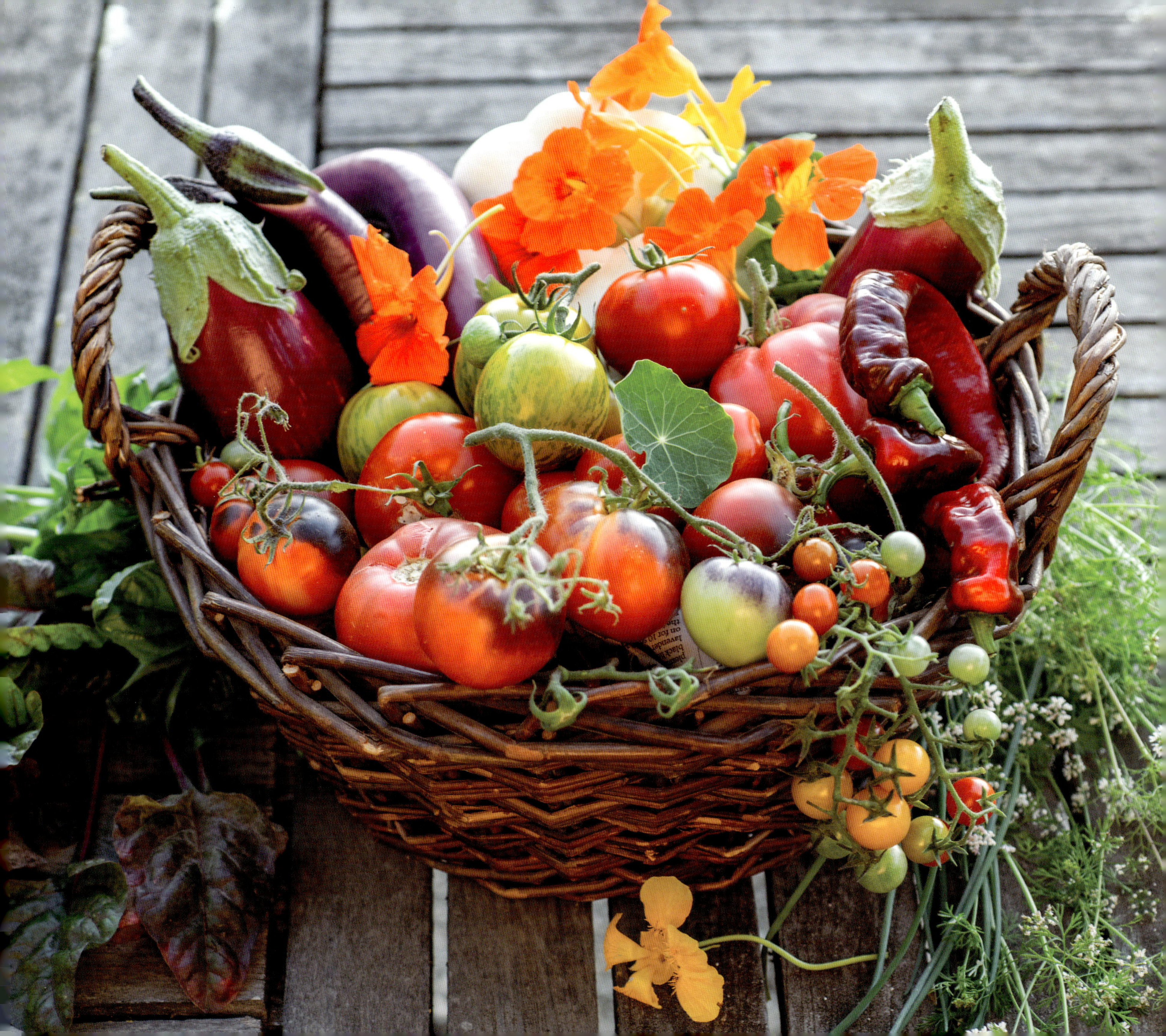

Trefethen Family Vineyards: *A Joyful Jumble*

Napa

Some wine country gardens look as if they are tidied around the clock, with nary a wilted leaf or pebble out of place. The Trefethen family takes a different approach in managing the flat, sunny plot that employees refer to as La Huerta—Spanish for a garden or small farm. This joyful jumble of clambering kiwi vines, sprawling squash plants, and towering tomatoes is more about nourishing people than impressing them. In a garden largely grown for employees, yield trumps tidiness.

"It's a bit of a wild garden," admits Hailey Trefethen, the third-generation vintner who oversees nearly an acre of beds behind the winery in Napa's Oak Knoll District. "We don't mind some weeds."

Even so, a lot more than weeds comes out of this fertile former vineyard: hundreds of pounds of chiles, eggplants, tomatoes, tomatillos, and green beans along with more esoteric heirloom produce, such as Jimmy Nardello sweet red peppers, Indigo Apple tomatoes, and Mexican sour gherkins. Although winery chef Chris Kennedy uses some of the harvest for guests, the vast majority goes straight to the staff.

Left and above: *Late-summer garden at Trefethen Vineyards yields heirlooms tomatoes, nasturtiums, eggplant, Jimmy Nardello sweet peppers, chard, and herbs; Janet Trefethen (left) and daughter Hailey*

Hailey grew up on garden produce—her mother, Janet, is an avid gardener and renowned home cook—and her grandmother Katie planted many of the fruit trees that still thrive at Trefethen. "Our family ate out of our garden most of the time," recalls Hailey. "So why didn't we do the same for employees? Why didn't we have a garden at the winery so people could go home with produce grown where they work?"

The family has always tried to promote wine as part of a healthy lifestyle; enabling employees to make better food choices seemed a good fit with that message. With that goal in mind, winery executive Jon Ruel initiated the garden program in 2008, and the garden now produces year-round, its harvest supplemented by the fig, persimmon, quince, kumquat, apple, and stone-fruit trees on the premises.

The produce is picked into bins and delivered to different departments on rotation; employees take what they want. "We switch it up so not all the zucchini are going to the tasting room," says Hailey, who also posts pictures, descriptions, and usage ideas for less-familiar produce. Chris often contributes an easy recipe, especially for an item, like the skinny Jimmy Nardello peppers or the mild shishito peppers, that staffers might otherwise pass up.

Many winery owners might look at this garden and see only an expense that's hard to defend, but the Trefethens think otherwise. "The employees value it," says Janet, "and we get paid back in their satisfaction."

Chiles, both hot and hotter, are the most in-demand crop, says Hailey; no matter how many seedlings she plants, it's never enough. Around Labor Day, an annual salsa-making competition encourages employees to flaunt their own creativity. All tomatoes, chiles, and tomatillos used in the salsas must come from La Huerta, and the winning entry is determined by popular vote of the staff. "We are trying to increase everybody's connection to the garden," says the vintner.

The prolific edible landscape at Trefethen was one of the lures for Chris when he accepted the job. What chef would not feel stimulated and challenged by the bounty this property yields? In Hailey and head gardener Paul Hoffman, he has found partners willing to experiment with planting African cucumbers, yellow wax beans, okra, and rhubarb. And Hailey can be sure that whatever Paul harvests, Chris will make it his mission to use every edible part.

"I like using what most people would get rid of," says the chef. In his toss-nothing kitchen, tender carrot tops aren't jettisoned for compost; they're chopped and used for *chimichurri* with peppery extra virgin olive oil pressed from Trefethen's own fruit. Nasturtium blossoms aren't merely strewn over salads. They're braised with the leaves and sautéed shallots, then blended, reemerging as a peppery, emerald-green sauce for fillet of beef. Convinced that toasted sunflower seeds make a great bridge to the winery's Chardonnay, Chris extracts the seeds from the mature sunflower heads by hand.

"The garden has honed my palate," says Chris, a longtime chef and restaurateur. Far more than most chefs, he pays close attention to how fruits and vegetables interact with wine (see sidebar, page 199). In regular wine-tasting sessions with Janet, he notes the scents and textures that might find an echo or complement in the garden: Riesling with citrus and cilantro, Merlot with fire-roasted red peppers, Chardonnay with melon and tarragon. From those tasting trials, he develops a wish list of wine-friendly fruits and vegetables to plant.

Above: *(clockwise from left) View of La Huerta, the staff garden; chili powders from dried garden chiles; dried Goat Horn peppers; salsa competition winners with Hailey Trefethen; jalapeño chiles; cherry tomatoes and cucamelons, a little-known vegetable*

"Our family ate out of our garden most of the time. Why didn't we have a garden at the winery so people could go home with produce grown where they work?"

"The thousand pounds of chiles we grow do not fit in that realm," jokes Hailey. But the chiles might find their way into the monthly "blue-plate lunches" that Trefethen hosts for small groups of employees, so staffers can connect across departments and get some fresh ideas for their own home meals.

Good cooking and home entertaining have been part of the Trefethen brand since at least 1973, when Janet and her mother-in-law, Katie, helped to start the Napa Valley Cooking Class at the winery. The valley had few good restaurants then, and vintners had visiting customers to entertain. Initially, the vintners' wives taught favorite recipes to one another, but the school's ambitions quickly grew, and over the next twenty-five years, many celebrity chefs held classes in the

Trefethen Family Vineyards

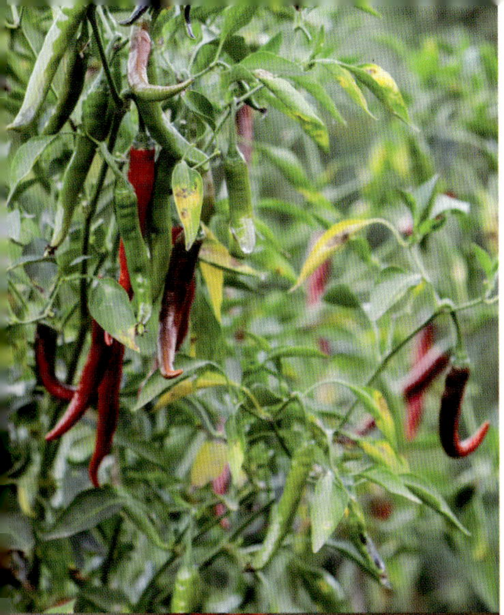
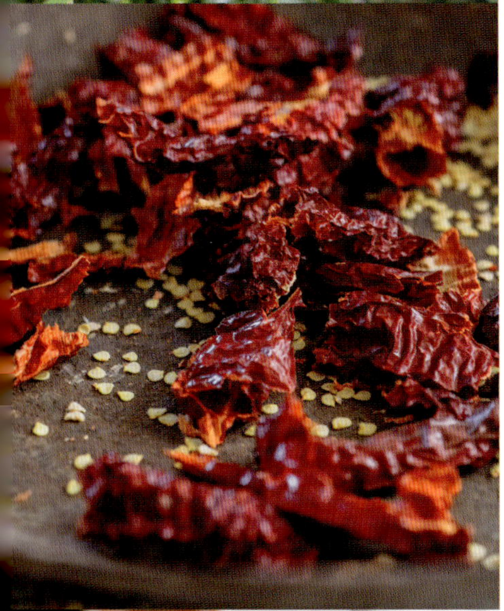
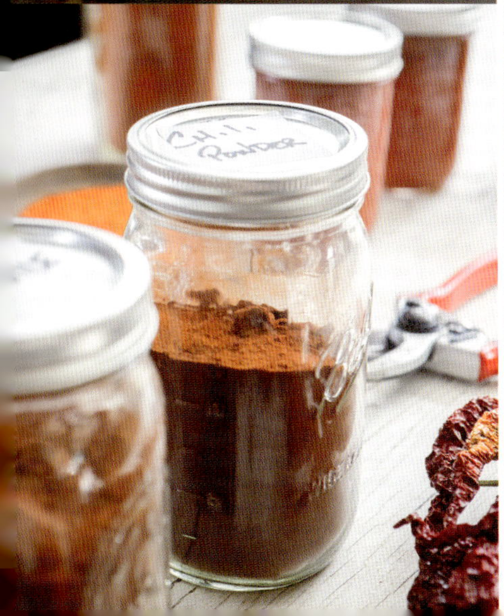
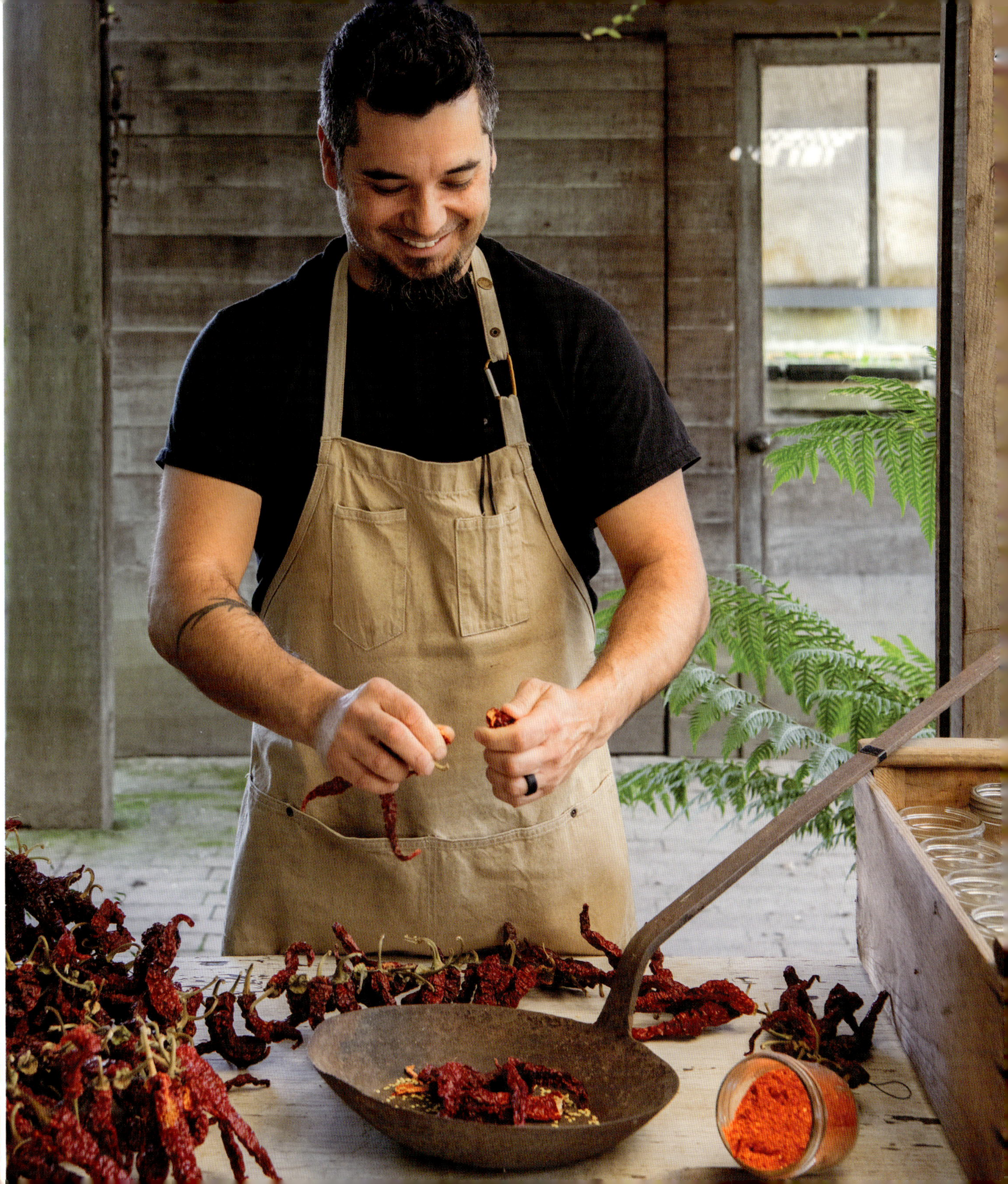

Trefethen winery kitchen. "I grew up on a stool there," says Hailey.

The valley has countless fine restaurants now, but many wine country visitors still seek to have a more personal wine-and-food experience at a winery. Weather permitting, Trefethen's guests get a quick tour of La Huerta, and they reap its benefits in the small seasonal bites that Chris prepares for the winery's Taste the Estate sessions.

"Chris continues to expand what we can pair with our wines," says Hailey. "He thinks up so many ways to process what we grow."

A serious student of food preservation—salting, drying, fermenting, pickling—Chris keeps testing the limits of where fruits and vegetables can go. In the fall, he makes *hoshigaki*, Japanese-style dried persimmons, but he has applied the same techniques to kiwis and apples. He hangs colorful *ristras* of Goat Horn peppers to dry in the potting shed and then grinds them for a sweet spice to use all year. He dries tomatoes, blueberries, apples, kale, and oregano. He pickles cucumbers and eggplants, cans hundreds of quarts of tomatoes, and makes wine vinegar and sweet-tart verjus from the juice of underripe grapes. Many cooks make salt-preserved lemons, but Chris makes salt-preserved kumquats scented with star anise for use in salads and vinaigrettes.

This informal garden is at its most riotous in late summer, when peppers, beans, squashes, and melons jostle for space. But every season here has its allure. For a late-spring menu, Chris makes the most of the garden's tender sweet carrots, beets, spring onions, and English peas and the leafy delicacy of spring cilantro and thyme. The meal opens, as it often does at Trefethen, with the winery's beloved Dry Riesling and concludes with its elegant Cabernet Sauvignon, a demonstration in five courses of the delicious possibilities when linking garden to glass.

Left and right: *Winery chef Chris Kennedy processing dried Goat Horn peppers; chard is one of the many crops that provide a treasured benefit to Trefethen employees.*

menu

Dungeness Crab Roll with Pickled Ginger, Cilantro, and Yuzu Crème

Trefethen Dry Riesling

Oven-Roasted Baby Carrots with Cumin Yogurt, Carrot Top Chimichurri, and Spiced Pumpkin Seeds

Trefethen Chardonnay

Handmade Pappardelle with Wild Mushroom Ragout and Peas

Trefethen Merlot

Spring Lamb Chops Scottadito with Charred Tomato and Black Olive Tapenade

Trefethen Dragon's Tooth

Black Pepper–Crusted Beef Ribeye with Balsamic Spring Onions and Smashed Beets

Trefethen Cabernet Sauvignon

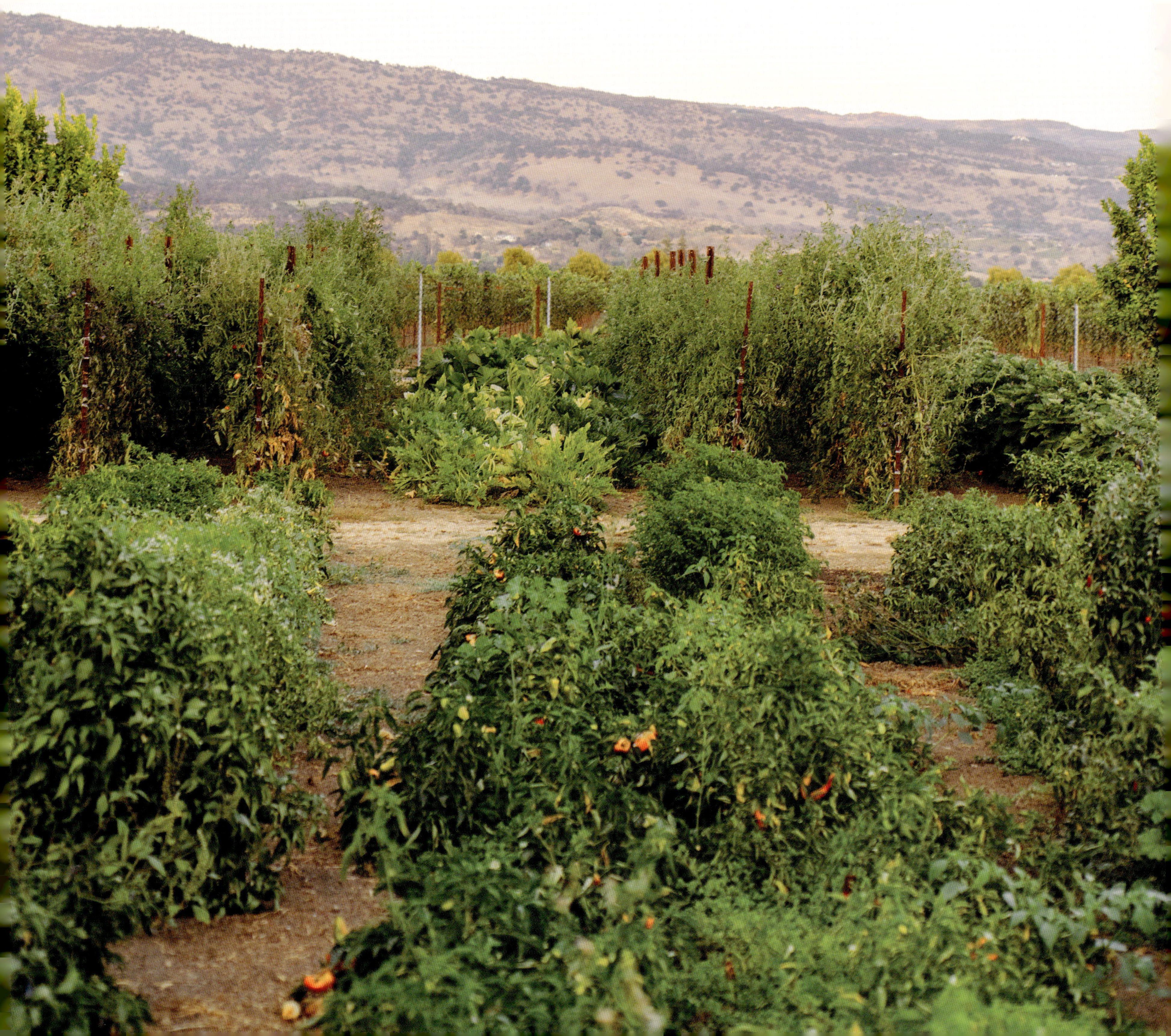

Dungeness Crab Roll with Pickled Ginger, Cilantro, and Yuzu Crème   **Makes 8 rolls; serves 4**

This West Coast spin on a lobster roll is a popular passed appetizer at Trefethen events. The winery's Dry Riesling, with its refreshing minerality, loves Dungeness crab, but Chris has found that cilantro and green apple create even more flavor bridges.

2 brioche hot dog buns

2 teaspoons unsalted butter, melted

¼ cup plain whole-milk Greek yogurt

1½ teaspoons crème fraîche

1½ tablespoons bottled yuzu juice or fresh lime juice

2 teaspoons coarsely chopped fresh cilantro, plus 8 whole leaves for garnish

½ teaspoon finely minced pickled ginger

½ apple, preferably a tart, crisp variety such as Granny Smith, peeled, cored, and diced small

½ pound fresh Dungeness crabmeat, preferably in large pieces, picked over for shells

Sea salt and freshly ground black pepper

Wine: Trefethen Dry Riesling

Preheat the oven to 375°F. Slice each bun crosswise into 4 equal chunks. Make a similar cut down the middle of each chunk (vertically, not horizontally) but do not cut all the way through. Brush these slots with the melted butter. Place on a baking sheet and bake until lightly toasted on the edges but not crisp, about 3 minutes. Set aside while you assemble the filling.

In a bowl, whisk together the yogurt, crème fraîche, yuzu juice, cilantro, and pickled ginger. Stir in the apple. Gently fold in the crab, trying not to break up the pieces. Season to taste with salt and pepper. Refrigerate for 10 to 15 minutes to allow the flavors to marry. Don't let the mixture sit too long or it will start to throw liquid.

Set aside 8 pretty pieces of crabmeat, then use the remaining crab mixture to fill the buns, dividing it evenly. Top each bun with a reserved piece of crabmeat, then garnish with a whole cilantro leaf. Serve immediately.

chef's tip:

If you can't find baby carrots, you can trim larger ones down, selecting those with the most tender, freshest greens. If your carrots don't have greens attached, replace with chopped fresh flat-leaf parsley, cilantro, or both.

Oven-Roasted Baby Carrots with Cumin Yogurt, Carrot Top Chimichurri, and Spiced Pumpkin Seeds Serves 4

Chris is a big advocate of using every edible part of a fruit or vegetable, including the tender leafy tops of young carrots. These frilly greens make a surprising substitute for chopped parsley in chimichurri, *the Argentine sauce often drizzled on grilled beef. In this dish, the* chimichurri *enlivens roasted baby carrots. Use any leftover sauce on a steak the following day.*

24 baby carrots with greens attached, about 1 pound after removing greens

Extra virgin olive oil, for drizzling

Sea salt and freshly ground black pepper

¼ teaspoon cumin seeds or ground cumin

¼ cup plain whole-milk Greek yogurt

Carrot-Top Chimichurri:

¼ cup white wine vinegar or verjus

1 small shallot, finely minced

⅓ cup finely chopped carrot greens

¼ cup olive oil (not extra virgin)

Spiced Pumpkin Seeds:

⅓ cup raw green pumpkin seeds (pepitas)

1 teaspoon extra virgin olive oil

Pinch of Spanish smoked paprika (pimentón de la Vera)

Wine: Trefethen Chardonnay

Position a rack in the upper third of the oven and preheat oven to 425°F.

Remove the carrot greens. Trim the greens, discarding the stems and keeping only the frilly leaves. Wash and dry the leaves well, then chop finely. Set aside ⅓ cup chopped leaves for the chimichurri.

Scrub the carrots under running water, then "polish" them with a rough dish towel to remove any clinging bits of soil, paying special attention to the area where the greens were attached. Place them on a heavy baking sheet, drizzle with just enough extra virgin olive oil to coat them lightly, and season with salt and pepper. Roast the carrots, shaking and rotating the pan halfway through to ensure even cooking, until the carrots are lightly caramelized and tender when pierced, about 20 minutes. Remove from the oven. Leave the oven on.

If using cumin seeds, toast in a dry small skillet over medium heat until darkened and fragrant. Let cool, then, with a mortar and pestle, pound until finely ground. Put the yogurt into a small bowl and whisk in the cumin, a pinch of salt, and a few grinds of pepper.

Prepare the chimichurri: In a small bowl, combine the vinegar and shallot. Add a pinch of salt and a few grinds of pepper and let stand for at least 10 minutes to soften the shallots. Add the carrot greens and olive oil, season with salt and pepper, and whisk well.

Prepare the spiced pumpkin seeds: Spread the pumpkin seeds in a pie pan and toast in the oven until lightly colored, about 5 minutes. Transfer them to a bowl and, while they are hot, add the olive oil and toss to coat well. Add the paprika, salt to taste, and a grind or two of pepper and toss again. Let cool.

At serving time, spoon the yogurt onto the bottom of a serving platter and spread thinly with the back of a soupspoon. Arrange the warm carrots on top in an artful mound, then put small dollops of chimichurri on the carrots, using as much as you like. Scatter the pumpkin seeds all over and serve immediately.

Handmade Pappardelle with Wild Mushroom Ragout and Peas

Serves 6

Pasta Dough:

3 large whole eggs plus 5 large egg yolks

1 tablespoon extra virgin olive oil, plus 2 tablespoons for the pasta water and more for drizzling

1½ teaspoons sea salt

2 cups Italian "00" flour or all-purpose flour, plus more for dusting

Ragout:

2 cups shelled English peas

1 tablespoon extra virgin olive oil

1 clove garlic, minced

1 large shallot, diced

Sea salt and freshly ground black pepper

1 pound wild mushrooms, cleaned and cut or torn into large pieces

1 tablespoon unsalted butter

½ cup Trefethen Chardonnay or other white wine

1 tablespoon chopped fresh flat-leaf parsley

1 teaspoon chopped fresh thyme

Chunk of Parmigiano-Reggiano cheese, for grating

Wine: Trefethen Merlot

Sweet, tender English peas are a fleeting treat in the Trefethen garden, so Chris makes sure they get star billing during that brief window. Spring morels would be his first choice for the mushroom ragout, but chanterelles or even cultivated oyster mushrooms will work.

Prepare the pasta dough: In a bowl, whisk together the eggs, egg yolks, oil, and salt. Place the flour on a large work surface and make a well in the center large enough to contain the eggs. Make sure the flour "walls" are high enough to keep the eggs from escaping. Pour the egg mixture into the well. With a fork, begin drawing in the flour from the sides and whisking it with the eggs. Take care not to let the runny eggs breach the flour walls. The mixture should come together into a slightly tacky dough. Dust with additional flour as needed and knead by hand until the dough is firm and no longer tacky.

Knead the dough by hand until it is smooth and elastic, 7 to 10 minutes. It should bounce back when poked with a finger. Divide the dough into 4 equal portions. Shape each portion into a ball, flatten slightly, and wrap in plastic wrap. Let rest at room temperature for about 1 hour.

(continued)

chef's tip:

Look for Italian "00" flour in well-stocked supermarkets and specialty stores. It is more finely ground than all-purpose flour. Fresh pasta made with "00" flour is easier to roll by hand and has a more pleasing texture.

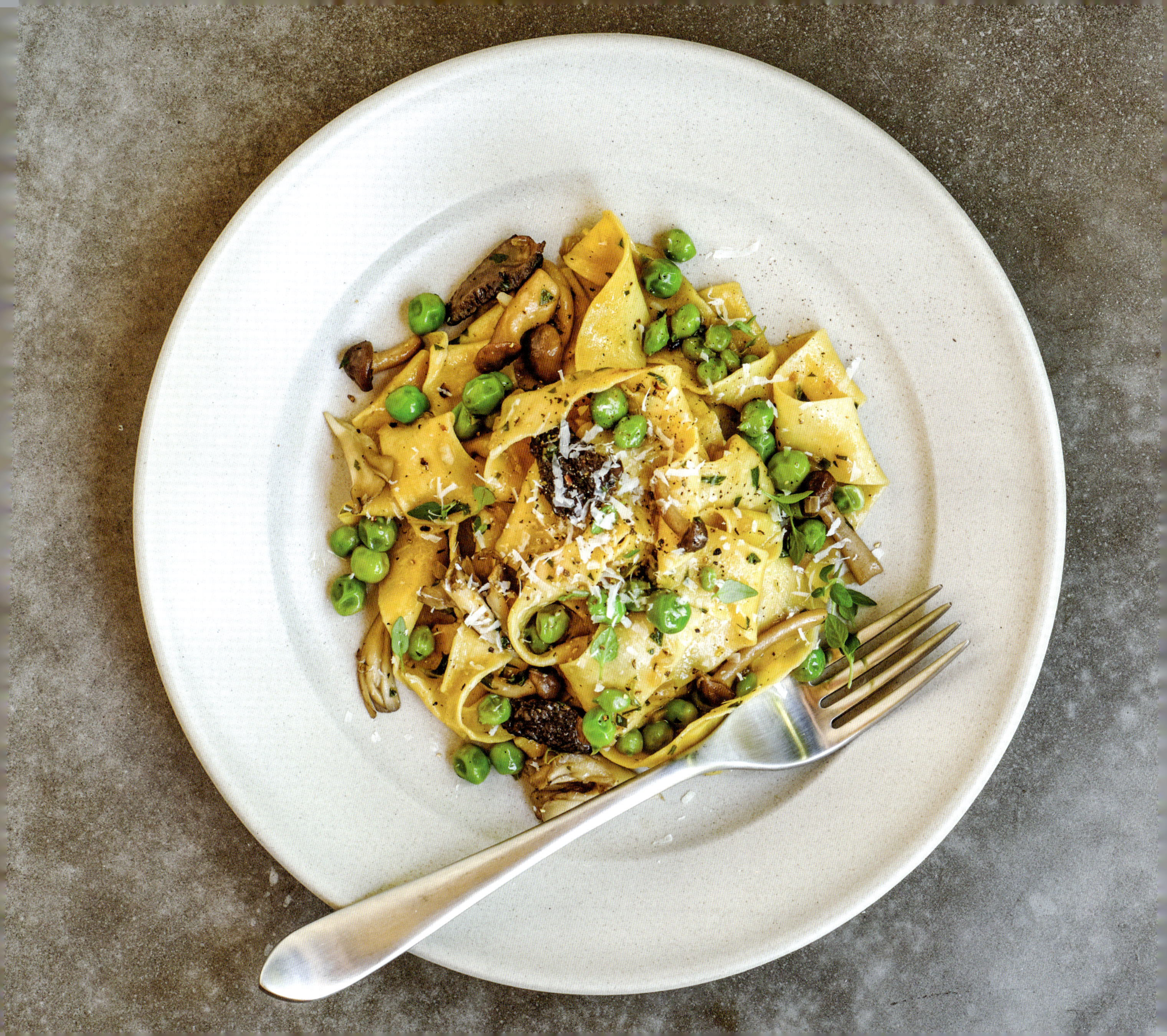

Handmade Pappardelle with Wild Mushroom Ragout and Peas

(continued)

Work with 1 dough portion at a time, keeping the others covered. With a pasta machine or by hand with a rolling pin, roll the dough into a sheet thin enough to see your fingers through it. Dust with flour as needed to keep it from sticking to the machine or work surface.

Starting at a narrow end, loosely roll the sheet like a jelly roll, leaving a 1-inch tail. With a sharp chef's knife, cut the roll crosswise into ¾-inch-wide ribbons. Grab the noodles by the exposed ends and lift them so they unfurl. Place them on a baking sheet, dust lightly with flour, and toss gently to separate. Repeat with the remaining 3 dough portions. Let the noodles dry while you prepare the ragout.

Prepare the ragout: Bring a small pot of water to a boil over high heat. Prepare a bowl of ice water. Boil the peas until barely tender, then drain and immediately immerse in the ice water. When cool, drain again and set aside.

Put the oil and garlic into a pot large enough to hold the pasta and place over low heat. Cook slowly, stirring occasionally, until the garlic begins to color, about 5 minutes; watch carefully to prevent burning. Add the shallot and a pinch of salt and cook over low heat, stirring occasionally, until the shallot is translucent, about 5 minutes. Raise the heat to medium-low, add the mushrooms, and season well with salt and pepper. Cook, stirring, until the mushrooms release their liquid, about 5 minutes. Add the butter, raise the heat to medium-high, and cook until the liquid has mostly evaporated and the mushrooms have begun to caramelize. Reduce the heat to medium-low, add the wine, and simmer until all the liquid has evaporated. Keep warm.

Bring a large pot of well-salted water to a boil over high heat. Add the 2 tablespoons oil to keep the noodles from sticking. Add the pasta and cook to desired doneness, about 2 minutes, depending on dryness. Add 1 cup of the pasta water to the mushrooms, then drain the pasta and return it to the warm pot, off the heat. Drizzle with a little oil and toss gently to keep the noodles from sticking.

Add the parsley and thyme to the mushrooms and simmer until the liquid is reduced by half. Add the peas and turn off the heat. Add the pasta, toss gently but well, and taste for seasoning. Divide among six bowls and garnish each portion with a generous amount of grated Parmigiano-Reggiano and pepper. Serve immediately.

what grapes want:

Although many cooks focus their wine pairing on the "center of the plate"—such as seafood, chicken, or beef— Chris finds that many fruits and vegetables can echo or complement the textures and aromas in a wine. Over frequent tastings with Janet, Chris has refined his ideas about the garden produce that flatters each of Trefethen's key wines.

Dry Riesling: green apples, Asian pears, Bosc pears, cucumbers, braised cabbage, quinces, kiwis, cilantro, citrus, chiles

Chardonnay: tarragon, melons, golden apples, fennel, butternut squashes, radishes, sunflower seeds, persimmons, brassicas, corn, carrots, delicata squashes, zucchini, romaine, white figs, oranges

Merlot: mushrooms, stewed tomatos, grilled peppers, nasturtiums, Swiss chard, sage, roasted squashes, figs, charred corn, polenta, green garlic

Dragon's Tooth (Bordeaux-style blend): mushrooms, toasted garlic, charred sweet peppers, Goat Horn peppers, parsley, nasturtiums, mustard greens, eggplants

Cabernet Sauvignon: thyme, carrots, mushrooms, potatoes, arugula, caramelized onions, toasted garlic, beets, chives, eggplants

Spring Lamb Chops Scottadito with Charred Tomato and Black Olive Tapenade **Serves 4**

4 lamb shoulder chops, each about 6 ounces and ½ inch thick

Sea salt and freshly ground black pepper

¼ cup extra virgin olive oil, plus more for drizzling

1 teaspoon minced fresh rosemary

3 teaspoons minced garlic

4 San Marzano or Roma tomatoes, halved lengthwise

½ teaspoon anchovy paste

⅓ cup pitted and neatly diced black olives, such as Niçoise or Kalamata

⅓ cup neatly diced caper berries

½ cup coarsely chopped fresh flat-leaf parsley

1 teaspoon fresh lemon juice

Wine: Trefethen Dragon's Tooth

The garden's beautiful old caper bush yields a lot of edible berries that Chris preserves for use all year. Its tiny buds are the familiar capers found bottled in brine. Left on the bush, they open into a gorgeous flower, which then sets an edible berry. Chris uses the berries in a zesty warm tapenade for lamb chops. Scottadito, *an Italian word, implies the pan-seared chops are so hot they will burn your fingers if you pick them up.*

Line a baking sheet with parchment paper. To keep the chops from curling as they cook, make a few small notches in the rim of fat on each chop. Season the chops on both sides with salt and pepper. In a small bowl, combine the oil, rosemary, 2 teaspoons of the garlic, and a pinch of salt. Put the chops on the prepared pan and spoon the seasoned oil evenly over them, coating both sides. Refrigerate uncovered for at least 2 hours or up to 24 hours. Bring to room temperature before cooking.

Heat a cast-iron or nonstick skillet over medium-high heat until very hot. Season the cut side of the tomatoes with salt, then place them, cut side down, in the hot skillet. Do not move them. Let them cook without moving or turning until they are soft to the touch and charred on the cut side, 7 to 8 minutes. Turn the heat off and let them rest in the pan while you cook the lamb.

Heat a large cast-iron or nonstick skillet over medium-high heat until very hot. Add the lamb chops in a single layer. Cook until they are well browned on the bottom, about 2 minutes, then turn and cook on the other side until they are well browned and fairly firm to the touch, 2 to 3 minutes longer. (Shoulder chops are best when cooked to at least medium.) Transfer the chops to a serving platter and reduce the heat to low. Discard any burnt garlic.

When the skillet has cooled a bit, add the remaining 1 teaspoon minced garlic and the anchovy paste and stir for about 30 seconds. Add the olives and caper berries and stir until aromatic, about 30 seconds. Add the parsley and cook, stirring, just until it wilts slightly, about 30 seconds. Stir in the lemon juice and remove from the heat.

Top each chop with 2 tomato halves and the olive mixture, dividing it evenly. Drizzle with a little oil, then serve immediately.

Black Pepper–Crusted Beef Ribeye with Balsamic Spring Onions and Smashed Beets **Serves 4**

Chris works many robust flavors into this dish—a peppery spice rub on the steaks, a balsamic marinade on the onions, and a tart poaching liquid for the beets—but Trefethen's elegant Cabernet Sauvignon can handle them. He harvests young onions from the garden when they resemble thick leeks, with a bulbous base that has just begun to swell. To use golden beets, substitute Chardonnay and white wine vinegar in the poaching liquid.

Beef:

2 beef ribeye steaks, about 1 pound each, trimmed of excess fat (leave some fat)

2 tablespoons sea salt

2 tablespoons chopped fresh thyme

2 tablespoons freshly ground black pepper

1 tablespoon olive oil

Spring Onions:

2 whole spring onions, roots removed, trimmed to 12 inches, and quartered lengthwise

1½ teaspoons sea salt

¼ cup extra virgin olive oil

¼ cup aged balsamic vinegar

1 teaspoon freshly ground black pepper

Beets:

4 cups water

½ cup Trefethen Cabernet Sauvignon

½ cup red wine vinegar

1 tablespoon sea salt

1 teaspoon freshly ground black pepper

12 small red beets, greens and roots removed

Olive oil, for searing the steaks

Vegetable oil, for frying the beets

Wine: Trefethen Cabernet Sauvignon

Prepare the beef: Season the steaks on both sides with the salt. Let rest at room temperature for 10 minutes to draw out moisture. Lightly pat the steaks dry but do not rinse or remove the salt.

In a small bowl, mix together the thyme, pepper, and olive oil to make a loose paste. Coat the steaks on both sides with the paste and put them into a lidded container. Cover and refrigerate for at least 4 hours or up to 24 hours, occasionally turning the steaks and massaging them lightly to encourage the seasonings to penetrate.

Prepare the spring onions: Season the onions with the salt and let rest at room temperature for 10 minutes to draw out moisture. Pat dry but do not rinse or remove the salt. In a small bowl, whisk together the olive oil, vinegar, and pepper. Put the onions and marinade into a lidded container and toss to coat. Cover and refrigerate for at least 4 hours or up to 24 hours, occasionally turning the onions and massaging them lightly to encourage the seasonings to penetrate.

Prepare the beets: In a pot, combine the water, wine, vinegar, salt, and pepper. Add the beets and bring to a simmer over high heat. Reduce the heat to maintain a gentle simmer and cook until the beets are just tender when pierced, about 30 minutes. They will be cooked more later so be careful not to overcook at this stage. With tongs, transfer the beets to a rack to cool. Try to keep the skins intact. Let cool to room temperature. With your palm, smack the beets to crack them and flatten them slightly.

(continued)

Black Pepper–Crusted Beef Ribeye with Balsamic Spring Onions and Smashed Beets *(continued)*

Remove the steaks from the container but do not pat them dry. They should still have bits of thyme and pepper on them. Bring them to room temperature. Heat a large cast-iron skillet over medium-high heat. Add enough olive oil to cover the bottom. When the oil is hot, add the steaks and let sear without moving them for 5 to 8 minutes to allow a crust to form. With tongs, turn the steaks and cook on the second side until done to your taste, another 5 to 8 minutes for medium-rare. Transfer the steaks to a cutting board to rest.

Pour off any fat in the skillet but do not wipe it clean. Return the skillet to medium heat. Remove the spring onions from their marinade, reserving the marinade. Add the onions to the warm skillet, cut side down, and cook, rotating as needed to keep them from burning, until they are richly caramelized and almost tender. Remove from the heat but leave the onions in the skillet.

Set another large cast-iron skillet over medium-high heat and pour in enough vegetable oil to come halfway up the sides of the beets. When the oil is hot, carefully add the beets to the pan. Cook until crisp on the bottom, 3 to 5 minutes, then turn and crisp the other side, 3 to 5 minutes longer. Drain on paper towels. Season with salt and pepper.

Divide the onions and beets evenly among four dinner plates. Slice the steaks to desired thickness and divide among the plates. Drizzle with the reserved spring onion marinade and serve immediately.

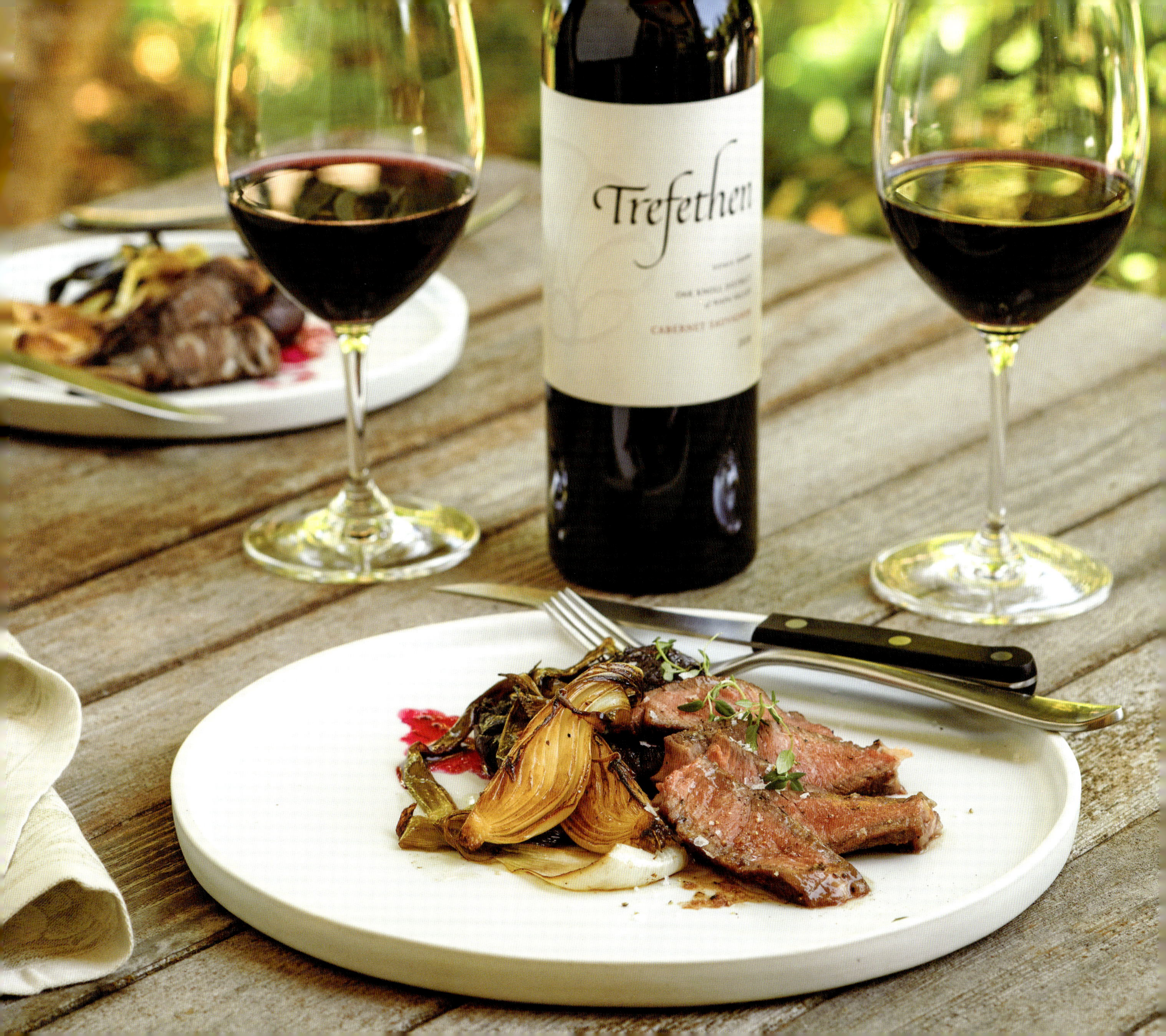
Trefethen

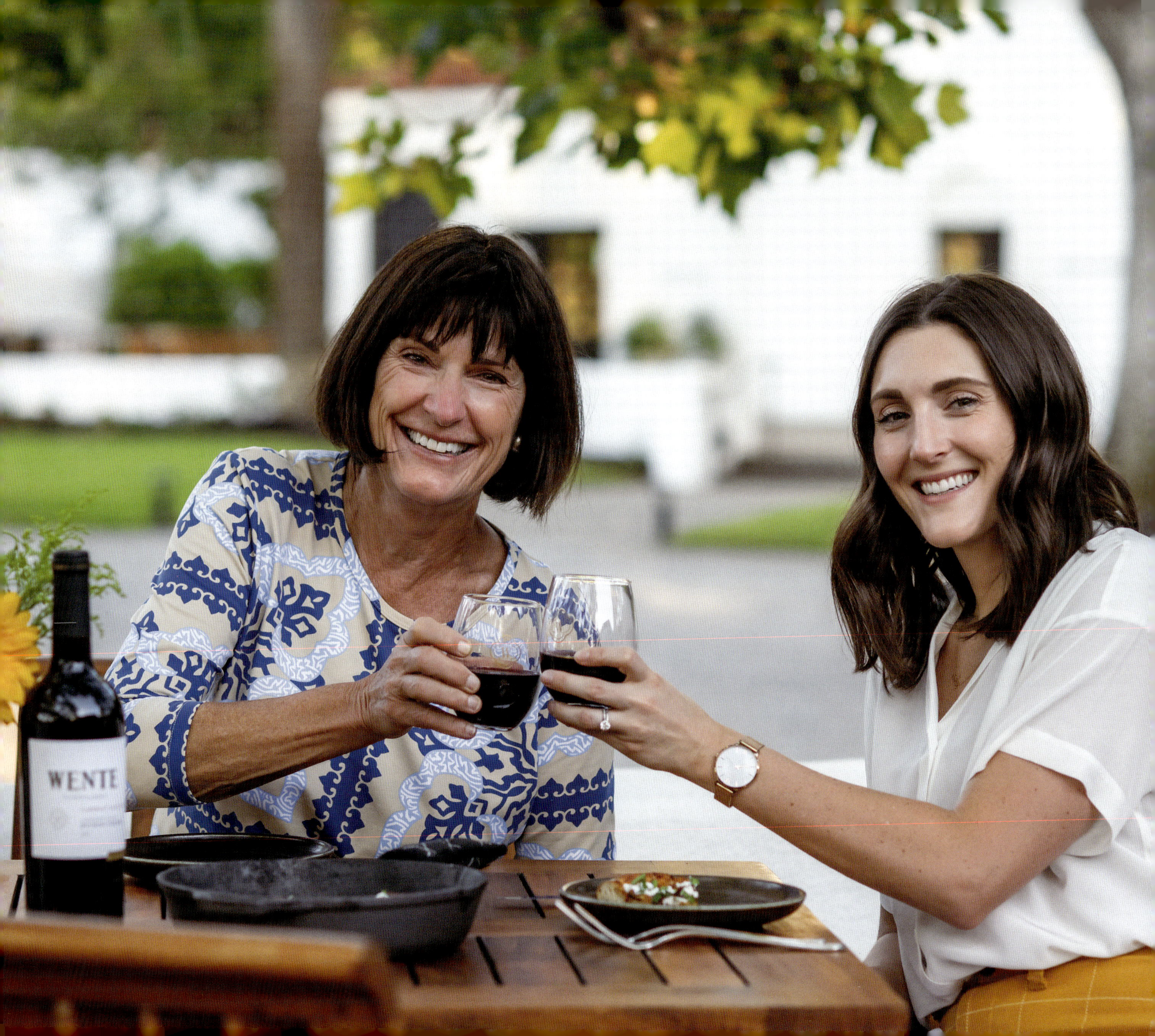
WENTE

Wente Vineyards: *Deep Roots in One Place*

Livermore

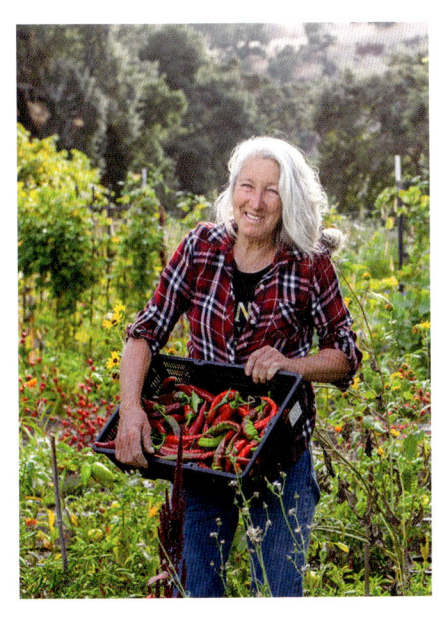

Gardens are forever evolving, their colors changing as plants come and go. They fall quiet in winter but perk up after a spring rain. They even look different at dawn and at dusk. And when a longtime caretaker moves on, a garden will shift shape, subtly or dramatically, again.

These images of the Wente Vineyards garden capture an especially sweet time in its life, the final season for its longtime manager, Diane Dovholuk, who retired at the end of 2019 after thirty-three years. How the garden will evolve is a story that hasn't been written yet, but Diane's long collaboration with the winery's culinary team has enhanced the experience of visiting this landmark Livermore Valley estate.

Fourth-generation vintner Carolyn Wente hired Diane in 1986 but not for the garden. Diane had been Carolyn's favorite server at a local steak house, and when Wente opened its own restaurant, Carolyn encouraged Diane to join the dining-room staff. She soon became its top salesperson and a keen observer of the restaurant kitchen.

Left and above: *Two generations of Wente women (CEO Carolyn and Aly Wente) share a patio meal near the winery's Cresta Blanca Room, a popular event center; garden manager Diane Dovholuk gathers sweet peppers in the autumn garden.*

"Carolyn, did you know you're spending $40,000 a year on herbs?" she asked one day. Diane was certain she could start an organic garden and deliver fresh herbs for much less than that, including her salary.

Carolyn and her brothers, Phil and Eric, agreed to transition a small vineyard parcel that was proving too shady for wine grapes. But Diane's herb garden thrived there, and her edible empire eventually grew to almost an acre. Predictably, fresh herbs were just the proverbial camel's nose under the tent. By the time she retired, Diane was harvesting two thousand pounds of tomatoes a year, plus eggplants, peppers, cucumbers, and specialties such as ground cherries, Italian Corona beans, and purple tomatillos. Along the way, a greenhouse went up so Diane, relentlessly frugal, could start plants from seed.

"The garden has paid for itself the entire time," says Carolyn, an avid home gardener herself whose family has deep roots in Livermore Valley agriculture. Her paternal grandfather, Ernest, who managed Wente's vineyards in his day, also cultivated citrus, avocado, fig, and persimmon trees at his Livermore home and started a cattle ranch to help the family survive Prohibition. "My grandparents lived from the land," recalls Carolyn, "and I remember working with them all the time in their garden." Returning an edible garden to the Wente estate would help visitors appreciate the profound connection to place that has long defined this pioneering wine family.

From the beginning, the garden's harvest has always remained on the property, supplying the restaurant, the golf-course grill, and, to a lesser extent, the winery's many catered events. Coordinating supply with kitchen demand is no easy task; nature throws curveballs and, despite the pampered soil and enviable climate, not every crop on the chefs' wish list is feasible. "In spring, I give them seed catalogs and they pick out what they want," says Diane. "Then I tell them what we can grow."

Fortunately for Wente's culinary team, Diane has rarely met a food plant she didn't want to grow. A stroll along the bark paths of this colorful, prolific garden turns up many novelties: baby butternut squash, long-necked Trombetta squash, holy basil, trendy Salanova lettuces with their tightly packed emerald and burgundy leaves, elderberries for syrup, hibiscus for tea, and red flint corn for polenta. Small fruit trees provide peaches, nectarines, apriums, and pluots for the pastry kitchen, as well as crisp Fuji apples and prized heirloom varieties, such as Cox's Orange Pippin and Hudson's Golden Gem.

The Wente garden is a compelling billboard for the sustainable growing methods that the family has long embraced in its vineyards. "We replenish our soil all the time," says Diane. All food waste from Wente events and the restaurant—ten thousand pounds a year—is composted and returned to the garden. Winter cover crops also nourish the soil, and the bark paths build humus, too, as the materials gradually decompose.

By planting densely, Diane has made the beds less welcoming for weeds. "You see how tight the basil and peppers are," she points out. "That's closer than what it says on the seed packets. Plus, I never walk by a weed. I pick it up."

Drifts of colorful blooms do more than beautify this sunny

Above: *(clockwise from far left) Cox's Orange Pippin; Wente Riesling with dessert; winery chef Jeff Farlow surveys the garden bounty; tomatillos; winery visitors on a garden tour; shucking red flint corn; chiles galore*

"My grandparents lived from the land," says Carolyn. "I remember working with them all the time in their garden."

parcel, a level plot embraced by hills. Asters, zinnias, hollyhocks, pansies, Maximillian sunflowers, and society garlic take their turn on the stage, luring pollinators and providing blossoms the chefs can use to garnish plates. Calendulas, dianthus, and bachelor's buttons are combined and delivered to the kitchen to scatter on salads. Aware that visitors routinely pocket seeds from unusual plants they admire—a trait shared by plant lovers the world over—guests are now treated to seed packets for garden standouts.

"Every herb we could need is out there," says Wente executive catering chef Jeff Farlow. Plus, he has access to every edible part of a plant—the pea tendrils, leafy pea greens, and the sweet peas

Wente Vineyards 207

themselves—at the ideal moment. In early spring, Wente guests might find a warm pea greens salad on the menu and, weeks later, sautéed peas with lavender.

"Before I worked with Diane, I wasn't nearly as comfortable with improv cooking," says Jeff. The garden has made him a more flexible and more creative cook, willing to make a temporary home on the menu for a small harvest of squash blossoms or to turn a surfeit of *ají amarillo* chiles into a fermented hot sauce.

Above and right: *(clockwise from left) Aly and Carolyn Wente enjoy cooking together; Aly in her aunt Carolyn's garden; Carolyn harvests navel oranges from her trees on the winery estate; Carolyn's citrus grove*

208   Gather

Carolyn maintains her own extensive edible garden, including a large collection of citrus, at her home on the winery estate. An accomplished cook, she hosts many philanthropic events on the winery's behalf and has a kitchen spacious enough to accommodate a catering crew when the occasion requires it. For her own dinner parties, she may re-create a dish from the winery's restaurant, but then round out the menu with courses drawn from her own repertoire.

Phil's daughter, Aly Wente, is part of the fifth generation running the winery and a self-confessed foodie who clearly inherited the interest, both from her aunt Carolyn and her mother, Julie, a skilled cook. Carolyn and Aly occasionally collaborate in the kitchen.

To showcase the early-autumn harvest from the winery garden, Carolyn and Aly settled on a menu with butternut squash hummus as the starter. A best seller at the winery's Tasting Lounge, the silky hummus makes a versatile dip—for homemade fried pita crisps, radishes, cucumber spears, roasted beets, or fennel wedges—and a casual companion for the evening's first glass of wine. For the next course, late-ripening tomatoes of many varieties are roasted with onions and blended for soup, a last hurrah before the vines decline. Risotto follows, prepared by Aly, who stirs in a handful of garden arugula at the last minute. Wente's famed Chardonnay accompanies the grilled halibut and its vegetable entourage.

As pioneer vintners in the Livermore Valley, the Wentes have been the region's most prominent and tireless advocates. Long before tasting rooms were widespread, the family was welcoming guests to the property. Carolyn's generation introduced the culinary experiences, and the fifth generation intends to build on them. "For decades, we've believed that wine and food belong together," says Aly. "That's how we live, and we try to share that lifestyle with visitors."

menu

Butternut Squash Hummus with Pepita Aillade and Pita Chips
Wente Vineyards Brut Sparkling Wine

Roasted Tomato Bisque
Wente Vineyards Sauvignon Blanc

Risotto with Pancetta and Arugula
Wente Vineyards Riva Ranch Vineyard Pinot Noir or Sandstone Merlot

Grilled Halibut with Cauliflower-Leek Puree, Roasted Zucchini, and Pistachio Pesto
Wente Vineyards Eric's Chardonnay

Blood Orange Crème Brûlée
Wente Vineyards Riesling

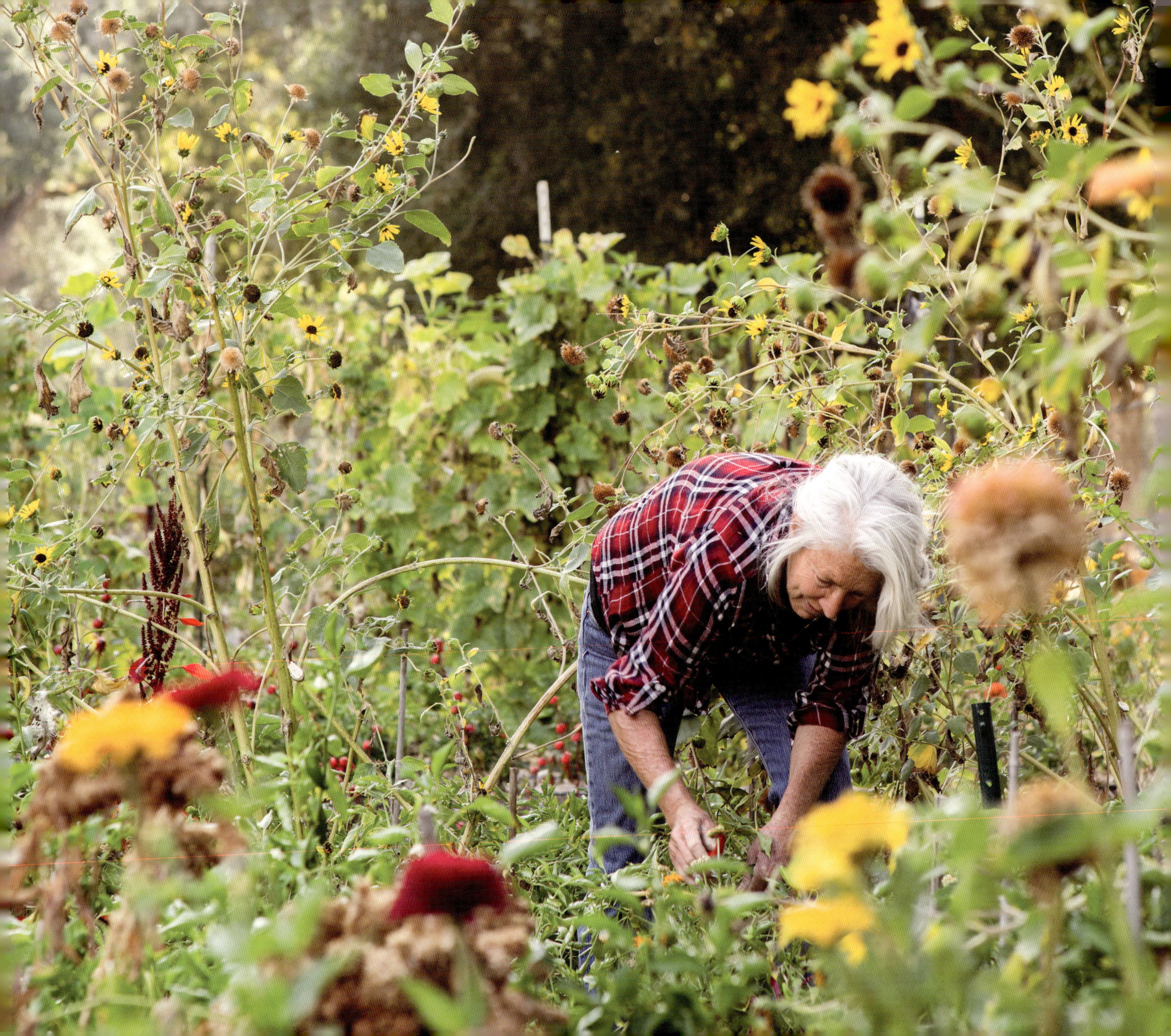

Butternut Squash Hummus with Pepita Aillade and Pita Chips Serves 8

Wente Vineyards chef Jeff Farlow dreamed up this hummus variation to use the deluge of autumn squashes from the garden. Beware: the fried pita chips are as addictive as the hummus. Jeff tops the hummus with a pumpkin seed aillade, a French word for a rustic, garlicky sauce. With garden vegetables for dipping—radishes, cucumbers, tomatoes, peppers—and some meaty olives, this appetizer could become a light meal.

Hummus:

2 pounds peeled butternut squash, in 1-inch cubes

2 cups drained home-cooked or canned chickpeas

½ cup tahini

3 tablespoons Champagne vinegar

2 tablespoons extra virgin olive oil

1 tablespoon honey

½ teaspoon ground nutmeg

¼ teaspoon ground turmeric

Juice of 1 to 2 lemons

Sea salt

Pepita Aillade:

⅓ cup roasted and salted pumpkin seeds, roughly chopped

1 small clove garlic, minced

¼ cup extra virgin olive oil

Red chile flakes

Canola oil, for deep-frying

4 pita rounds, cut into triangles

Wine: Wente Vineyards Brut Sparkling Wine

Make the hummus: Preheat the oven to 425°F. Line a baking sheet with parchment paper. Spread the squash cubes on the prepared pan. Bake until tender and lightly browned in spots, 25 to 30 minutes.

In a food processor, combine the squash, chickpeas, tahini, vinegar, olive oil, honey, nutmeg, turmeric, the juice of 1 lemon, and a large pinch of salt. Process until smooth. Taste and adjust with more lemon juice or salt if necessary.

Make the pepita aillade: In a small bowl, stir together the pumpkin seeds, garlic, olive oil, and chile flakes to taste.

Pour canola oil to a depth of 3 inches into a heavy saucepan and heat to 360°F. Working in batches, add the pita triangles and fry, turning once with tongs, until golden brown on both sides, about 1 minute. As they are done, use the tongs to transfer them to a rack. Sprinkle with salt and let cool.

To serve, spread the hummus on a platter. With the back of a spoon, make a well in the center and spoon the aillade into the well. Serve with the pita chips for scooping.

Roasted Tomato Bisque

Makes 6 cups, to serve 4 to 6

The annual tomato harvest from the Wente garden is almost overwhelming—hundreds of pounds of lemon-yellow, sunset-orange, pink, carmine, and purple fruits. What to do with this river of ripeness? Carolyn freezes some and dries some, and many pounds become soup. This bisque is a family favorite. Roasting concentrates the tomato flavor, and garden herbs round out the scent.

3 pounds tomatoes of any color, including some cherry tomatoes for garnish

6 cloves garlic, peeled

2 large yellow onions, halved and sliced

½ cup extra virgin olive oil

Sea salt and freshly ground black pepper

1½ cups chicken broth

½ cup dry white wine

1 teaspoon minced fresh thyme

1 teaspoon minced fresh rosemary

4 tablespoons unsalted butter

Crème fraîche or thinned sour cream, for garnish (optional)

Thinly sliced fresh basil leaves, for garnish (optional)

Wine: Wente Vineyards Sauvignon Blanc

Preheat the oven to 450°F. Line two baking sheets with parchment paper. Core the large tomatoes and cut into quarters. Leave the cherry tomatoes whole. In a large bowl, combine the tomatoes, garlic, onions, oil, and salt and pepper to taste. Toss gently, then spread the vegetables on the two prepared pans. Roast until the tomatoes have softened and begun to caramelize and the onions are lightly colored, 25 to 30 minutes. Set the roasted cherry tomatoes aside.

Scrape the remaining vegetables and any juices into a soup pot and add the broth, wine, thyme, rosemary, and butter. Bring to a simmer, adjust the heat to maintain a simmer, and cook uncovered until the volume has reduced by about one-third and the tomatoes are completely soft. Remove from the heat and let cool for a few minutes.

Working in batches, puree the mixture in a blender until smooth. Strain through a fine-mesh sieve to remove the tomato skins and seeds, pressing hard on the solids with a rubber spatula. Adjust the seasoning with salt and pepper.

Return the soup to the pot and reheat gently. Ladle into bowls and garnish with the reserved cherry tomatoes and with a drizzle of crème fraîche and a scattering of basil, if desired.

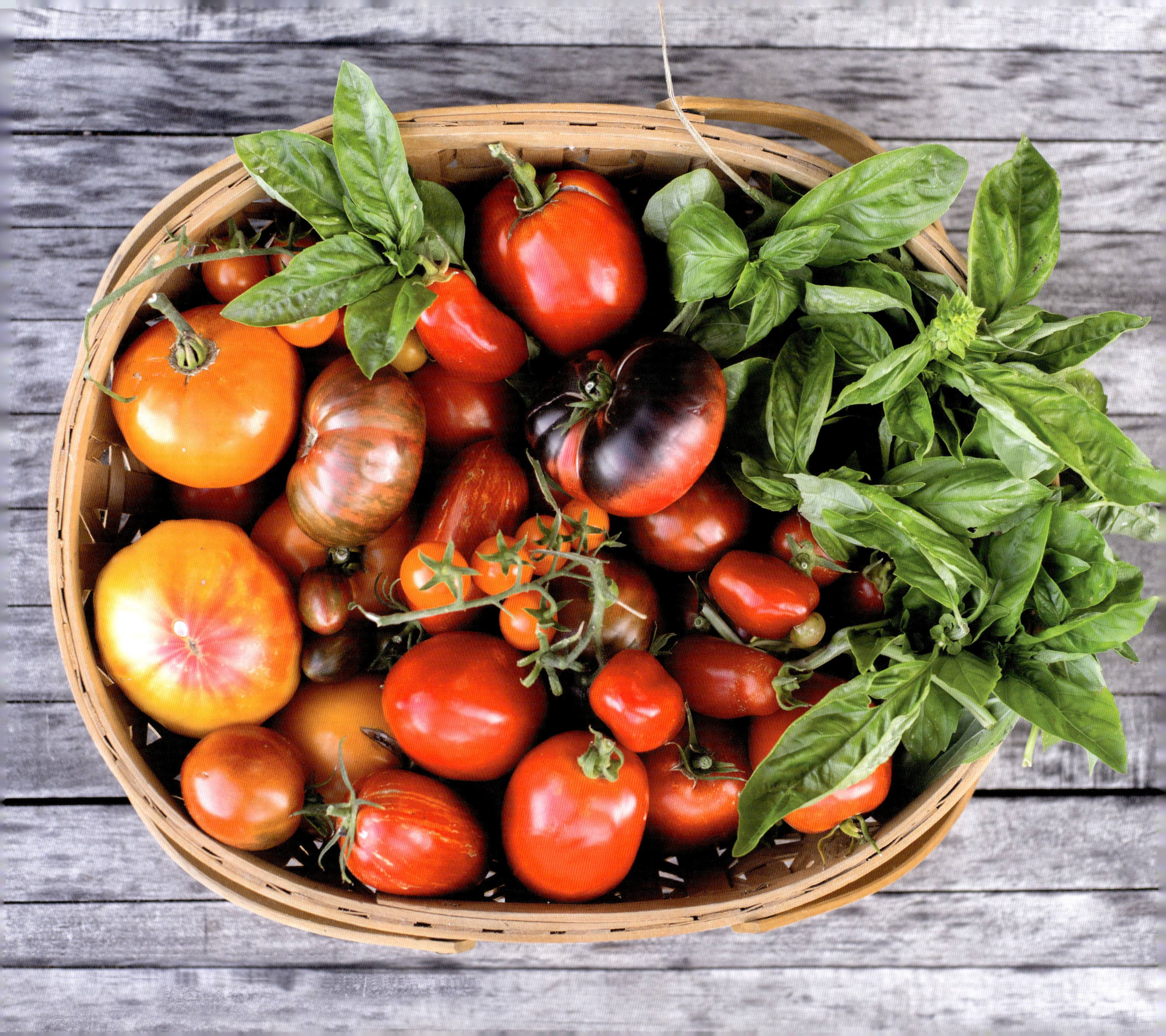

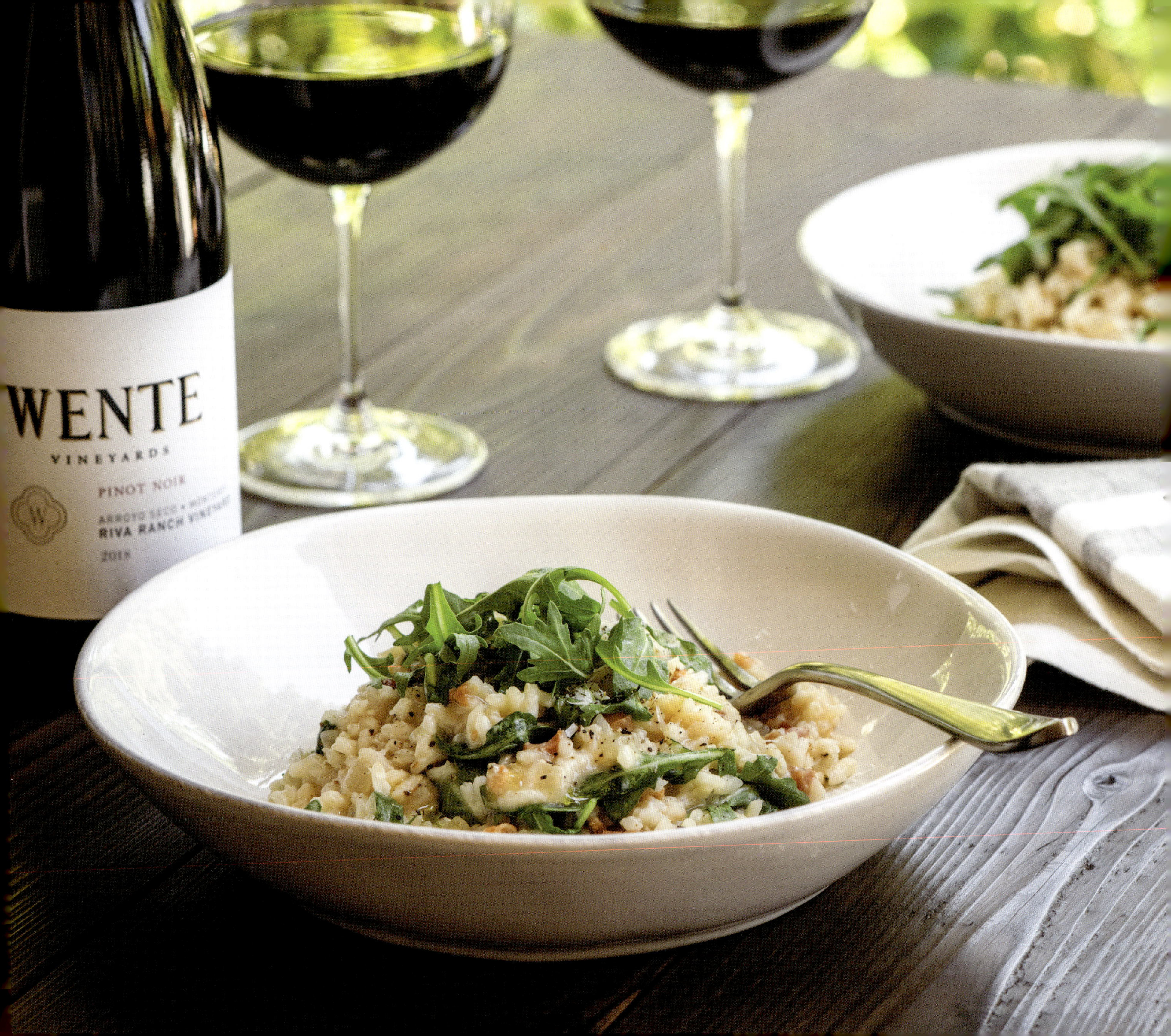
WENTE
VINEYARDS
PINOT NOIR
RIVA RANCH

Risotto with Pancetta and Arugula Serves 4

1 tablespoon extra virgin olive oil

¼ pound pancetta, diced

1 small yellow onion, minced

1 clove garlic, minced

1 cup Carnaroli or Arborio rice

4 to 5 cups chicken broth, simmering

2 cups baby arugula

⅓ cup freshly grated Parmigiano-Reggiano cheese, plus more for topping

Fresh lemon juice

Sea salt and freshly ground black pepper

Wine: Wente Vineyards Riva Ranch Vineyard Pinot Noir or Sandstone Merlot

---

Warm the oil and pancetta in a heavy saucepan over medium heat. Cook, stirring, until the pancetta has rendered most of its fat and is almost crisp. With a slotted spoon, transfer the pancetta to paper towels. Add the onion and garlic and sauté until the onion has softened, about 5 minutes. Add the rice and cook, stirring, until the grains are coated with oil and have just started to color, about 2 minutes.

Begin adding the hot broth ½ cup at a time. Adjust the heat to maintain a gentle simmer and cook, stirring frequently and adding more broth only when the previous addition has been absorbed. It should take 20 to 25 minutes for the rice to absorb most of the broth and become al dente. Taste often and stop cooking when the rice is just tender enough for your taste. It will soften a bit more as it rests.

Aly learned to make risotto from her aunt Carolyn and has gradually mastered the technique, a useful one for gardeners because almost any vegetable can find a home in risotto. For this autumn version, she stirs in a handful of arugula when the rice is almost done. The greens wilt during the few minutes the rice needs to rest.

Stir in the pancetta, arugula, cheese, and the lemon juice to taste. Season with salt and pepper. Stir in another ¼ cup of the broth, cover, and let rest for about 3 minutes.

Divide the risotto among four bowls, sprinkle a little more cheese on top, and serve immediately.

wine-pairing tips from two pros:

Vintners are often more casual about wine pairing than their customers might imagine. "For me, it's more about the wine I want to drink that evening," admits Carolyn Wente. "Then I think about what's in the garden and open the fridge." The pairing dos and don'ts that make many people self-conscious are often relaxed in her household. "There were so many rules when I was growing up," recalls Carolyn. "'You can't have asparagus with wine; you can't have artichokes with wine.' Well, I think you can."

Her niece, Aly, concurs. "I like to drink what I'm in the mood for and eat what I'm in the mood for," says the fifth-generation vintner. If you want to serve a steamed artichoke with white wine, marinate it in olive oil and vinegar, then finish it on the grill, suggests Aly. "I'm a believer that salt and acid can fix anything."

Grilled Halibut with Cauliflower-Leek Puree, Roasted Zucchini, and Pistachio Pesto Serves 4

Carolyn often gets inspiration from the Wente Vineyards restaurant for her own home entertaining. This recipe is one example: a restaurant-caliber dish that any home cook can do. The cauliflower–leek puree is simple. Young garden zucchini roast in the oven while the halibut is on the grill. An impressive dinner-party dish, it gets a big assist from the garden and from a bottle of Wente Vineyards Chardonnay.

Pistachio Pesto:
1 cup loosely packed fresh basil leaves
½ cup loosely packed fresh flat-leaf parsley leaves
½ cup unsalted roasted pistachios
1 tablespoon chopped garlic
1 teaspoon sea salt
½ cup extra virgin olive oil
Freshly ground black pepper

1 cup chicken broth
1 large leek, white and pale green parts only, thinly sliced
1 medium cauliflower, cored and separated into florets
Sea salt and freshly ground black pepper
½ lemon
2 small green zucchini
2 small yellow zucchini
2 tablespoons extra virgin olive oil, plus more for the fish
1 tablespoon sherry vinegar
4 cloves garlic, minced
4 skin-on halibut fillets, 5 to 6 ounces each

Wine: Wente Vineyards Eric's Chardonnay

Make the pistachio pesto: In a food processor, combine the basil, parsley, pistachios, garlic, and salt and pulse to blend. With the motor running, add the oil in a thin, steady stream, blending until smooth. Stop and scrape down the sides of the work bowl once or twice. Transfer the pesto to a bowl and stir in pepper to taste.

In a saucepan, heat the broth over medium-high heat. Add the leek and simmer until softened, about 5 minutes. Add the cauliflower florets, season with salt, cover, and adjust the heat to maintain a simmer. Cook until the cauliflower is tender, about 10 minutes. Drain into a sieve set over a bowl, reserving the liquid. Transfer the leeks and cauliflower to the food processor and puree until very smooth, thinning as needed with the reserved cooking liquid. Return the puree to the pan and season with salt, pepper, and a squeeze of lemon juice. Cover and keep warm.

Preheat the oven to 400°F. Prepare a medium charcoal fire or preheat a gas grill to medium. Preheat the grill rack to prevent the fish from sticking.

Line a baking sheet with parchment paper. Slice all the zucchini lengthwise about ⅜ inch thick. In a bowl, toss the zucchini slices with the oil, vinegar, and garlic and season with salt and pepper. Arrange them on the prepared pan and roast until tender and golden, 15 to 20 minutes. Keep warm.

Coat the halibut on both sides with oil and season with salt and pepper. Place the halibut, skin side down, on the preheated grill rack. Cook for about 5 minutes, then turn and cook on the flesh side until the fish barely flakes, about 3 minutes longer. The fish will continue to cook as it cools.

To serve, spoon some of the cauliflower-leek puree on each plate. Arrange the zucchini slices alongside and top them with the fish. Spoon the pesto over all and serve immediately.

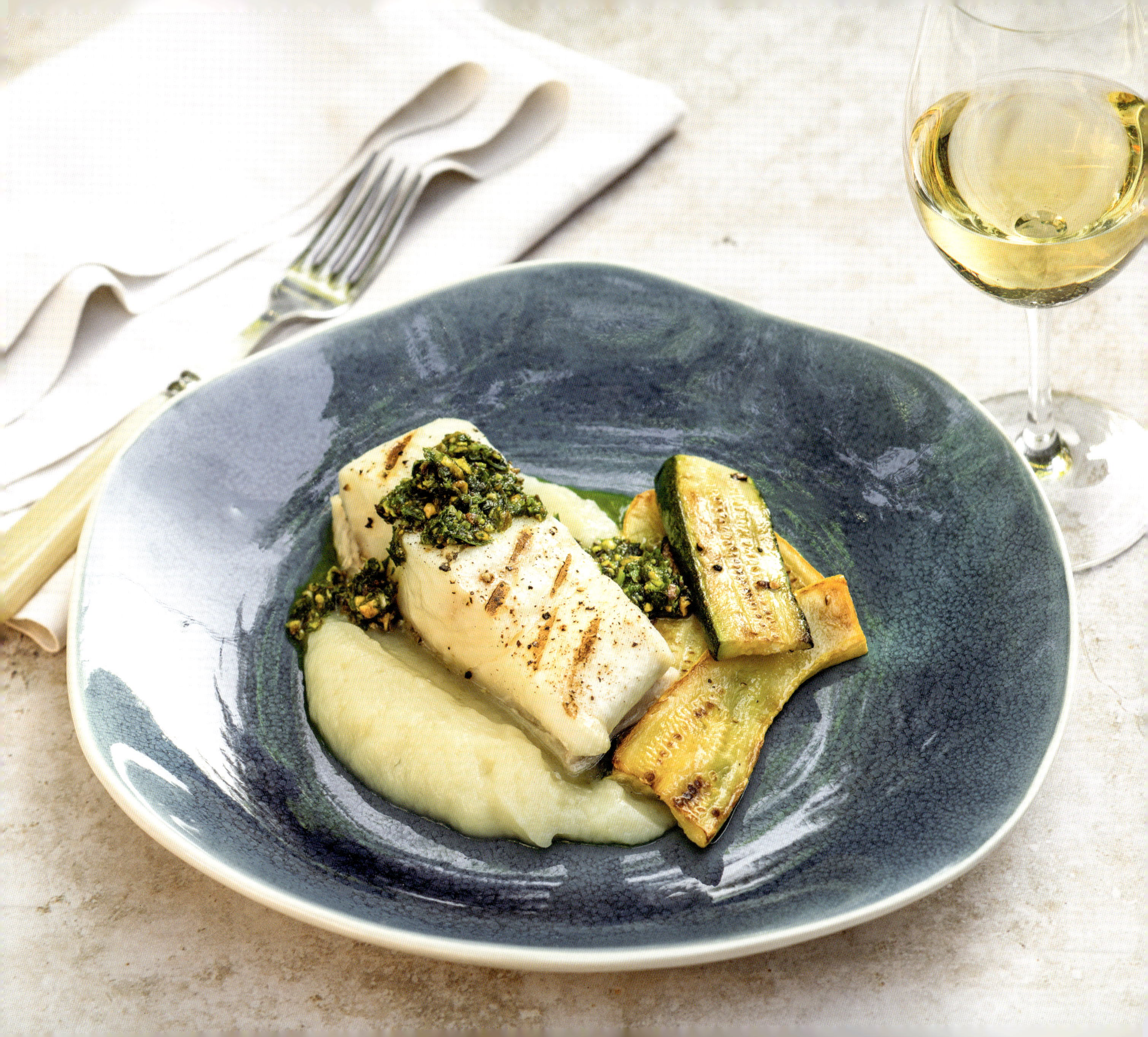

WENTE
VINEYARDS
ESTATE GROWN
Riverbank
RIESLING
ARROYO SECO • MONTEREY
2018

Blood Orange Crème Brûlée

Serves 6

4 blood oranges

2 tablespoons Wente Vineyards Riesling

6 tablespoons granulated sugar

2 cups heavy cream

1 vanilla bean

6 large egg yolks

Pinch of sea salt

6 tablespoons superfine sugar

Wine: Wente Vineyards Riesling

Carolyn has a potted blood orange tree just outside her kitchen door—convenient for breakfast juice—and another in her hillside orchard. No wonder she dreamed up this gorgeous crème brûlée, with Riesling-steeped oranges on the bottom of the ramekin and a ruby-red orange slice on top.

With a rasp grater, grate enough blood orange zest to yield 1 tablespoon. Working with 1 orange at a time, cut a thin slice off both ends so it will stand upright. Stand the orange on a cutting surface and, using a sharp knife, remove all the peel and white pith by slicing from top to bottom all the way around the orange, following the contour of the fruit. Cut along the membranes to release the individual segments and place them in a small bowl. Repeat with 2 more of the oranges. Remove any seeds.

Add the Riesling and 1 tablespoon of the granulated sugar to the segments and toss gently.

Pour the cream into a small saucepan and add the orange zest. Halve the vanilla bean lengthwise and, with the tip of a small knife, scrape the seeds into the saucepan. Add the pod as well. Bring just to a simmer over medium heat. Cover, remove from the heat, and let steep for 5 minutes, then remove the pod.

In a bowl, whisk together the egg yolks, the remaining 5 tablespoons granulated sugar, and the salt. Add the warm cream ½ cup at a time, whisking constantly.

Drain the orange segments and divide them evenly among six 6-ounce heatproof ramekins. Pour the custard mixture into the ramekins, dividing it evenly. Place the ramekins in a baking dish just large enough to hold them. Add boiling water to come halfway up the sides of the ramekins. Cover the baking dish tightly with aluminum foil and bake until the custards are just set, about 30 minutes. They will be slightly puffy on top and still a bit jiggly. With a jar lifter or pot holders, carefully lift the ramekins out of the hot water and set on a wire rack to cool. When cool, cover and refrigerate until chilled, at least 4 hours or up to overnight.

Preheat the oven to 350°F. Remove the peel and pith of the remaining blood orange as described for the first 3 oranges. Then, instead of removing the segments, slice the orange crosswise into 6 thin slices. With the tip of a knife, remove the white pith at the center of each slice. Remove any seeds.

Place an orange slice on each chilled custard. Top each custard with 1 tablespoon of the superfine sugar in an even layer. With a kitchen torch, heat the sugar until it melts and caramelizes; do not allow it to burn. Let cool briefly, then serve.

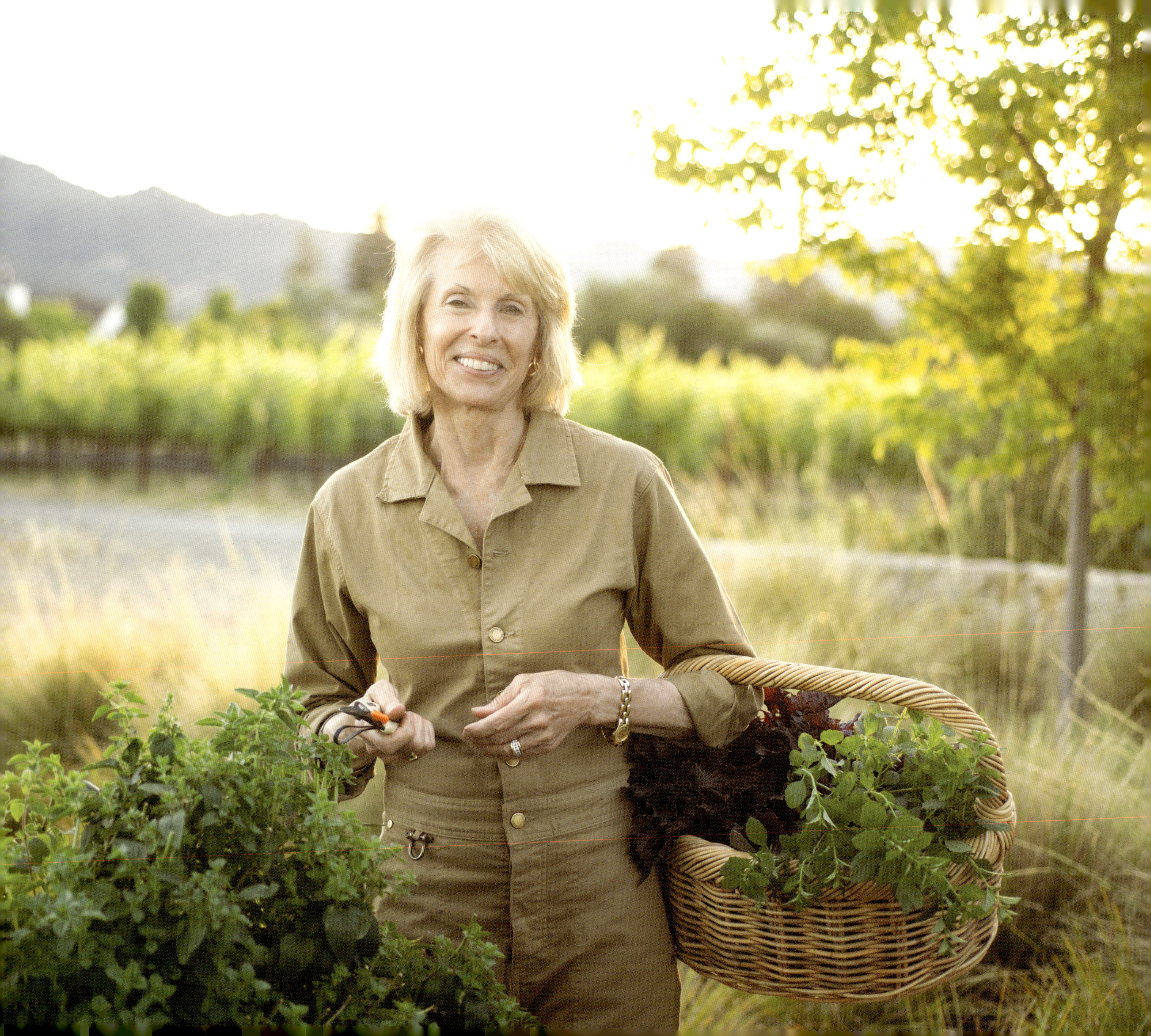

Wheeler Farms: *Restoring Diversity*

St. Helena

Most people place their vegetable gardens out of visitors' sight, knowing that tomato vines and melon patches can look ragged by season's end. Keeping an edible garden camera ready year-round takes persistence and the ability to see beauty in autumn's decline and winter's comparative bareness.

"We put in front what most people put in back," acknowledges Daphne Araujo about the landscape plan she settled on for Wheeler Farms, the estate she purchased with husband, Bart, and partners in 2014. From their experience at Araujo Estate, the Calistoga winery they formerly owned, the couple knew that an edible garden, front and center, should be a key feature of their new venture.

"Gardens are such a magnet," says Daphne, a former landscape architect. At Araujo, tasting-room visitors would hear the chickens and then want to see the chickens. "It dawned on us that the people who were coming to wine country wanted the whole 'country' experience," says the vintner. "We want to give them that experience at Wheeler Farms."

Left and above: *Wheeler Farms proprietor Daphne Araujo is a former landscape architect and avid gardener; Daphne and husband, Bart, enjoy a glass of the winery's Sauvignon Blanc in the garden at sunset.*

Working with San Francisco landscape architect Ron Lutsko, the Araujos have restored the agricultural diversity that defined the property when J. H. Wheeler owned it in the late 1800s. Inheriting part of a large Spanish land grant, Wheeler cultivated wine grapes as well as fruit, nut, and citrus trees on more than one hundred acres. The family's holdings dwindled over the decades, and the parcel the Araujos and their partners purchased is only a sliver of the original farm. But by reviving the Wheeler name, the Araujos are signaling their commitment to preserving the land's farming past. Adding a state-of-the-art winery and planting Cabernet Sauvignon and Sauvignon Blanc grapes, the couple has created a nearly self-sufficient estate.

"We took out vineyard to make room for the orchard," says Daphne, "and that was not a hard decision. We wanted fruits and vegetables coming into the kitchen that you could cook with and decorate with."

That orchard now supplies the kitchen with more than twenty different heirloom fruits, from prized (and endangered) Royal Blenheim apricots to Elephant Heart plums, Northern Spy apples, and sought-after Suncrest peaches. Growing winter cover crops in the orchard has helped restore the soil's tilth, and in keeping with the Araujos' commitment to organic and biodynamic practices, weeds are managed by hand. California poppies and other wildflowers carpet the orchard with color in spring and provide habitat for beneficial insects. A thriving beehive generates honey for the kitchen, but its occupants are valued more for their contribution as pollinators.

Lutsko, known as a brilliant plantsman as well as for his genius with hardscape, designed steel planter boxes of varying heights to give the garden a strong visual structure. Filled with ornamental plants and edibles and surrounded by decomposed granite paths, the burnished copper-colored beds occupy a sunny walled courtyard with views of the Mayacamas Mountains. "Even if the beds are empty, the garden looks good," says Daphne. "When things grow, the joy is in the growth, and when the trellises come down, you can see the garden's bones again."

But these handsome, deep raised beds are rarely empty. Soft mounds of white alyssum bloom almost nonstop, wafting a gentle, honeyed scent that bees love. Ladybugs, butterflies, and other desirable visitors know they will always find blooming plants here, from cheery violas and pansies in late winter to sweet peas, nasturtiums, bachelor's buttons, sunflowers, salvias, and cosmos as the seasons progress. "A lot of what goes on in that garden is about attracting beneficial insects," says Daphne.

But fundamentally, the garden is about farm-to-table eating and celebrating the synergy between good cooking and fine wine. Wheeler Farms' Cabernet Sauvignons draw serious collectors to its Hospitality House for tasting, and the Araujos initially viewed the property as something of a demonstration farm, a model of sustainable Napa Valley living. But their ambitions grew with the arrival of Sarah Heller, a talented and energetic young chef and experienced gardener.

"She is a perfectionist on the French Laundry level," says Daphne, who soon delegated garden management to Sarah. "Every now and then I'll make a suggestion, but she knows what to do."

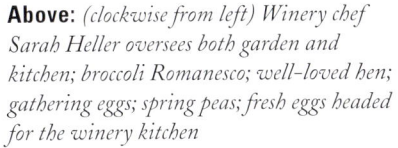

Above: *(clockwise from left) Winery chef Sarah Heller oversees both garden and kitchen; broccoli Romanesco; well-loved hen; gathering eggs; spring peas; fresh eggs headed for the winery kitchen*

"Gardens are such a magnet," says Daphne. *"The people coming to wine country want the whole 'country' experience, and we want to give them that."*

Following a monthly planting calendar, Sarah has greatly expanded the garden's variety, preferring smaller harvests but more diversity. A greenhouse on the premises allows her to start seeds for specialty produce rarely available in nurseries, such as purple jalapeños; Mr. Stripey, Blondkopfchen, and Hawaiian Pineapple tomatoes; Gadzukes zucchini; Graffiti and Fairy Tale eggplants; six varieties of cucumber; and eight types of basil.

In spring, the beds are flush with tender herbs like chervil, chives, and lime thyme; mild spring onions, spring garlic, and garlic flowers; baby kale; five types of radishes; and blossoming fava beans and peas, whose delicate blossoms Sarah plucks to garnish plates. By summer, the onslaught of tomatoes, peppers, eggplants, beans, and basil means

Wheeler Farms 223

long days for Sarah in the farm's light-filled contemporary kitchen making tomato sauce, fermenting hot peppers, and pickling cucumbers.

Now, Wheeler Farms visitors have a more elevated tasting experience, engineered by a chef who understands the harmonies between garden produce and wine. "I try to make the food complement the wine instead of mimic the flavors," says Sarah. "If the wine tastes of tropical fruit, I won't make a dish with tropical fruit, but I'll use complementary ingredients like shrimp and green vegetables."

Above and right: *(clockwise from left) Sarah preserves much of the garden harvest for visitor gifts; the chef discusses the dinner menu with the Araujos; Daphne in the garden; Wheeler Farms' handsome kitchen; Sarah's edible flower cookies*

224   Gather

The winery's powerful Cabernet Sauvignons love rich red meats, but the garden supplies pairing options, too. "You can cook a carrot to go with Cabernet if you grill it and use complex spices," says the chef. The Cabernet-friendly dishes she makes for vegetarian guests often include roasted or grilled eggplant, caramelized onions, roasted peppers, and sturdy herbs like rosemary, oregano, and lavender.

"So much of the food that goes with red wine is brown and white," says the chef, "but I like to make pretty food." The garden, with its riot of color, solves that dilemma, offering golden beets, flowering mint, Thumbelina carrots, purple bean blossoms, and other edibles in gemstone hues for her plates.

Even the chicken eggs are colorful here. The Wheeler Farms flock resides in the Taj Mahal of coops, a pristine residence for heirloom-variety laying hens that looks as if a housekeeper tidies up daily. Many Wheeler Farms visitors go home with a half dozen of these exceptional eggs, or a jar of Wheeler Farms apricot preserves, or a cellophane bag of sugar cookies stamped with pressed flowers.

For a dinner showcasing the late-spring garden and built around Wheeler Farms wines, Sarah first surveys what the raised beds have to offer: English peas, fresh-dug potatoes, fava beans, fragrant mint, spring onions and garlic, tender broccoli shoots, and, from the orchard, the first apricots. From that inventory, a menu takes shape: chilled spring vegetable soup with a lemony shrimp garnish to show off the Sauvignon Blanc; a poached egg on potato puree with fava bean pesto and fried shallots, a dish robust enough for a vineyard-designated Cabernet Sauvignon; and for the main course, well-marbled short ribs with broccoli di cicco and farro— a Cabernet Sauvignon slam dunk. Apricots in lemon verbena syrup and a dainty quenelle of olive oil–sea salt ice cream reflect Sarah's tendency to end meals on a light note. A parting gift of flower cookies sends guests home with a souvenir of a wine estate with a distinctive vision and purpose.

menu

Chilled Spring Garden Soup with Bay Shrimp
Wheeler Farms Sauvignon Blanc

Poached Farm Egg with Potato Crème, Fava Bean Pesto, and Crispy Shallots
Wheeler Farms Beckstoffer Georges III Cabernet Sauvignon

Slow-Roasted Beef Short Ribs with Broccoli di Cicco and Farro
Wheeler Farms Beckstoffer Missouri Hopper Cabernet Sauvignon

Lemon Verbena Apricots with Olive Oil–Sea Salt Ice Cream

Edible Flower Cookies

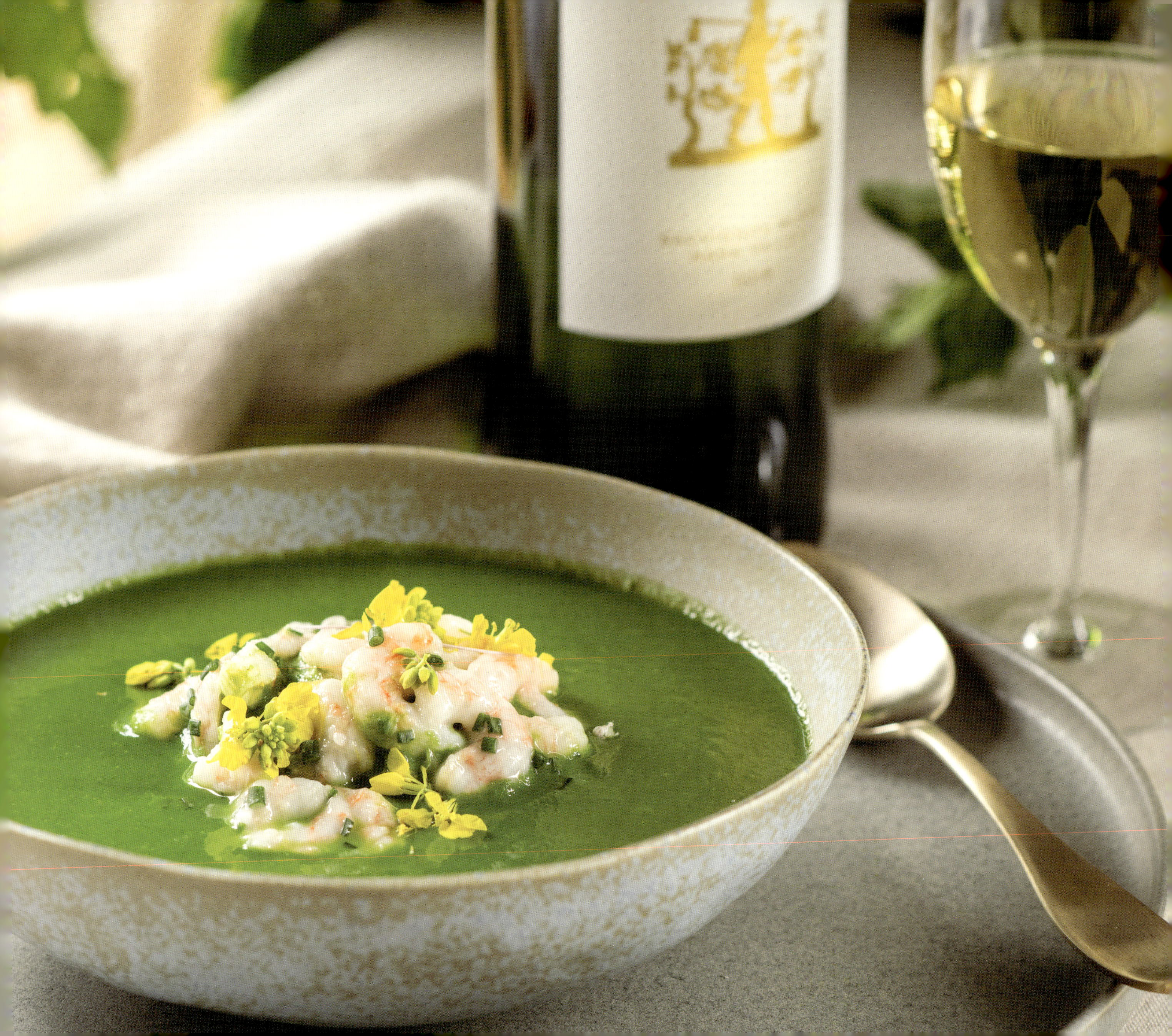

Chilled Spring Garden Soup with Bay Shrimp Serves 4

In spring, the Wheeler Farms garden is flush with delicate leafy greens and tender fresh herbs. Sarah likes to blend them together in an emerald-green cold soup brightened with Meyer lemon. Low-fat milk keeps the texture airy; even so, the soup has depth and plenty of body. Sugar snap peas, asparagus, leeks, or dill could also play a role if you have them. A spoonful of lemony shrimp salad on top dresses up the soup and supplies a bridge to the winery's seafood-friendly Sauvignon Blanc.

¾ pound English peas, chopped into ½-inch pieces (including the pods)

2 spring onions

1 small bunch spinach (about 6 ounces), stemmed

½ bunch fresh flat-leaf parsley, stems included

4 fresh mint sprigs

2 tablespoons extra virgin olive oil

2-inch piece green garlic, coarsely chopped

Kosher or sea salt and freshly ground white pepper

2 cups low-fat milk

½ teaspoon grated Meyer lemon zest

Fresh Meyer lemon juice, as needed

Shrimp Salad:

¼ pound bay shrimp (about ¾ cup), halved crosswise

2 tablespoons plain Greek yogurt

1 teaspoon fresh Meyer lemon juice

¼ teaspoon grated Meyer lemon zest

1 teaspoon thinly sliced fresh chives

Sea salt and freshly ground white pepper

Fresh chive blossoms or mustard blossoms, for garnish (optional)

Wine: Wheeler Farms Sauvignon Blanc

Bring a pot of salted water to a boil over high heat and prepare a large bowl of ice water. Add the peas to the boiling water and boil until the pods are just tender, about 2 minutes. With a wire skimmer, transfer the peas to the ice water to chill quickly.

Cut the leafy green tops from the spring onions. Chop the green tops and the white stalks coarsely but keep them separate. Add the green tops to the boiling water along with the spinach, parsley, and mint. Boil just until the onion tops are tender, about 1½ minutes, then drain and transfer to the ice water. When cool, drain well.

Heat the olive oil in a saucepan over medium-low heat. Add the green garlic and white spring onion stalks, season with salt and pepper, and sauté until translucent, about 5 minutes. Add the milk and lemon zest, bring to a simmer, then reduce the heat to low and cook gently for about 10 minutes to infuse with flavor. Remove from the heat.

In a blender, combine the boiled herbs and vegetables and the milk mixture and puree until smooth. Blend only as long as necessary to avoid overheating the mixture, which can dull the color. Strain the mixture through a fine-mesh sieve, pressing on the solids. Cover and chill.

Make the shrimp salad: In a small bowl, combine the shrimp, yogurt, lemon juice and zest, and chives and mix gently. Season to taste with salt and pepper.

Taste the soup for salt and add a squeeze of lemon juice to brighten the flavor if needed. Divide the soup among four bowls. Spoon the shrimp salad on top of each portion, dividing it evenly. If desired, garnish with chive blossoms. Serve immediately.

Poached Farm Egg with Potato Crème, Fava Bean Pesto, and Crispy Shallots Serves 4

Potato Crème:

1 large russet potato, about 10 ounces, peeled, in ¾-inch cubes

Kosher or sea salt

¾ cup low-fat milk

2 tablespoons unsalted butter

¼ teaspoon freshly grated nutmeg

Freshly ground black pepper

Fava Bean Pesto:

2½ pounds fava beans

⅓ cup freshly grated Pecorino Romano cheese

1 tablespoon extra virgin olive oil

1 tablespoon fresh Meyer lemon juice

½ teaspoon grated Meyer lemon zest

Fried Shallots:

Canola oil, for deep-frying

1 large shallot, peeled

Unbleached all-purpose flour, for dusting

Sea salt

Eggs:

6 cups water

1 tablespoon kosher salt

1 tablespoon white wine vinegar

4 large farm eggs

Extra virgin olive oil

Sliced fresh chives, for garnish

Wheeler Farms' heirloom chickens supply golden-yolked eggs that deserve center stage. In spring, Sarah poaches them and presents them on a bed of potato foam (a simple potato puree works, too) with tender spring fava beans transformed into pesto. On another occasion, spoon the fava pesto on ricotta-topped crostini.

Wine: Wheeler Farms Beckstoffer Georges III Cabernet Sauvignon

Make the potato crème: In a saucepan, combine the potato, 1 tablespoon salt, and cold water to cover and bring to a simmer over medium heat. Cook at a gentle simmer until the potato is tender, about 20 minutes. Drain, reserving about ½ cup of the potato water. While the potato cooks, in a small saucepan, combine the milk, butter, nutmeg, several grinds of black pepper, and ½ teaspoon salt. Warm over low heat until the butter melts; keep warm.

In a blender, combine the boiled potato and the warm milk mixture and blend just until smooth, adding enough reserved potato water—about ⅓ cup—to make a creamy, pourable puree. Do not overblend or the potato may turn gummy. Taste for salt. Transfer the puree to a whipped-cream dispenser or to a small saucepan.

Make the pesto: Shell the fava beans. You should have about 2 cups beans. Bring a small saucepan of water to a boil over high heat and prepare a bowl of ice water. Add the beans to the boiling water and blanch for about 30 seconds (a little longer if they are large), then drain and transfer to the ice water. When cool, drain again. Peel the beans; the skins should slip off easily. You should have a scant 1 cup peeled beans. Put the beans into a food processor and add the pecorino, olive oil, and lemon juice and zest. Pulse a few times to make a coarse but blended mixture. It should not be smooth.

Make the fried shallots: In a small saucepan, pour canola oil to a depth of 2 inches and heat to 325°F. While the oil heats, slice the shallot thinly on a vegetable slicer. Toss the shallot slices in flour, shaking off the excess. Add the slices to the hot oil and fry, agitating constantly, until deep golden brown, about 2 minutes. With a wire skimmer, transfer the slices to paper towels to cool; sprinkle with salt.

Cook the eggs: In a wide saucepan, combine the water, salt, and vinegar and bring to a simmer over medium heat. Adjust the heat to maintain a bare simmer. Break each egg into a small ramekin or cup. Stir the simmering water to create a vortex, then slide the eggs in one at a time. Adjust the heat to make sure the water does not boil; it should barely bubble. Poach until the egg whites are set, 3 to 4 minutes. Meanwhile, put about 2 teaspoons olive oil into a shallow bowl. With a slotted spoon, lift the eggs out of the water and into the bowl. The oil will keep them from sticking.

If the potato puree is in a whipped-cream dispenser, activate the charger. If the puree is in a saucepan, reheat it gently. Divide the puree among four plates. Top with the fava pesto, dividing it evenly. Put a poached egg on top of the pesto, then scatter the fried shallots and chives over the top. Serve immediately.

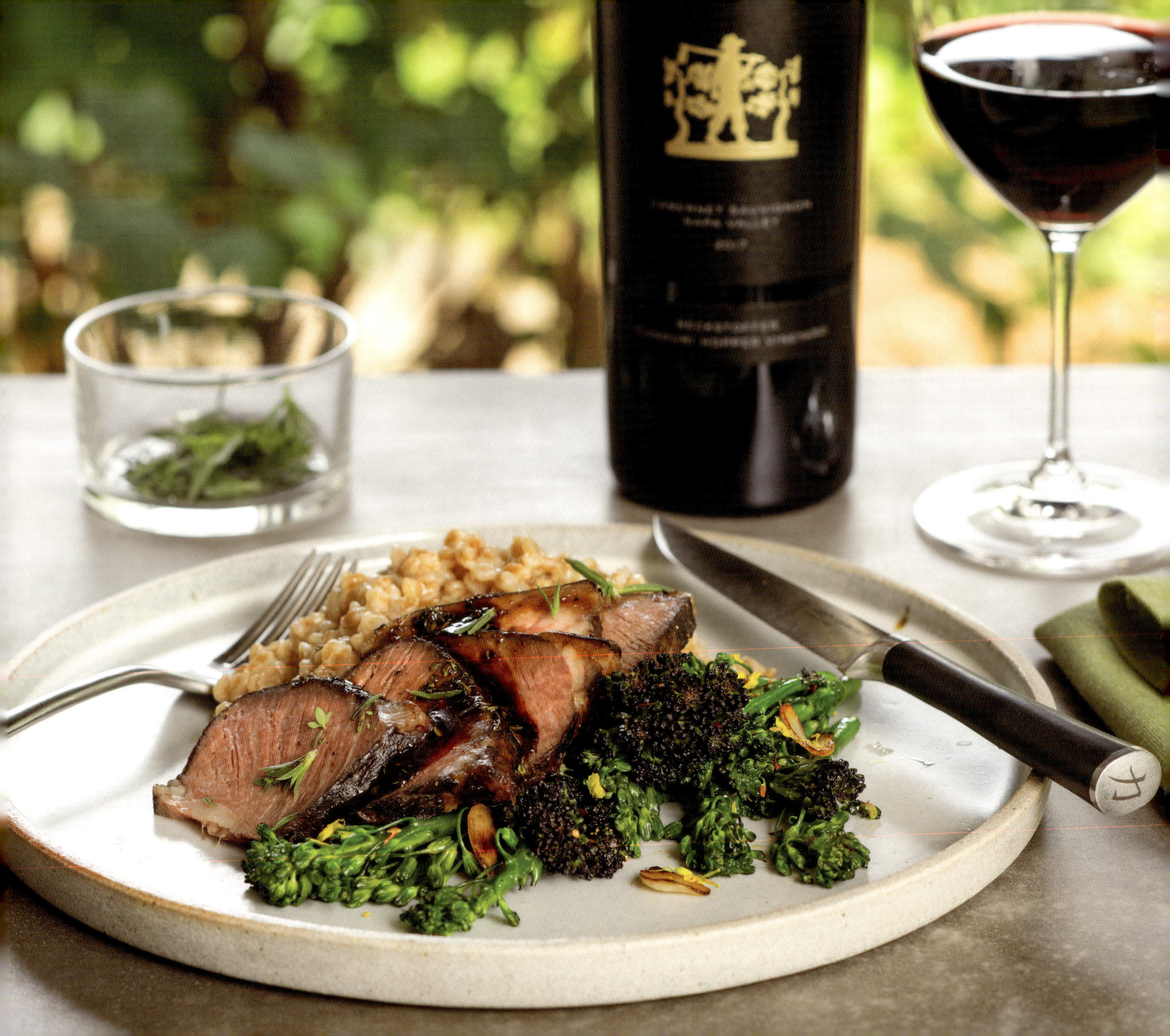

Slow-Roasted Beef Short Ribs with Broccoli di Cicco and Farro

Serves 4

No recipe for beef could be easier than this slow-roasting method. The ribs aren't even browned first, but after four hours in a slow oven, they are the color of mahogany. To balance their richness, Sarah serves them with nutty farro and broccoli di cicco, an Italian variety that produces tender side shoots rather than a single head. This prized crop thrives in the Wheeler Farms raised beds in late spring and again in fall.

1½ pounds boneless beef short ribs, preferably USDA Prime, trimmed of silverskin

Sea salt and freshly ground black pepper

Farro:

¼ cup extra virgin olive oil

1 cup farro

2 fresh thyme sprigs

⅓ cup finely diced red onion

1 large clove garlic, peeled

1 tablespoon unsalted butter

3 cups chicken broth or water

1 teaspoon balsamic vinegar

Kosher or sea salt

Broccoli:

3 tablespoons extra virgin olive oil

1 large clove garlic, very thinly sliced

4 cups loosely packed broccoli di cicco (sprouting broccoli) or broccolini florets

Wheeler Farms ground chile ají amarillo or other mildly spicy ground chile

Kosher or sea salt

¼ cup veal demi-glace (optional)

1 teaspoon finely minced mixed fresh herbs, such as oregano, thyme, and savory (optional)

Wine: Wheeler Farms Beckstoffer Missouri Hopper Cabernet Sauvignon

Preheat the oven to 200°F. Pat the short ribs dry, then season all over with salt and pepper. Arrange the short ribs, not touching, in a single layer in an ovenproof skillet or on a baking sheet. Roast uncovered for 4 hours without opening the oven door. They will release some fat and turn a deep, dark brown. Let rest for at least 30 minutes before slicing. (Note: You can cool the ribs and refrigerate them, covered, overnight. Shortly before serving, slice the meat ¼ inch thick, stack the slices against one another in a baking dish, and reheat in a preheated 350°F oven until hot, 3 to 5 minutes.)

Make the farro: Heat the oil in a saucepan over medium heat. Add the farro and cook, stirring constantly, until it smells like toasted wheat, about 3 minutes. Add the thyme, onion, garlic, and butter and cook, stirring, for about 2 minutes. Then add the broth and bring to a simmer. Adjust the heat to maintain a gentle simmer and cook uncovered until the farro is tender and the liquid has been absorbed, about 40 minutes. Remove the thyme sprigs, stir in the vinegar, and season to taste with salt. Keep warm.

Make the broccoli: Heat a large skillet over medium-low heat. Add the olive oil and garlic, and when the garlic begins to color, add the broccoli, chile, and salt to taste. Cook, tossing often with tongs, until the broccoli is tender but not soft, about 5 minutes.

If using the demi-glace, warm it in a small saucepan over low heat. Stir in the mixed herbs.

Slice the short ribs about ¼ inch thick. Divide the broccoli and the farro evenly among four dinner plates. Top with the sliced short ribs. Brush the meat with demi-glace, if using. Serve immediately.

Lemon Verbena Apricots with Olive Oil–Sea Salt Ice Cream

Serves 4

Ice Cream:

3 cups half-and-half

1 cup sugar

1 teaspoon vanilla bean paste, or seeds from 1 vanilla bean, halved lengthwise

½ teaspoon sea salt

5 large egg yolks

3 tablespoons extra virgin olive oil

Lemon Verbena Apricots:

½ cup sugar

2 tablespoons fresh Meyer lemon juice

1 tablespoon vanilla bean paste, or seeds from 1 vanilla bean, halved lengthwise

½ cup water

20 fresh lemon verbena leaves, chopped medium-fine, or 2 tablespoons chopped dried lemon verbena leaves

2 large or 4 medium apricots, halved, pitted, and sliced

Flaky sea salt, such as Maldon, for garnish

Make the ice cream: In a saucepan, combine the half-and-half, sugar, vanilla paste, and salt. Bring to a simmer over medium heat, whisking to dissolve the sugar. Remove from the heat. Put the egg yolks into a blender and, with the motor running, gradually add the hot half-and-half mixture, blending well. Return the mixture to the saucepan and cook over medium heat, stirring constantly, until the mixture visibly thickens and coats a wooden spoon. Do not let it boil or it may curdle. Transfer the custard to a clean bowl, let cool, and then chill.

Apricots aren't the easiest fruit to grow in Napa Valley, but Wheeler Farms has a tree that yields enough for two to three weeks of desserts and out-of-hand eating. Sarah likes to toss the sliced fruit in a light lemon-verbena syrup and pair it with olive oil ice cream. You can replace the apricots with pitted cherries, blackberries, nectarines, strawberries, or figs.

Churn the custard in an ice-cream maker according to manufacturer's directions, adding the oil when the ice cream is almost frozen. Transfer to a container and freeze for at least 1 hour to firm.

Make the apricots: In a small saucepan, combine the sugar, lemon juice, vanilla, and water and bring to a simmer over medium heat, stirring to dissolve the sugar. Remove from the heat. If using dried lemon verbena, add to the syrup while it is hot. If using fresh lemon verbena, let the syrup cool, then add the leaves. Let steep for at least 10 minutes, but overnight is better.

Put the apricots into a small bowl and add about 2 tablespoons of the syrup, enough to coat them lightly. Toss gently. Divide the apricots evenly among four dessert plates. Spoon a little more syrup over the apricots. Place a scoop of ice cream alongside. Top the ice cream with a few salt flakes. Serve immediately.

Edible Flower Cookies

Makes forty-eight 2½-inch round cookies

Visitors to Wheeler Farms often go home with a gift bag of these exquisite cookies, each one decorated with a pressed edible flower from the garden. The buttery cookies make a memorable accompaniment to ice cream, sorbet, poached fruit, or a pot of hot tea.

48 fresh edible flowers of any type

1¼ pounds plus 2 tablespoons unsalted butter, in small cubes, at room temperature

2 cups powdered sugar, sifted

1 large egg

1 teaspoon sea salt

1 teaspoon vanilla bean paste

½ teaspoon violet extract

8 cups sifted all-purpose flour

Egg Wash:

½ cup granulated sugar

½ cup water

1 large egg white

½ teaspoon citric acid or 1 tablespoon lemon juice

Place the flowers in a single layer between two sheets of parchment paper and put heavy weights, such as books, on top to flatten them. Press overnight.

In a stand mixer fitted with the paddle attachment, cream together the butter and powdered sugar on medium speed until light. Add the egg and mix until fully incorporated. Add the salt, vanilla, and violet extract and mix well. On low speed, add the flour and mix until just combined. Cover and chill the dough for at least 2 hours or overnight.

Preheat the oven to 325°F. Line four heavy baking sheets with parchment paper.

Make the egg wash: To make a simple syrup, combine the sugar and water in a small saucepan and bring to a simmer over medium heat, stirring to dissolve the sugar. Remove from the heat, let cool, and then chill well. In a small bowl, whisk together ¼ cup of the simple syrup, the egg white, and citric acid until well blended. Reserve the remaining simply syrup for another use.

Roll out the dough ½ inch thick. Brush the entire dough sheet with the egg wash. Using a 2½-inch round cutter (or a cutter of another desired size), cut out as many cookies as possible. Transfer them to the prepared baking sheets, spacing them 1 inch apart. Carefully place a flower in the center of each cookie and brush again with the egg wash.

Place the baking sheets in the freezer for 10 minutes, then bake the cookies, in shifts if necessary, until they just start to brown around the edges, about 12 minutes. Transfer the cookies to a wire rack to cool.

daphne's garden tips:

Keeping a vegetable garden attractive all year takes attention to detail. Daphne's advice:

Create an aesthetically pleasing structure—"good bones"—so even if the beds are empty, the garden looks inviting.

"Tidy is important," say Daphne. "It takes discipline to constantly deadhead and thin and remove wilted leaves, but you have to get them out of there." A neat garden is more sanitary, too, which keeps disease at bay.

Plan to have something in bloom always. Orange cosmos, poppies, and alyssum are among Daphne's favorites. "If not much else is happening, the eye goes to color," says the vintner.

Plant a cover crop to conceal bare ground and improve the soil.

Left and right: *Sarah snips pansies and other edible flowers for her captivating butter cookies; Daphne's ambitious objective is to have these handsome garden beds productive, tidy, and beautiful year round.*

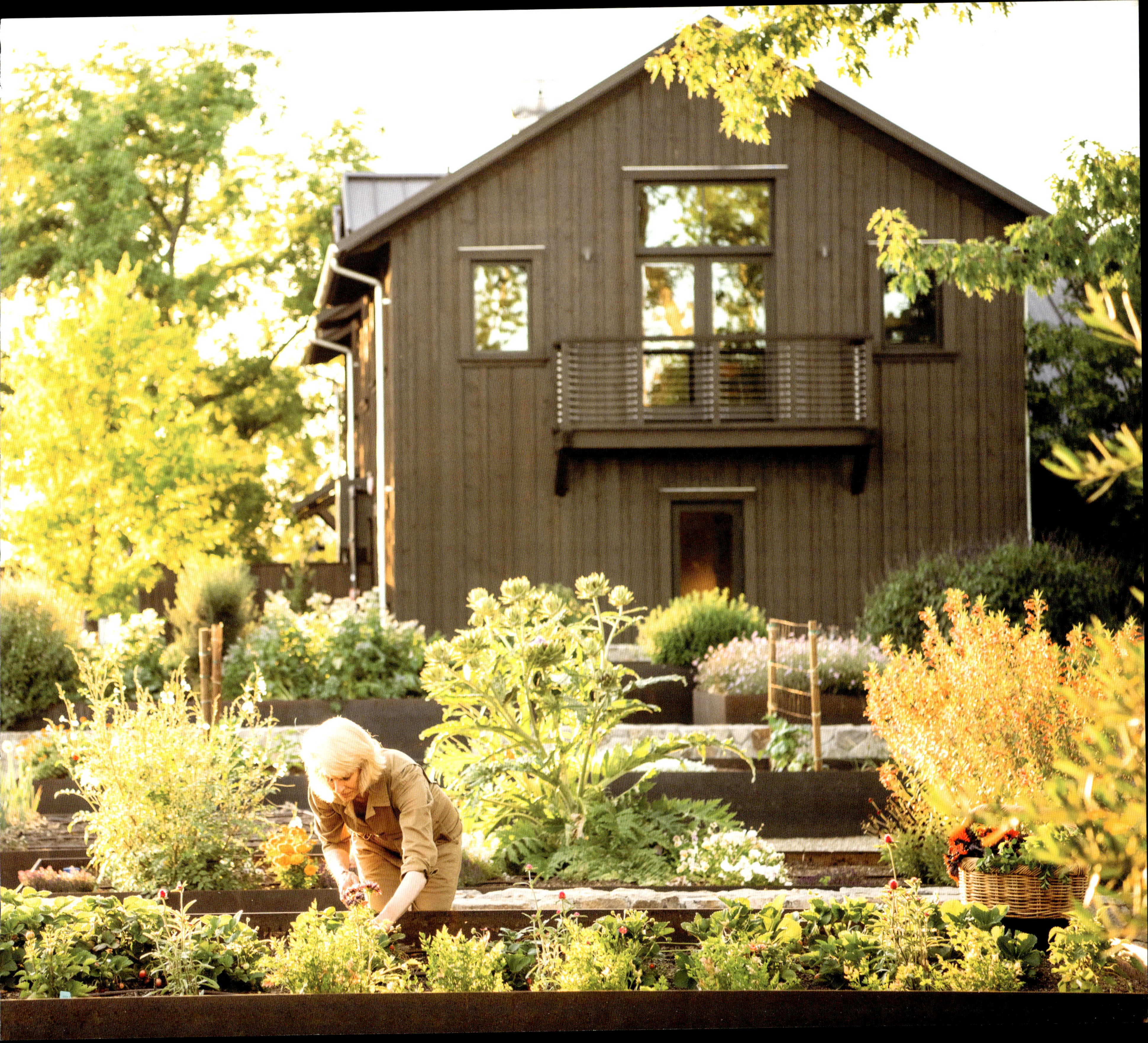

visitor guide

All of these wineries welcome visitors, although most require a prior appointment. Check the website for guest policies and hospitality programs. Many of the wineries offer experiences that include a tour of the garden.

Alexander Valley Vineyards
8644 Highway 128
Healdsburg
707-433-7209
www.avvwine.com

B Cellars
703 Oakville Cross Road
Napa
707-709-8787
www.bcellars.com

Beringer Vineyards
2000 Main Street
St. Helena
707-257-5771
www.beringer.com

Cakebread Cellars
8300 St. Helena Highway
Rutherford
800-588-0298
www.cakebread.com

Clif Family Winery
709 Main Street
St. Helena
707-968-0625
www.cliffamily.com

HALL Wines
401 St. Helena Highway South
St. Helena
707-967-2626
www.hallwines.com

The Prisoner Wine Company
1178 Galleron Road
St. Helena
877-283-5934
www.theprisonerwinecompany.com

Regusci Winery
5584 Silverado Trail
Napa
707-254-0403
www.regusciwinery.com

Robert Mondavi Winery
7801 St. Helena Highway
Oakville
888-766-6328
www.robertmondaviwinery.com

Skipstone
2505 Geysers Road
Geyserville
707-433-9124
www.skipstonewines.com

Trefethen Family Vineyards
1160 Oak Knoll Avenue
Napa
707-255-7700
www.trefethen.com

Wente Vineyards
5565 Tesla Road
Livermore
925-456-2305
www.wentevineyards.com

Wheeler Farms
588 Zinfandel Lane
St. Helena
707-200-8500
www.wheelerfarmswine.com

Above and right: *A scarecrow encourages a happy harvest at Regusci Winery; spring garden radishes at Robert Mondavi Winery*

acknowledgments

This book was a dream project that brought together my three principal interests: cooking, wine, and gardening. My greatest pleasure in writing it was meeting so many others who share these passions and who were generous in sharing what they knew. I am indebted to Cate Conniff for the magazine assignment on winery gardens that planted the seed for this book, and I am deeply grateful to all the vintners, winery chefs, winery gardeners, and their teams who took time to work with me and educate me. The beauty you create in your gardens and kitchens will inspire my own gardening and cooking for years to come.

    I have been privileged to collaborate on this book with a team of top-tier professionals. Photographer Meg Smith and her assistant, Antonio Fernando, produced images more beautiful than I dared to imagine. Thank you to food stylist Abby Stolfo; her assistant, Natalie Drobny; and prop stylist Thea Chalmers for interpreting the recipes with such care and style. Copy editor Sharon Silva has an attention to detail and concern for clarity that always make my manuscripts better.

    Designer Jennifer Barry made these gardens come to life with her creative vision and good taste. Jenny has been my partner on this book from the beginning, as producer and general wrangler on a project with many moving parts. The trains run on time when Jenny is in charge and *Gather* would never have happened without her.

—Janet Fletcher

index

A
Alexander, Cyrus, 15, 19
Alexander Valley Vineyards, 7, 10, 15–19, 23, 236
Almond and Semolina Cake with Quince Spoon Sweet, 183
Antipasto Platter with Southern-Style Pickled Okra, 141
Apples, Brussels Sprouts with Bacon, Pistachios, and, 143
Apricots, Lemon Verbena, with Olive Oil–Sea Salt Ice Cream, 232
Araujo, Bart, 221, 224
Araujo, Daphne, 4, 221–24, 234
Armagnac-Soaked Prunes, 77
arugula
    Autumn Squash, Pear, and Arugula Salad, 71
    Risotto with Pancetta and Arugula, 215
Asparagus, Potato Gnocchi with Black Trumpet Mushrooms and, 128–29
avocados
    Avocado Salsa Verde, 21
    Hamachi Crudo Tostada with Finger Limes and Avocado, 158

B
Bachor, Jim, 135, 138, 146
bacon
    Brussels Sprouts with Bacon, Apples, and Pistachios, 143
    Spring Pizza Flambé with Bacon, Leeks, and Fromage Blanc, 126–27
Baldridge, Gina, 51
Barrett, Laura, 92
basil
    Greek dwarf, 86
    Thai, 130
B Cellars, 10, 31–36, 44, 47, 236
beans
    Butternut Squash Hummus with Pepita Aillade and Pita Chips, 211
    Crostini with White Bean Puree and Fava Bean Pesto, 55
    Pan-Seared Pork Chops with Shelling Bean and Wild Mushroom Ragout, 110–13
    Parsley Fettuccine with Fava Beans, Peas, Spring Onions, and Parmesan Cream, 162
    Poached Farm Egg with Potato Crème, Fava Bean Pesto, and Crispy Shallots, 228–29
    Winter Vegetable and Bean Soup with Tuscan Kale Pesto, 73
    Zeytinyagli Green Beans with Olive Flatbread, 178
beef
    Black Pepper–Crusted Beef Ribeye with Balsamic Spring Onions and Smashed Beets, 201–2
    Grilled Rib Eye with Grilled Spring Vegetables and Salsa Verde, 165
    Slow-Roasted Beef Short Ribs with Broccoli di Cicco and Farro, 231
beets
    Beet and Citrus Salad with Charred Citrus Crème Fraîche, 106
    Black Pepper–Crusted Beef Ribeye with Balsamic Spring Onions and Smashed Beets, 201–2
    Golden Beet Gazpacho, 59
    Seared Scallops with Parsnips Two Ways, 40–41
Beringer, Frederick, 49, 50
Beringer, Jacob, 50, 62
Beringer Vineyards, 9, 49–53, 56, 59, 60, 62, 236
Bittner, Stefani, 118
Blackberry, Pear, and Granola Crisp, 29
blueberries
    Cheesecake with Blueberry Gelée, 166–67
    Red Wine–Macerated Blueberries, 96–97
Borsack, Jim, 31, 35
bread. *See also* crostini
    Bruschetta with Brassicas, Peas, and Burrata, 89
    "Cacio e Pepe" Croutons, 90
    Italian Cornbread Dressing, 145
    Olive Flatbread, 180
Brisoux, Alex, 117, 119, 121
broccoli
    Bruschetta with Brassicas, Peas, and Burrata, 89
    Grilled Rib Eye with Grilled Spring Vegetables and Salsa Verde, 165
    Slow-Roasted Beef Short Ribs with Broccoli di Cicco and Farro, 231
Bruschetta with Brassicas, Peas, and Burrata, 89
Brussels Sprouts with Bacon, Apples, and Pistachios, 143
Butter, Roasted-Tomato, 74

C
"Cacio e Pepe" Croutons, 90
Cadamatre, Nova, 151–53
Cakebread, Dolores, 7, 9, 65–66, 68–69
Cakebread, Jack, 65
Cakebread Cellars, 4, 7, 9, 12, 65–71, 73, 236
cakes
    Almond and Semolina Cake with Quince Spoon Sweet, 183
    Cheesecake with Blueberry Gelée, 166–67
    German Honey Cake with Orange Mascarpone, 62
carrots
    Carrot and Parsnip Slaw with Lemongrass-Ginger Oil, 109
    Crostini with Garden Carrots, Goat Cheese, and Dukkah, 70
    Oven-Roasted Baby Carrots with Cumin Yogurt, Carrot Top Chimichurri, and Spiced Pumpkin Seeds, 194–95
    Spring Lettuces with Sugar Snap Peas and Roasted Carrots, 56
cauliflower
    Bruschetta with Brassicas, Peas, and Burrata, 89
    Grilled Halibut with Cauliflower-Leek Puree, Roasted Zucchini, and Pistachio Pesto, 216
cheese
    Bruschetta with Brassicas, Peas, and Burrata, 89
    "Cacio e Pepe" Croutons, 90
    Cheesecake with Blueberry Gelée, 166–67
    Crostini with Garden Carrots, Goat Cheese, and Dukkah, 70
    Elk Sugo with Herb Cheese Tortellini and Kale Chips, 42–43
    German Honey Cake with Orange Mascarpone, 62
    Heirloom Tomato and Peach Salad with Burrata, 39
    Katie's Pimiento Cheese, 20
    Parmesan Cream, 162
    Spring Pizza Flambé with Bacon, Leeks, and Fromage Blanc, 126–27
    Spring Vegetable Salad with Ricotta, Nasturtium Pesto, and Edible Flower Croccante, 159–61
Chernick, Ryan, 52
Chicken, Maggie's Ranch, 24
Chicory Caesar, Mixed, with "Cacio e Pepe" Croutons, 90
Chimichurri, Carrot Top, 195
Chocolate-Caramel Sauce, 76–77
Christophel, Michael, 32–33
Clif Family Winery, 9, 81–86, 89, 92–94, 96, 236
Coffee Ice Cream, 76
Cookies, Edible Flower, 233
Cornbread Dressing, Italian, 145
Couscous, Garden-Vegetable, Lamb Rib Chops with, 60–61
Crab Roll, Dungeness, with Pickled Ginger, Cilantro, and Yuzu Crème, 193
Crawford, Kit, 81–83, 85–86
Crème Brûlée, Blood Orange, 219
Crêpes with Sautéed Strawberries, 114
Crisp, Pear, Blackberry, and Granola, 29
crostini
    Crostini with Garden Carrots, Goat Cheese, and Dukkah, 70
    Crostini with White Bean Puree and Fava Bean Pesto, 55
Croutons, "Cacio e Pepe," 90
Cyprus Potatoes, 181

D
Diner, Constance, 10, 169–73
Diner, Fahri, 10, 169–73, 180, 183
dips
    Butternut Squash Hummus with Pepita Aillade and Pita Chips, 211
    Caramelized Spring Onion Dip with Spring Vegetable Crudités, 122
Dovholuk, Diane, 205–6
Dressing, Italian Cornbread, 145
Dukkah, 70

E
Eggplant Bayildi with Tomato, Saffron, and Pine Nut Sauce, 177
eggs
    Fingerling Potato "Tostones" with Olive Salsa Verde and Farm Eggs, 93
    Poached Farm Egg with Potato Crème, Fava Bean Pesto, and Crispy Shallots, 228–29
Elk Sugo with Herb Cheese Tortellini and Kale Chips, 42–43
Erickson, Gary, 81–82, 85–86

F
Farlow, Jeff, 207–8, 211
Farro, Slow-Roasted Beef Short Ribs with Broccoli di Cicco and, 231
finger limes, 47
    Hamachi Crudo Tostada with Finger Limes and Avocado, 158
fish
    Cedar Plank Salmon with Roasted-Tomato Butter, 74
    Grilled Halibut with Cauliflower-Leek Puree, Roasted Zucchini, and Pistachio Pesto, 216
    Hamachi Crudo Tostada with Finger Limes and Avocado, 158
    Lightly Cured Salmon with Salmon Roe, Zhug, and Persimmons, 174
    Strawberry Salmon Tartare, 36

flowers
    Edible Flower Cookies, 233
    Edible Flower Croccante, 159–61
    Nasturtium Pesto, 159–61
Frank, Ken, 101, 103, 105–6, 109–10, 114

G
Gallaccio, Anya, 101
Garay, Lissette, 155
gardens
    habitat plants for, 149
    tips for, 79, 234
garlic
    Garlic Confit, 44–46, 61
    Green Garlic Fried Rice with English Peas and Scallions, 123
Gazpacho, Golden Beet, 59
German Honey Cake with Orange Mascarpone, 62
Gnocchi, Potato, with Asparagus and Black Trumpet Mushrooms, 128–29
granola
    Katie's Granola, 29
    Pear, Blackberry, and Granola Crisp, 29
ground cherries, 86

H
Halibut, Grilled, with Cauliflower-Leek Puree, Roasted Zucchini, and Pistachio Pesto, 216
Hall, Craig, 99, 101–3, 109, 113
Hall, Kathryn, 99, 101–3, 109, 113
HALL Wines, 99–103, 109–10, 114, 236
Hamachi Crudo Tostada with Finger Limes and Avocado, 158
Heller, Sarah, 9, 222–25, 227–28, 231–32
Henry, Tessa, 81–82, 84–85
hibiscus, 47
Hoffman, Paul, 188
huckleberries, 47
    Dijon-Crusted Lamb Chops with Pistachio Puree, Chard, and Huckleberry Gastrique, 44–46
Hummus, Butternut Squash, with Pepita Aillade and Pita Chips, 211

I
ice cream
    Coffee Ice Cream, 76
    Olive Oil–Sea Salt Ice Cream, 232
Italian Cornbread Dressing, 145

K
kale
    Kale Chips, 42–43
    Tuscan Kale Pesto, 73
kalette, 47
Kamman, Madeleine, 50

Kennedy, Chris, 9, 187–88, 191–93, 196, 199–201
Keys, Duffy, 31, 33, 35
kumquats
    Beet and Citrus Salad with Charred Citrus Crème Fraîche, 106
Kuntz, Derick, 31–36, 39, 40, 42, 44, 47
Kusch, Shelley, 99–103, 109

L
lamb
    Dijon-Crusted Lamb Chops with Pistachio Puree, Chard, and Huckleberry Gastrique, 44–46
    Grilled Lamb Shoulder Chops with Cyprus Potatoes, 181
    Lamb Rib Chops with Garden-Vegetable Couscous, 60–61
    Spring Lamb Chops Scottadito with Charred Tomato and Black Olive Tapenade, 200
Lee, Euming, 117
leeks
    Grilled Halibut with Cauliflower-Leek Puree, Roasted Zucchini, and Pistachio Pesto, 216
    Spring Pizza Flambé with Bacon, Leeks, and Fromage Blanc, 126–27
Lemongrass-Ginger Oil, 109
lemon thyme, 130
lemon verbena, 130
    Lemon Verbena Apricots with Olive Oil–Sea Salt Ice Cream, 232
lettuce
    Little Gem Lettuces with Radishes, Fennel, and Verjus-Umeboshi Vinaigrette, 125
    Spring Lettuces with Sugar Snap Peas and Roasted Carrots, 56
Lutsko, Ron, 221–22

M
McConnell, John, 81–86, 89–90, 92–94, 96
Melka, Philippe, 171
Meyer Lemon Curd Parfait with Poppy Seed Crust and Red Wine–Macerated Blueberries, 96–97
Mondavi, Margrit, 151, 154–55, 166
Mondavi, Robert, 151–52, 154
Moore, Lisa, 155
Mosher, Jeff, 151–55, 159, 162, 165
Murphy, Katie Wetzel, 12, 15–21, 24, 26, 28, 29
mushrooms
    Grilled Rib Eye with Grilled Spring Vegetables and Salsa Verde, 165
    Handmade Pappardelle with Wild Mushroom Ragout and Peas, 196–98
    Pan-Seared Pork Chops with Shelling Bean and Wild Mushroom Ragout, 110–13

Porcini Crème Fraîche, 105
Potato Gnocchi with Asparagus and Black Trumpet Mushrooms, 128–29

N
Nasturtium Pesto, 159–61
nepitella, 86

O
oats
    Katie's Granola, 29
Oil, Lemongrass-Ginger, 109
Okra, Southern-Style Pickled, Antipasto Platter with, 141
olives
    Olive Flatbread, 180
    Olive Salsa Verde, 93
    Spring Lamb Chops Scottadito with Charred Tomato and Black Olive Tapenade, 200
onions
    Cabernet red, 86
    Caramelized Spring Onion Dip with Spring Vegetable Crudités, 122
    Pickled Onions, 56
    Pickled Red Onions, 39, 159–61
oranges
    Beet and Citrus Salad with Charred Citrus Crème Fraîche, 106
    Blood Orange Crème Brûlée, 219
    German Honey Cake with Orange Mascarpone, 62
    Golden Beet Gazpacho, 59
    Seared Scallops with Parsnips Two Ways, 40–41
oregano, Mexican, 130
Ozyilmaz, Laura and Sayat, 171, 177

P
Pancetta, Risotto with Arugula and, 215
Parsley Fettuccine with Fava Beans, Peas, Spring Onions, and Parmesan Cream, 162
parsnips
    Carrot and Parsnip Slaw with Lemongrass-Ginger Oil, 109
    Lamb Rib Chops with Garden-Vegetable Couscous, 60–61
    Seared Scallops with Parsnips Two Ways, 40–41
pasta
    Elk Sugo with Herb Cheese Tortellini and Kale Chips, 42–43
    Handmade Pappardelle with Wild Mushroom Ragout and Peas, 196–98
    Winter Vegetable and Bean Soup with Tuscan Kale Pesto, 73
Patino, Javier, 16, 17

Peach Salad, Heirloom Tomato and, with Burrata, 39
pears
    Autumn Squash, Pear, and Arugula Salad, 71
    Pear, Blackberry, and Granola Crisp, 29
peas
    Bruschetta with Brassicas, Peas, and Burrata, 89
    Chilled Spring Garden Soup with Bay Shrimp, 227
    Green Garlic Fried Rice with English Peas and Scallions, 123
    Handmade Pappardelle with Wild Mushroom Ragout and Peas, 196–98
    Parsley Fettuccine with Fava Beans, Peas, Spring Onions, and Parmesan Cream, 162
    Spring Lettuces with Sugar Snap Peas and Roasted Carrots, 56
peppers
    espelette, 47
    Katie's Pimiento Cheese, 20
    Pickled Peppers, 36
Perez, Adriana, 145
Perez, Angel, 9, 134–35, 138–39, 142, 145
persimmons
    Lightly Cured Salmon with Salmon Roe, Zhug, and Persimmons, 174
    Steamed Persimmon and Walnut Pudding, 146
pesto
    Fava Bean Pesto, 55, 228
    Nasturtium Pesto, 159–61
    Pistachio Pesto, 216
    Tuscan Kale Pesto, 73
Phinney, David, 117
pineapple guava, 47
pistachios
    Brussels Sprouts with Bacon, Apples, and Pistachios, 143
    Dijon-Crusted Lamb Chops with Pistachio Puree, Chard, and Huckleberry Gastrique, 44–46
    Dukkah, 70
    Pistachio Pesto, 216
Pizza Flambé, Spring, with Bacon, Leeks, and Fromage Blanc, 126–27
pluots, 86
Polenta, Creamy, Clif Family Porchetta with, 94–95
Pomegranate, Roasted Butternut Squash Soup with Pumpkin Seeds and, 142–43
pork. *See also* bacon; pancetta
    Clif Family Porchetta with Creamy Polenta, 94–95
    Pan-Seared Pork Chops with Shelling Bean and Wild Mushroom Ragout, 110–13

Index 239

potatoes
- Fingerling Potato "Tostones" with Olive Salsa Verde and Farm Eggs, 93
- Grilled Lamb Shoulder Chops with Cyprus Potatoes, 181
- Lamb Rib Chops with Garden-Vegetable Couscous, 60–61
- Poached Farm Egg with Potato Crème, Fava Bean Pesto, and Crispy Shallots, 228–29
- Potato Gnocchi with Asparagus and Black Trumpet Mushrooms, 128–29

The Prisoner Wine Company, 9, 117–23, 125–26, 130, 236

Profiteroles with Coffee Ice Cream, Armagnac-Soaked Prunes, and Chocolate-Caramel Sauce, 76–77

Prunes, Armagnac-Soaked, 77

Pudding, Steamed Persimmon and Walnut, 146

pumpkin seeds
- Pepita Aillade, 211
- Roasted Butternut Squash Soup with Pomegranate and Pumpkin Seeds, 142–43
- Spiced Pumpkin Seeds, 194–95

Q

quince
- Quince Raspberry Dressing, 56
- Quince Spoon Sweet, 183

R

Raspberry Dressing, Quince, 56
Regusci, Jim, 133–35, 137, 139
Regusci, Laura, 9, 133–34, 137–39, 141, 145, 148
Regusci Winery, 4, 9, 133–35, 137–39, 141, 146, 236

rice
- Green Garlic Fried Rice with English Peas and Scallions, 123
- Risotto with Pancetta and Arugula, 215

Robert Mondavi Winery, 10, 151–55, 236
Ruel, Jon, 187

S

salads
- Autumn Squash, Pear, and Arugula Salad, 71
- Beet and Citrus Salad with Charred Citrus Crème Fraîche, 106
- Carrot and Parsnip Slaw with Lemongrass-Ginger Oil, 109
- Heirloom Tomato and Peach Salad with Burrata, 39
- Little Gem Lettuces with Radishes, Fennel, and Verjus-Umeboshi Vinaigrette, 125
- Mixed Chicory Caesar with "Cacio e Pepe" Croutons, 90
- Spring Lettuces with Sugar Snap Peas and Roasted Carrots, 56
- Spring Vegetable Salad with Ricotta, Nasturtium Pesto, and Edible Flower Croccante, 159–61
- Summer Garden Salad with Linda's Dressing, 23

salmon
- Cedar Plank Salmon with Roasted-Tomato Butter, 74
- Lightly Cured Salmon with Salmon Roe, Zhug, and Persimmons, 174
- Strawberry Salmon Tartare, 36

sauces and salsas. *See also* pesto
- Avocado Salsa Verde, 21
- Carrot Top Chimichurri, 195
- Chocolate-Caramel Sauce, 76–77
- Olive Salsa Verde, 93
- Parmesan Cream, 162
- Pepita Aillade, 211
- Salsa Verde, 165
- Yogurt Tahini Sauce, 56
- Zhug, 174

Scallops, Seared, with Parsnips Two Ways, 40–41
Schneider, Sally, 76
Scott, Sarah, 10
Shrimp, Bay, Chilled Spring Garden Soup with, 227
Skipstone, 10, 169–74, 181, 183, 236
Slaw, Carrot and Parsnip, with Lemongrass-Ginger Oil, 109
Snow, Marcy, 65–67, 73, 79

soups
- Chilled Spring Garden Soup with Bay Shrimp, 227
- Golden Beet Gazpacho, 59
- Roasted Butternut Squash Soup with Pomegranate and Pumpkin Seeds, 142–43
- Roasted Sunchoke Soup, 105
- Roasted Tomato Bisque, 212
- Winter Vegetable and Bean Soup with Tuscan Kale Pesto, 73

squash. *See also* zucchini
- Autumn Squash, Pear, and Arugula Salad, 71
- Butternut Squash Hummus with Pepita Aillade and Pita Chips, 211
- Roasted Butternut Squash Soup with Pomegranate and Pumpkin Seeds, 142–43

strawberries
- Crêpes with Sautéed Strawberries, 114
- Strawberry Salmon Tartare, 36

Streeter, Brian, 7, 65–69, 71, 73, 76
Strohl, Curtis, 31, 33, 35
Sunchoke Soup, Roasted, 105

T

tarragon, Mexican, 130

tomatillos
- Avocado Salsa Verde, 21

tomatoes
- Eggplant Bayildi with Tomato, Saffron, and Pine Nut Sauce, 177
- Elk Sugo with Herb Cheese Tortellini and Kale Chips, 42–43
- Heirloom Tomato and Peach Salad with Burrata, 39
- Roasted Tomato Bisque, 212
- Roasted-Tomato Butter, 74
- Spring Lamb Chops Scottadito with Charred Tomato and Black Olive Tapenade, 200
- Winter Vegetable and Bean Soup with Tuscan Kale Pesto, 73
- Zeytinyagli Green Beans with Olive Flatbread, 178

Tostada, Hamachi Crudo, with Finger Limes and Avocado, 158
Trefethen, Hailey, 187–89, 191
Trefethen, Janet, 187–89, 199
Trefethen, Katie, 187, 189
Trefethen Family Vineyards, 9, 10, 187–89, 191–93, 196, 236

V

vegetables. *See also individual vegetables*
- Caramelized Spring Onion Dip with Spring Vegetable Crudités, 122
- Crudités with Avocado Salsa Verde, 21
- Grilled Rib Eye with Grilled Spring Vegetables and Salsa Verde, 165
- Lamb Rib Chops with Garden-Vegetable Couscous, 60–61
- Spring Vegetable Salad with Ricotta, Nasturtium Pesto, and Edible Flower Croccante, 159–61
- Summer Garden Salad with Linda's Dressing, 23
- Winter Vegetable and Bean Soup with Tuscan Kale Pesto, 73

Verjus-Umeboshi Vinaigrette, 125

W

walnuts
- Katie's Granola, 29
- Steamed Persimmon and Walnut Pudding, 146

Wente, Aly, 205, 208–9, 215
Wente, Carolyn, 205, 207–9, 212, 215–16, 219
Wente, Eric, 205
Wente, Ernest, 205
Wente, Julie, 209
Wente, Phil, 205, 209
Wente Vineyards, 9, 205–9, 211, 216, 236
Wetzel, Hank, 10, 15–19
Wetzel, Harry, 19, 24
Wetzel, Linda, 15, 19, 23
Wetzel, Maggie, 15, 19, 24
Wetzel, Robert, 19, 24
Wheeler, J. H., 221
Wheeler Farms, 4, 9, 221–25, 227–28, 231–33, 236
wine pairing, 53, 92, 199, 215
Wittmann, Chrissy, 117

X

xanthan gum, 125

Y

Yogurt Tahini Sauce, 56
Young, Brett, 117–18, 120–23, 125, 127–28, 130

Z

Zeytinyagli Green Beans with Olive Flatbread, 178
Zhug, 174

zucchini
- Grilled Halibut with Cauliflower-Leek Puree, Roasted Zucchini, and Pistachio Pesto, 216
- Lamb Rib Chops with Garden-Vegetable Couscous, 60–61
- Winter Vegetable and Bean Soup with Tuscan Kale Pesto, 73